MUSIC AT THE LIMITS

EDWARD W. SAID

MUSIC
at the LIMITS

Columbia

University

Press

New York

COLUMBIA UNIVERSITY PRESS
Publishers Since 1893
New York   Chichester, West Sussex
Copyright © 2008 Edward W. Said

Library of Congress Cataloging-in-Publication Data
Said, Edward W.
   Music at the Limits / Edward W. Said ; foreword by Daniel Barenboim.
      p. cm.
   Includes index.
   ISBN 978-0-231-13936-6 (cloth : alk. paper)—ISBN 978-0-231-51155-1 (electronic)
   1. Musical criticism.   2. Opera—Reviews.   3. Operas—Performances—20th
century.   4. Concerts—Reviews.   5. Music—Book reviews   I. Title.
   ML3785.S34 2007
   780.9—dc22
2007002276

Columbia University Press books are printed on permanent
and durable acid-free paper.

Designed by Lisa Hamm

This book is printed on paper with recycled content.
Printed in the United States of America
c 10 9 8 7 6 5 4 3 2 1

Contents

PART III: 2000 AND BEYOND

Foreword

Daniel Barenboim

E DWARD SAID was a scholar with a remarkable breadth of interest. In addition to being well versed in music, literature, philosophy, and the understanding of politics, he was one of those rare people who sought and recognized the connections between different and seemingly disparate disciplines. His unusual understanding of the human spirit and of the human being was perhaps a consequence of his revelatory construct that parallels between ideas, topics, and cultures can be of a paradoxical nature, not contradicting but enriching one another. This is one of the ideas that I believe made Said an extremely important figure. His journey through this world took place precisely at a time when the value of music in society began to decline. The humanity of music, the value of musical contemplation and thought, and the transcendence of the idea as expressed through sound are all concepts that regrettably continue to decline even further in the modern world. Music has become isolated from other areas of life; it is no longer considered a necessary aspect of intellectual development. Just as in medicine, the music world has evolved into a society of specialists who know more and more about less and less.

His fierce anti-specialization lead him to criticize very strongly, and in my opinion very fairly, the fact that musical education had become increasingly poor, not only in the United States—which, after all, had imported the music of Old Europe—but also in the very countries that had produced music's greatest figures. Both Germany, that cradle of musical creation that produced Beethoven, Brahms, Wagner, Schumann, and many others, and France, the home of Debussy and Ravel, were, according to Said, allowing the quality and availability of their musical education to deteriorate. Furthermore, he perceived a trend that unsettled him exceedingly (an observation that united us very quickly): that musical education was becoming increasingly specialized and limited, even where it was readily available. In the best of cases, this type of education produces highly competent instrumentalists who possess little knowledge of theory and musicology but are highly advanced in the technical execution essential for a professional musician. What Said recognized, however, was the lack of a fundamental ability on the part of the musician to delve into, comprehend, and express the essential substance of music. After all, the nature of music is such that its content is inexpressible except through sound. Musical education today has moved further and further away from the deep and complex mystery of this essential truth and now focuses increasingly on the separation of the physical dexterity required to produce sound on an instrument and the sterile science of dissecting music structurally and harmonically without any active participation or experience of its power. Said deplored this development in the music business, and his concert reviews are full of the evidence of this antipathy.

No one could have exemplified the opposite of this microscopic focus more completely than Edward Said, which is not to say that he was uninterested in detail. On the contrary, he understood perfectly that musical genius or musical talent requires tremendous attention to detail. The genius attends to detail as though it were the most important thing and, in so doing, does not lose sight of the big picture; in fact, this attention to detail enables him to manifest his vision of the big picture. In music, as in thought, the big picture must be the result of the precise coordination of small details. When Said attended a concert or performance, he focused his attention on these details, some of which have gone unnoticed by many professionals. As a critic, he distinguished himself in many ways from his colleagues, of whom it can be said that some lack the knowledge to write about their subject matter intelligently and others lack the ability to listen without preconceptions. Of this second category it is clear that such critics have, at best, forged for themselves an idea of the "correct" interpretation of a certain work and are therefore capable only of making comparisons, favorable or otherwise, between the current performance and their own preconceptions to which they have become enslaved. Said, on the other hand, listened with open ears and a depth of musical knowledge that allowed him to hear, and attempt to understand, the intention of the performer and his approach to the music. Thus when reviewing a concert given by Celibidache and the Munich Philharmonic, he meanders into the philosophical realm of the nature of public performance, observing and comparing the performers who have had the imagination to question the tradition of the two-hour concert. His comments on Celibidache's notoriously slow tempi and theatrical pauses between movements are contemplative, insightful, and fair; they represent not a personal reaction to a deviation from the norm but an attempt to enter the mind of the performer and to understand his motivations.

Said had a refined knowledge of the art of composition and orchestration. He knew, for example, that at a certain moment in the second act of *Tristan und Isolde,* the horns withdraw behind the stage. A few bars later, the same note they played reemerges in the clarinets of the pit orchestra. I have had the honor and pleasure of collaborating on that piece with a great number of illustrious singers who were unaware of that detail and always looked behind them to see where the sound was coming from! They didn't know that the note no longer came from behind the stage, but from the pit. He took interest in such things; it was part of his meticulous interest in detail, which conferred upon his understanding of the whole an otherwise unimaginable grandeur. Edward Said's understanding of the world made it impossible for him to see only the obvious, the literal, the readily graspable: in his writing and in his life he continually discovered and brought forth evidence of the interconnected nature of all things, a notion he most probably derived from music. In music, there are no independent elements. One would like to believe it possible to take independent action in personal, social, or political realms that would have no further consequences, and yet one is constantly confronted with evidence to the contrary. It came naturally to Said, for example, to quote Keats when analyzing a performance of Bach or to compare the performance of Wagner in Israel with the reading of Joseph Conrad's *Heart of Darkness* by a contemporary African. There were, for Edward Said, no two aspects of being human that were not related to one another.

As a musician, he knew and believed, as I do, that logic is inseparable from intuition, rational thought from emotion. How often do we succumb to the temptation of abandoning all logic for the sake of satisfying an emotional need or whim? In music, this is impossible, since music can be made neither exclusively with reason nor solely with emotion. In fact, if these elements are separated, we are left not with music but a collection of sounds. His belief in the concept of inclusion as opposed to exclusion also derived from his understanding of music. Just as it violates the principle of counterpoint in music to emphasize one voice while excluding all the others, so he believed it impossible to settle a conflict, political or otherwise, without involving all parties concerned in the discussion of a solution. The same could be said of the principle of integration, applicable to all sorts of problems from acoustic balance in an orchestra to peace talks in the Middle East. These brilliant and unlikely connections are responsible for Said's reputation as a great thinker. He was a fighter for the rights of his people and an incomparable intellectual and musician in the deepest sense, having used his musical experience and knowledge as a base for his convictions about politics, morality, and intellectual thought. His writings on music and musical performance are at the very least entertaining and informative, if somewhat far-fetched in the scope of the associations he conjures. They are always expressed with great elegance of language, and at best they are brilliant, original, witty, and full of unexpected revelations that he alone could uncover.

Preface

I N THE introduction to *Musical Elaborations*, Edward's first book on music, he writes that his "primary interest [in music] is to look at Western classical music as a cultural field that has meant a great deal to [him] as a literary critic and a musician." I, on the other hand, saw his interest and relation to music as a dynamic, changing phenomenon, whose origins were intensely personal.

In his memoir *Out of Place*, Edward describes how he felt about music as a child. To him "music was, on the one hand, a dissatisfying boring drill of piano exercises . . . and, on the other hand, an enormously rich and haphazardly organized world of magnificent sounds and sights." Edward discovered this world through his parent's eclectic collection of records and by listening every Sunday evening to the radio broadcasts *Nights at the Opera* on the BBC.

Classical Western music was part of our daily life. Edward listened to music when he worked and played the piano when he took a break or when he needed to relax; his leisurely reading included an enormous amount of literature about music. His knowledge of music was immense, and he had a coterie of friends who, like him, were either intellectuals passionate about music or simply music buffs, with whom he chatted about it. Musical examples and citations abound in his various writings, but I believe that it was Glenn Gould's death in 1982 that impelled Edward to write seriously about music. The realization that Glenn Gould's early demise ended an eccentric pianist's brilliant career compelled Edward to probe deeply into Gould's life and musical achievements. He indulged himself in listening to every recording of Gould that he could get hold of and read everything written about and by him. He also saw all the films made of Gould's recordings and those that were made about him. Gould became an obsession, and Edward seemed unable to let go of his beloved genius.

In January 1983, a few months after Gould died, our son, Wadie, had a freak accident, a terrifying brush with death for our nuclear family. The day we learned that Wadie had a serious infection and needed hospitalization I was completely paralyzed with fear. Edward absorbed the news and then half an hour later said we should get ready for the concert we had tickets to that night. I stayed at home, afraid and puzzled, while Edward attended the concert. Many years later I realized how important it was for him to seek out music when faced with the fear of death.

While Wadie was in the hospital, Edward learned that his mother had been diagnosed with cancer and had to have an operation. He associated music with his mother because of the many musical experiences they had shared. "It is to my mother's own wonderful musicality and love of the art that I owe my earliest interest in music," he wrote in *Musical Elaborations*. In May 1983 the first piece in this collection, on Glenn Gould, appeared. In 1986 Edward became music critic of *The Nation*, and from that moment the study of music merged with his personal passion about it. He began to amass a huge collection of different recordings of the same concertos, symphonies, operas, and other musical works. He spent many hours listening to these recordings, and he attended as many performances as possible of certain operas, recitals, and concerts on both sides of the Atlantic. It was as though the deeply varied themes in music and the complexity of musical compositions were connected to his struggles to face the reality of his mother's illness and death. During this period we drove as a family from New York to Washington, D.C., to visit his mother. Edward, who normally insisted on conversing during long car rides, had brought a canvas bag full of cassettes, which he deposited at my feet in the front seat. When I objected, he felt wounded. Wagner's *Ring* was our companion for the five-hour drive. Meanwhile the children sat in the back, both with earphones listening to their own kind of music. It was almost surreal. Then suddenly it dawned on me that the only way Edward could deal with his pain over his mother's illness and impending death was to drown himself in the sounds of magnificent, beautiful music—no doubt a reminder of his childhood with her. Edward's mother passed away in 1990. *Musical Elaborations* was published in 1991 and dedicated to her memory.

One year after his mother died, Edward was diagnosed with leukemia. Music became his constant companion. In the summer of 1998 he had to undergo a rigorous and horrible experimental treatment, just when Christopher Herrick was scheduled to perform fourteen concerts of Bach's complete organ works. Edward arranged his treatment days around the concerts. Not only did he attend all the concerts, but he managed to write a review of them that is included in this collection.

At the same time Edward was exploring the idea of "late style." He determined that what composers wrote toward the end of their lives was characterized by "intransigence, difficulty, and unresolved contradictions," thoughts that evolved into his book *On Late Style*, which touches on a number of late works by various composers. In the section from *Out of Place* in which Edward relates his musical experiences as a child, he goes on to describe the pleasure he derived from these experiences. He adds details about all the things he listened to and how his interest and curiosity led him to learn more and more about these pieces and about the artists who performed them. Then, after a long reflection on Wilhelm Furtwängler, whom Edward saw conducting in Cairo, Edward writes "Time seemed forever against me." This introduces a prolonged passage linking music and time. Time had always preoccupied Edward—its fleetingness, its inexorable march forward, and the challenge it posed to accomplish important things while it continued to exist. To him music occupied this same world. The last essay in this collection, a review of Maynard Solomon's book on late Beethoven, was published in September 2003, two weeks before his death. It is ironically titled "Untimely Meditations."

In early June 2003, three months before Edward passed away, he called his cousin, a Presbyterian minister, and asked him where in the Bible the phrase "the hour cometh and is now" appears. When his question was answered, Edward put the phone down, turned to me, and said that he was worried I wouldn't know what music to play at his funeral. I was taken aback by this statement and waited before replying, because I realized that he was telling me that this was the beginning of the end and that he was dying.

Mariam C. Said

Acknowledgments

M OST OF the essays collected in this book were written by Edward when he served as music critic for *The Nation.* The rest of the essays appeared in *Raritan,* the *London Review of Books,* the *New Yorker, Vanity Fair, Harper's,* the *Observer,* the *Washington Post Book World,* the *New York Times,* the *New York Times Book Review, Al Ahram Weekly, Al Hayat,* and *Le Monde Diplomatique.* The piece appearing in the appendix is a book proposal that Edward thought he would write one day. Later on he abandoned this project.

I am particularly grateful to the many friends whose help was invaluable in publishing this collection—especially Richard Poirier to whom I am indebted for his invaluable advice, Daniel Barenboim for writing a most perceptive foreword, and Ara Guzelemian for reading the manuscript. I also would like to thank Sandra Fahy, who helped me collect and assemble these essays; Sarah Chalfant, Jin Auh, and Tracy Bohan at the Wylie Agency; Jennifer Crewe of Columbia University Press, who has been a most patient and helpful editor; and her colleagues Anne McCoy and Timothy Clifford.

MUSIC AT THE LIMITS

PART I
The Eighties

CHAPTER 1

The Music Itself: Glenn Gould's
Contrapuntal Vision

G LENN GOULD is an exception to almost all the other musical
performers in this century. He was a brilliantly proficient pianist (in a world of brilliantly proficient pianists) whose unique
sound, brash style, rhythmic inventiveness, and, above all, quality of attention seemed to reach out well beyond the act of performing itself. In the
eighty records he made, Gould's piano tone is immediately recognizable. At
any point in his career you could say, this is Gould playing, and not Alexis
Weissenberg, Vladimir Horowitz, or Alicia de Larrocha. His Bach stands in
a class by itself. Like Gieseking's Debussy and Ravel, Rubinstein's Chopin,
Schnabel's Beethoven, Katchen's Brahms, Michelangeli's Schumann, it defines the music, makes that artist's interpretation the one you have to have if
you are to get at the composer definitively. But unlike all those pianists and
their individual specialties, Gould playing Bach—no less sensuous, immediate, pleasurable, and impressive as music making than any of the others
I've mentioned—seems like a species of formal knowledge of an enigmatic
subject matter: it allows one to think that by playing the piano Gould is
proposing some complex, deeply interesting ideas. That he did all this as
the central focus of his career made that career more of an aesthetic and
cultural project than the short-lived act of playing Bach or Schoenberg.

Most people have treated Gould's various eccentricities as something to
be put up with, given that his performances were often so extraordinarily
worthwhile. Exceptional critics, Samuel Lipman and Edward Rothstein
principally, have gone further than that, saying that while Gould's uniqueness manifested itself in different, but usually erratic ways—humming,
strange habits of dress, playing that is unprecedented in its intelligence

Vanity Fair, May 1983; reprinted in John McGreevy, ed., *Glenn Gould: Variations*
(New York: Doubleday, 1983).

and grace—it was all part of the same phenomenon: a pianist whose work was an effort to produce not only performances but also statements and criticisms of the pieces he played. And indeed Gould's numerous writings, his departure from concert life in 1964, his single-minded attention to the details of record production, his garrulous, rococo way of being a hermit and ascetic, reinforce the notion that his performances could be connected to ideas, experiences, and situations not normally associated with the career of a virtuoso pianist.

That Gould's career truly began in 1955 with his recording of Bach's *Goldberg Variations* is, I think, apparent, and the move, in some sense, foreshadowed nearly everything he did thereafter, including his rerecording of the piece not long before his death. Until he put out the record, few major pianists except Rosalyn Tureck had played the *Goldberg* in public. Thus Gould's opening (and lasting) achievement was, in alliance with a major record company (a liaison Tureck never seemed to have), to place this highly patterned music before a very large public for the first time, and in doing so to create a terrain entirely his own—anomalous, eccentric, unmistakable.

You have the impression first that here is a pianist possessed of a demonic technique in which speed, accuracy, and power are subordinate to a discipline and calculation that derive not from a clever performer but from the music itself. Moreover, as you listen to the music you feel as if you are watching a tightly packed, dense work being unfolded, resolved almost, into a set of intertwined lines held together not by two hands but by ten fingers, each responsive to all the others, as well as to the two hands and the one mind really back of everything.

At one end of the work a simple theme is announced, a theme permitting itself to be metamorphosed thirty times, redistributed in modes whose theoretical complexity is enhanced by the pleasure taken in their practical execution. At the other end of the *Goldberg,* the theme is replayed after the variations have ceased, only this time the literal repetition is (as Borges says about Pierre Menard's version of the *Quixote*) "verbally identical, but infinitely richer." This process of proceeding brilliantly from microcosm to macrocosm and then back again is Gould's special accomplishment in his first *Goldberg:* by doing it pianistically he also lets you experience the sort of understanding normally the result of reading and thinking, not simply of playing a musical instrument.

I don't at all mean to denigrate the latter. It is simply that from the beginning Gould tried to articulate music in a different mode than was the case when, say, Van Cliburn—his near contemporary, a fine pianist—played Tchaikovsky or Rachmaninoff concertos. Gould's choice of back at the outset, and his subsequent recording of most of Bach's keyboard works, is central to what he was trying to do. Since Bach's music is preeminently contrapuntal or polyphonic, this fact imparts a really astonishingly powerful identity to Gould's career.

For the essence of counterpoint is simultaneity of voices, preternatural control of resources, apparently endless inventiveness. In counterpoint a melody is always in the process of being repeated by one or another voice: the result is horizontal, rather than vertical, music. Any series of notes is thus capable of an infinite set of transformations, as the series (or melody or subject) is taken up first by one voice then by another, the voices always continuing to sound against, as well as with, all the others. Instead of the melody at the top being supported by a thicker harmonic mass beneath (as in largely vertical nineteenth-century music), Bach's contrapuntal music is regularly composed of several equal lines, sinuously interwoven, working themselves out according to stringent rules.

Quite apart from its considerable beauty, a fully developed contrapuntal style like Bach's has a particular prestige within the musical universe. For one, its sheer complexity and frequent gravity suggest a formidable refinement and finality of statement; when Beethoven, or Bach, or Mozart writes fugally the listener is compelled to assume that an unusual importance is given the music, for at such moments everything—every voice, every instant, every interval—is, so to speak, written out, worked through, fully measured. One cannot say more in music (the tremendous fugue at the end of Verdi's *Falstaff* comes to mind) than in a strict fugue. And consequently the contrapuntal mode in music is, it seems, connected to eschatology, not only because Bach's music is essentially religious or because Beethoven's *Missa Solemnis* is highly fugal. For the rules of counterpoint are so demanding, so exact in their detail as to seem divinely ordained; transgressions of the rule—forbidden progressions, proscribed harmonies—are specified in such terms as *diabolus in musica*.

To master counterpoint is therefore in a way almost to play God, as Adrian Leverkühn, the hero of Thomas Mann's *Doctor Faustus,* understands. Counterpoint is the total ordering of sound, the complete management of time, the minute subdivision of musical space, and absolute absorption for the intellect. Running through the history of Western music, from Palestrina and Bach to the dodecaphonic rigors of Schoenberg, Berg, and Webern, is a contrapuntal mania for inclusiveness, and it is a powerful allusion to this that informs Mann's Hitlerian version of a pact with the devil in *Faustus,* a novel about a polyphonic German artist whose aesthetic fate encapsulates his nation's overreaching folly. Gould's contrapuntal performances come as close as I can imagine to delivering an inkling of what *might* be at stake in the composition and performance of counterpoint, minus perhaps any grossly political import. Not the least of this achievement, however, is that he never recoils from the comic possibility that high counterpoint may only be a parody, pure form aspiring to the role of world-historical wisdom.

In fine, Gould's playing enables the listener to experience Bach's contrapuntal excesses—for they are that, beautifully and exorbitantly—as no other pianist has. We are convinced that no one could *do* counterpoint, reproduce and understand Bach's fiendish skill, more than Gould. Hence he seems to perform at the limit where music, rationality, and the physical incarnation of both in the performer's fingers come together. Yet even though Gould's playing of Bach is so concentrated on its task, he manages also to suggest different kinds of power and intelligence that would appear in later recordings. In the course of recording Bach's keyboard works integrally, Gould produced a disc of Liszt's transcription of Beethoven's Fifth Symphony and, still later, his own versions of orchestral and vocal music by Wagner, late romantic music that was contrapuntal in its own overripe way, made even more artificial by being set in a chromatic polyphony that Gould forced out of the orchestral score and onto the piano keyboard.

The records, like all of Gould's playing, accentuate the overwhelming unnaturalness of his performances, from his very low chair to his slump, to his semi-staccato, aggressively clear sound. But they also illustrate the way in which Gould's predilection for contrapuntal music gave him an unexpectedly novel dimension. Sitting at his keyboard, doing impossible things all alone, no longer the concert performer but the disembodied recording artist, didn't Gould seem to become his own self-confirming, self-delighting hearer, a man who replaced the God that Albert Schweitzer suggested that Bach was writing for?

Certainly Gould's choice of music to play bears this out. He has written of his preference not only for polyphony in general, but also for the composer, like Richard Strauss, "who makes richer his own time by not being of it; who speaks for all generations by being of none." Gould's dislike of middle-period Beethoven, Mozart, and most of the nineteenth-century romantics whose music was intensely subjective or fashionable and too instrument-specific, is balanced by his admiration for pre- and post-romantics like Orlando Gibbons and Anton Webern, as well as for polyphonists (Bach and Strauss) whose all-or-nothing attitude to the instruments they wrote for made for a total discipline lacking in other composers. Strauss, for example, is Gould's choice as the major twentieth-century musical figure. Not only was Strauss eccentric, he was also concerned "with utilizing the fullest riches of late-romantic tonality *within* the firmest possible formal disciplines"; thus, Gould continues, Strauss's "interest was primarily the preservation of the *total* function of tonality—not simply in a work's fundamental outline, but even in its most specific minutiae of design." Like Bach then, Strauss was "painstakingly explicit at every level of . . . architectural concept." You write music in which every note counts and if like Strauss you have an explicit function in mind for each: whereas if like Bach you write simply for a keyboard instrument, or in the *The Art of the Fugue* for four unspecified voices, each voice is carefully disciplined. There are no strummed *oompahs* (although, alas they exist in Strauss), no mindlessly regular chordal accompaniments. The formal concept is articulated assertively and consciously, from the large structure to the merest ornament.

There is a good deal of exaggeration in these descriptions, but at any rate Gould's playing aims to be as explicit and detailed as he thinks the music he plays is. In a sense his performances extend, amplify, make more explicit the scores he interprets, scores that do not as a matter of principle include program music. Music is fundamentally dumb: despite its fertile syntactic and expressive possibilities, music does not encode reference, or ideas, or hypotheses discursively, the way language does. So the performer can either be (or play) dumb, or, as in Gould's case, the performer can set himself a great deal to do. If this might mean controlling the performance space to the extent of articulating, taking over his environment (by dressing and appearing to be against the grain), conducting the orchestra despite a conductor's presence, humming over and above the piano's sound, talking and writing as if to extend the piano's reach into verbal language via a whole slew of essays, interviews, record jacket notes, then Gould did so enthusiastically, like a mischievous, unstoppably talkative little prodigy.

The most impressive of the numerous Gould events I attended was his appearance in Boston in October 1961 with Paul Paray and the Detroit Symphony Orchestra. In the first half Gould did the Fifth *Brandenburg* with the Detroit's leading violinist and flutist. He was partially hidden from view, but his arms and head were visible, bobbing and swaying to the music, although his playing was suitably small-scaled, admirably light, and rhythmically propulsive, perfectly conscious of the other performers. Music with eyes, ears, and a nose, I remember thinking. (All of Gould's recorded concerto performances—especially the Bach concertos—are the same in one respect: so athletically tensile and rhetorically inflected is his playing that an electric tension is kept up between what seems often to be a heavy, rather plodding orchestra and a darting, skipping piano line that dives in and out of the orchestral mass with marvelous aplomb.) After the intermission Gould reemerged to play the Richard Strauss *Burleske,* a horrendously busy one-movement work that is not exactly a repertoire staple; Gould incidentally never recorded the piece. Technically his performance with the Detroit was stunning; one wouldn't have believed it possible that an essentially Bach-ensemble pianist would all of a sudden have become a whirlwind post- and hyper-Rachmaninoff-style virtuoso.

But the real wonder was more bizarre still, and as one reflects on Gould's later career, what he did in the Strauss besides playing the piano seems like a prefiguring of subsequent developments. As if to enlarge his part as a soloist, Gould conducted the orchestra extravagantly, if not intelligibly. Paray was there too, and he of course was the actual conductor. Gould, however, conducted to himself (plainly disconcerting though the sight of him was), doubtless confusing the orchestra and, unless Paray's occasionally murderous glances at Gould were part of some prerehearsed routine, annoying Paray. Conducting for Gould seemed to be an ecstatic, imperialistic widening of his reading of the *Burleske,* at first through his fingers, then by means of his arms and head, then finally by pushing out from his personal pianistic space into the orchestra's territory. Watching Gould do all this was a skewed lesson in the discipline of detail, the artist being led where the fanatically detailed, expansively inclined composer led him.

There is more to a Gould performance than that. Most critics who have written about him mention the clean dissections he seems to give the pieces he plays. In this he strips the piano literature of most of its inherited traditions, whether these have come down in the form of liberties taken with tempi or tone, or from declamatory opportunities that issue as a sort of profession deformation from the great line of piano virtuosos, or again that are ingrained in patterns of performance certified by famous teachers (Theodor Leschetizky, Rosina Lhevinne, Alfred Cortot, etc.). There is none of this in Gould. He neither sounds like other pianists, nor, so far as I can determine, has anyone succeeded in sounding like him. It is as if Gould's playing, like his career, is entirely self-made, even self-born, with neither a preexisting dynasty nor an extra-Gouldian destiny framing it.

The reason for this is partly the result of Gould's forthright egoism, partly the result of contemporary Western culture. Like many of the composers and pieces he has played, Gould wants to appear beholden to no one as he goes his own way. Not many pianists will take on and make sense of so formidable a mass as both books of Bach's *Well-Tempered Clavier,* all his partitas, the two- and three-part inventions, the toccatas, the English and French suites, the *Art of the Fugue,* all the keyboard concertos including the Italian, plus such oddities as Bizet's *Variations chromatiques,* Sibelius's sonatas, pieces by Byrd and Gibbons, Strauss's *Enoch Arden* and his *Ophelialieder,* the Schoenberg concerto, transcriptions of Wagner's "Siegfried Idyll" and Beethoven's Pastoral Symphony. What Gould sustains in all this is (to use a phrase he once applied to Sibelius) a style that is "passionate but antisensual." It allows the listener to observe Gould's "gradual, lifelong construction of a state of wonder and serenity" not only as an independent aesthetic phenomenon, but also as a theatrical experience whose source is Gould himself.

In 1964 Gould left the concert world and was reborn as a creature of the technology he exploited to permit more or less infinite reproduction, infinite repetition ("take-twoness," he called it), infinite creation and re-creation. No wonder he referred to the recording studio as "womblike," a place where "time turns in upon itself," where a new "art form with its own laws and its own liberties. . .and its quite extraordinary possibilities" is born with the recording artist. A highly readable book by Geoffrey Payzant, *Glenn Gould: Music and Mind,* copiously describes this rebirth, as well as Gould's skill in managing to keep the spotlight on himself. Gould's post-concertizing afterlife was passionate, antinatural antisensuality carried very far indeed, and it certainly flowed from his cheery penchant for being lonely, original, unprecedented, and somehow immensely gregarious, someone who curiously never tired of himself.

In less metaphysical terms, what occurred in his career after 1964 was a displacement in emphasis. In the concert hall the emphasis had been on the reception by the audience of a live performer, a commodity directly purchased, consumed, and exhausted during two hours of concert time. Such a transaction had its roots in eighteenth-century patronage and the class structure of the *ancien régime,* although during the nineteenth century, music performance became a more easily acquired mass commodity. In the late twentieth century, however, Gould acknowledged that the new commodity was a limitlessly reproducible object, the plastic disc or tape; as performer, Gould has transferred himself back from the stage to the studio, to a site where creation has become production, a place where he could manage to be creator and interpreter simultaneously without also directly submitting to the whims of a ticket-purchasing public. There is no small irony in the fact that Gould's new bonds were with technicians and corporate executives, and that he spoke of his relationship with them (and they of him) in emotionally intimate terms.

In the meantime, Gould was able to push his contrapuntal view of things a bit further. His aim as an artist would be, like Bach or Mozart, to organize the field completely, to subdivide time and space with utmost control, to "speculate the elements" (Mann's phrase in *Doktor Faustus*) in such a way as to take a row of elementary notes and then force them through as many changes as possible, changes that would come from splicing bits of tape together to make new wholes, from displacing sequences (for instance, the different enunciations of the *Goldberg* theme in Gould's 1981 version were recorded out of order), from using different pianos for different sections of the same music, recording and living without paying attention to the time of day, making an informal studio space into the opposite of the concert hall's crippling formality. This, Gould said, was giving additional enrichment to the idea of process, to carrying on more or less forever.

It was also, perhaps poignantly, a way of trying to undermine the biological and sexual bases of the human performer's life. For the late-twentieth-century musical artist, recording would be a form of immortality suited not only to a noncomposer (nineteenth-century-style composers being now both rare and rarefied), but to what the German cultural critic Walter Benjamin called the age of mechanical reproduction. Gould was the first great musical performer of the twentieth century unequivocally to choose that fate. Before Gould, performers like Stokowski and Rubenstein had self-consciously lived in the hybrid world of wealth and romantic cliché created by spectators, impresarios, and ticket sellers. Gould saw that such a choice, however admirable it was for those two, wouldn't do for him. Yet for someone so self-aware, Gould never reflected on the unflattering complicities of an enterprise such as his, which depended ultimately on giant corporations, an anonymous mass culture, and advertising hype for its success. That he just did not look at the market system, whose creature to some degree he was, may have been cynical prudence, or it may have been that he somehow couldn't fit it into his playing. It was as if the real social setting of his work was one of the things that Gould's contrapuntal skills were not meant to absorb, however much these skills assumed the system's complaisance.

Yet he was far from being a pastoral idiot-savant despite his affinity for the silence and solitude of the North. As the critic Richard Poirier has said of Frost, Lawrence, and Mailer, Gould was a performing self whose career was the cultivated result of immense talent, careful choice, urbanity, and, up to a point, self-sufficiency, all of them managed together like a polyphonic structure in relief. The last record to be released in Gould's lifetime—the rerecorded *Goldberg Variations*—in almost every detail is a tribute to an artist uniquely able to rethink and replan a complex piece of music in a new way, and yet keep it (as much as the earlier version) sounding recognizably like a performance by Glenn Gould.

Child and partner of the age of mechanical reproduction, Gould set himself the task of being at home with what Mann calls "the opposing hosts of counterpoint." Despite its limitations, Gould's work was more interesting than nearly all other performing artists of this era. Only Rachmaninoff, I think, had that special combination of lean intelligence, magnificent dash, and perfectly economical line that Gould produced in nearly everything he played. Technique in the service of an inquiring understanding, complexity resolved without being domesticated, wit relieved of philosophical baggage: Glenn Gould plays the piano.

CHAPTER 2

Remembrances of Things Played:
Presence and Memory in the Pianist's Art

PIANISTS RETAIN a remarkable hold on our cultural life There are the crowd-pleasing "superstars" as well as a somewhat lesser order of pianists who nevertheless have sizable followings. Recordings enhance and amplify out involvement in what the performing pianist does: they may evoke memories of actual recitals—live audiences coughing and clapping, live pianists playing. Why do we seek this experience? Why are we interested in pianists at all, given that they are a product of nineteenth-century European culture? And further, what makes some pianists interesting, great, extraordinary? How, without being either too systematic or absurdly metaphysical, can we characterize what it is that sustains the distinguished pianist before us, claiming out attention, bringing him or her back to us year after year?

For although there is an immense piano repertory, there is little in it that can be called new; the world of the piano is really a world of mirrors, repetitions, imitations. And what actually gets performed is a relatively small part of the repertory—Beethoven, Schubert, Chopin, Schumann, Liszt; some Debussy and Ravel; some Bach, Mozart, and Haydn. Alfred Brendel has said that there are only two performing traditions with regard to the piano; one built on the works of Chopin and a few related composers, the other and richer one made up of the works of Central European composers from Hamburg to Vienna, and from Bach to Schoenberg. A pianist who attempts to build a career performing the works of, say, Weber, MacDowell, Alkan, Gottschalk, Scriabin, or Rachmaninoff usually ends up as little more than a peripheral artist.

My own enjoyment of today's pianism, an enjoyment involving not only the pianist's presence but also my ability to play the instrument and to

Harper's, November 1985.

reflect on what I play and hear, is pointed toward the past. That is to say, to a large degree it is about memory. That my pleasure should be so strongly linked to the past (more specifically, my understanding of it) is not hard to understand. Despite the energetic immediacy of their presentation, pianists are conservative, essentially curatorial figures. They play little new music, and still prefer to perform in the public hall, where music arrived, via the family and the court, in the nineteenth century. It is private memory that is at the root of the pleasure we take in the piano, and it is the interesting pianist who puts us in touch with this pleasure—who gives the recital its weirdly compelling power.

On March 23 and March 31 of this year, Maurizio Pollini performed at Carnegie Hall and Avery Fisher Hall. Pollini, a Milanese, is forty-three years old, and from the very beginning his career has been extraordinary: at the age of eighteen he won the Warsaw Chopin Competition, the first non-Slav to do so. His programs for the New York recitals—Beethoven and Schubert in the one, Schumann and Chopin in the other—were the typically Pollinian mix of familiar, even hackneyed, pieces (the "Moonlight" Sonata, Chopin's "Funeral March" Sonata) and difficult and eccentric works (the Schubert Sonata in C Minor and Schumann's last piano work, the *Gesänge der Frühe*, written during, and some would say exemplifying, the final stage of his mental illness). More important than the programs, though, was the way Pollini demonstrated once again that he is an *interesting* pianist, one who stands out in the enormous crowd of first-rate pianists filling the New York concert agenda.

To begin with there is Pollini's technical prowess, which comes across as neither glib facility nor tedious heroic effort. When he plays especially difficult pieces like the Chopin Etudes or one of the complex Schumann or Schubert compositions, you do not automatically remark on how cleverly he has solved the music's challenge to sheer dexterity. His technique allows you to forget technique entirely. Nor do you say, This is the *only* way Chopin, or Schubert, or Schumann ought to sound. What comes through in all of Pollini's performances is an approach to the music—a direct *approach*, aristocratically clear, powerfully and generously articulated. By this I also mean that you are aware of him encountering and learning a piece, playing it supremely well, and then returning his audience to "life" with an enhanced, and shared, understanding of the whole business. Pollini doesn't have a platform manner, or a set of poses. What he presents instead is a totally unfussy *reading* of the piano literature. Several years ago I saw him, jacketless, and with the score before him, perform Stockhausen's intransigently thorny *Klavierstück X;* I could perceive in his playing some of the marginality and playful anguish of the composition itself—music that takes itself to limits unapproached in the work of other contemporary composers.

Even when Pollini does not achieve this effect—and many have remarked on his occasionally glassy, tense, and hence repellent perfection—the expectation that it will occur in another of his recitals remains vivid. This is because there is for the listener the sense of a career unfolding *in time.* And Pollini's career communicates a feeling of growth, purpose, and form. Sadly, most pianists, like most politicians, seem merely to wish to remain in power. I have thought this, perhaps unfairly of Vladimir Horowitz and Rudolf Serkin. These are men with tremendous gifts, and much dedication and energy; they have given great pleasure to their audiences. But their work today strikes me as simply going on. This can also be said about fine but much less interesting pianists like André Watts, Bella Davidovitch, Vladimir Ashkenazy, and Alexis Weissenberg. But you could never say that Pollini's work just goes on, any more that you could say that about the work of Alfred Brendel; nor could you so neatly write off Sviatoslav Richter or Emil Gilels or Arturo Benedetti Michelangeli or Wilhem Kempff. Each of these pianists represents a project unfolding *in time,* a project that is about something more than playing the piano in public for two hours. Their recitals are opportunities to experience the exploration, interpretation, and, above all reinterpretation of a major portion of the pianistic repertory.

All pianists aspire to be distinctive, to make an impression, to have a unique aesthetic and social imprint. This is what we call a pianist's "personality." But pianists are thwarted in their desire to sound "different" by the fact that audiences today take for granted a very high level of technical competence. It is assumed that pianists will be sophisticated performers, and that they will get through the Chopin or Liszt Etudes flawlessly. Thus pianists must rely on the equivalent of special effects to establish and sustain their pianistic identities. Ideally, a listener should be able to recognize the sound, style, and manner of another individual pianist, and not confuse them with those of other pianists. Still, resemblances and comparisons are crucial to the outlines of any interesting signature. Thus we speak of schools of pianists, disciples one or another style, similarities between one Chopin specialist and another.

No contemporary pianist more brilliantly established himself through an extraordinarily distinctive identity than Glenn Gould, the Canadian pianist who died in 1982 at the age of fifty. Even Gould's detractors recognized the greatness of his gifts. He had a phenomenal capacity to play complicated polyphonal music—preeminently Bach's—with astonishing clarity and liveliness. András Schiff has rightly said of Gould that "he could control five voices more intelligently than most [pianists] can control two."

Gould's career was launched with a stunning recording of Bach's *Goldberg Variations,* and so rich was his pianistic resourcefulness that one of the last records he made was still another *Goldberg* interpretation. What is remarkable is that the 1982 version is very different from the earlier one—and yet it is patently the work of the same pianist. Gould's interpretation of Bach was meant to illustrate the music's richness, not simply the performer's ingenuity—without which, of course, Bach's fertile counterpoint would not have emerged in so startlingly different a way in the second recording. Gould's performances of Bach—cerebral, brilliantly ordered, festive, and energetic—paved the way for other pianists to return to the composer. Gould left the recital stage in 1964 and confined himself to recording. But a string of other pianists, all of them influenced by Gould—András Schiff, Peter Serkin, Joao Carlos Martins, Charles Rosen, Alexis Weissenberg— have become known for performing the *Goldberg Variations.* Gould's Bach playing caused a seismic (by pianistic standards) shift in ideas about performance. No longer would Bach be ignored in favor of the standard repertory—Beethoven, Chopin, Liszt, Brahms, Schumann. No longer would his work be created as inoffensive "opening" material for recitals.

Gould's playing was noteworthy for more than mere keyboard virtuosity. He played every piece as if he were X-raying it, rendering each of its components with independence and clarity. The result was usually a single beautifully fluid process with many interesting subsidiary parts. Everything seemed thought out, and yet nothing sounded heavy, contrived, or labored. Moreover, he gave every indication, in all that he did, of being a mind at work, not just a fleet pair of hands. After he retired from the concert stage Gould made a number of records, television films, and radio broadcasts that attest to his resourcefulness beyond the keyboard. He was at once articulate and amiably eccentric. Above all, he always surprised. He never contented himself with the expected repertory: he went from Bach to Wagner to Schoenberg; back to Brahms, Beethoven, Bizet, Richard Strauss, Grieg, and Renaissance composers like Gibbons and Byrd. And, in a perverse departure from the tradition of playing only those composers and pieces one likes, Gould declared that he *didn't* like Mozart, then proceeded to record all of his sonatas, playing at exaggerated speeds and with unlovely inflections. Gould presented himself to the world meticulously. He had a sound all his own; and he also had arguments about all kinds of music, arguments that seemed to find their way into his playing.

Of course intelligence, taste, and originality do not amount to anything unless the pianist has the technical means to convey them. In this respect, a great pianist is like a great tennis player, a Rod Laver or a John McEnroe, who can serve strongly, volley accurately, and hit perfect ground strokes—every day, against every opponent. We should not underestimate the degree to which we respond to a fine pianist's athletic skill. The speed and fluency with which Josef Lhevinne could play thirds and sixths; the thundering accuracy and clangor of Horowitz's octaves; the rhythmic dash and chordal virtuosity of Alicia de Larrocha's Granados and Albéniz; Michelangeli's transcendentally perfect rendering of Ravel's *Gaspard de la Nuit*, Pollini's performance of Beethoven's *Hammerklavier*, with its finger-bending fugue and its meditative slow movement; Richter's strong but ethereally refined performances of Schumann, especially the long episodic pieces like the *Humoresque*—all these, in their bravura and virtuosic elaboration, lift the playing of the notes above the ordinary. These are physical achievements

But the intelligent audience cannot be satisfied by what might be called loud-and-fast playing. There is virtuosity of style, too, in Brendel's Beethoven performances, where we feel intellect and taste allied with formidable technical command; or in Murray Perahia's Schubert, where a gentle singing line is supported by a superbly controlled chordal underpinning; or in Martha Argerich's sinuous filigree work in a Chopin scherzo. Similarly, the resolution of great musical complexity holds our interest, whether we find it in Charles Rosen's performances of Elliott Carter, in Jerome Lowenthal's performances of Bartók concertos, or in the incandescent purity of Edwin Fischer's Bach or Mozart. Above all, the pianist must physically shape sounds into form—that is, into the coherent interlocking of sonority, rhythm, inflection, and phrasing that tells us: *this* is what Beethoven had in mind. It is in this way, at such a moment, that the composer's identity and the pianist's are reconciled.

Pianists' programs are put together with greater or lesser degrees of thought and skill. While I would not go to hear an unknown pianist only because he or she has an interesting program, I would also not go to hear a distinguished pianist offering an obvious or carelessly put together program. One looks for programs that appear to *say* something—that highlight aspects of the piano literature or of performance in unexpected ways. In this, Gould was a genius, whereas Vladimir Ashkenazy, his very gifted near-contemporary, is not. Ashkenazy first announced himself as a "romantic" pianist specializing in Chopin, Liszt, and Rachmaninoff, and he confirms his prowess in that field every time he plays. Yet his programs do not reveal new meanings or new connections, at least not those of the sort Gould revealed when he linked Bach and Richard Strauss, or Sweelinck and Hindemith (the contrapuntal elaborations of the latter two composers, similar in their learned determination and often graceless length, occur almost three centuries apart).

Some programs are interesting because they present the audience with a narrative. This narrative maybe conventional, moving historically from Bach or Mozart to Beethoven, the Romantics, and then the moderns. Or a program may have an inner narrative based on evolving forms (sonatas, variations, fantasies), tonalities, or styles. Of course, it is the pianist who makes the narrative come alive, consolidates its lines, enforces its main points.

Each of Pollini's programs last March focused on a pair of near-contemporary composers: Beethoven and Schubert in the March 23 recital, Schumann and Chopin in the performance on March 31. In both recitals the older composer was represented by works whose formal structures are "free"—Beethoven's two Op. 27 sonatas, which he described as *quasi una fantasia,* and Schumann's *Gesänge der Frühe* and *Davidsbündlertänze,* made up of loosely connected mood pieces. The younger composers were represented by two kinds of works: a shorter, rigorously symmetrical piece, intended as a *divertissement* but revealing a strong minor-key pathos (Schubert's C Minor Andante, Chopin's Scherzo in C-sharp Minor), and a major sonata (Schubert's late Sonata in C Minor, Chopin's Sonata No. 2 in B-flat Minor) that recalled the episodic material featured earlier. Thus Pollini's programs made clear the rigorously structured, almost Bach-like logic in Beethoven's and Schumann's free, or "fantastic," forms, as well as the way in which Schubert's and Chopin's sonatas, in the grip of a great musical intelligence, almost overflow their formal restrictions The "almost" is a tribute to Pollini's restraint in observing the significant, if small, difference between fantasy and sonata in the early Romantic idiom. It hardly requires saying that such complete satisfaction as offered by Pollini's consummately demonstrative but unpretentious performances is very rarely found.

Most programs are divided into halves, each with its own introduction and climax. It is rare for a program not to end with a bang, although pianists generally make some effort to link the fireworks with the rest of the performance. Usually this is done by including something substantial—a big Chopin group, for example—as a way of impressing the audience with the pianist's power. Encores, in my opinion, are appalling, like food stains on a handsome suit. They serve to illustrate that the art of building a program is still a primitive one. In fact, the typical program, constructed out of little more than the most simple-minded contrasts (a reflective piece followed by a showy one), is often a reason for *not* attending a recital.

Some pianists tend to put together didactic programs—all the Beethoven or Schubert sonatas, for example. Last March, at the Metropolitan Museum, András Schiff did an especially noteworthy sequence of three Bach recitals, culminating in the *Goldberg Variations.* The first pianists to attempt such programs were Ferruccio Busoni and Anton Rubinstein, whose recitals offered a history of piano music on a truly heroic scale. All-Chopin or all-Schumann recitals are not in themselves arresting, in part because they are not that uncommon, but the sequence of sixteen concerto performances presented by Artur Rubinstein in the 1960s *was* interesting. While the performances were noteworthy in illuminating the various transformations of the concerto form, that was not the chief source of their power. What was so gripping was the spectacle of a feat combining aesthetic range and athletic power and spanning a number of weeks.

But such interesting programming is rare. Most pianists plan their recitals around a repertory stamped by their predecessors, hoping—generally without any basis, in my opinion—to capture the music for themselves. What aesthetic identity can a pianist possibly have if he allows himself to be billed as "the new Schnabel" or "the twentieth-century Tausig"? Even worse are those who try to imitate the sounds of the one pianist who for half a century has been the model of dynamic and, I would say, strident pianism, Vladimir Horowitz. None has succeeded, in part at least because Horowitz himself has gone on playing.

Adding to the limitations of the pianistic repertory is the fact that most of the piano literature is very familiar and pretty well fixed: the notes are written down and, in almost all cases, the pieces have been recorded. Thus to play the four Chopin ballades, as Emanuel Ax recently did at Carnegie Hall, is not just to play the pieces, but to replay them. The hope is that the pianist does so with variations that reveal his or her imagination and taste—and that show no sign of copying others or distorting the composer's text. Most interesting pianists, even when working through a conventional program, give the impression that their playing of a piece is also a commentary on it, much as an essay on a great novel is a commentary, and not simply a plot summary. A successful performance of the Schumann Fantasy, such as Pollini's, makes the listener feel two disparate things *together:* you feel that this is the work Schumann wrote; and you feel that Pollini, in responding to its infinitely variable rhythmic and rhetorical impulses, accents, phrases, pauses, and inflections, is *commenting* on the piece, giving us his version of it. Thus do pianists make their statements.

The world of pianism is a curious amalgam of "culture" and business. Some would argue that the cultural context (no less than the ticketseller's booth) is a distraction from the *sound* of the pianist. But that view too easily dismisses as distractions some of the circumstances that actually stimulate what we would term interesting pianism. The very prominence of modern pianists is in fact a result of the fraying, described fifty years ago by Theodor Adorno, of the connection between the three essential threads of music making: the composition and production of music, its reproduction or performance, and its consumption. Most pianists have no time for contemporary music; conversely, not much music is being written with the piano in mind. The public is saturated with mechanically reproduced music. Moreover, musical literacy is no longer a requirement for the educated person. As a result, audiences are by and large removed from the acts of playing and composing.

Musical competitions, which were established as a way of launching virtuoso careers, have also contributed to specialization. Most of these contests are run by an odd assortment of philanthropists, musicians, and concert managers, and they have tended to foster a kind of pianistic triumphalism. To those like myself who are aghast at what takes place in most competitions, this triumphalism brings to mind the world of sports, where amphetamines and steroids are routinely taken to improve performance. Occasionally pianists will survive the paranoid atmosphere that is a feature of all competitions. The pianism of these few is not ruined by their having to adopt the bravura techniques and paced-down and neutral style favored by juries. Pollini is one of the survivors, in part, I believe, because after he won the Warsaw Chopin Competition he did not immediately go on tour to launch a "major career." Instead he spent several years studying and, not incidentally, maturing as a pianist. When I speak of survival I am not suggesting that prizewinners fizzle out after a while. The roster of successful prizewinners and competition pianists is very large: Ashkenazy, Malcolm Frager, and André Michel Schub come to mind. What I am suggesting is that hardly any of them do interesting work.

"Star" pianists command great fees, and when this money is combined with the income from their records it can amount to a sizable fortune. Some pianists seem to benefit from the system: their success allows them to play less often, to take sabbaticals, to learn new (and riskier) material. In general, however, there seems to be a scramble for more concerts, better recording contracts, greater "opportunities." The stars struggle to maintain their positions and lesser luminaries try desperately to move up a rung. All this results in little pleasure for the mass audience, although it produces much profit for the agents, middlemen, and media manipulators.

There is not much hope that composer, performer, and listener will once again work together—without the distraction of recording deals and prizes—in a real community, the kind of community for which the Bach family has always served as an attractive model. Nor is the public likely to become less susceptible to hype and commercialism. But there *are* signs, both within the piano world and outside it, that many people feel the need to reestablish links between piano playing and other human activities, so that the mindless virtuosity of the whizbang pianist might be superseded by something more interesting. Certainly Pollini's success has something to do with this, as does Brendel's. And Glenn Gould, in everything he did, expressed dissatisfaction with piano playing as such: his project was an attempt to connect pianism with the larger society.

All of this is evidence of a pianism trying to break out of its intellectual silence, its fetishes and rituals, its "beautiful" sounds and athletic skill. We will always admire those sounds, that skill; and we will always take pleasure in listening to pianists perform the standard repertory. But the experience of the piano is intensified when it is joined to the other experiences in which we find nourishment.

How do pianists transport us from the performance itself to another realm of significance? Listen to the record of Sergei Rachmaninoff. Rachmaninoff fairly bristles with interest; everything he does strikes us as an intervention into a piece of music that would otherwise be a score dead on the page. We feel there is a point he is trying to make. In playing the Schumann *Carnaval*, for example, he makes us aware of the composer working the piece out, bringing it to statement; and yet the chaos of Schumann's merely private vision is plainly in evidence. We feel the same thing about the playing of Alfred Cortot.

This sort of pianism is not simply a matter of taking risks, playing at outrageously fast tempi, introducing highly inflected lines. Rather—and this is the central matter—such pianism draws us in because its processes are apparent, compelling, intelligently provoking. The same point can be made negatively. There is nothing less stimulating than a pianist whose sole concern is perfection, perfection of the sort that causes one to say: How perfect is this playing. The emphasis on winning prizes certainly encourages an aesthetic of "accomplishment," as does the desire to remove from the performance everything but the pianist's dazzling finger-work. Put differently, piano playing that seems so finished as to be solely about itself (the work of the formidable Josef Lhevinne comes to mind) pushes the listener away and isolates the pianist in that sterile environment reserved for "pros."

The kind of playing that encourages me is playing that lets me in, so to speak: the pianist, by the intimacy of his or her playing, makes me feel that I would want to play that way too. The work of Dinu Lipatti, who turned out burningly pure performances of Mozart and Chopin, exudes that sense, as does the work of a relatively obscure school of British pianists—Myra Hess, Clifford Curzon, the great Solomon, and the equally fine Benno Moiseiwitsch. Today Daniel Barenbboim, Radu Lupu, and Perahia carry on in that vein.

One could argue that the social essence of pianism is precisely the opposite: it *ought* to alienate and distance the public, thereby accentuating the social contradictions that gave rise to the virtuoso pianist, the preposterous result of the overspecialization of contemporary culture. But this argument ignores what is just as apparent, and no less a result of the alienation produced by consumerism—namely, the *utopian* effect of pianistic performances. For the performer traffics between composer and listener. And insofar as performers do this in ways that involve us listeners in the experience and processes of performing, they invite us into a utopian realm of acute awareness that is otherwise inaccessible to us. Interesting pianism, in short, breaks down the barriers between audience and interpreter, and does so without violating music's essential silence.

When a performance taps into its audience's subjective time, enriches it and makes it more complex, it becomes more than a couple of hours of good entertainment. Here, I think, is the essence of what can make the piano and pianists interesting. Each listener brings to a performance memories of other performances, a history of relationships with the music, a web of affiliations; and all of this is activated by the performance at hand. Every pianist does this differently. Gould seemed actually to invent himself and his playing; it was as if he had no antecedents. The counterpoint seemed to speak to you directly, intelligently, vividly, forcing you to leave your ideas and experiences in abeyance. Pollini, on the other hand, lets you hear in his Schumann not only the composer's episodic genius but also the performances of other pianists—Michelangeli, for instance—from whom Pollini has learned, and gone beyond. The intellectual rigor of both pianists compares, in strength and cogency, with the prose of first-rate discourse.

Thus the greatest pianists somehow bridge the gap between the unnaturally refined, rarefied world of the recital stage and the world of music in human life. Surely we have all been tremendously moved by a piece of music, and have imagined what it must be like to feel compelled to perform it, to be disturbed into expressing it aloud, to be urged into articulating it, note by note, line by line. It is this experience which the best pianists can stimulate: the conviction of their playing, the beauty and nobility of their sound, make me feel what I might feel were I able to play as they can.

This is not all a matter of the performer meeting one's expectations. Just the opposite: it is a matter of the performer giving rise to expectation, making possible an encounter with memory that can be expressed only in music performed this way, now, before one.

Many years ago in Europe I heard the great German pianist Wilhelm Kempff perform. To my knowledge Kempff has played in America only once recently, a Carnegie Hall recital about ten or twelve years ago which was not very successful. He has not been much celebrated in this country, overshadowed perhaps by lesser contemporaries such as Wilhelm Backhaus and Serkin. Kempff's music has a unique, singing tone, and his playing, like Gould's, is unusual in not bearing the imprint of his teachers, or of other pianists. What you do hear in his playing is an unfolding interpretation. Kempff is someone for whom technique has been subordinated to discovery, for whom the piano is an instrument sharpening perception, rather than delivering perfectly fashioned sounds. This is true of all his work, from the rigorous counterpoint of the terminal fugue in Beethoven's Op. 110 to the fantastic, broken energy of Schumann's *Kreisleriana.*

The surface finish of Kempff's playing never impresses us with either its assertiveness or its strength. Rather, we are aware of him bringing a literal reading of the notes to its fulfillment, much the way, over a longer period of time, we learn a piece of music, grow to understand it, and finally know it, as the beautiful phrase has it, "by heart."

To understand what I mean, listen to Kempff's 1976 performance of Bach's "Jesu, Joy of Man's Desiring." Most people know this piece from Dinu Lipatti's transparent and pure recording. But while Lipatti uses Myra Hess's transcription, Kempff uses his own, thereby heightening the intimacy of his performance. Bach's work is a serene elaboration of chorale melody with a sinuous triplet obbligato, which Lipatti renders in a legato encompassing infallibly stated inner voices; this execution is envied by most other pianists. Yet the listener is always aware of one effect or another claiming his attention. This is especially apparent when one compares Lipatti's interpretation with that of Kempff. By the time Kempff reaches the final statement of the choral tune, obbligato and melody have been expanded to embrace the pianist's lifetime of attention to Bach's music. The disciplined line of the performance reaches its conclusion without pious triumphalism or trite melancholy. The music's outward evidence and inner movement are experienced as two forms articulated together. And we realize that while much of the pianistic enterprise as we know it—through playing (if we play), and through listening—takes place in the public sphere, its fullest effects are felt in a private sphere of memory and association which is the listener's own. This sphere is shaped, on the one hand, by the enveloping sphere of performances, patterns of taste, cultural institutions, aesthetic styles, and historical pressures, and, on the other, by far more personal pleasures.

I am speaking here of the quite considerable musical world that was explored and illuminated by Proust in *A le recherche du temps perdu* and by Thomas Mann in *Doktor Faustus,* those extraordinary monuments to the convergence of literary, musical, and social modernism. It is an indication of how powerfully the three spheres still interact that Glenn Gould seemed to be the embodiment of Mann's Adrian Leverkuhn, and that the robust theatricality of Artur Rubinstein's pianism seems to come straight out of the salons and *musicales* of Proust's Hôtel de Guermantes in the Faubourg Saint-Germain.

That the corporate world of the music business has replaced bohemia and the *beau monde* as the environment for concert music tells us of marketable commodities, yes; but it also testifies to the durability of a tradition served and often ennobled by the contemporary pianist, who, when he or she functions on the level attained by Pollini, attests to the tradition's variety and seriousness.

The greatest performances provide the invaluable restatements and forceful interpretations of the essay, a literary form overshadowed by the grander structures of epic and tragedy. The essay, like the recital, is occasional, re-creative, and personal. And essayists, like pianists, concern themselves with the givens: those works of art always worth another critical and reflective reading. Above all, neither pianist nor essayist can offer final readings, however definitive their performances may be. The fundamental sportiness of both genres is what keeps them honest, as well as vital. But there is an irreducible romance to the pianist's art. It is suggested by the underlying melancholy in Schumann's *Humoresque* and Chopin's Ballade in F Minor; by the lingering authority of legendary pianists—Busoni, Eugen d'Albert, Franz Liszt, Leopold Godowsky—with magical names; by the sonorous power that can encompass the solidest Beethoven and the most slender Fauré; by the curious, almost audible mixture of dedication and money circulating through the recital's atmosphere.

CHAPTER 3

Pomp and Circumstance (on Musical Festivals)

READING THE brief but intelligent article on festivals in Grove's *Dictionary*, you become aware of the deep divergence between premodern music festivals as symbolic rituals connected with religion and agriculture and modern music festivals as commemorations of great composers or as commercial and tourist attractions. From the great theatrical festivals of fifth-century Athens to the druidic Eisteddfod and the thirteenth-century Puy in France, the first type has now receded into a dim anthropological past. The second type is very much with us, too much so. With a few exceptions, its extraordinary proliferation and degradation have further weakened a musical life that seems to be getting more disablingly eccentric as time goes on.

Modern musical festivals began during the nineteenth century as worshipful commemorations of great composers—Handel, Mozart, Bach, Beethoven and, later, Wagner. Wagner's Bayreuth Festival, which opened in 1876, was unusual in that it was originally planned as a revolutionary celebration, not as a monument to the high bourgeoisie and its authorized cultural memory. In a review of Wagner's letters, Thomas Mann noted that the composer's intention was to

proclaim the necessity of putting a torch to the whole of bourgeois civilization along with its commercialized theatre industry. In the wake of this fiery cleansing, an isolated enthusiast here and there (like [Wagner] himself) might summon together the survivors of this despicable world and ask them: "Which of you would like to help me put on a drama?" Then only men of truly disinterested motives would come forward, since it would no longer be possible to make money out of the enterprise. They would then gather

The Nation, August 30, 1986.

together in a rapidly erected wooden building to show people what art really is. . . . The building was to be placed on a hill, a temple of art visible for miles around. The people would come together from the four corners of the land to be edified by a beauty pure and sublime. Only the most sublime works were to be given, in productions of the very highest standards.

After the sublime performances ("with no charge for admission, of course") the project would end, and the theater would be torn down.

No such thing happened. By the end of the nineteenth century, Bayreuth was a place of social pilgrimage—Proust's unworthy Odette, not a knowledgeable music lover at all, irritated Swann by wanting to attend and to rent one of King Ludwig's castles as a nice place to stay—and by the 1930s the festival had become a symbol of the 1,000-year Reich. When it was reopened by Wilhelm Furtwängler in 1951, with a cleansing performance of Beethoven's Choral Symphony, it was quickly established as the standard by which all performances of Wagner are measured. Directed by Wolfgang and Wieland Wagner, Richard's grandsons, Bayreuth attracted such major conductors as Hans Knappertsbusch, Andre Cluytens, Karl Böhm and, more recently, Pierre Boulez. If performance standards have slipped in recent years, the festival nevertheless remains an extraordinarily durable and expensive one; to get in during July and August for a complete *Ring* cycle (no easy task) is to incur ticket and hotel expenses in the thousands of dollars.

Salzburg's Festival, begun in 1877, is no less durable, expensive and mortuary, although the charms of little Mozart—who in his day seemed to detest nearly everything about the place: its notables, its horrid *Gemütlichkeit*—have been superseded by the Mercedes-like power and efficiency of Herbert von Karajan, the General Music Director of Europe. Although Salzburg is still supposedly dedicated to Mozart, other composers (Verdi, Strauss, Beethoven) are represented there, all herded under the driven and totalizing personality of von Karajan, who once dreamed of preparing productions of fifty operas in a central European location and then sending them forth to tour the world. Bayreuth and Salzburg both conform to the pattern of festivals expressing the special aesthetic and political personality of one ego; others are Menotti's at Spoleto, Britten's at Aldeburgh, Menuhin's at Bath, Serkin's at Marlboro, Casals's at Prades and San Juan.

Such festivals often suffer from atrophy, or the kind of traditionalism that is associated with dictatorships and cabals. The alternative, however, festival-by-committee, usually works no better. The most common type of summer festival is essentially an extension of an orchestra's or opera company's regular season. Some are more blatantly commercial than others. In

Vienna and Munich the so-called summer opera festival offers exactly the same set of works, with most of the same performers, as the winter repertory—but at considerably higher prices, pegged to the gullible tourist's dollar. Mostly Mozart in New York is a catchall which includes bits and pieces of the winter season but at somewhat lower prices (and performance levels), whereas Ravinia and Tanglewood are routine prolongations of the orchestra seasons in Chicago and Boston, respectively, translated to "rustic" settings, with the same extremely mixed results. The rest of the major festivals—the Maggio Musicale in Venice, Santa Fe, Aix-en-Provence, Lucerne, Glyndebourne, to name a few—fall somewhere between these two types. Their claim on the public, apart from their attractive locations, is based largely on their reputation for a distinctive and meticulous excellence.

It is certainly true that a great musical experience can occur at one of these festivals, and that a spectacular setting can enhance the enjoyment of routine performances. My only Bayreuth experience occurred in 1958, and so stunning was the impression on me of those ten days that I have never wished to return for fear of spoiling it. And for about twenty years, until 1976 or so, the Baalbeck Festival in Lebanon was wonderful to visit, set in the great Roman ruins of the temples of Jupiter and Bacchus in that eastern Lebanese town, now a Shiite militia center and detention point for various hostages. But I wonder whether festivals, even at their very rare best, can offer anything more than isolated moments savored and recollected in tranquillity. At their customary worst, they provide performances bathed in an entirely misleading light, that of an extraordinary occasion whose intimidating glare allows skillful but sometimes routine going-through-the-notes to pass for inspired and dedicated music making.

There are now so many summer music festivals that aesthetic rationales for them seem to have been discarded entirely. Check the listings in *The New York Times* and you will find at least fifteen festivals in the New York area alone. One gets the feeling that ambitious impresarios and directors try to fill out the year by stuffing the dead summer months with programs designed to convince consumers that they are getting something special, while allowing musicians new occasions for engagements and income. Is there a big festival today that doesn't feature Alfred Brendel or James Levine or Emanuel Ax or Christopher Hogwood? You might be lucky enough to hear a marvelous recital by, say, Murray Perahia at Aldeburgh, which can be anchored aesthetically in the musical and pedagogical performance practice created there by Benjamin Britten and Peter Pears. But what are you to make of a performance of Beethoven's Third Piano Concerto at Tanglewood by Seiji Ozawa and Brendel when you know that Brendel will perform the same piece a week later at Edinburgh with a different orchestra and conductor but in more or less the same way, and that Ozawa will conduct it next season much as he did last in Symphony Hall? There seems to be nothing festival-like in such performances, even if you allow for indifferent acoustics, inordinately high ticket prices, heat, bugs and a seven-hour drive.

Music for the multitudes, someone will mutter; or music in a charming locale; or music performed at a restful time, inside a withdrawn or informal or massively concentrated framework. Perhaps. But consider the following. First, there are virtually no festivals whose aim it is to bring contemporary music into sharper relief. All successful festivals today are essentially reconsecrations of the mainstream mid-eighteenth- to early twentieth-century central European tradition. Some, like Tanglewood, do have an estimable component of contemporary work, but these concerts seem to be curtained off from the main crowd-drawing events: the big performances of Beethoven and Brahms, and the occasional but laudable curatorial attempts to perform rarely heard works (Weber's *Oberon* in its original English version this season at Tanglewood) for a large audience. Big names are what count, plus relatively familiar repertory.

Second, the acceleration in the number of performances has had the effect of diminishing the aesthetic and augmenting the socially significant dimensions of the playing. (Mostly Mozart runs for almost two months, on nearly every night of the week.) These occasions do provide an opportunity to hear a large body of work during a musically arid season. But it is the spectatorial, the acquisitive tastes of the metropolitan crowds that sustain summer festivals. Most people go to them for a few concerts, the way they go for walks in a city park; rarely if ever does anyone, except the reviewing staff of the big daily newspapers, attend a festival from start to finish. The pedagogical point of scheduling large swatches of repertory by a single composer is lost. Instead, we get the musical equivalent of a weekend outing.

In his excellent book *The Painting of Modern Life: Paris in the Art of Manet and his Followers*, T. J. Clark describes the emergence of a middle-class habit of experiencing nature in the suburbs at a time when growing and hyperorganized cities like Haussmann's Paris were beginning to dominate their inhabitants' lives. The irony, as recorded by the painters of the 1860s and 1870s, is that even during these outings, industrial life would make an appearance, for example in the smokestacks and rail lines of Manet's suburban paintings. In turn, Monet and others chose to focus on weeds, streams, trees, as if deliberately to ban industry, to re-experience nature unnaturally, at close quarters. In this cycle of suburban "landscapes arranged for urban use," of the Sunday outing celebrated as "a ritual of bourgeois identity," Clark detects the appearance of "leisure as a great symbolic field in which the battle for bourgeois identity was fought."

No less than the realistic painting of Paris's environs, music festivals took hold in the second half of the nineteenth century as part of that mode by which, according to Clark and Thorstein Veblen leisure became performance. To go to Bayreuth meant not only to admire Wagner but to be able to spare the time, to travel a fair distance, to stay away from home and routine, and, above all, to expect a better-than-average performance of music one could certainly hear at home in less expansive circumstances. It also meant experience in music that, like all difficult art, requires the luxury of special attention and effort. Nowadays, the intimidating and even authoritarian aspects of the early festivals have been overwhelmed by the sheer attention-getting expense of having star performers playing star works, day after day after day. Roger Vaughan says in his recent biography, *Herbert von Karajan,* that in 1983 the Salzburg Festival dished out the following sums:

For *Fidelio,* it was reported that $110,000 had been spent for costumes; $280,000 for sets. For *Così fan tutte,* $140,000 for costumes; $305,000 for sets. The totals reported were $500,000 for hair and wardrobe; $1 million for lighting; $2.65 million for administrative and technical personnel. The 147 year-round personnel at the Festspielhaus consumed $3.6 million. Maazel received $50,000; Sawallisch $40,000; Levine $100,000. Karajan reportedly received $11,000 per evening for conducting, and $20,000 for producing. The soloists shared $1.75 million. Each of the Vienna Philharmonic's 147 players was receiving $7,500. The total festival subsidy was around $6 million.

Not even von Karajan would suggest that such sums of money guarantee commensurately fine performances, or that the spirit of Mozart and Beethoven requires so astonishing an outlay of wealth. Half a million for "hair and wardrobe" highlights the stars, who perform before an admiring audience that can then flatter itself that being at Salzburg, pleasantly cowed into accepting display in lieu of musicianship, is better than not being there. In other words, the festival is a structure of alienation by which highly specialized musicians, hairdressers, lighting technicians, etc., distance themselves from the public, which "consumes" music rather than makes it.

At festivals, then, the music is mostly subordinated to the occasion. Norms for "live" performance are borrowed from the spectacle and from the recording. As Adorno says in his aptly titled essay "On the Fetish-Character in Music and the Regression of Listening," when it is excellent, "the performance sounds like its own phonograph record," A long series of performances, such as those at a festival, are like many records in one's library—available, accessible, ready for instant use. Festivals at which teaching and new compositions occur are therefore quite rare. The great summer courses at Darmstadt after the war, when Stockhausen, Boulez, Cage, Berio, Steuermann and others came together, are now a thing of the past.

I would not want to imply that festivals are bad, or that all musical performances there are flawed, tawdry and somehow unworthy of serious attention. Certainly, as I shall explain in a subsequent article, there are some worthwhile festival concerts to be heard. But festivals and the music they present cannot be divorced from the social circumstances in which they occur. Whether at Salzburg, Lincoln Center or Santa Fe, musical performance has been streamlined, essentialized, pared down in all sorts of ways to suit the consumer's ear and pocket—as well as, it might be added, the daily reviewer's commentary. As for the music festival as Wagner intended it at Bayreuth, or as Nietzsche described it in *The Birth of Tragedy*, that is now almost as difficult to imagine as it is to experience.

CHAPTER 4

On Richard Strauss

NEARLY HALF a century after his death, Richard Strauss's role in twentieth-century music remains an unresolved matter. No one disputes his talents, his professionalism, his often unusual musical imagination. Yet his work, after an initial flirtation with advanced chromaticism, remained solidly within the tonal tradition established by Wagner and Brahms, even though it is also true that he elaborated that tradition as no one else could or did. He went on writing songs, operas, chamber music and occasional orchestral pieces well into and even after the Third Reich, leaving questions as to his complicity with or his innocence about the going order; at the same time he seemed to develop his fairly narrow aesthetic into an expressiveness roughly comparable to that attained by the early Viennese school, Stravinsky and Bartók. His brooding and deeply affecting string work, *Metamorphosen,* is a case in point, one of the summits of twentieth-century music, written in the early 1940s in an idiom that had matured four decades earlier.

Strauss's opera *Die ägyptische Helena* is one of the most problematic of his works. A product of the remarkable collaboration between Strauss and the great Viennese poet Hugo von Hofmannsthal, *Helena* took five fitful years to complete. It had its premiere in 1928, but has not been staged in this country for more than fifty years. This summer, however, it was one of the operas presented by The Santa Fe Opera, now in its thirtieth season.

There are few places as fitting as Santa Fe for performing anomalous and unusual works, and fewer still where a summer festival is held with such conviction and interest. The stunningly designed opera house stands a few miles outside the town; although its sides and part of its top are open to the winds its acoustics are fairly lush. Set designers routinely employ the surrounding twilit mountains and valleys as a backdrop to suggest the distances of legend on which many operas are based, or, when the summer light has disappeared altogether, to project the darkness of the sea, the mystery of the desert, as in Acts I and II of *Helena.*

Most things about the Santa Fe Opera festival accentuate, rather than mute, the extraordinary contradictions at work in the music business today. One can fly there in about three hours, and yet Santa Fe is about as far from New York and the East Coast in general as it is possible to get, and this distance is emphasized by its unusually interesting and thoughtfully selected repertory, its well-prepared productions and the absence in its roster of big-name stars, whether singers or conductors. Why, you ask yourself, has it been possible for Santa Fe to put on successful performances of Britten, Henze, Zemlinsky, Virgil Thomson, Stravinsky, Berio, Ravel, Janáček and Villa-Lobos, plus a fair complement of Puccini, Verdi, Rossini and Mozart, while the Met and the other establishment houses hardly even try?

Performances of Richard Strauss's operas—including the rarely seen *Daphne, Die Liebe der Danae* and *Capriccio,* plus standard favorites like *Elektra* and *Der Rosenkavalier*—lead the Santa Fe list in number and frequency. Perhaps this is because John Crosby, the festival's director and chief instigator, is a Strauss fancier and a devoted (if not always inspired) conductor of his music. *Helena* is certainly the rarest of the lot. It belongs with the group formed by *Ariadne, Daphne* and *Danae,* operas whose subject matter is classical myth treated either as commentary on aesthetic problems of interest to Strauss and von Hofmannsthal, or as an elucidation of domestic paradoxes which exposes the instability of sexual as well as social identity. Von Hofmannsthal and Strauss worked intermittently on *Helena* for five years without ever resolving the oddities in it. These peculiarities, I believe, are an important part of the opera which, alone among Strauss's later work, shows his astounding musicianship and competence—plus his unique talent for writing what the late Glenn Gould has called ecstatic music—constrained by material of a lesser order. Taking it on strikes me as an ideal procedure for summer festivals, which ought to (but rarely do) heighten the tensions and issues of interest woven into the fabric of twentieth-century music.

Menelaus was Agamemnon's brother and Helen's husband, and as such is a pivotal figure in the bloodiest and arguably the most famous pair of episodes in classical Greek culture: the Trojan War, the subject of Homer's *Iliad,* and the fall of the house of Atreus memorialized in Aeschylus's *Oresteia.* Yet in Book IV of *The Odyssey* Menelaus turns up as a rather comfortable king, with Helen once again at his side. Hofmannsthal was understandably fascinated by the transformation of Menelaus from a husband hellbent on revenge for the loss of his wife into a placid Spartan king thoroughly at peace with his lovely middle-aged spouse. In his extraordinary 1928 preface to the opera (reprinted in Ulrich Weisstein's valuable but out-of-print collection *The Essence of Opera*), Hofmannsthal says that the thought of Menelaus wandering through Priam's ruined palace the night Troy fell, looking for his wife—"this woman who was his beloved, abducted wife and, besides, was the most beautiful woman in the world, the cause of this war, of these frightful ten years, of this plain filled with dead men, and of this conflagration"—gripped him totally:

> What a situation for a husband! It transcends all imagination—no lines, not even lines which Shakespeare might have written, would be equal to it, and I am certain that Menelaus carried this woman . . . down to his ship in silence.

The libretto of *Helena* was Hofmannsthal's attempt to render what had occurred in the interval between *The Iliad* and *The Odyssey*. Characteristically, however, Hofmannsthal invents a third figure, the sorceress Aithra, whose house and machinations on a Mediterranean island near Egypt supply the poet with two acts in which to effect the transformation. Menelas (as he is called in the German text) and Helena stagger onto Aithra's island after the ship transporting them from Troy is wrecked. Just before Menelas is about to slit Helena's throat with the very dagger he had used to kill Paris, Aithra greets them, and using her magic powers to dissipate the conflict between the pair changes Helena into a beautiful young maiden. When Menelas sees her a few moments later he does not recognize her; he accepts a drink of magic lotus juice from Aithra who convinces him that the real Helena was never in Troy but had been spirited away to Egypt during the offending decade. The young and lovely woman before him is his wife, and the two go off to a nuptial reunion.

Neither librettist nor composer could end matters there. Act II is one of the most unintentionally comic and tangled conclusions in any of Strauss's works: each episode engenders another, more improbable one, until, sensing the uselessness of extending the proceedings even further, composer and librettist manage a ceremonial finale with the entirely unanticipated appearance of Hermione, the couple's daughter, at its center. Along the way Strauss and Hofmannsthal devise an episode with Helena and two Arabian warriors, Altair and his son, Da-Ud, who appear out of the desert and are smitten by the woman's beauty; Da-Ud is killed during a hunting expedition, and Altair finally realizes that Helena is not to be his. This section of the opera is the occasion for the sort of "Eastern" music Strauss first tried out in *Salome,* but for the librettist, Altair and Da-Ud surely accentuated the curious polarity at work in the relationship between Helena and Menelas. Hofmannsthal writes in the preface that Menelas's morality and sense of guilt made him "to me the fatal embodiment of everything occidental, while in her, I saw the inexhaustible strength of the Orient." This rather pompous Orientalism is used, I think, to hide the difficulty of getting Menelas to change his mind convincingly, since in most of Act II he is as murderous as he was before drinking the lotus juice at the end of Act I. Even after a fantastic night with Helena he is still furious enough to kill her.

Often strident or glib, empty and almost unbearably complex, Strauss's music is at its most interesting when he is either letting one of the women soar away in "ecstatic" cantilena passages which no other romantic composer could match, or when two or more women sing together so sinuously as to suggest that his fascination with soprano voices in combination reflects an extraordinary obsession with the displacement of the male by the female. Rarely do any of the men in *Helena* have anything compelling to sing, and whatever ingenuity there is in Strauss's always flowing, disturbingly nonplussed line is reserved for orchestral color and his endlessly clever rhetorical skills. But in *Helena* his writing is so loaded with devices calling attention to themselves that one isn't even sure whether to listen or take notes on the resolutions he provides to various problems.

In point of fact, *Die ägyptische Helena* is a vast tissue of anomalies, contradictions and impossibilities; it is a strangely interesting opera for that reason. Hofmannsthal, for example, dreamed up a character called "alles wissende Muschel," or the all-knowing Mussel, a sort of resident prophetic shellfish in Aithra's employ who also happens to be a mezzo-soprano. Never one to be fazed by the most ludicrous challenges, Strauss wrote skillfully amiable music for this beast, although he was heard to whisper aloud during a dress rehearsal that the damn thing looked too much like a gramophone. Clearly then, with mussels, a sorceress and Arabian warriors jostling Greek heroes and heroines, the opera cannot be staged or witnessed as what it purports to be; there are too many crazy things going on, too many fatally confusing situations for it to be played as somberly as, say, *Die Frau ohne Schatten* usually is. The question as to what is to be done about it offers reason enough to attend one of its infrequent stagings. Perhaps the best thing about the Santa Fe production—beside the fact that it actually took place—was its design, predominantly blue (for the sea) in Act I, yellow (for the desert) in Act II. Crosby is a dutiful rather than an interesting conductor, although it must be said that he certainly commands the various Straussian mannerisms or tics. In his monumental study of Strauss,

Norman del Mar remarks that during rehearsals under the conductor Fritz Busch the musical effect of the whole seemed choppy since Strauss kept tinkering with the score. After a while everything went awry. Then Strauss took over and conducted with "one big, broad line" to totally different and apparently successful effect. This, at bottom, is what Strauss needs—and just missed getting in Santa Fe—a kind of willful suspension of disbelief not only in the laws of reality and history, but also in the laws of musical evolution: otherwise how could so many anachronistic and atavistic statements be made so brilliantly? There was some attempt to approach this effect at Santa Fe. The major problem was that no one—except the stunningly fluent Aithra, played by Sheryl Woods—was really first-rate and heedlessly soaring: not Helena (Mildred Tyree) who had a tendency to struggle at the top; not Menelas (Dennis Bailey) who just couldn't manage the long tessituras in the part; not Altair and Da-Ud (Michael Devlin and Glenn Siebert) who understandably never seemed to figure out what they were doing there. Clarity James as the Mussel was mellifluent and somber, although I couldn't help wondering how she explained the character to herself as she sang.

Hermann Broch argues in his often pitiless analysis of Hofmannsthal that operas like *Helena* belonged to the poet's denial of the real world and to his desire to give Vienna "a farewell festival" as its 1,000-year-old reign was ending. For his part Adorno, who respected Strauss's ability to "produce spontaneity by technique," saw in the "unfounded style" and suppleness of his later work what he called the Bazaar of the World, which stands next to the Grand Hotel: everything offered for display and sale, everything accommodated. Certainly it seems to me that any performances of the Strauss-Hofmannsthal works today have to take into account their dense cultural context, plainly referred to in the rich decadence of their aesthetic hermeticism, and the entire gamut of issues, both political and aesthetic, that these two supremely gifted and oddly unbalanced artists always touch upon. As an emanation of the desert sunset, Santa Fe's *Helena* seemed to inch toward an intellectually interesting statement because it was put on in so innocent and careful a way, and yet the statement never got made, since the ideology of undeveloped, un-self-conscious performance was allowed to predominate.

Little of the sort can be said about New York's Mostly Mozart Festival, a hodgepodge of miscellanies if ever there was one. The festival's impresarios have shined up the proceedings to a great gleaming finish, with, alas, very little of interest to be discovered there. I attended some eight concerts, which seemed far too many. Avery Fisher Hall is positively awful if you have to go there more than once a month; nothing sounds really good in that hall and one is encouraged neither to hear acutely nor to think there.

Add to that the routine performances with no guiding intelligence behind them and no perceivable style either to admire or to disagree with, and you have a thoroughly dispirited summer ritual put on for mostly well-behaved and appreciative crowds.

Something should be said about Gerard Schwarz, who is rapidly becoming our favorite music director. He runs a number of festivals, programs and orchestras, from one end of the country to the other, and yet nothing I have heard *him* do seems to have any gravity or imprimatur at all. He conducts with about the same level of competence at all times and is amazingly available to more or less anything on the stand before him. He and Rampal bustled through the Mozart G major Flute Concerto with an almost insulting incongruence, and when near the end of the festival Schwarz and his overworked orchestra played out Mozart's opera *La Finta Giardiniera,* the result was, in Alexander Pope's phrase, "a universal yawn." It's hard to justify lusterless, uninflected, poorly thought-out performances of terribly uneven Mozart just because one might hear predictions of *Cosi fan tutte* in a few passages.

The absence of any coherent stylistic personality in the performances was noticeable throughout unless, as was the case with Charles McKerras's, it *was* noticeable for flaccid, disastrously sloppy and, in my opinion, scandalous work. The irony was that the redoubtable Alicia de Larrocha had to contend with Sir Charles first in the Mozart A major Rondo, where her ever-reliable fingers and superbly acute sound triumphed, then in the D minor Concerto; in that piece, she had already resorted, perhaps out of fatigue (she seems to play more concerts than anyone alive) or boredom, to "pearly," tinkly Mozart. There were some other fine moments: the great Richard Goode in Mozart's Piano Concerto No. 25 in C major (K. 503), and Heinz Holliger sculpting an extraordinary oboe performance—a lot of it wonderful acting and physical gestures—out of a totally forgettable piece by one Franz Krommer.

The extent to which apparently extra-musical factors such as personality, memory and gesture enter into the creation of powerful music-making was borne out during the concert led by Robert Shaw. Currently the conductor of the Atlanta Symphony, Shaw came to public attention thirty years ago as the founder of the Robert Shaw Chorale and, especially in the choral sections of Toscanini's rendition of Beethoven's *Missa solemnis,* as the person responsible for producing the most accomplished choral singing in this country. He has the mannerisms of a modest man, but his work is anything but that: I was impressed by his broad, often overstated lines and massive climaxes in the Mozart C minor Mass (easily the pinnacle of Mozart's church music), and the strength of his work in the Beethoven Choral

Fantasia for which Rudolf Firkusny was the seemingly unwilling soloist. Robert Shaw is a throwback to something earlier in musical life, especially when compared with young whizzes like Edo De Waart and Schwarz. He is clearly a musician who thinks that he is there to make a statement, to suggest an idea, while the younger breed give the impression of efficient businessmen who can read through any score and get by any difficulty, on their way to the airport. It's difficult to accept the second sort of musicianship at all, since the very notion of a two-month "festival" filled with dozens of pieces by (as the program has it) M, B and H (Mozart, Beethoven and Haydn), in no particular order, calls for some overall purpose and pattern to emerge from the fuss. But no: it's concert after concert, a routine for which no great music was ever written.

CHAPTER 5

Die Walküre, Aida, X

WHILE IT is true that grand opera is essentially a nineteenth-century form, and that our great opera houses now resemble museums which preserve artifacts by Wagner and Verdi for twentieth-century spectators, it is also a fact that some of the nineteenth-century repertory was already reactionary in its own time, whereas some was musically and theatrically revolutionary. In either case, however, nineteenth-century performances maintained vital contact with the cultural and aesthetic practice of the time: composers like Verdi, Wagner and Puccini were often around to influence what was done to their work, audiences and performers usually understood the language in which the opera was sung, and in the main, a musical idiom was shared by all concerned.

Very little of this obtains today. No real distinctions are made between, say, the repertory performance of a fundamentally conservative work like *Aida* and a revolutionary one like *Die Walküre.* "Four fat people singing interminably and incomprehensibly in the dark," a wag once said of a performance of *Tristan und Isolde* at the Metropolitan Opera. With minor variations, the same can be said of almost any Met performance. No doubt the costly, heavy-handed show is thought to be exactly what the audience wants. Virtually every singer of note who draws crowds at the Met is a kind of freak who sings in an unfamiliar language, exhibits an outdated musical style and is dramatically unconvincing. As for most of the designers and directors, their job seems to be nothing more than putting funny clothes on the singers, and getting them to move around looking serious and urgent.

At the risk of offending many opera-goers I shall add that much of the problem today comes from the Italian repertory which, aside from Rossini, who was a genius, is mostly made up of second-rate work. The very promi-

The Nation, December 6, 1986.

nence of a grotesque like Pavarotti is itself an indictment of the repertory that suits him so well. Such singers have reduced opera performance to a minimum of intelligence and a maximum of overpriced noise, in which almost unbelievably low standards of theater combine with equally low standards of musicality and direction. This is an environment inhospitable to ideas or aesthetic conceptions.

Much of what I am saying in so extreme a form is the result of my having seen one extraordinary contemporary opera, Anthony Davis's *X (The Life and Times of Malcolm X)* at the New York City Opera, sandwiched between two exceptionally problematic Met performances—*Die Walküre*, this season's opening-night attraction, and *Aida*. Even if Davis's opera wasn't running concurrently with the two at the Met, I would still have found the Met's relentless avoidance of the interesting and the contemporary exasperating. I am not speaking of the fact that 80 percent of the repertory is usually made up of *La Bohème, Tosca, Rigoletto, Lucia di Lammermoor, Norma* and the like. What I am objecting to is the way in which the Met performs and reperforms the nineteenth-century repertory guided by a concept it seems to have borrowed from the opera sequences in 1930s Hollywood films—all the heroes and heroines are pudgy, loud and stupid, the music they sing equally so. Inevitably then the avant-garde work of the nineteenth-century is flattened into a semblance of its conservative counterpart. Even if allowances are made for the narrow range of the repertory, there is little excuse for collapsing the possible effect of those operas into caricature.

Take *Die Walküre*, which although it is the second of the four operas in Wagner's *Der Ring des Nibelungen*, was chosen to begin the Met's new cycle of the tetralogy. The Met got the services of Hildegarde Behrens, a competent and occasionally fine Brünnhilde; Jeannine Altmeyer, a superbly passionate Sieglinde; and Aage Haugland, a vocally secure but curiously remote—which is perhaps the last thing he should be—Hunding. In addition, the Met's orchestra is now one of the finest ensembles around, certainly a cut above the New York Philharmonic when it comes to accuracy, intonation, refinement and responsiveness. But Wagner requires more than a few good singers and an excellent orchestra, and this is where the Met's aesthetic comes in. Unlike Verdi, whose "naïvité is celebrated by his devotees, Wagner (to his undying discredit, according to some) was also a philosopher and, above all, a musical and aesthetic pioneer. By 1870, when Verdi was working on *Aida*, Wagner's influence had spread throughout Europe, and it was an influence that, as composers like Verdi acknowledged, inspired opera toward more reflection, sophistication and attention to detail. What irony therefore that the Met's *Walkure* was more influenced by its notion of *Aida* than vice versa.

The *Ring* remains the largest operatic conception ever attempted. It was Wagner's effort to convey a historical/mythic account of the origins of modern culture and, as readers of Nietzsche will remember, was modeled on the great cycles of Attic tragedy. Wagner's musical intelligence was profound and his understanding of the orchestra, the voice and artistic structure brings to a culmination the course of Austro-German music from Bach and Handel through the Viennese classicists, to Beethoven, Schubert and Schumann. Two more things make Wagner exceptionally challenging to a twentieth-century opera company. One is that no operatic composer has generated more interpretive theories and practices than he, partly because of Bayreuth (which as the center of Wagnerology was designed by Wagner to serve as a point of reference for all work on or about him) and partly because of the musical giants who devoted themselves to his music. It is perhaps more intimidating than illuminating for a young conductor like James Levine leading his first *Walküre* to realize that von Bülow, Nikisch, Strauss, Toscanini, Furtwängler, Knappertsbusch, Solti and Boulez went before him.

The second difficult but rewarding thing about Wagner's work is that his mode was essentially, if not irreducibly, narrative. He is, I believe, most fruitfully compared not with his operatic contemporaries but with Flaubert, James, Mann and Proust (the latter two were mesmerized by him). And his narratives are, like the Nibelung's ring itself, circular, reflective, somberly recapitulatory: each episode alludes to earlier ones, and those in turn confirm and doom the later ones. The density of the musical line is such that in moving forward it also moves backward, downward and across, gathering stress and intensity all the time until by the end of the cycle everything is so locked up, heavy and self-conscious as to collapse under its own weight: Wagner seems to have invented and set Freud's theory of overdetermination to music, using chromaticism and polyphony to such demonic effect as in theory to explode the conscious and rational material holding the tonal world together.

The upshot is that for better or worse, putting on a *Ring* cycle is a formidable undertaking—one which was last attempted with the requisite intelligence by Pierre Boulez and Patrice Chereau at Bayreuth a decade ago. Let us grant that such talents were not available to the Met's *Walküre;* but should the opera therefore be given a directionless and ultimately purposeless production?

The first difficulty is that Levine's musical conception, allied with Otto Schenk's dramatic realization, ignores every postwar advance in Wagnerian performance. There's nothing symbolic, Jungian, Freudian, Marxist or structuralist here—just a "naturalist" presentation, circa 1900, of some

Nordic types whose idea of dramatic gesture is an impassioned run from stage center to the door and back to stage center. Peter Hofmann (Siegmund), glorious-looking in abbreviated costume and flowing blond hair, exemplifies this approach in its purest form. (Although he is incapable of anything above a G or A, he does sing decently, using his essentially high baritone voice to considerable advantage in Act I.)

Second, Wagner must be performed with the closest attention to what is going on dramatically. Long stretches of the *Ring* are recitations that advance the narrative and reveal character; for such passages you must have actors and directors who convey the sense that matters of significance are taking place. Act II is a perfect instance. Here Wotan retells the story of his early life, his descent into the earth, his rape of Erda, the birth of Brünnhilde, his compact with Fafner and Fasolt, his contest with Alberich, and now, his search for a device (which will be the hero, Siegfried) for extricating himself from the network of promises and laws in which, as a god, he has become imprisoned. Wotan's narrative is the center of *Walküre*; it dramatizes the cultural and political predicament of a consciousness free to create, unable to free itself of its creation, and yet endlessly in search of a means to get to new and amoral levels of freedom. This is perhaps *the* German statement, in all its horror and exaltation. It can only be performed by a supremely intelligent artist, with a conductor who does not regard the long orchestral silences as empty gulches to be relieved by an occasional plunk of sound. (To listen to the recording of Hans Hotter, one of the greatest twentieth-century Wagnerians, delivering this forty-minute narrative, is to be overwhelmed by his intensity, his craftsmanship, his understanding of the words and score.)

Simon Estes, who sang Wotan at the Met, is a fine light bass who has sung a few non-*Ring* Wagner roles. Wotan, however, is a commanding figure (Hotter was about 6 feet 5 inches, and a great stage presence), but Estes did not command; his smallish voice could get the middle and high notes, but floundered on the lower ones. His narrative did not seem inward enough, and he appeared to have no guiding idea for his singing and acting. To make matters worse, Estes—as well as the other performers—was singing complex, poetical words which no one in the audience would possibly understand. The Met has been ridiculously adamant about not using supertitles. Why do audiences stand for this? Would they pay $100 to watch a bad performance of Shakespeare chanted in Esperanto?

Levine's musical direction was, to say the least, streamlined, the orchestra responding sensitively to his warmth in the *Wintersturme* scene, his noisy bravado in the Ride of the Valkyries, his quite poetic expansiveness in the Magic Fire (which provided the puniest lighting display imaginable). But all in all, Levine's conception of the piece was like a rapid sketch for some future performance. The irritating thing about Levine is that he is damnably gifted, and yet prefers somehow to ignore most of the reflective, intellectual dimensions in music that is steeped in thoughtful reflection.

He seems to have shrewdly abandoned the current production *of Aida* to lesser hands. Aside from the redoubtable Grace Bumbry, an Amneris fiery enough to wipe out her slave rival, the by now pathetic and vocally nonexistent Martina Arroyo, this production is an irretrievable loss. Verdi's miscalculations in *Aida*—his overdeveloped score and underdeveloped story, his lifeless attention to an Orientalist Egyptology, his callous disengagement from the place (Cairo) for which the piece was intended—were made plainer and more painful by the Met's alternately strutting and stuttering performance. Why the Egyptian interiors of a triumphant Pharonic court at the height of its powers should be in jagged ruins, friezes and bas reliefs decomposing before you, is left to conjecture.

But all is not lost. There's *X*, with music by Anthony Davis and libretto by Thulani Davis from a story by Christopher Davis. *X* is a riveting work, uncompromising politically, interesting if not always stylistically coherent in its music, splendidly theatrical. The odd thing is that it was put on in these reactionary times. The opera is based on *The Autobiography of Malcolm X*, which it follows fairly closely. Divided into three acts of three, four and five scenes respectively, the opera deals with Malcolm's early years, 1931 to 1945, from his father's death in Lansing to his street life in Boston and his sentencing to prison; then in the middle section, from 1946 to 1963, the story proceeds to his conversion to Islam and his discipleship to Elijah Muhammad; finally we are shown Malcolm during his Mecca trip, his separation from Elijah Muhammad and his assassination.

The action abounds in historical allusions: the vogue of Garveyism; the rise of black separatism and the Black Muslims; the Kennedy assassination; pan-Africanism; the murders of Medgar Evers and Patrice Lumumba. Moreover the opera utilizes a large, superbly orchestrated cast to represent different black communities at various levels of consciousness. The overall effect is of an amalgam of epic theater, classical opera and jazz ensemble. And although there is an unresolved tension between Malcolm and the oppressed nation which he alternately leads and represents, I found it a fertile tension. Ben Holt, who plays Malcolm, has in his own manner the self-limiting restraint and the personal force of the very dilemma he represents. In contrast there is the bravura performance of Thomas Young, who plays both Street, a flamboyant street tough, and a preachy, faintly menacing Elijah Muhammad. It's rare to encounter so strong a pair of performances.

Unquestionably *X*'s greatest impact is in the varied and often large ensembles, especially those in the first and third acts; the prison scenes seem
to be less strong, as does a good bit of Act II, which is often flatly discursive
as if the librettist was trying to get a lot of information about Malcolm's
conversion to Islam across before she has him make his notorious remark
about "chickens coming home to roost" when John Kennedy was assas-
sinated. The particular strengths of Act III lie in Malcolm's confrontation
with Elijah Muhammad and in his second conversion in Mecca. In the
latter scene, Davis is remarkably successful in sustaining a long, ritualistic
representation of the *fatiha,* the Koranic opening to prayer in the mosque.
The dramatic rightness of the two scenes succeeding each other is that Malcolm's coming to consciousness in Islam is synonymous with his liberation
from all the bonds of racial exclusivism. Malcolm's solitude and eventual
acceptance of Islam's universalism seems to be influenced by Schoenberg's
Moses und Aron, although the divine anger represented by Schoenberg as
being in Moses from God, is displaced almost unilaterally to Malcolm's time
in history: "a tide rises at your back and sweeps you in its path." Moreover,
Davis explicitly associates Malcolm's self-liberation with freedom fighters
from Mozambique, Angola, Zambia, Zimbabwe, even from South Africa,
lending a broader significance to Malcolm's redemptive vision and his sacrificial assassination.

The City Opera's production of *X* shows every sign of having been wonderfully responsive to the Davises' music, story and libretto. The cast is
uniformly well-trained and sharp, which may be a measure of how urgently
contemporary the opera is. I'm not suggesting that only contemporary political operas are worth doing. But operas do need to be done with some
vital conception that informs the whole and with some sense of their own
history or their relevance to the history of our time. Though it may seem a
backhanded way of getting at Anthony Davis's music itself, we should note
the difficulties of creating a musical idiom for so affectingly contemporary a
work as *X.* Christopher Keene conducted the score with dispatch and obvious authority, but I sensed an incompletely achieved musical synthesis of
two warring idioms, twelve-tone and jazz. On the other hand, Davis does
have a coherent—that is to say accomplished—rhythmic pulse, more lively
and topical than aesthetic and reflexive. This makes *X* a spellbinding work.
The fact is, however, that Davis's recourse to politics and not, say, to any
obvious musical model, as well as his ultimate failure to produce a musical
style (as opposed to a dramatic statement of great force), makes itself apparent in the wavering between the rigor of the twelve-tone row and the
freedom of the improvisatory jazz flow that characterizes the score of *X.*

X has many external obstacles to overcome, even though it is an authentically important and original work. One is that it is oppositional and not reassuringly conformist; Malcolm himself is not easy going for white opera audiences. Second, it is costly to produce precisely because there isn't yet anything to succeed it. Third, few singers are likely to invest the time necessary to learn such difficult music when the money is in Puccini and Mascagni. Short of having an opera company like the Berliner Ensemble which can inspire better productions, repertory opera houses must be goaded into more adventurous attitudes. By performing *X* they can make a start.

CHAPTER 6

Music and Feminism

I T IS an interesting fact about feminism, and about the place of music in contemporary culture, that very little has been done to map the female role in the production and performance of music. Mainstream classical music is dominated by men in almost every economic, political and social respect, yet women play prominent and varied roles in the artistic sphere. The most traditional is that of inspirational muse, and later helpmeet, adjunct, adoring (but lesser) partner, to some prominent male composer: Clara and Robert Schumann, Cosima and Richard Wagner. The figure of woman as unattainable ideal preoccupied Beethoven; its obverse, woman as destructive seductress, is more frequently to be found in representations of women in music (Berg's Lulu, for instance, or Strauss's Salome) than in the lives of famous musicians. The rise of women performers from the ranks of a socially unacceptable underclass (dancing girl, actress, courtesan, etc.) to luminous fame as divas, star instrumentalists and teachers in the nineteenth century is of paramount importance in the history of music; witness the repertory of great works for and about women, such as Schumann's *Frauenlibe und Leben*, Bizet's *Carmen*, Poulenc's *Dialogues des Carmélites*.

Music criticism and musicology, as well as the worlds of performance and composition, are strikingly removed from the main fields of cultural criticism. In a recently published exchange between Pierre Boulez and Michel Foucault the latter remarks that, except for a passing but idle interest in jazz or rock, most intellectuals who care about Heidegger or Nietzsche, about history, literature and philosophy, regard music as too elitist, irrelevant or difficult for their attention. Musical discourse is probably less available to Western intellectuals than the obscurer realms of medieval,

Chinese or Japanese culture. It is therefore predictable and yet odd that feminism, much concerned with almost all the humanities and sciences, has offered little in the way of music criticism. Feminism in music seems to be roughly at the stage where literary feminism was twenty years ago: a sort of separatist enterprise which attempts to identify women musicians of the past who spoke with a voice of their own. Beyond that, there is a void. But it would be wrong to fix the blame exclusively on music criticism or on feminist theory. The problem is that music today is as massively organized a masculine domain as it was in the past. Without significant exception, women play a crucial but subaltern role.

This is true in almost any random sampling of recent events—operas, recitals, orchestral performances—in which issues of interest to feminism are in evidence, but for which feminist critical responses are not likely to be encountered. The question of whether there is a "feminine" musical style, for example, emerges when female instrumentalists perform. In October the pianist Alicia De Larrocha played the Mozart Concerto in C Major (K. 503) with Klaus Tennstedt and the New York Philharmonic; she also gave a recital in Avery Fisher Hall which featured Books 1 and II of Albeniz's *Iberia*. Compared with the late Lili Kraus, De Larrocha is a more assertive pianist; her Mozart (long thought to be a "feminine" composer, unlike Beethoven who was always "masculine") is not pearly, trilling, fading or gentle. Yet except for the Spanish music that she practically owns, De Larrocha tends to play music more readily identified with female performers (because of its smallness and intimacy) than with male: Scarlatti, Chopin, Mozart, even Bach. Even so, K. 503 is the largest and most expansive of Mozart's concern, the one most identified as a forerunner of Beethoven's concerti, and therefore the most "masculine." On the other hand, the Beethoven piece she played at her recital was the Opus 110 Sonata in A flat Major, a less "masculine" piece than the Hammerklavier, or Opus III.

The question of patterns of gender and sexuality in music itself is a hugely complicated one. It is most conveniently at hand in Romantic program and operatic music, in which representations of women animate the proceedings from start to finish. As an example, I would offer Bellini's *I Puritani*, recently performed by Joan Sutherland at the Metropolitan Opera. What an odd, even kinky spectacle this opera presents, with its interminable vocal acrobatics, its vacant plot, its pointless allusions to seventeenth-century England. At its center stands a fluttery teenager who has gone "mad" in her love for a man she thinks has betrayed her; the lovers' music is based upon an inhumanly elongated treble melody set above an unabatedly monotonous and minimal bass, punctuated by militaristically concerted brasses. Exhibitionist display, an utterly precious and exhausting idiom, endlessly

forestalled climaxes, men's and women's voices rising and falling indiscrimi-
nately in constant imitation of each other: this surely adds up to a vision of
sexuality that requires some skeptical attention, not least for its enduring
capacity to captivate large audiences of men and women.

At the opposite extreme is Mahler's *Kindertotenlieder* with its formidable
economy of means, its understatement and calm, its almost total control of
its difficult material. The cycle of songs was performed by Zubin Mehta and
the New York Philharmonic with Marilyn Horne as soloist, and although
one could have wished for a more committed reading by Horne, there was
much to admire in her singing. The deep quiet of these anguished poems
by Friedrich Rückert is matched by Mahler's dense but always somehow
transparent contrapuntal orchestration. Like Schoenberg's *Erwartung,* the
songs are a dramatic dialogue for female voice that expresses various stages
of grief—prophetically in Mahler's case, since he finished the songs in 1904,
three years before his oldest daughter died—and ends in reconciliation. The
range of emotions offered in the cycle, as in Gerard Manley Hopkins's late
sonnets, is intense but not great, and for this Horne's restraint was perfectly
suited. She seemed to me to falter only once, in the great strophic repetitions of "In diesem Wetter, in diesem Braus" (Song 5), each one varied by
Mahler with differing instrumentation and inflections. Horne's imagination failed her after the climax, I thought, and she misconstrued the final
strophe, seeing in it a kind of helpless fatigue instead of the peace of benign
rest.

One could call these songs ventriloquism, a male composer representing
and perhaps animating the female, but it would be reductive to describe
them thus. There is identification and symbiosis here, as between Mahler's
songs and his symphonies, not mere manipulation. A more convincing case
for manipulation might be made about two nineteenth-century Dionysiac
works recently performed in New York: Beethoven's *Fidelio* at the Met,
with Hildegard Behrens in the title role, and Berlioz's *Damnation of Faust,*
with Charles Dutoit leading the Pittsburgh Symphony at Avery Fisher Hall.
I had never seen Dutoit in action before, and I was hypnotized by his work.
If ever there was a toreador-cum-Valentino style of conducting, Dutoit embodies it: he is all narrow hips, svelte torso, stiff legs and darkly menacing
features. Between Dutoit and his Mephistopheles (the Greek bass Dimitri Kavrakos, who has a powerful but unpolished, unfocused instrument
and still manages to project great charm) there stood the poor Marguerite,
Katherine Ciesinski, a decent but small-scaled mezzo-soprano who hardly
had a chance.

Berlioz's conception, or rather transcription, of Goethe's epic is odd;
with its lyrics translated into Gerard de Nerval's French, it is designed as a

one-shot affair not to be succeeded by any imitators, a genre entirely of its own. As with all redemptive visions it is more interesting for its demonism than its piety. Berlioz's imagination is largely instrumental and episodic: individual vocal production is subordinated to an astonishingly inventive ensemble sense, which Dutoit and Kavrakos exploited to the utmost, Berlioz had no intention whatever of dutifully following Goethe; instead he wished to draw out of his poem those elements that suited his own heterodox approach to drama, neither operatic nor oratorical but scenic, atmospheric, allusive. The *Damnation* is not only full of open spaces, receding armies, wandering students but also of learned devices (a fugue about fugues, for example) and surprising shifts in mood and tone.

Except for her modal ballad "Le Roi de Thulé," Berlioz's Marguerite is more interesting sung about than singing. Dutoit's adept theatricality was at its dashing best when the Devil wins as Faust acknowledges that the woman, who is only a function of his "devorant desir," has satisfied him: "L'amour en t'enivrant doublera ta folie." There is at this moment a textbook case of the nineteenth-century predilection for representing woman as the destructive angel in the house: Marguerite is to be imprisoned for accidentally poisoning her mother. Through Mephistopheles, Berlioz tries to temper this punishing vision by blaming Faust for various excesses, almost convincing us with the red-blooded jibberish of "Pandemonium" that the Devil's scholar-victim is destined for a pretty bad time in the hereafter. The trouble is that the music for male naughtiness and crime is much more interesting than the sugary pap used for feminine goodness, a besetting problem in all French music since Berlioz (Saint-Saëns, Frank, Fauré and even Messiaen come to mind). So we are left, in effect, with a celebration of misogyny—woman as the source of a male pleasure that can quite easily turn into hatred.

Finally, we come to Beethoven's *Fidelio,* less a dramatic representation of redemptive woman than an enactment of various principles: loyalty, conjugal bliss (the opera is based on Bouilly's play *L'Amour conjugale*), hatred of tyranny. Originally finished in 1806, the opera was not successful until eight years later, when Beethoven shortened it considerably and changed its name from *Leonore* to *Fidelio.* I've heard the earlier version on records, and it comes across as much more tuneful than taut, its characters all-too-human and genial. By 1814 Beethoven had compressed everything so much as to leave only the essentials intact, with very little in the way of charm or stage business left to distract the audience.

Fidelio is perhaps the one standard repertory opera capable of surviving the very worst performances, even though it requires the gifts of at least four first-class singers and one really inspired conductor. There is something naïve and enthusiastically straightforward about the work, which defies partisanship as well as partiality. Beethoven's admiration for the French Revolution (from which in a sense his text for *Fidelio* was borrowed) pays little heed to actual revolutionary life; what he achieves is the much more special advantage of using a political motif to get beyond politics altogether, and beyond history as well. Ernst Bloch has made the inspired claim that *Fidelio* is an apocalyptic work oriented to the future; thus the famous trumpet call releasing Florestan from Pizarro just after Leonore has made herself known is the "*tuba mirum spargens sonum*, pronouncing the Savior's arrival." By the end of the opera, Bloch continues, Beethoven's music has proved itself to be "militant-religious, the dawning of a new day so audible that it seems more than simply a hope . . . Thus music as a whole stands at the farther limits of humanity, but at those limits where humanity, with new language and haloed by the call to achieved intensity, to the attained world of 'we,' is first taking shape."

The Met's ungracefully aging production scarcely gives one any such glimmerings, but it is still worth going to, if only because almost any *Fidelio* is worth going to. Christof Perick substituted gallantly as conductor for the ailing Tennstedt, and the singers surrounding Behrens were adequate. I suppose it is a kind of gargantuan egoism on Beethoven's part to pretend that he was capable of going beyond humanity into the realm of the timeless and the principled. But his egoism, his carefully constructed subjectivity, his aesthetic norms are all part of the attempt to rise out of the particular, the historical, the political. Early Romantic art is full of this disenchantment with the worldly, even in supposedly political works; it is fascinating not because it is humanistic as it pretends but precisely because its aims are to dehumanize and depoliticize. As to whether *Fidelio* achieves a flattering portrayal of the feminine as Beethoven intended or whether there is a chilling derogation of women in Leonore's supplementary status, the music, in its obsessively patterned structures of aspiration and blockage, does not appear to furnish a conclusive answer. It is worth considering whether feminist criticism can find one.

CHAPTER 7

Maestro for the Masses

UNDERSTANDING TOSCANINI

T HE SELLING of classical musicians by record companies and concert hall managers is an enormously lucrative business—which,
however, is bound to affect standards of performance adversely.
In 1964 the Canadian pianist Glenn Gould, who had been extremely successful as a concert musician, retired from live performing; until his death
in 1982, he confined his work to records, radio and television. One of the
reasons he gave for his decision was the distorting effect of the audience
on his playing; he felt he had to keep wooing its attention by forcing the
classical restraint of Bach's polyphony into rhetorical emphases and stresses
that did not really belong there. Nevertheless, all artists, producers and
performers need an audience. The problem is how to balance the inner
obligations to one's art with the outer claims of a society whose demand for
satisfaction, entertainment and excitement cannot really be ignored.

Such a problem inevitably draws one into further reflection about
whether the issue of art and society can ever be resolved neatly, especially
since substantial economic interests are so regularly at stake. The marketing
apparatus now available to record companies and musical impresarios is so
powerful that it can catapult a pianist or a singer from respectability into a
career worth millions. No longer are artists likely to be satisfied with doing
their work quietly and conscientiously. If the film "Amadeus" can translate
Mozart's already considerable achievements into an endless number of
tickets and tapes, if a record company can derive millions out of billing an
unusual performer as "the world's greatest," there is a strong probability that
some artists will be tempted to go after fame and reputation, whatever the
cost to their artistic integrity. While it would be ridiculous to try to convert
a mediocre talent into a Luciano Pavarotti or an Itzhak Perlman, there is

good reason to suppose that both of these men have become superstars by sacrificing the nuances and refinements that other, less "successful" performers have stubbornly retained.

Joseph Horowitz's massively detailed study, "Understanding Toscanini," provides a compelling argument that "the world's greatest conductor" was a largely American success story, an astonishingly gifted man who—thanks to RCA, to a variety of what Mr. Horowitz calls "conservative popularizers" and "high culture populists," as well as to an authoritarian and insecure musical personality—achieved an artistic quasi dictatorship in this country for almost 50 years. Since his death in 1957, Arturo Toscanini's reputation has diminished somewhat, partly because the proliferation of records and tapes has drawn attention to a large number of other conductors, partly because the demanding but unsatisfying standards Toscanini represented have been discredited. Yet, during the years of his greatest ascendancy (1937–54), as conductor of the NBC orchestra (which was created for him), Toscanini was like nothing else in American musical life—the subject of a cult whose uncontested rule according to Mr. Horowitz, eliminated all rivals and made his every demand a law.

As he chronicles Toscanini's rise our of the Italian provinces to his directorship at La Scala in Milan and his years at the Metropolitan Opera (1908–15) and the New York Philharmonic (1927–36), Mr. Horowitz emphasizes a number of motifs in the man's career. Together these made up what Mr. Horowitz calls the "definitive midcult phenomenon for music in this century." First, of course, was a preternaturally acute musical faculty, an infallible ear and memory accompanied by a penchant for the dramatization of every piece he performed—all music for Toscanini tended to the condition of Verdi's whether it was a Beethoven symphony, a Brahms overture or a Tchaikovsky serenade. Second was a social tendency in the United Slates to simplify and reduce culture to a set of dead and imported masterpieces served up by hucksters, public relations men, Philistines and uncritical zealots. These people battened on the essentially uncontroversial and serviceable Toscanini and made a hero of him; they turned him into the master interpreter of the classics. This transformation, Mr. Horowitz says, was not entirely unjust, since Toscanini was patently well endowed as a musician and could legitimately symbolize the better traditions of Europe.

The third, and more problematic, theme is the musical or esthetic result of the convergence between Toscanini and that prevalent social tendency in America. Mr. Horowitz puts forward the claim—and this is the main argument of the book, as well as the reason for its enormous detail—that not only did art and music generally suffer, but Toscanini the musician did too. "His personality is what attained unprecedented stature among conductors" Mr. Horowitz writes. "And to speak of his legacy is to speak primarily in extramusical terms. Toscanini the conductor influenced mere generations of heirs and epigones; the Toscanini cult, with its unprecedented machinery and machinations, exerted the more lasting impact." By the time Toscanini and David Sarnoff of RCA were collaborating on the NBC orchestra, the maestro was 70 years old and he had pared down his repertory to a relatively small selection of canonical 19th century works, to the neglect of contemporary music and, by his reckoning, works that were too complex, peripheral or contrapuntal. All of Toscanini's efforts were now concentrated on mass appeal of a highly restricted type—"all-purpose performance excitement correlative with Verdian visceral mechanics." In Studio 8H a NBC—symbolic of the maestro's aloofness, his invisibility and inaccessibility, the quasi-scientific ballyhoo of the corporation's "merchandizing mindset"—Toscanini and the orchestra churned out their weekly "legendary" performances, performances whose shrunken content was embellished with the hype and worshipful commentary of a battery of corporate flunkies.

Mr. Horowitz's argument, extreme though it is, is by no means as simple as this. The idea of Toscanini as a cult figure is perceptive. It originates, I think, in a brilliant short essay about him published in 1958 by Theodor Adorno, the German philosopher, musicologist and social critic, cited by Mr. Horowitz. Adorno treats Toscanini as a disorder of late capitalism, his *Meisterschaft*, or mastery, symbolizing the authoritarian and yet mechanically streamlined perfection of a soulless leader whose will to domination is expressed in a performing style that loses the human spirit of the music.

Although Mr. Horowitz does not have all the subtlety of Adorno's metaphysical wit, he does have a large arsenal of descriptive resources with which to render the Toscanini phenomenon. Many of the most interesting pages in the book reproduce in discursive language the highly charged effect of Toscanini's performances; many more pages, all of them informed and provocative, suggest the ways in which Toscanini's influence imposed "standardized" norms on performance; prevented great European musicians like Gustav Mahler, Wilhelm Furtwängler (before World War II as well as after), Eugen Jochum and Hans Knappertsbusch from doing well in America; and propelled the careers of Toscanini acolytes like George Szell and Fritz Reiner. Toscanini was in the same sphere as the "music appreciation" vogue, *Good Housekeeping* and *Reader's Digest*, Bob Hope and Earl Wilson, and barkers for "the world's biggest drum."

But whereas one can agree with much of Mr. Horowitz's antipathy for Toscanini worship, and with his sympathy for anti-authoritarianism and native creativity as manifested in the work of Charles Ives, John Cage, Paul

Bowles, Henry Cowell and others (he even cites Walt Whitman), heaping inordinate blame on Toscanini for what is wrong with American culture presents problems. Surely what he calls "the Lincoln Center syndrome" is not ascribable to Toscanini alone, and it is not acceptable to make Toscanini a far more important and all-encompassing figure in American culture than he is. Mr. Horowitz is simply too linear and repetitive, too single-minded and too homogenizing in his analyses; one senses an almost unrestricted explanatory urge in his always intelligent writing, as if everything about Toscanini could be collapsed into the American corporate ethos, and vice versa. After all, by the terms of Mr. Horowitz's own argument, culture is more than the sum of its social determinants. Why then whittle Toscanini down entirely to the level of a commodity that was marketed and sold?

Mr. Horowitz's book ought to be read less as an entirely successful analysis of Toscanini than as a *cri de coeur* about the philistinism and commercialism of contemporary society. Toscanini himself is, I think, more positive and estimable a figure than Mr. Horowitz allows. Although he died too early to benefit from the great recent advances in audio technology, his legacy as the man who stripped phony traditionalism and sentimental sloppiness from musical performances will endure. To call his sinewy, taut readings of some orchestral masterpieces "literalism" is unfair to the electrifying experience of actually listening to Toscanini at his best; this would be like confusing his claim on an audience's attention with the syrupy clichés of an NBC announcer.

The difficulty with Mr. Horowitz's undertaking, and with satisfactorily assessing Toscanini's work, is a theoretical problem: how is it possible to connect such complex things as style and performance with the history and social reality of their moment? It is an index of the relatively undeveloped and impoverished intellectual state of American music criticism that this problem has not been adequately studied or answered; compared with literary or art criticism, music criticism infrequently concerns itself with social context, and when it does it is often unsophisticated and rudimentary. That Mr. Horowitz has taken on so redoubtable a figure as Toscanini is vastly to his credit, even though his shortcomings as a critic are very evident. Nevertheless, the challenge of such musicians as Toscanini is not only that their presence tends to overwhelm most schematizations, but that they require the critic to understand their force and precision in terms of a comprehensive theory of interpretation. Mr. Horowitz has not done much on this front. But his considerable labors to illuminate aspects of Toscanini's effect on American society are impressive, enough of a start to get a lot of critics moving.

CHAPTER 8

Middle Age and Performers

IDDLE AGE, like everything that stands between more clearly defined times or things, is not an especially rewarding period. One is no longer a promising young person and not yet a venerable old one. To be a rebellious child after the age of forty is frequently silly, and yet to assume the authority of old age prematurely is to risk the awful pomposity and rigidity of an institution. Dante produced his greatest work out of the crisis of the middle years, but so grand and detailed is his vision as to reduce the crisis of lesser people to a piddling whine, and although in his career T. S. Eliot made serviceable use of Dante and middle age, the model remains good for only a small minority. Middle age is uncertainty and some lostness, physical failings and hypochondria, anxiety and nostalgia; for most people it is also the time that affords the first sustained look at death.

Those, at any rate, are some of the empirical realities. In the arts there is sometimes a surprising sentimentality about the glorious middle years. Middle-period Beethoven is celebrated well beyond the merits of the sonatas and symphonies of that time, as if to suggest that Beethoven's true heroism begins then, with the underlining and italicizing of phrases that go on for too long or accents that make their point well past good taste or balance. Wordsworth too is praised for his middle years, as are Stravinsky and Victor Hugo. But to anyone actually living through those years, there is a good deal more to think about—in finding your way again, in adjusting your failing animal energies to the new realities, in learning from your past without repeating or (alas, more likely), betraying it—than to cheer. As with all clichés, there is some truth to the boring or frumpy or faded quality that one associates with middle age.

The Nation, March 14, 1987.

For the pianist who is no longer a prodigy or a recent contest winner, and with the rewards of old age nowhere in sight, the perils of middle age are considerable. But so too are the possible achievements. Maurizio Pollini is the middle-aged pianist par excellence (as, for the violinists, is the somewhat older Menuhin) in his willingness to explore and risk new repertory, in his quite conscious attempt to alter the horizons, and the aesthetics, of his playing. He was known first as a Chopin pianist, but quickly branched out into the rest of the nineteenth-century repertory. Soon he had added the great twentieth-century classics (Schönberg, Berg, Webern, Stravinsky), and immediately afterward he started to perform his major European contemporaries, Berio, Boulez and Stockhausen. In 1985 he did a surprising about-face and presented Bach's *Well-Tempered Clavier, Book I,* in Europe and the United States. In March of this year, with Claudio Abbado and the Vienna Philharmonic Orchestra, he will perform the five Beethoven concerti at Carnegie Hall.

Although I am an admirer of Pollini's playing, there was a lot to criticize in his Bach, which seemed driven by a severe, narrowly focused wish to avoid any trace of the influence of Glenn Gould. Instead Pollini reverted to a distinguished Italian predecessor, Ferrucio Busoni—perhaps the most underrated, underconsidered composer and personality in twentieth-century music—and performed Bach as he did, that is, as a contemporary of Brahms. Nowhere did Pollini's playing flag either in intensity or concentration and, especially in the more extended fugues (C sharp minor, A minor and B minor), there was a deep logic at work as he constructed a spacious intellectual architecture for each of these tightly woven contrapuntal textures. The sound, however, was often muddy, and the polyphonic lines unclear, as if Pollini were trying to accomplish an impossible montage—to let the voices move horizontally and, at the same time and with equal force, to build their sound vertically. But at least one felt that the whole enterprise was governed by an aesthetic decision (to finesse Gould by recourse to Busoni) which had not worked out very successfully, not because it hadn't been thought through, but because it had been thought too much and too hard. In its clotted busyness, Keats's line "the wreathed trellis of a working brain" suggests the curious achievement of Pollini's Bach.

With Alfred Brendel, who seems to be Pollini's implicit rival whenever eminent middle-aged pianists are mentioned, there is a lesser, or perhaps a less attractive, achievement to note. Brendel's work is notable for its solidity, its carefulness, its well-prepared, reliable and often noble interpretations. Brendel is also an articulate and scholarly occasional writer on music; he has a particularly high status among intellectuals. For him the middle years constitute an age of consolidation, typified in the complete

Beethoven sonata cycle he played in New York and in Europe a few years ago. If Pollini's failures are the result of overreaching, Brendel's are the opposite, the result perhaps of wanting to do a job thoroughly without sufficient regard for the exigencies of temperament and mood. His unaffecting Schumann strikes me as the work of a pianist adding a handful of masterpieces to his repertory in order to have covered Schumann the way he covered Schubert, Mozart, Beethoven and Liszt. Similarly, those pieces by Beethoven and Schubert—the *Eroica* Variations and the *Wanderer* Fantasy, respectively—that are peripheral to the central metropolitan block of sonatas, are assimilated by Brendel to a style perfected elsewhere but not applicable here, with not enough whimsy and fantasy, and too much dutiful or fussy exposition and precious emphasis.

Pollini and Brendel are both remarkably interesting pianists for whom middle age is neither a slough of despond nor a repetition ad nauseam of earlier triumphs. At a minimum, their playing attempts to render the context of meaningful development that gives their careers distinction, an enterprise that entails risk as well as victory. At their best, they involve their audiences in a movement that suggests a sustained and elevated look beyond the performance and the occasion. This is also the case with Charles Rosen, whose lesser career as a performer seems the result of a choice to expand into other fields (writing and teaching, for instance), which has taken a toll in sheer finger dexterity. It is hard not to take interested notice of him, however, just as one would never want to miss recitals by Martha Argerich, Peter Serkin, Malcolm Frager, Ursula Oppens and a few others. The finest middle-aged pianists I ever heard—each vastly different—are Solomon, Arturo Benedetti Michelangeli and the redoubtable Sviatoslav Richter.

This is a long way of getting around to Vladimir Ashkenazy, whose first U.S. recitals I heard over twenty-five years ago. Phenomenally gifted and wonderfully natural and instinctive in his playing, he seemed incapable of an ugly or awkward performance of the pieces he chose, which were all clustered in the post-1835 Central European and Russian repertory. The first time I heard Ashkenazy, he played the Brahms-Handel and the Rachmaninoff-Corelli variations, large and brilliantly textured pieces that the barely 20-year-old pianist performed with genuine style and finesse. Later came the Tchaikovsky Medal and his defection from the Soviet Union, and as he wandered the world's concert halls nearly every recital he gave was a disappointment, as much for the strangely lumpish and inexpressive perfection of his playing as for the impression he conveyed of having very little to say or to venture. More recently he has been doing chamber music, accompaniment and conducting, as if to prod his gifts into new territory.

He seems now to embody the quandary of middle age in its rawest, least successfully resolved form.

I heard him most recently at Carnegie Hall, as conductor and performer with the Royal Philharmonic Orchestra, an excellent group whose darker sound and slightly sloppy attacks are a nice change from the better American ensembles. Ashkenazy began the concert with Berlioz's *Corsaire* Overture, a busy, colorful piece arranged to display a variety of choirs in full-throated battle. It's not as headstrong and dashing as much of Berlioz's best music, but it serves orchestras very well as an opener. Ashkenazy's conception was alarming, a clarification of what is awry in his current state. There seemed no previously designed balance in the sound, a fault to be attributed exclusively to the conductor: in his enthusiasm to have the orchestra playing at its most acute, Ashkenazy had simply forced every mass in it to the front, so that strings, brasses and winds seemed to be clamoring for attention all at once. In the absence of either a principle of subordination or a sense of drama, the orchestra seemed both eager and lost. The overall impression was of a crowded blare, all foreground and display.

After the Berlioz the musicians regrouped for Beethoven's Third Concerto, in a semicircular arrangement that permitted Ashkenazy to face the orchestra from the piano stool. Thus surrounded on three sides he launched into a performance of this quintessential middle-period work, which can veer quite easily into graceless stolidity. The results, again, were symptomatic. The orchestral introduction, for example, was a pastiche of recorded versions—a bit of von Karajan, some Toscanini, etc.—and the music became gradually more distended as the tight rhythmical impulse which holds the first movement together disappeared. Ashkenazy as a conductor focuses on embellishing the smaller units, a sign of inexperience and insecurity. In his pianism, on the other hand, one got a demonstration of the old pro at work: the opening scales were blurred because covered by the orchestra, the first cadence was overaccented to contrast with the tutti, and so forth. The second movement *largo* in particular was almost totally without rhythmic organization and was reduced to a swooning *molto adagio*. But Ashkenazy's wonderful fingers saved the last movement, although by then the orchestra was, I thought, dispirited, reduced to playing pretty much on its own.

To say that Ashkenazy is a disappointment in middle age is to remark not just on the failures of intelligence and competence that mar his conducting but also on his capitulation to anachronistic performing instincts that are unguided by any apparent aesthetic conception. One has no sense of any interesting movement in his career, as if his prodigious talents were only commodities to be displayed before audiences several nights a week. He seems to have very little held in reserve, very little musically or intellectually to draw on, except the perfected techniques he has relied on for so many years. Perhaps to go on doing what you've always done, and to do it as well as before, is another solution to middle-age doldrums. But this not only leaves the audience's memory and perception out of the musical equation; it also refuses to acknowledge the dwindling spiritual satisfactions of so narrowly specialized and dull a project.

At its worst, middle-aged performing is scarcely to be endured, in part because it cannot easily be justified by a programmatic rationale imposed on the actual performance. Young pianists, after all, are like emanations out of nature, and old performers either suggest an ageless athleticism or the precious insight afforded by aesthetic closure. One of the great virtues of recordings is that they provide reference points to phases in a career, thus enabling us to compare early with middle Richter, or Kempff's Beethoven with Brendel's. Yet too often records are extensions of the recital stage, made with an eye toward immediate effect, interesting in a limited way (as Ashkenazy is) for the momentary pleasures afforded by fine execution. In the best of middle-aged performances, on stage and on record, one listens for signs of that dialectic between self and other, between performer and work, whose purpose is to reveal something about both as they undergo change in time. Thus the performer makes a statement about the unending process of interpretation itself, which is what all performance is finally about. Yet unless the listener can sense the perils and the rare grace of such an enterprise in its groundless effort and its groping for definition, the experience is a stale and flat one.

CHAPTER 9

The Vienna Philharmonic:
The Complete Beethoven Symphonies and Concertos

OWARD THE end of E. M. Forster's *A Passage to India,* as the spiritually exhausted Fielding is sailing home, he comes through the Suez Canal into the Mediterranean, "the human norm." The relief he feels derives from that region, where "harmony between the works of man and the earth that upholds them" has been achieved. It is an insidious comparison that Forster intends between India, all muddles and unsatisfying mysteries, and Europe, a "civilization that has escaped muddle, the spirit in a reasonable form."

Something like that experience of Fielding's (minus its offensive aspects) occurs in anyone who tries to grasp the significance of Beethoven's life and music. The heroic element so central to them resides entirely within human proportions: the life is neither too long nor too short, the *oeuvre* seems exactly large enough, with clearly defined outlines, periods, developments. As we enter the nineteenth century we leave behind composers like Bach, with his twenty children, his 200-plus cantatas, his innumerable instrumental works and his unendingly complex and inventive counterpoint; or Mozart, with his inhuman productivity, his forty-nine symphonies and twenty-one piano concertos, his operas, masses, quartets, trios and sonatas, all exuding formal perfection and grace; or Haydn, with his more than one hundred symphonies and dozens of works in every conceivable genre; or Handel, like Bach in his vast output, exuberant, repetitious, gallant. Such men both express a kind of murmuring anonymity and evoke a distinct aesthetic signature; the net effect is that the twentieth-century listener is awed and mystified, above all unable to identify with musical careers that were fashioned as subaltern structures framed by court and church.

The Nation, May 9, 1987.

Beethoven is the musical vanguard of what Charles Morazé has called *les bourgeois conquérants.* His aristocratic supporters were, he believed, his subordinates, not his overlords. A man of the middle classes, his were the stubborn, almost entrepreneurial successes of a thoroughly worldly individual who rose well above the circumstances of his birth. Everything about his music, from the large cache of sketchbooks to the laboriously worked and reworked scores, argues effort and development on a human scale. The difficulties of his life are understandable—illness, debt, loneliness, an unpleasant family, unhappy love affairs, creative blocks—and, if we except his extraordinary gifts and accomplishments, his artistic achievements as a whole belong to a creaturely realm: they have a dimension no lesser mortal needs to feel is theoretically unattainable. Beethoven's music is vitally committed either to sonata forms or to variation forms, the former dramatic and developmental, the latter exfoliative and circular; in both instances, his hallmark is work, not shattering insight, and although the so-called late-period style, which so fascinated Adorno and Thomas Mann, alternates between the demonic and the quasi-ethereal, there is always a healthy modicum of gritty technical effort to be appreciated.

Proust once said that every artist has a particular tune *(chanson)* that can be found in every work: a special cadence, theme, obsession or characteristic key absolutely the artist's own. Mozart's key may be the way configurations of the human voice enter all his melodic phrases; Bach's, the combination of rhythm and polyphonic statement (the "dance of God," said musicologist Wilfred Mellers) that informs all his writing. In Beethoven's case, it is an immediately recognizable tension between simple melody and insistent, sometimes explosive developmental sequences, a tension whose result is the almost visible realization of a conventional form (sonata, symphony, quartet). Beethoven sets the form, as a dramatist sets a play—on a stage, before the audience and for a concrete span of time.

So powerful and so focused was Beethoven's attention to his musical goals that great units, such as the thirty-two piano sonatas, nine symphonies, seventeen quartets and five piano concertos, emerge from his career with rock-like integrity, as wholes anchored in the secular and human elements, and attractive for that reason. Even at his most sublime, however, he rarely resists interrupting an elevated moment with some jarring sforzando recollection of a vulgar reality, "the uncontrollable mystery on the bestial floor." Not surprisingly, the last movement of his last symphony opens with a parade of themes from earlier movements, each of which is greeted with noisy bass rejections, a routine repeated when the baritone soloist enters. There are other examples: the repeated C sharp minor interruptions in the last movement of the Eighth Symphony; the discordant, asymmetrical and offbeat punctuations of the first movement development of the *Eroica* Symphony; or, to take an instance from Beethoven's life as a virtuoso, his sudden blow to the piano keys succeeded by raucous laughter, in order to break the audience's tearful and rapt admiration of an improvisation. All of these moments form part of a drama of fused wholes whose elements are humble and whose artistic ethic is inclusive, not programmatically homogenizing.

Performances of the complete cycle of symphonies or piano concertos are rare, not only because symphony organizations thrive on subscriptions, which demand variety, but also because there is no way to attempt them without venturing a statement through or about them. In fact, just to announce and perform these works is to make a statement, so powerfully established is their centrality by years of venerated performance. That both cycles were performed in six Carnegie Hall concerts in March by the Vienna Philharmonic under Claudio Abbado and with Maurizio Pollini as soloist was itself meant as a gesture extending the Viennese traditions associated with Beethoven (and, of course, with the other great symphonists) authoritatively into the New World. Like all performances, these were socially determinate. Prices for good seats were exceptionally high at $75 and $60 per concert, and the whole burnished-wood-and-leather phenomenon that stands metaphorically for the Old World (the Mercedes-Benz is its automotive equivalent) included unusually well-dressed, prosperous and European-looking audiences, and a generally festive ambiance. By attending these performances one established contact with a reconstructed *fin de siècle* Vienna. Europe still has the prestige to offer its music on its terms.

I mention these outward-seeming things because the managerial production of the concerts, as well as the aura of tradition and carefully aged beauty still attached to the all-male Vienna Philharmonic, were so much more integral than the performances themselves. Of Beethoven the revolutionary innovator and coarse parvenu there were occasional hints here and there, and the orchestra still seduces one with the gorgeous warmth and shine of its sound, its unforced unanimity, its idiomatic inwardness to the music. But Abbado's highly dedicated technical grasp of the cycle was not absorbed into any coherent vision. One reviewer of the first concert (the Egmont Overture, the Fourth Piano Concerto, the *Eroica*) attributed Abbado's insufficiencies to his nationality, an astonishingly idiotic and racist assumption. The fact is that to conduct all the symphonies and concertos from memory as Abbado did, to hold such an immense amount of difficult music before one and to play through it, is an immense feat, not given to many musicians to attempt. But it is hard to deny that Abbado's work was best characterized as vacillating between highly intense and often rushed music-making on the one hand, and inattentive, routine playing on the other.

The most satisfying of all his performances was the *Eroica*, especially the first movement, in which the confidence of the phrasing, the clarity of the voicing, the rhetorical justice of the work's pacing from beginning to end, were profoundly affecting. Yet overall, the fine moments were only intermittent: a splendidly robust final movement of the Fifth, with each dotted note right on target, each climax as joyously full as possible; a luxuriously expansive *Pastoral*, the second movement played almost as if it stood as a source for Bruckner's symphonies; an exceptionally clear and unsentimental rendition of the great allegretto movement of the Seventh; a marvelously paced opening movement for the Eighth, lyrical and extroverted at the same time. The indifferent performances were all similar in their afflictions, although the Fourth, perhaps Beethoven's least accessible symphony, was played with an almost insulting, scampering gaucherie.

Abbado's main problem was that his ideas about Beethoven's nervous, Dionysiac music seemed not to take into account its pulse or its almost blind insistence on itself. Nowhere was his failure more apparent than in the Ninth, which along with the *Eroica* remains, in my opinion, the only completely satisfying symphony. Neither Abbado nor the orchestra seemed able to get the A minor tonic-dominant sequence right in the first movement, and their playing got more tattered as the symphony progressed. By far the worst movement was the scherzo, in which Abbado's beat was sodden and uninflected, and the attacks insufficiently marked. In most of the headstrong and festive concluding moments of the symphonies Abbado whipped the orchestra up into a disproportionately loud accelerando, with results in the closing choral moments of the Ninth that verged on the raucous.

All in all, this cycle of the nine seemed to be premised on a vision that never appeared; perhaps it was that Abbado was unable to translate his view of the symphonies into execution. Expecting a hedgehog, one got a ragged fox. Having admired Abbado's conducting of Mahler and Verdi in the past, I wonder whether in Carnegie Hall he allowed the magnificence of the orchestra and the surroundings to do some of the work for him. It would be a great pity if the ethos of contemporary performance, with its exorbitant costs and fees, its star system, its ballyhoo and advertising, had come to dominate even so apparently principled and serious an artist.

No such doubts linger over Pollini's performances of the five concertos. Pollini remains, in my opinion, *the* pianist of today, for confidence, for unerring directness, for rigor of interpretation, for technique and no-nonsense power. He took an extraordinarily inventive position on the works, treating them as five separate aesthetic units, each with its own tonal quality, degree of tension, attitude toward the piano-orchestral relationship. It did not matter whether Pollini provoked, or Abbado's often haphazard conducting caused, the tension between the two, because in the end Pollini pulled out the performances brilliantly. Thus an extra drama attached to the Second Concerto—perhaps the least substantial of the five—in which Abbado's opening tutti dragged noticeably as he persisted in landing the orchestra on the middle or the tail end of each beat. Pollini's entering statement of the theme immediately shifted the emphasis to the quick side of the same basic pulse, and this contrast persisted throughout the concerto, with some particularly light and scintillating double thirds at the end of the last movement rounding out the miniature tug-of-war.

The great thing about Pollini's work was how widely he varied the quality of his tone, how unassumingly and yet definitively he manipulated his instrument to achieve contrasting results. The grace and elegance of the last movement of the Fourth were exhilarating and elevated at the same time, with the intimacy of music played in a smallish hall; by contrast, the Third was taut and almost dark, with none of the usual mooning about in the second movement largo. Somehow Pollini minimized the worst aspects of Beethoven's middle-period style, instead drawing out the thematic economy of each episode with surgical precision. Nowhere was he more overwhelming than in his *Emperor,* whose grandeur and sheer tonal massiveness I have never heard matched, except by Michelangeli. What was so breathtaking about the great C flat minor chords in the first movement development, and the E flat minor octave scales that follow those sledgehammer blows, was how unexpectedly their power appeared. Thus the extreme contrast between the Fourth and Fifth concertos framed a wonderful mapping of the classical concerto form in all its Beethovenian ardor and intelligence.

So Pollini's performances and the sound of the Vienna Philharmonic made coherent sense, although the Beethoven cycle as a whole did not. The greatest virtue of the series was its concentrated presentation of the works themselves, and if Abbado's aesthetic purpose was limited, there was no reason why the symphonies and concertos could not be admired as individual compositions by one particularly forceful composer. The recent death of Eugen Jochum, the last of the Furtwängler-type seers, convinces me that a truly complete cycle of these fundamental works is unlikely to be performed in the foreseeable future. Perhaps all attempts at the larger aesthetic undertakings in classical music—the *Ring,* the Beethoven Symphonies, the Bach Passions and *Well-Tempered Clavier*—are doomed, for now, to fragmentary recapitulation or elegiac failure.

CHAPTER 10

The Barber of Seville, Don Giovanni

M UCH OF the great outburst of intellectual energy in recent literary criticism has focused on the difficulty, even the impossibility, of interpretation. Psychoanalysis, semiotics, linguistics, deconstruction, feminist theory and Marxism have so expanded our notions of what a text or an authorial performance is that buying what was meant in *King Lear* or *Ulysses* is now an enormously complex enterprise. At its best, interpretation has therefore become inventive, a form of deliberate misreading, supplying all sorts of frankly conjectural possibilities as a way of rendering the work's historical distance, the author's silence, the critic's manifest power over the work. Texts that are subject to the tyranny of the unconscious or the tactics of class are no longer read for their lifelike depiction of characters, setting or history. "Wordsworth" has become a convenient shorthand for the writer whose text—a much more significant word—is the tangled meeting place for innumerable and unstable forces, none of them renderable "realistically" in the way that a photograph of a waterfall represents a real waterfall.

Musical performance is, of course, an art of interpretation. Yet it isn't plausible to expect a pianist playing a Beethoven sonata or an opera director staging *Wozzeck* to produce creative misreadings of these works. Most musical performance is still held in by mimetic norms. The pianist tries to play as exactly as possible what he or she thinks Beethoven actually wrote, in the order that he wrote it, first movement first, last movement last. Similarly, opera productions, although they give the director considerable leeway, must still respect character and plot. It would be impossible to do *Aida* without an Aida, although in a famous Frankfurt production Wieland Wagner had her skulking in the background, leaving the central position to

Amneris. Directors and audiences (to say nothing of singers and dancers) retain a common realistic expectation of what the intactness of a piece is, otherwise there would be no opera, and no paying audience.

So it has been the case that musical revivals have tended to be conservative, trying to get back to some lost or forgotten original. The vogue for early music played on original instruments, the revival of bel canto repertoire and style, the return to Mahler: All these have embodied not just the idea of recuperation but a usually unstated ideology of authenticity. The musical results are often satisfying. But it is not generally noted that even so apparently harmless and "correct" a notion as faithfulness to an original is itself already an interpretation, in which a slew of unverifiable entities (the composer's intention, an original sound, etc.) are set up and bowed to as if they were facts of nature.

Take as an illustration the current Rossini revival. With the exception of *The Barber of Seville*, Rossini's operas were scarcely performed in this country until about thirty years ago. A number of factors—the interest in bel canto, the advent of singers like Joan Sutherland and Marilyn Horne, the massive re-editing of Rossini's scores undertaken by Ricordi, the pioneering historical research of scholars like Philip Gossett—stimulated interest in the other operas, which are now available on records and occasionally performed with some educated attention to his extraordinary music. Rossini's work is still not appreciated as it ought to be or performed with the frequency it deserves, but it is rare to encounter even *The Barber* today without also noting a salutary change in interpretive attitudes to Rossini's music and drama.

As a performance of *The Barber of Seville* at London's Covent Garden in July revealed, even the most well-known Rossini is no longer played as simple comic entertainment, fit for children or softheaded adults. The contemporary Rosina, sung in London with a wryly confident maturity by Lucia Valentini-Terrani, is a cynical mezzo, not a soprano ingénue. The conductor, Gabriele Ferro, one of the Rossini revivalists, converted the orchestra of the Royal Opera House into a brasher, less mellifluous instrument, as if to reflect the chattily rhetorical characteristics of Rossini's ensemble writing: the strings were toned down, the higher winds and brasses (piccolos and trumpets especially) were given prominence and the percussion team was required to perform with sharp accentuation. Aside from Paata Burchuladze, a young Georgian with a tremendously large and resonant bass, as Don Basilio, the cast was unexceptional, but the overall effect was of a new, politically complex and intelligent Rossini. How rewarding it is to see this familiar opera staged not as a semimoronic farce but as a shrewdly calculating and inventive piece of class provocation. It might also be noted that the Covent Garden program was packed with useful historical and cultural information culled from Beaumarchais's correspondence, the memoirs of the Duc de Saint-Simon and Alberto Zedda's editorial notes for the Ricordi edition; so literate a program is not to be encountered at the Met, which treats the intellectual content of its programs condescendingly, like mere commercial filler.

Few critics or audiences today object to the results of the Rossini revival, partly because, to my knowledge, his works have not yet been given the kind of revolutionary and antimimetic revision given to Wagner and a few others. Quite the opposite was the case with Mozart's *Don Giovanni* as directed by Peter Sellars at this year's PepsiCo Summerfare festival in Purchase, New York. *The New York Times'* Donal Henahan was greatly offended by Sellars's staging of the opera as a ghetto drama of pushers and junkies, an idea, according to Henahan, that traduced Mozart completely. Sellars's *Così fan tutte*, set in Despina's Diner circa 1970, was somehow forgiven its licenses by most critics because *Così* is considered a lighter, less consequential work. (Although, as I was reminded by Professor Fred Grab of Bard College, the great director of the East Berlin Komische Opero Walter Felsenstein never attempted a realization of *Così* because he considered it too difficult to pull off.)

Henahan, and Andrew Porter in *The New Yorker*, who found Sellars's *Don Giovanni* the most electrifying he'd ever seen, were touching on important questions about the interpretation of music. How far can one go in transforming a work, and what is it about the work itself that appears to permit some changes but not others? Why are ideological notions about authenticity or fidelity to a text allowed to rule performance standards, and what is it about Mozart's operas in particular (some Strauss and Wagner operas also qualify) that inspires the conservatism of some viewers and the enthusiasm of others when the works are staged with startlingly new, even shocking force?

The great virtue of Sellars's productions is that they can provide some direct insight into these matters. Almost immediately, they put you in touch with what is most eccentric and opaque about Mozart: the obsessive patternings in the operas, patternings that have little to do with showing that crime doesn't pay or that the faithlessness inherent in all human beings must be overcome before true union can occur. Mozart's characters in *Don Giovanni* and *Così* can be interpreted not as individuals with definable characteristics but as figures driven by forces outside themselves that they don't comprehend and make no effort to examine. These operas, in fact, are about power and manipulation that reduce individuality to a momentary identity in the vast rush of things. There is very little room in them for providence, or for the heroics of charismatic personalities. Compared with Beethoven, Verdi or even Rossini, Mozart depicts an amoral Lucretian world, in which power has its own logic, undomesticated either by considerations of piety or verisimilitude. What is it that keeps Don Giovanni bound irrecusably to his licentiousness—exposed with such cold, quantitative abandon by Leporello in "Madamina, il catalogo questo"—or Don Alfonso and Despina to their schemes and fixings? Nothing in the operas provides an adequate answer.

Instead, I think, Mozart has tried to embody an abstract force that drives people without the consent of their mind or will, through the use of stories whose moral pointlessness is highly in evidence. It is for this reason that Beethoven, ever the Enlightenment enthusiast, disliked Mozart's operas. When in *Così* Guglielmo sings his questioning aria "Donne mie, la fate a tanti," he is meant literally and unenlighteningly to be asking why women behave as they do; in the context the aria also refers to the behavior of men, which Guglielmo's own actions do nothing to illuminate. Sellars had the aria sung in the audience, as if the character playing Guglielmo had become a Phil Donahue, getting different answers with equally uninformative results in each case.

Power in Mozart's operas is managed or brokered by enigmatic older men (Alfonso, Sarastro) and by willful aristocrats (Almaviva, Don Giovanni). Their power is arbitrary and cannot be characterized simply; it works according to elaborate protocols which are both headstrong and self-sustaining. Because he lived in the late eighteenth century in a society whose modes of power were feudal, ecclesiastic and increasingly urban, Mozart deployed the elements that were familiar to him—gentlemen and ladies, peasants, servants and (in the case of Sarastro) Masonic pseudo-priests. But there is no reason to suppose that he meant these embodiments of power to exhaust the possibilities of social force forever after. Moreover, Mozart's characters are engaged not in action, but in the gamelike activity that ensues after a pattern has been set in motion. Theoretically, it is quite possible to imagine the process continuing into the twenty-first century.

And so, why not a diner and Vietnam vets for *Così*, followed by a drug addict *Don Giovanni*? Are these two fictions really any less plausible than Mozart's "originals," as if the original *Così*—mutilated beyond recognition by editors and *régisseurs*—or *Don Giovanni* were somehow easier to understand in eighteenth-century costume? What Sellars has picked up with great brilliance is the void at the center of both operas, a void that allows an infinite series of substitutions, so long as each is internally consistent in its patterns and conceits. *Così* functions in symmetries, with three pairs of men and women acting in concert; hence, the choreographed movements, the synchronized gestural excesses, the topical beach-bumming casualness of Sellars's conception. In *Don Giovanni* Mozart's imagination focuses on the serial and linear quality of the action, in which one episode is like another, one adventure follows another without real development or fixed purpose. Sellars's choice of the drug scene, with a darkened stage and frequently indistinguishable figures, struck me as shatteringly, chillingly pertinent. Don Giovanni's love life is as romantic as a dingy subway platform inhabited by outcasts and misfits who lie in wait for the occasional trick; the attitude of the confirmed junkie shooting up every time he gets a chance is perfectly comparable to the driven rake in his view of women. And so Sellars portrayed it.

But there is another, more exigently contemporary and practical reason for interpreting Mozart as Sellars has. Consider that Sellars himself is the product of a culture with no continuous and independent opera tradition. Until now mainstream American opera production has derived mainly from Europe, and a boring *verismo* (i.e., mimetic) Europe at that. For such a tradition to work here you need money and stars, neither of which are handily available. Sellars's means are therefore modest. His singers in *Così* and *Don Giovanni* were young and of average (even mediocre) voice, with the women in general better than the men. What they lacked in musical polish, they more than made up for in physical agility; many arias were sung by characters rolling around on the stage, with results in pure vocal production that were not always satisfying. Thus it is difficult to pick out anyone from the ensemble who was truly outstanding. In fact, so strong is Sellars's conception of his singers as functionaries in his productions that you can only imagine them singing for him, rather as Dickens's characters remain fixed forever in the stylized world of his novels.

The greatest misgiving I have about Sellars's Mozart concerns his conductor, Craig Smith. Granted that the orchestra at Smith's disposal is both a sparse-sounding and a less than first-class one, and granted also that romanticizing Mozart to make him more beautiful and heavenly than he is is no good outside *Amadeus*. But do we then have to have Mozart at seventy-five miles an hour? The oddest thing about Smith's performances was how similar every aria and ensemble sounded. Invariably the opening tempo was fast and got faster. Invariably the singers could not keep up. Invariably the number was uncadenced and uninflected, leaving the singers a thankless job of pattering out semi-inarticulate words in an imperfectly understood language. Whereas Sellars's notion of style is imaginative and plastic, Smith's seems mechanical and, alas, both unmusical and unfinished.

I must confess to being flabbergasted by the disparity between these two collaborators. Quite possibly I have missed something in Smith's conducting that may be particularly relevant to Sellars's vision. Nevertheless it is a pity that dramatic intelligence of such high quality is served by so uninteresting and heedless a musical execution. Perhaps a greater equivalence will occur when Sellars comes to the Met and James Levine next season, but there will remain for him a puzzling question which his brilliant work has hitherto only begun to answer: how to make congruent Mozart's musical fluency, his astonishingly idiomatic compositional style, his endless melodic invention with the starkly uncompromising severity of his major comic plots. Does the music mock the action? Is the music meant to accentuate the plot's socially acceptable conventions, thus disguising Mozart's subversiveness? Or is there some as yet undiscovered notion of counterpoint or accompaniment that yokes the two elements together so strangely? These questions require interpretations of considerable depth and subtlety, which is why Sellars's work, with its often lurid explicitness and its ingenious distortions of the "original," is so interesting.

CHAPTER 11

Glenn Gould at the Metropolitan Museum

ON SEPTEMBER 26 and 27, the Metropolitan Museum of Art in New York City screened eight one-hour television films of Glenn Gould playing a wide range of repertory. Arranged by the Met's concerts and lectures manager, Hilde Limondjian, this was the third such screening in New York since Gould's death in October 1982. Judging by the healthy turnout, Gould remains a compellingly attractive figure. He was that almost impossible creature, both a pianist of staggering talent and a man of effortlessly articulate opinions, some so arguable as to seem merely quirky, others profoundly insightful and intelligent. His work invariably offers musical and intellectual satisfactions encountered in the performances of no other contemporary musician.

The Met screenings began with performances recorded by Gould as a very young man in the middle 1950s; they ended with the last film he made, his 1981 performance of the *Goldberg Variations,* subsequently released as a record. The selections presented were mainly of Bach and Beethoven solo and ensemble works, and with the exception of a spectacularly, relentlessly, sadistically boring massacre of a Mozart sonata (K. 333), all the performances showed off Gould to great advantage. (I am now convinced that aside from the concerti, most of Mozart's piano works are fundamentally unplayable; Gould succeeded in demonstrating that point by the way he interpreted the sonatas throughout his career.)

There is an estimable mixture of eccentricity and surprise to be enjoyed in Gould's playing: he could always be depended on to do *something* in a performance that would make it completely unusual. The earliest of the films, a 1954 CBC broadcast of the first movement of the first Beethoven concerto, contains a dazzling cadenza by Gould in the form of a complex four-part fugue based on part of the movement's main theme. Beethoven, of course, provided cadenzas for the concerti; Gould, in a characteristic act of lese majesty, inserts his own. Two back-to-back performances of Sergei Prokofiev's 7th Sonata, from 1961 and 1976, show totally different conceptions of the pieces, the first startlingly lyrical and expansive, the second (which comprised only the opening movement) brittle and tense, with a nervousness of attack much more characteristic of Gould's mature style.

In spite of his flamboyance, Gould also seems to have been a perfect chamber musician, effortlessly accommodating himself to other ensemble players (as he does in the Shostakovich Quintet) or matching soloists in perfectly scaled virtuosity and sheer professional skill. Particularly notable are his performances of Beethoven's A major Cello Sonata with Leonard Rose, and a set of somewhat uneasy but always interesting traversals with Yehudi Menuhin of Bach's C minor Violin Sonata, Schoenberg's Violin and Piano *Fantasy* (a late and tremendously complex work played rather anxiously and unwillingly by Menuhin and with great authority and passion by Gould, who had the piece committed to his apparently flawless memory) and Beethoven's late middle-period G major Sonata, Opus 96, one of Menuhin's specialties. To the best of my knowledge none of the music from these videotapes was ever released on disc (although Gould did record the *Fantasy* in 1964 with Israel Baker).

Yet the most riveting part of these eight films was Gould's performance of contrapuntal pieces and variations. One hour-long program devoted to the fugue comprised selections from Bach's *Well Tempered Clavier,* the last movement of Beethoven's Sonata in A flat major (Op. 110) and a daemonic rendition of the last movement of Paul Hindemith's Sonata No. 3, a fine piece hardly ever played in concert today because of the intellectual cowardice of most contemporary musicians. The program of variations climaxed with performances of Webern's *Variations* and Beethoven's Sonata in E major (Op. 109). Gould linked the two by a brilliant highlighting of the structural finesse and expressive detail in both works—a considerable achievement, since the pieces are written out of diametrically opposed aesthetics, one exfoliative and elaborate, the other concentrated and crabbed. The program also included a severely restrained performance of a Sweelinck organ Fantasy, which I first heard during a Gould recital in 1959 or 1960. I was struck then, and again watching the film, by the way Gould could disappear as a performer into the work's long complications, providing an instance of what he called "ecstasy," the state of standing outside time and within an integral artistic structure.

By far the most moving and affecting of the films was director Bruno Monsaingeon's record of Gould speaking about and then playing the

Goldberg Variations. Here, Gould is no longer the lean and youthfully eager intellectual, the caustic wit who could say of Beethoven that he was always going to meet his destiny at the next modulation. He has now become a pot-bellied, bald and somewhat mournful middle-aged aesthete whose jowly face and slightly decadent lips suggest too many rich meals. Even his fingers, which have retained their fabulously efficient elegance and economy, are now evidently older, more worldly. And indeed Gould's performance of these thirty extraordinary pieces has acquired layers of sophistication and cleverness, in added ornaments, in oddly varied and usually slower tempi, in surprising repetitions, in more sharply inflected lines—for example, the heavily strummed base line in variation one, or the underlinings of the theme in Bach's unison canon in variation three.

This is one of the few films I've seen of Gould which is in color and quite obviously the work of a filmmaker, not simply a TV cameraman. Its autumnal hues are made sadder by the realization that this was to be Gould's last performance of the work that first brought him widespread attention. I was told last year by Professor Geoffrey Payzant of Toronto University (a philosopher whose excellent 1978 book *Glenn Gould, Music and Mind* is the only work on the pianist to begin to do him justice) that Monsaingeon has a cache of fifty-two hour-long films of Gould performances that he has tried unsuccessfully to sell to TV companies in Europe and the United States. In spite of the stations' indifference, I think Monsaingeon was right to want so singlemindedly to film Gould at work—the man was, quite literally, a full-scale cultural enterprise.

None of the remarkable things that Gould did, however, would have been possible without a truly rare digital mechanism that easily rivals those of legendary technicians like Horowitz, Bolet or Michelangeli. Gould always seemed to achieve a seamless unity between his fingers, the piano and the music he was playing, one extending into the other until the three became indistinguishable. It was as if Gould's virtuosity finally derived its fluency from the piece and not from a residue of technical athleticism built up independently over the years. Pollini has something of this quality, but it is the wonderfully intelligent exercise of his fingers in polyphonic music that separates Gould from every other pianist. Only a great Bach organist communicates in the same way.

But the most interesting thing about Gould, as Monsaingeon saw, is the way he constantly overstepped boundaries and burst confining restraints. Last year Monsaingeon published a book in France called *Glenn Gould: Non, je ne suis pas du tout un excentrique,* whose last section is a "video montage" of the pianist being interviewed by five critics after his death: clearly Monsaingeon sees him as a man for whom ordinary mortality was no limit at all. And Gould certainly cultivated this notion in his audience. Not only was it clear that he could, and did, command the entire range of Western music from the Renaissance until the present—there are instances in the films of Gould talking about a series of musical examples and then turning to the piano to illustrate them from memory—he also could do with that music what he liked.

Most good musicians do have at their fingertips, or lips, a lot more music than they perform in public. Memory is part of the gift every performer carries within. Yet we normally see performances only on the stage, in a program. Gould went to very great lengths after he left the concert stage in 1964 to communicate his diverse talents to a wide audience, spilling out his knowledge, his articulate analyses and his prodigious technical facility well beyond the concert experience. Thus in addition to performing for the camera, Gould wrote dozens of articles; he produced, wrote and directed radio scripts; he interviewed people; he did television work; and, of course, he continued to produce records. And whenever he seemed to have settled into a niche, say, as a Bach pianist, he would up and record Wagner transcriptions, or the Grieg sonata—repertory that could not have been more unexpected.

Gould had a rare and astonishing talent for doing one thing brilliantly and suggesting that he was doing something else too. Hence his predilection for contrapuntal or variational forms or, on a slightly different level, his habit of playing the piano and conducting and singing, or his way of being able to quote both musically and intellectually more or less anything at any time. In a sense, Gould was gradually moving toward a kind of untheatrical and anti-aesthetic *Gesamtkunstwerk*, or universal artwork, a description which sounds ludicrous and contradictory. I am not sure how deliberately he was trying to achieve this, or how conscious he was of Rimbaud's *déracinement du sens* as an aesthetic project. But those are the ideas that seem to me best to sum up the disturbing and yet attractive postmodern qualities of Gould's highly unusual enterprise.

CHAPTER 12

Giulio Cesare

O F ALL the great Western classical composers Georg Friedrich Handel has been the most consistently misrepresented and generally underestimated. An exact contemporary of J. S. Bach, Handel has routinely suffered in comparison with him. I recall frequent discussions with a musicologist friend who used Bach's elevated polyphonic style, his apparent intellectualism and severity, his affecting religiosity, to denigrate Handel's less complex style and his irrepressible, thumping floridity. Certainly one senses Handel's music a certain worldliness and even courtliness of a sort not likely to engage contemporary audiences. But taken on his own, extraordinarily complex terms, Handel is certainly Bach's equal in technique and finish. Moreover, Handel's eighteenth-century colleagues all commented on his religious devotion, which rivaled Bach's, and although the aesthetic of his dramatic oratorios—*Israelites in Egypt, Messiah, Judas Maccabeus,* etc.—is brashly theatrical and realistic, there is no gainsaying the authentic splendors and unending inventiveness of his work.

There are, however, two problems with Handel that keep him from being as appreciated today as he has been by other great composers (remember, for example, how on his deathbed Beethoven spent hours leafing through Handel scores, venerating him above all his redoubtable predecessors). One problem is that Handel's major achievement was as an operatic composer in an admittedly constrained and specialized form, the *opera seria*. During the fifty years (1710 to 1759, the year of his death) he spent in England, Handel composed about thirty operas, produced and directed most of them and was almost until the end of his life a working man of the theater. Virtually none of this material is included in the modern operatic repertory, which has avoided it in preference to the (equally stylized and limited) *bel canto* and *verismo* traditions.

The Nation, November 14, 1988.

The other reason for Handel's relative eclipse is that whereas he began as a composer for an essentially aristocratic audience, with the decline of that audience he became the composer for an expanding and triumphant English middle class. In the nineteenth century Handel was treated as a thoroughly Victorian composer and was celebrated in ways that distracted from the genius of his music. His work was known in grotesquely large choral extravaganzas—descriptions of 2000-voice Handel choirs and 500-instrument woodwind and brass ensembles are not uncommon—or as a ceremonial composer for royal occasions. Not even his spectacular anthems (like *Zadok the Priest*) and bravura arias (who can forget Kiri Te Kanawa, in an absurd flowerbonnet, singing "Let the Bright Seraphim" at Charles and Di's wedding) have been immune from unintentional comedy.

Thus Handel has had the worst of it, despite the immense strengths of his music. Neither has he been considered an abstract, pure musician of the Bach-Palestrina type, nor, as with Mozart, Haydn and Beethoven, a model of the mature classicism that points the way toward romanticism. Handel seems completely enclosed by his period, except for the middle-class and royal associations that do not endear him to today's engaged music-lovers, who seem to regard him as an adolescent or low-brow taste. Handel does require a major effort at understanding, although ironically he is one of the most easily and directly likable of all composers. Handel has, however, been fortunate in that most of his modern scholarly interpreters have written informative and eminently readable books. There are few musicological studies to rival the intelligence and lucidity of Winton Dean's great books on Handel, and even in less specialized work—that of Paul Henry Lang and H. Robbins Landon—Handel emerges as a remarkably humane genius. He was worldly, yes, and always professional, and as has often been suggested, he seems to have taken from the English enough of their irony and common sense to undercut pretentiousness and give his profile a competence that is dismayingly unneurotic.

But Handel's greatness as a composer is in the end fascinatingly evident in his music. In everything he wrote there is a unique relationship between, on the one hand, counterpoint that could be as brilliantly organized as Bach's (with a slightly less opulent harmonic diversity) and on the other, a melodic, textural quality that often overtakes the counterpoint and commands the form. Some of his chaconnes and variational structures fuse the two modes, but on the whole Handel seems always to go from, say, fugues to arias to ensembles: This is true in his keyboard suites, the Opus 6 concerti grossi and many of his finest choral works. It is as if the strictness of polyphony were being coaxed by his power of dramatic and emotional expression into song, moving from the imitation of music by itself (counterpoint) to the imitation by music of a mood. In Handel one senses an enactment of musical invention that goes—to reverse Michael Fried's formulation for eighteenth-century painting—from the absorption of music with itself to the theatricality of music that seeks to show audiences what it can do mimetically by way of drama, dance, melody and formal organization.

Handel, more so than Bach, Mozart or Beethoven, was a composer whose method included a great deal of borrowing, substituting and reworking. Those who adhere to the cult of Mozart and Bach as endlessly and even effortlessly fertile composers have looked askance at Handel, who trails behind him a milewide stream of plagiarisms and casual thefts. Handel is even more unlike Beethoven, whose introspective struggles, tortured sketchbooks and tragic self-awareness seem written all over his music. Handel's is an art not so much of concealment as, paradoxically, of containment and adequacy. He could, as scholars have noted, say anything, represent any mood, any situation, without a single seam showing. And yet he haunts one by the protean restlessness of his work. He seems never to be *there*, and yet his unmistakable sound and range regularly stand out. In no composer is originality harder to pin down and yet easier somehow to experience intelligently. The instinctual drives present in all music are educated and tamed by Handel almost completely, although in rare moments (in the Dionysian excesses of the late oratorios, for example) they do burst forth.

The real obstacle to appreciating Handel remains, however, his absence from the operatic stage today. There are few recordings of the operas to help remedy that gap: the only available version of *Giulio Cesare*, which the Metropolitan Opera has just staged for its 1988–89 reason, is an unsatisfactory performance by Beverly Sills and Norman Treigle taken from the old New York City Opera production twenty years ago. I own a strangely disordered, but in its own way preferable, set of recorded extracts performed in 1964 by Joan Sutherland and Marilyn Horne with Richard Bonynge conducting, but that recording is no longer in print. By and large, then, Handel's operas are kept from contributing to his reputation. This is like excluding Beethoven's quartets or Mozart's piano concerti from the repertoire.

The usual reasons given for this omission are that Handel's conventions are cripplingly antimodern, antidemocratic and antirealistic, or that there aren't singers around who can handle either the virtuosity or the improvised ornamentation required for the performance of his work. There is enough truth in both these charges to make them stick—for about a minute. Mozart is equally difficult but he gets performed; similarly, the demands on the voice exacted by Verdi, Donizetti or Strauss are as great as what is required by Handel, and yet those composers are often performed. But today's opera culture—ruled as it is in New York by people who consider the Metropolitan's mission to be fulfilled by repeated productions of Puccini and Verdi—has disallowed Handel not because he is stylized, but because his stylizations cannot be explained or performed away, so to speak. Most of the literature on opera—Paul Robinson's excellent *Opera and Ideas*, for instance—doesn't touch Handel, and when such books do (as in *A Song of Love and Death* by the egregious Peter Conrad) he is reduced to clichés that render him a boring imitation of Molière. Handel's modernity may be found in the rigor with which he, like Schönberg or Webern, sticks to a prescribed mode, as well as the intelligence with which he always saves himself from mere routine or self-parody.

The original conditions for the performance of a Handel opera cannot be replicated today: Aristocratic coteries, castrati, card-playing audiences, Italianate literature and the like are in short supply, and the musicians trained in or capable of his rarefied manner of performance soon discover that the money is elsewhere. Yet the operas can be performed, and when they are, they are usually successful. But the essennal point about Handel's operas is that intelligence and style are central to them; no amount of bellowing and emoting can help singers who can get through *Don Giovanni* but who can get absolutely nowhere with *Rodelinda* or *Cesare*. Short of hearing or seeing good performances of the operas, the best way for audiences and performers to get closer to Handel's world is to read the first two chapters of Winton Dean's *Handel and the Opera Seria*, and to play through a piano-vocal score, imagining Handel's full might.

Mercifully, someone at the Met has done that, with the result that the current *Giulio Cesare* is actually first-rate. The night I went, Kathleen Battle, slated most nights to sing the role of Cleopatra, was ill and replaced by Barbara Kilduff, a singer who in physique, agility of voice and technical security closely resembles Battle. Handel's Caesar and Cleopatra (mezzo and soprano) are not Shavian but Shakespearean, and Cleopatra in particular is wonderfully seductive and operatic—a mature woman capable of intrigue and murder, not a precocious teen-ager who sounds like a flute abandoning itself to unbelievable trills and runs. Kilduff wasn't ideal, but she got through creditably.

The plot of *Giulio Cesare* unfolds in Egypt in the aftermath of Pompey's defeat and subsequent murder by Tolomeo (castrato or countertenor), Cleopatra's brother, who also has designs on Caesar's life. So while Cleopatra plots to seduce Caesar, Caesar is also trying to escape Tolomeo's attempts on his life; the subplot concerns the efforts by Achilla, Tolomeo's general, to possess Cornelia, Pompey's widow, and destroy her vengeful son, Sesto.

It all works out well of course—Achilla is killed, Tolomeo foiled, Caesar and Cleopatra united, Sesto and Cornelia rescued. As the only conventionally male voice in the ensemble, Julien Robbin's Achilla was good enough, and once in a while affecting, but it was Tatiana Troyanos's Caesar that dominated the proceedings with admirable, although not always successful consistency. Of her singing, it could be said that it was sublime, although in Caesar's first act aria "Va tacito e nascosto"—a piece that sets out Caesar's determined plan of revenge—her meticulous phrasing and ensemble delicacy (the aria is unique for its horn obbligato) went too far in communicating majestic transcendence and not far enough in cold-blooded vengeance. This is the difficulty with Handel: So finely calibrated are the effects of his words to his music that if the tempo is even a hair too fast the music sounds foolishly jolly; too slow and it sounds lugubrious.

The well-known British harpsichordist and conductor Trevor Pinnock led *Giulio Cesare* in his Metropolitan conducting debut. The sound he drew out of the confident orchestra was what we have come to recognize as Baroque authentic, with plentiful harpsichord continuo and somewhat thinned-out strings. There wasn't much flair to his conception, though it was idiomatic, sensible, well crafted. As with some of the principals in the cast—Martine Dupuy as Sesto and Sarah Walker as Cornelia—one felt that a serious idea of the music hadn't quite developed before the performance; only Jeffrey Gall, an impressive American countertenor, as Tolomeo treated Handel's music with the bold mixture of pleasure and art it requires, but his voice took almost a whole act to warm up.

John Copley's production was adequate, and except for tacky Egyptian costumes obviously borrowed from *Aida*, neither offended nor stirred me. Handel's operas work by extremely well-defined parts—recitatives, *da capo* arias, occasional ensembles that build into immediately discernible dramatic units, each of them cut off (and this is hard for modern audiences) by relentless exits. When the opera finally resolves itself into a conclusion with all the "good" characters onstage, Handel's method of deferred satisfaction is vindicated in a majestic concluding chorus, which in the Metropolitan production was a really great moment. For reasons I cannot fathom, almost a third of the audience left before the end, perhaps because they couldn't follow what was happening; in the Met's idiotic refusal to use supertitles, audiences are supposed either to sit passively or to have memorized the libretto. Nevertheless, should *Giulio Cesare* return to Lincoln Center, I would urge you to see and stay to the final curtain of this splendid example of an unusually great opera.

CHAPTER 13

Bluebeard's Castle, Erwartung

ÉLA BARTÓK'S *Bluebeard's Castle* and Arnold Schoenberg's *Erwartung* make for an unusual and often gripping evening at the Metropolitan Opera House despite their flawed production. Their relatively unfamiliar and specialized idioms are rarely encountered in a house that is, ironically, better placed to produce twentieth-century opera than the rigorously mediocre *verismo* repertory it seems always to prefer. Both these works date from about the same period, *Erwartung* (Expectation) from 1909, *Bluebeard's Castle* from 1911; both had to wait several years before they were performed. They are what have loosely been called expressionist or symbolist works in that both are antirealistic, elusive in meaning, very much the products of an eccentric, personal vision of the world in which alienation, anxiety and exaggerated loneliness are the main features. Sexuality (and not sex) is at the heart of both short operas (Bartók's is an hour long, Schoenberg's barely half that). In each, it is a woman—played and sung by the redoubtable Jessye Norman—whose travails stand at the work's center.

In the first opera, Judith has just been brought to the castle by Bluebeard (Samuel Ramey), as his new wife. Determined to unlock seven doors that line one of his walls, she cajoles him into consenting. As each door is opened by Judith it reveals first power and wealth, then brutality and horror; thus, for instance, the third door presents a hoard of gold and jewels that a moment later appears to be covered with blood. The last door releases the three wraiths who are Bluebeard's former wives, and at that instant Judith realizes what her own fate is to be. The opera ends with a mournful exit of the women: Judith is the last wife in a procession watched contemplatively by Bluebeard, their lord and murderer.

The Nation, March 6, 1989.

Judith and Bluebeard are quite explicitly in love, yet it is she who forces him to uncover secrets that, we gather, he would prefer to leave alone. Nevertheless, Bartók presents the unfolding action as taking place inevitably, almost ritualistically; both characters seem driven by forces they neither understand nor command, although Bluebeard—the sound of the original Hungarian name Kékszakállú communicates this better—is tinged with a sinister power that finally overcomes the questioning woman. One thinks of Pandora here, though Bartók took this drama from a fairy-triptych by Maurice Maeterlinck (which included *Peléas et Mélisande,* set by Claude Debussy, and *Ariane et Barbe-Bleue,* set by Paul Dukas). Thus the world of *Bluebeard's Castle* is hieratic, coded, magical; even enough its main action is the striking revelation of terror induced by the need for intimacy and sexual knowledge. This was explicitly underlined in Goran Jarvefelt's production by having Bluebeard shed an item of clothing each time one of the doors is opened.

As is evident from my summary, Bartók's opera is highly patterned, almost predictable from beginning to end. So to the music, which belongs to a period in Bartók's career when his research in Hungarian folk culture accompanied his recoveries of other avante-garde composers, principally Richard Strauss. Indeed one of the things that impresses one overwhelmingly about both operas is not so much how they relate to their composer's later careers (this is often and justifiably explored in discussing *Erwartung*) but how they bear the stylistic imprint of Richard Strauss, whose *Salome* (1905) and *Elektra* (1909) were so electrifying an advance over Wagner. Strauss, like Bartók and Schoenberg, took Wagner's extraordinary chromaticism and pushed it to expressive lengths, flirting with a nontonal universe that was little short of scandalous.

Interestingly, however, Wagner's own experiments with nontonal music were associated with feverish, transgressive sex, so powerfully embodied in *Tristan und Isolde.* Yet *Meistersinger* comes after *Tristan* and, partly because of its "healthier" subject matter (the robust state of Germanic art as embodied in the friendship of Hans Sachs with Walther and Eva), Wagner's musical idiom is correspondingly healthy, and foursquare too. True, the style of diatonic polyphony and Lutheran church music used in *Meistersinger* is occasionally interspersed with deviant harmonic digressions, but the work's overall musical profile underlines the equation between sexual normality and conventional harmony. Thus, there is a straight line from the fevers of *Tristan* to Salome's depravity, Electra's matricidal obsessions, Judith's unfortunate fixations and the hysteria of *Erwartung's* unnamed "Frau"; a line of increasingly untonal, "abnormally" psychological music whose final release from any fidelity to classical tonal norms Schoenberg soon accomplished when he promulgated his twelve-tone method.

Bluebeard's Castle is less harmonically and aesthetically aggressive than *Erwartung,* and less demanding, less uncompromising as well. I should say that I have never been completely convinced by Bartók. Like Schoenberg, he is one of the giants of twentieth-century music. His later works, including the Fifth and Sixth Quartets; the Music for Strings, Percussion and Celesta; the Concerto for Orchestra; and the Second and Third Piano Concerti are manifestly powerful scores with a tremendous declamatory and rhythmic effectiveness, and with a melodic generosity unlike anything in the music of that period. Yet I have also felt that there is in Bartók an appeal to, or a residue of, a romantic (mostly, but not always nationalist) project imperfectly and unsatisfyingly realized in the music; compared with Debussy, the early Strauss or Schoenberg, Bartók seems an unwilling avant-garde artist, perhaps less reflective and well thought through.

In the Met's *Bluebeard* these aspects of Bartók's music emerged as half tacky, half schmaltzy. For example, in displaying his kingdom to Judith, Bluebeard waves down an entire wail of his house, accompanied by loudly italicized modal chords that Bartók, I think, wanted us to suspect for their brassy assertiveness, but which, delivered by James Levine and the orchestra, sound like Miklos Rosza at M.G.M. As Bluebeard, Samuel Ramey was impressive, always dignified and convincing—even when, half undressed, he was required to assume the fetal position on a ridiculous little round platform placed asymmetrically at stage right. He has the finest legato phrasing of any male singer at the Met, and this aspect of his singing is always a function of the drama, not of posturing or "beautiful" voice production. His part is static and enigmatic, just as to a degree the action is. His demeanor and noble sound, however, disguise the opera's misogyny, making it seem as if both he and Judith are caught in a plot of someone else's making.

Although I am pleased to see the Met put on Bartók and Schoenberg, there are some real problems with these performances. Jessye Norman is undoubtedly a superb singer, at her best in German and French romantic lieder, as well as certain operas (again French, German and, in the case of Purcell's *Dido and Aeneas,* British) in which there is a premium on eloquence, stability and a narrow range of vocal as well as dramatic acting. She is incapable of ugly or badly phrased sounds, and cannot be surpassed in Strauss or Berlioz. But in the Met's twentieth-century double billing she fared badly, I thought, getting worse and worse in *Erwartung.* She does not move well, and produces fluttering, restless gestures that are supposed to connote everything from fear to hysterical excitement, passion, love and ecstasy.

In *Bluebeard* Norman was overshadowed, but admirably supported, by Ramey, whose presence gave her gesticulations and assured singing a focal point. One could reluctantly forgive the Hans Schavernoch sets, with their monumental Art Deco style, garish colors and an occasional jarring note, such as the space ship from *Star Trek* that obtrudes itself from behind one of the doors, which resemble store-front steel shutters. Norman could also be forgiven her somewhat erratic performance as a woman whose early enthusiasm for life and marriage is gradually reduced to a pathetic compliance with her lord's cruel will. She at least had the descending line of her fortunes before her, and pursued it more or less faithfully.

Schoenberg provides no such theatrical clarity in *Erwartung*, which is where Norman's limitations became increasingly apparent. The "Monodrama," as Schoenberg called it, is one of his greatest scores, the musical parent of Alban Berg's *Wozzeck* in its unforgiving, unsparing account of human despair and neurotic expressivity. The piece was written with Mozartean speed and definitiveness in about two weeks, and set to a four-part text by a medical student, Marie Pappenheim. An unnamed woman is seen in a forest looking for her lover; she finds him as a corpse, and it has been argued that she may have escaped from a mental institution and killed him in a jealous fit. The text comprises not set speeches but fragments, bursts of hysterical energy that reveal (as Boulez said of it) an unraveling sensibility.

Like the polytonal *Bluebeard's Castle*, *Erwartung* is a work that brings earlier portraits of unbalanced women—from Isolde to Salome and Electra—into realms excavated by Freud, Schoenberg's Viennese contemporary. (Theodor Adorno somewhere makes the analogy between the form of Freud's case studies and *Erwartung*, suggesting further that the monodrama was to the twelve-tone method what, by way of presentation, the case studies were to the full-fledged psychoanalytic method.) It is a remarkably gripping work, with a score of as much delicacy, passion and intensity as Schoenberg ever wrote. Minutely realized in its subtly nuanced effects, its four scenes are increasingly long and complex: The woman wanders deeper and deeper into the forest, her mind straying further from everyday reality into "a dream without limits and colors." Nature, history, self and other are gradually knit together in a paranoid web and, as the piece ends, she is totally without perspective, searching.

Listening to this work attentively is an experience quite without equivalents. Schoenberg's somewhat reduced orchestra is in effect a chamber ensemble of soloists, and part of the startling pleasure of the music is his inventiveness in combining instruments around, but never in, a centralizing tonality. The result is an immensely rapid and yet deliberate series of choices, moves and tactics, each of them adroitly expressive, rigorously harnessed to the quasi-hallucinatory dramatic situation. I believe that to stage *Erwartung* is already to reduce these effects and to turn the inner drama into a dated and almost comic spectacle. And, alas, between them Norman and set designer Schavernoch made matters even worse. Schoenberg's directions specify a forest, but instead of leaving it at that, contenting himself with trees, leaves and a couple of benches, Schavernoch plants an enormous grand piano, complete with candelabra and artily draped cloth, in the middle of the stage. Thus we get a forest with grand piano, in which Jessye Norman—all alone—has to sing difficult music *and* act.

No one can survive such a challenge elegantly. Not only could Norman not figure out what to do with the piano (who could blame her?), she also didn't appear to have completely internalized the part. She certainly got all the words end notes, but the very correctness and beauty of her rendition seemed to highlight almost all the incongruities around her. It was as if her busy dutifulness in getting the notes and phrasing right, moving up and down and wringing her hands, created a massive distraction from the fineness of Schoenberg's inner drama of a hysterical woman confronting her disintegrating selfhood. This is the musical world whose correlative is not only Freud's case studies but also Adorno's negative dialectic and Georg Lukács's theories of alienation and reification. Yet what the Metropolitan's scheme allowed for was a remarkably intelligent orchestral performance— masterfully conducted by James Levine—accompanied by a truly botched stage picture, with Jessye Norman, a great singer, its sometimes all too willing victim.

CHAPTER 14

Extreme Occasions (on Celibidache)

THE TWO-HOUR classical concert performance has solidified into an unchangeable commodity, bought and sold by managers, performers and audiences alike. One reason for this development is that the performance and composition of music have been severed from each other almost completely. Since Georges Enescu, Sergei Rachmaninoff and Ferruccio Benvenuto Busoni earlier this century, the performer has become a specialist only in performing, the composer only in composing (although composition has become even more specialized, confined by and large to a comparatively small, often academic audience). Pierre Boulez and Leonard Bernstein are the only two major performers today who are also recognized composers, but it is not as performers of their own music that either of them made his career. The mass public spectacle is therefore pure performance, governed by a fairly rigid set of rules and rituals.

Carnegie Hall remains one of the best places in the United States to witness performances at a fairly high level of competence—and, alas, routine. So all-encompassing is the performance regime—it covers dress, program, physical deportment, style of playing, audience behavior, ticket prices, type of performance, identity of performer—that one can observe, I believe, a correlation between the genuine merit of the performance and the performer's comfort. The higher the level of the performer's excellence, the greater his or her dissatisfaction with the occasion. For the most unusual musicians, the performance occasion, although more or less a given in advance, furnishes an opportunity to push against, assault, expand or otherwise change its tyrannical limits and protocols. The least interesting work is almost always provided by musicians who passively accept the unnatural confines of the two-hour performance, and operate within them uncomplainingly.

The Nation, June 26, 1989.

This is why the visit to Carnegie Hall of Sergiu Celibidache and the Munich Philharmonic was so extreme an experience for a New York audience accustomed to accomplished but relentlessly unvaried performances of the great eighteenth-and nineteenth-century orchestral classics. Celibidache is now 76, a Rumanian eccentric who has been loitering on the fringes of the concert world since a brief career of some prominence with the Berlin Philharmonic right after World War II. Requiring five times more rehearsal time than any orchestra has been willing to provide, he has also refused to make recordings on the ground that mechanical reproduction bears no significant resemblance to the act of interpreting music. This, he contends, occurs with an inevitability and metaphysical rightness—the music, he has said, is *there*—only possible once, in the concert hall. In addition, Celibidache is known for extraordinarily slow tempos, as evidenced by the performance of the Bruckner Fourth Symphony I attended at Carnegie Hall on April 22. The Bruckner Fourth is never scheduled as the only piece on the program because it is approximately an hour long, but that was the only work that Celibidache offered.

It was certainly unlike most other musical performances I have heard—richer in many ways, more detailed, leisurely, plotted, planned, extended. Bruckner's symphonies rely on sheer length and inordinate repetition for their aesthetic effect; indeed, Bruckner's innovation as a symphonist was that he made size an integral, rather than an incidental or formal, aspect of the work's musical content. This Celibidache underscored with astonishing perseverance and, I think, effect. It was as if he had refused the forward logic of sonata form as it was forged during the late eighteenth and early nineteenth centuries and decided instead to see music as an essentially lateral, exfoliating fabric, unfolding with infinite leisure rather than developing in time. You often experience the music in what seems to be an unnaturally slowed-down and gigantically distended passage of time, but Celibidache's Bruckner never failed to grip me totally, render me completely attentive and persuade me that the music was, in fact, there. I can no longer imagine Bruckner performed any other way, even though as I recall sections of each of the symphony's four movements I hear them separately and discretely, rather than connected in a continuous line. That is a disability or dysfunction in my memory, however, and not, as some critics have argued, a failure in Celibidache's conception: At the time, I *was* convinced. Paradoxically, I don't remember that Celibidache's rhetorical impulse flagged at all, or that what he delivered was only a disconnected set of beautiful, if drawn out, sounds. Celibidache's orchestra was perfectly adequate to his design, with a particularly impressive performance by the solo horn, which plays the major role in the symphony.

This was not all, however. Celibidache's conception included immense pauses between the movements, so that by the end of the evening the Bruckner Fourth had been stretched to about an hour and twenty minutes. Add to that his extremely slow and deliberate walk to and from the podium, the courtly and deliberate manner in which he and the orchestra take curtain calls (first he signals the horns to stand, then the flutes, then horns and flutes together, then trumpets, then trombones, then horns, flutes, trumpets, trombones, and so on) and you have a complete two-hour evening. The point in all this, I think, is to force the boundaries of the performance occasion, and to transform it into something more focused and thought-through. One has the impression that Celibidache's is a continuously worked-out performance encompassing and welding together musical and performance duration, and this, I believe, makes for an extraordinarily interesting transfiguration of time.

Performance thus becomes an inclusive and highly self-dramatizing phenomenon, not just a two-hour period that frames a ritual of virtuosity and applause. The more one looks at contemporary musical performance the more one notes that by far the most arrestingly brilliant performers are the ones who have selfconsciously gone over, worked through, incorporated the empty stretches of the two-hour interval in ways that draw attention to it. This is not really an enormous accomplishment, but it testifies at least to the performer's intelligence and will, neither of which is in very great supply these days. And in some instances—Arturo Benedetti Michelangeli, Sviatoslav Richter, the late Glenn Gould, Horowitz during the 1950s and early 1960s—so powerful is the tension between performer and performance time that the virtuoso simply quits performing altogether. It's as if he or she no longer can accept domination by the formalistic reification provided by the concert occasion.

What makes far too many musicians uninteresting is that their playing merely conforms to what is automatically offered by the concert episode itself: a stage, an instrument, performance, applause, various monetary and social rewards. Take Murray Perahia, who used to be a very fine pianist. At Carnegie Hall on April 10 he played one of the most boring and safe recitals on record. He was like the votary of an unknown cult coming to an altar decorated like a nineteenth-century ballroom, surrounded by admiring people dressed up like admiring people. His Beethoven was too academic and cautious, his Rachmaninoff like a parody of Rachmaninoff, his Liszt too loud and arid for his essentially miniaturist technique. The coarseness that has defaced his tone now seems to be a permanent feature of his style.

But at least here and there one can hear traces in Perahia's playing of what was once an agreeable idiom: not so with the lamentable André Watts, who was incongruously matched with the excellent Leipzig Gerwandhaus Orchestra under Kurt Masur, a good but far from great German conductor. At Carnegie Hall Watts performed three of the Beethoven concertos, of which I heard only the second, on April 14. Watts clearly fancies himself a very stylish man, but the phrase that echoed through my mind as I sat through his effortless athleticism was "meaningless fluency." Watts is one of the few performers whose technique and apparent popularity keep provoking the question, Why does he play the piano? So utterly pointless does the whole exercise seem, so without thought or even care, so without statement or plan is his playing.

Pianists far exceed any other instrumental soloists in number, which is why there are fewer compelling performers among them. Watts and Perahia are thus a kind of norm—a more or less constant low point, generous with physical prowess, parsimonious with the sort of performance delivered by Celibidache. For this reason, the virtues of Maurizio Pollini seem quite stunning. A little distracted and quizzical in appearance, Pollini gallops out on the stage, sits at the edge of the piano bench and proceeds to push and pull the two hours at his disposal with greater and greater, more and more improbable intensity. In the second of his two Carnegie recitals, on March 14, he began with Brahms's Opus 119 (a group of intermezzos and the E flat major "Rhapsody"), went on to sets of Schönberg and Stockhausen *Klavierstücke* (as if plotting the fortunes of Austro-German Romanticism from tonalism to post-tonalism) and concluded with a hair-raising performance of the Beethoven "Hammerklavier," rendered more diabolically and yet plainly than I have ever heard—the final unplayable fugue especially.

The fugue is, by any standard, the ultimate Pollini piece. Pollini's virtuosity is more like Swift's, say, than Johnson's: It keeps getting simpler and more powerful in vocabulary at the same time. I was also especially impressed by Pollini's interpretation of the slow movement, which is often allowed to slide off into an early version of a Chopin nocturne whose idiom is often startlingly predicted by Beethoven. Pollini read the movement as part of his relentless teleological impulse—that is, as a prologue to the fugue—and it worked.

Pollini's major competitor is Alfred Brendel, who performed at Carnegie Hall a short time before his Italian rival. Brendel's distinction is that he has laid claim to the chair vacated by Artur Schnabel, although in fact his repertory is slightly more varied (Brendel still schedules some Liszt and Schumann along with the inevitable Beethoven, Mozart and Schubert). Like Pollini, Celibidache, Gould, Michelangeli and Richter (who has returned to performing in Europe but insists on darkening the hall and stage except for a tiny reading lamp over the keyboard, above which, unlike any other major performer today, he props a score), Brendel doesn't seem especially at ease during the performance. His playing has never seemed to me really attractive: It doesn't drive off the competition as Pollini's does. Brendel is a decent, earnest pianist, much admired by literary people for his seriousness and apparent intelligence, unusual among touring virtuosos, but he isn't theatrically exciting. In the narrow world of recital programs, however, Brendel makes his effect through his choice of works, and the way he plays them against each other, dialectically and critically. (As a clue to the way he plays, see his essay on Schubert's last sonatas in *The New York Review of Books* for February 2, in which his main interest is how the three works interact with one another.) At his February 12 recital in Carnegie Hall, Brendel performed four sets of themes and variations: Mozart's group on "M. Duport's Minuet"; Brahms's transcription of the second movement of the Opus 18 string sextet; Liszt's variations on Bach's "Weinen Klagen Sorgen Zagen"; and Beethoven's "Diabelli" variations. Because the variation form is essentially digressive and relational, unlike classical sonatas, which are dramatic and developmental, Brendel afforded a view of the four works that seemed to stretch outward rather than press forward relentlessly inside the program's framework. The "Diabelli" was superbly performed, as if a test of the pianist's skill against Beethoven's obduracy and wit as he spins more and more material out of the silly little waltz theme. Brendel's playing was notably fleet and economical, more of a distillation than an affirmation, and curiously unassertive as a result. The oddest thing was that, unlike Pollini's "Hammerklavier," Brendel's "Diabelli" went out of its way not to make a statement about Beethoven's late style, a novel approach to that extremely portentous music. Although I was aesthetically dissatisfied, I found myself admiring the lengths to which Brendel goes in fighting against the grain.

CHAPTER 15

Peter Sellars's Mozart

P ETER SELLARS'S detailed scene-by-scene notes and interpretive
essays on *Don Giovanni, Così fan tutte* and *The Marriage of Figaro*
were handed out at his productions of those works at Pepsico's
Summerfare at the State University of New York at Purchase. This unusual
and commendable practice not only helped the audience to understand
what the director had in mind but was also part of the difficult job of per-
suading audiences to accept extremely uncommon views of these very commonly performed masterpieces. I had seen and written in these pages about
Sellars's earlier productions of *Don Giovanni* and *Così fan tutte* [September
26, 1987], which were then also put on at Pepsico's Summerfare. But I welcomed the occasion to see them again this year, performed as a cycle with
The Marriage of Figaro. This was Pepsico's tenth and last year; the occasion
therefore recommended itself as a summation of Sellars's work on these
remarkable, extremely worldly and complex operas.

What connects the three productions is not the much-remarked-on cleverness of conception (or gimmickry, or, according to *The New York Times'*
relentless Donal Henahan, "directorial hybris," if you don't like them), nor
Sellars's madcap exuberance, nor the startling juxtaposition of truly classical
eighteenth-century music and Italian words with twentieth-century American semi-pop allusions. It is rather that Sellars's views have a specifically
political tendency. He argues first that all three operas were self-conscious
products of a society on the verge of revolution; then he translates them into
an unmistakably broad late-twentieth-century American idiom in order to
suggest that the "*ancien régime* [here] is crumbling, whether it cares to ad-
mit it or not." Thus *Figaro* is set in Trump Tower, in which Count Almaviva
is a wealthy but lecherous tenant who employs Figaro and Susanna as driver

The Nation, September 18, 1989.

and maid; *Don Giovanni* is set in a New York ghetto, its hero a black pusher and addict who is seen as parasitical on the "oppressive class structure that Mozart depicted"; *Così*—the finest of Sellars's productions—is set in Despina's Diner, with its manager, Don Alfonso, a "Vietnam vet who is having trouble hanging on," and the two couples portrayed as silly yuppies.

I happen to be in general agreement with Sellars's premises and his bold and innovative schemes for the three operas. Yet, I don't feel able to pretend that the cycle is terrific all the way through, or that Sellars is on the mark all the time. However brilliantly daring it may be as a translation from eighteenth-century Seville, *Don Giovanni* as produced by Sellars is, I felt this time, disturbing, unpleasant and monotonously haranguing. While Mozart fastidiously distinguishes between aristocracy, urban dwellers and peasants, most of the action in Sellars's version takes place on an ill-lit ugly stoop, and all the characters are drawn from the dregs of the earth—thereby rendering the politics of the work both primitive and, ultimately, unengaging. Despite Sellars's discovery of a pair of identical black twins, Eugene and Herbert Perry, to sing Don Giovanni and Leporello splendidly—a dazzling masterstroke that underlines the opera's amorality and disregard of ordinary conceptions of identity—there is a claustrophobic dissonance throughout that finally overwhelms the work. The characters fade into one another, the action is muddled, the extraordinarily contrapuntal stage logistics planned by Mozart are garbled in the extreme. Sellars is not helped by Craig Smith, his conductor. Smith's time-beating is regular enough, but his tempi (mostly too fast, especially in *Così*, or else nondescript and aimless) and balances are either indifferent to the music or simply coarse.

Sellars's obvious regard for Smith increases my suspicions that, as a director with a strong political vision to render theatrically, he wants the music kept as streamlined and innocuous as possible. This isn't to say, however, that his singers are not adequate; they are wonderful to look at, and in a couple of cases excellent. Sellars makes you realize that Mozart's male figures are consistently more interesting than the females, and certainly when it comes to that combination of airy competence, endearing sonority and suave musicality necessary for Mozart's swaggering macho poses (always complicated with either self-criticism or misanthropy) Sellars's baritones and tenors are more convincing than, in their own ways, the sopranos are. As Figaro and Don Alfonso, Sanford Sylvan—bald, overweight, eerily effective, with wraparound smiles and appealingly awkward flourishes—is the one international-class singer in the cycle. He is seconded by James Maddalena as Almaviva and Guglielmo. Maddalena's voice has a rougher edge, but he is somehow always in control even though he occasionally overstates and overexpresses. Frank Kelley (Don Basilio and Ferrando) has a piercing, nasal timbre to his tenor, but he carries off his part with a strikingly serene musical confidence that is charmingly undercut by a campy slouch.

Aside from Despina, who is tough, Mozart's heroines tend to a weepy complaining that Sellars, this time around, rather misogynistically accentuates. This emphasized the relative thinness or reediness in their voices; thus Susan Larson, spritely and endlessly inventive as the page boy Cherubino, returns as a despairing Fiordiligi, whose anguish at self-discovery keeps dissolving into aimless hysteria. It's hard to do much of that to Mozart without mercilessly exposing *all* a singer's weaknesses at the same time. Yet I still find it difficult to tell whether those problems—much greater in *Don Giovanni*—are the fault of Mozart, who viewed women as either girlish pranksters or teary shrews, or of Sellars. I suspect the former, but we have become so accustomed to the lush and cloying archness of Elisabeth Schwarzkopf or Lisa Della Casa as models for these roles that we ignore their inherent (and deeply despairing) limits.

There is nevertheless an unsettling insouciance about the way Sellars treats musical matters, which leaves no doubt that he is trying to do for opera what is rarely attempted: Wagner was the last serious composer, librettist and producer to study the tension between words and music and opera and decide that music was the most important. Since his time, everyone has continued to believe that opera is mainly a musical genre. Sellars has the idea of treating the work, as a full-scale intellectual, social and aesthetic project, and *not* mainly a musical one. Dramatic details and production values are always changed by Sellars in different versions of the same opera; this is why the unity or purpose in his productions often emerges only later, by retrospective illumination, even though one has the impression of a great deal of thought and practice having gone into them. No less important, his opera conceptions, of which the Mozart/da Ponte cycle is his biggest and most integral, are clearly intended as a full-scale assault on the conventions that currently prevail nearly everywhere on opera stages in the United States. His restless and brilliantly critical imagination keeps running up against and taking pitiless aim at the idea (much vaunted at the big houses) that opera performances ought to provide the occasion for ceremonies of veneration and slavish repetition. The turns that Sellars rings on Mozart's courtly operas make you wonder why wooden delicacy and affectations of authenticity have satisfied us for so long. We learn through Sellars that they never did satisfy us, not just because their silly conventions leave Mozart untouched but also because they protect the laziness and incompetence of most opera companies.

I wish I could easily appraise the final political or even theoretical import of what Sellars does. O.K., so he is post-modern, deft, creative. But there is the bothersome question of his, and our, complicity with the cultural establishments that have made him successful. I'd like to think he has an ironic sense about that—for instance, when he mocks capitalism on a stage that has been munificently subsidized by Pepsico. He's an extraordinarily gifted man, and his opera productions outstrip any others in the United States. I am always stimulated by what Sellars does, but I'm still not entirely convinced that he has really gone beyond the handful of arresting gestures that have made his Mozart/da Ponte work so striking and at the same so curiously inconclusive. Is there a whole vision or theory there?

A clue to that will come when Sellars takes more of a position on the music. So far he seems to confine it rather antiseptically, as if he were letting it take care of itself (which it can't, with Smith doing so little to help). He now has a fine company of amiable and hugely competent regulars to work with, but what would he do with a roster of truly excellent singers? Then, I think, Sellars would have to deal with the challenges to conventional performances provided for classical music by people like Roger Norrington and, an earlier instance, Glenn Gould. And then maybe we would know the extent and the depth of his vision.

CHAPTER 16

András Schiff at Carnegie Hall

T HE FRENETIC clarity and prodigious technical dexterity of Vladimir Horowitz have been much talked about in the wake of his death on November 5. Nevertheless, he rarely seemed to be interesting or arresting because of what he did musically; rather it was his *crescendi,* or his capacity for steel-like and massive sonority, or the sheer speed and accuracy of his octaves, thirds or scales that drew attention. Of course, in his later years it was the dreadful cloying image of "Volodya," the national asset celebrated in the White House, seen on television with worshipful commentators and reporters in tow. He seemed to have built his career and reputation around what no other pianist could dare to attempt or pull off, so formidable were his powers.

Yet, great pianist though Horowitz was, his pianism was often effective but unpersuasive: You could marvel and gape, but you couldn't really learn or emulate without hurting yourself. When some pianists about thirty years ago tried to do what he did, the results were extraordinarily unsuccessful (for example, Ivan Davis or Byron Janis). Horowitz's closest virtuoso competitors in the group that matured before World War II—Sviatoslav Richter, Arthur Rubinstein, and Arturo Benedetti Michelangeli—were altogether more satisfying artists. Richter now seems to be perhaps the most astonishing in his powers of communication, his almost mystical interpretive genius and his supernal virtuosity.

The infrequency of Richter's appearances in the United States is therefore very regrettable, but his absence, the deaths of Rubinstein and Horowitz and Michelangeli's virtual disappearance compel one to look at new forces and configurations in today's roster of regularly appearing young pianists. Besides Alfred Brendel and Mauricio Pollini, two or three younger figures rise above the others: Radu Lupu, Martha Argerich and András Schiff. For the first time in several years the 48-year-old Argerich, who is unquestionably the finest woman pianist around, will appear as soloist at Carnegie Hall (with the Orchestre de la Suisse Romande); Lupu has not played in New York City for almost two years. Schiff, on the other hand, has been a regular performer here, most recently in an October 19 recital at Carnegie Hall.

Schiff's earlier work of note was his Bach, particularly a series of three recitals at the Metropolitan Museum a few years ago that culminated in a memorable Goldberg Variations. He is a cherubic-looking 36-year-old Hungarian who left Budapest after he completed his training and has since settled in Salzburg and London. The influence of Glenn Gould was clearly observable in Schiff's Bach performances, though unlike Gould he was eminently capable of legato playing, with a subtly varied dynamic range and a much more moderated, less brittle and severe rhythmical impulse. Schiff's besetting problem had been his tendency to sweeten and prettify both his interpretations and his sound, so that in performances of the English and French Suites, for instance, he would use very pianistic and italicized mannerisms either to loosen up one of Bach's exuberently long but tightly articulated contrapuntal phrases, or end a piece, say, with rather tightly contrived diminuendo or subtly produced but obvious deceleration. Since Schiff's recitals have tended to occur in the smaller New York halls, he has therefore communicated an impression of domestic music making, more like a chamber recitalist with a penchant for thoughtful, tasteful playing in classical pieces, rather than a thunderer who, according to the model provided by Horowitz and company, performed Liszt and Rachmaninoff to enormous, adulatory and usually uncritical crowds. Paradoxically, however, there has been no doubt about Schiff's extraordinarily fluent and complete technical attainments; yet they always seemed subordinated to an aesthetic of modesty, affability, introverted musicality, and were not made to serve the virtuosic demonism we associate with bravura and egoistic display.

All musical performance involves domination, of course, since no instrumentalist can command (the military metaphors entirely apt) the public's attention and the instrument's resources without disciplined and self-serving force. The two different styles of playing to which Horowitz and Schiff belong achieve domination through choice of repertory and degree of assertion. The first category is based in a style of extroverted display, in works whose claims are principally pianistic as opposed to musical, in the prominence of the performer's interpretive personality (a high rhetorical profile, willful extremes of tempo and dynamics, a sense of instinctual freedom in performance rather than a studied or deliberate manner). The ideal repertory for this category of pianists consequently is highly restricted—

much Chopin (excluding nocturnes, most mazurkas and all but three po-
lonaises), some Schumann, much Liszt, Prokofiev, Scriabin, Rachmaninoff,
Bartók, Stravinsky's *Petrouchka*, some Ravel, and very occasionally the Berg
sonata. Thus pianists of this type would include Horowitz, Rubinstein, Jorge
Bolet, Shura Cherrkasky, Ivo Pogorelich, Van Cliburn, Andre Watts and, at
times, Vladimir Ashkenazy.

The central figures in the second category are Artur Schnabel, Dinu
Lipatti and Edwin Fischer and, in classical romantic and impressionistic
music, Wilhelm Kempff, Solomon and Walter Gieseking; their disciples
today would include the wonderfully gifted Mitsuko Uchida, Peter Serkin
(who has always seemed a more refined and gifted musician than his father)
and Richard Goode, as well as Schiff, Lupu, Argerich and Zoltan Kocis. The
danger to their work, as indeed to that of all performers, is that worldly success in one idiom or repertory brings pressure on the performer to persist
in that course until what was fresh and interesting becomes coarse and
mindless (as is the case, I think, with Murray Perahia). What makes for
optimum results is when pianists in one category demonstrate their powers
in the other; in this, of course, Pollini, Brendel, Argerich and, sometimes,
Ashkenazy are triumphantly transgressive.

But so too is András Schiff. His October 19 program was as remarkable for its structure and content as for its stunning execution. There was
intelligence and vision in the choice of Haydn's F Minor Variations, the
rarely performed Janáček sonata ("October 1, 1905"), the Bartók Dance Suite
and the very late Schubert C Minor Sonata (D.958)—a brace of difficult
and dark, entirely Central European works, whose peculiar brooding eccentricity is perhaps their main feature. As Schiff performed the elaborate
configurations of the Haydn, it was late Beethoven and Mahler that came
to mind, particularly in the angular severity of the work's final measures,
and in its unembarrassed declamatory thrust. Janáček's only sonata is a
two-movement torso originally composed (like Yeats's poem "Easter 1916")
to commemorate a nationalist uprising against foreign hegemony; Janáček
later destroyed the score in a despondent fit, but copies of it survived
thanks to two friends, and the text remains available among his handful of
collected piano compositions.

Schiff's performance was mesmerizing: controlled, passionate, intelligent, compelling. Janáček's fundamental line is very lyrical (the traces of
Dvořák and Smetana are readily decipherable), but there is an interven-
tionary, dislocating wildness to his writing that is especially affecting in the
sonata, which works through an alternation of placidly repeated sequences
and terrifyingly agitated piano virtuoso patterns that recall the *Glagolitic
Mass* and both his quartets. Janáček, like the early Strauss, stands at the

precipice before the advent of atonality and after the almost total exhaustion of tonality. His musical forms, therefore, are unsettlingly patched together; a classical sonata structure, for instance, is regularly made to serve autobiographical and deeply private purposes. The result is an *inscape* of disquieting volatility, moving from placid flowing statements to suddenly dark sonorities and then back again. Schiff's superior technical gifts were well up to the challenges of this quite extraordinary work, yet he never deviated from the task of unfolding the sonata's complexities with a kind of transfiguring patience that is rarely encountered.

The Bartók and Schubert works drew the whole program together into a set of piano works constituting a counternarrative running next to the conventional one that bridges the passage from Viennese classicism to twentieth-century mainstream modernism. I had the impression that Schiff was trying to provide a musical experience that was located neither in royal court nor established church nor aristocratic coterie but in some entirely authentic and as yet unformalized site in European culture—partly pastoral and rural, peripheral and strangely emergent, all but forgotten and unexplored.

Experiences like this dignify concert life with a rare coherence. To juxtapose and perform interesting pieces; to allow them to produce unexpected pleasures; to enable audiences to perceive configurations of style and sound that have not yet acquired a reified status in the much traversed and official resplendencies of nineteenth- and twentieth-century Western music—these are signal accomplishments, and that they can now be expected from András Schiff is an index of how his new eminence now places him significantly above the affectations and limitations of his earlier recitals. He is still essentially a modest stage presence, with few of the mannerisms of the crowd-pleasing soloists. What testifies to the depth of his mark as an interpreter is that one retains from what is after all a two-hour episode a sustained tonal structure that persists in, and permanently alters, the internal record of a lifetime of musical experiences.

When, a couple of days later, on October 21, the estimable Bella Davidovich also came to Carnegie Hall, so dominant was the effect of Schiff's playing that it scaled down the effect of hers. She is a Schumann-Chopin player whose clean execution and unprissy elegance at their best put her in some amalgam of the Solomon tradition with the classy virtuosity of Russian predecessors like Gilels. At Carnegie Hall, however, she began with two of the Opus 21 Schumann *Novelettes* disfigured by uncertain, awkward phrasing; she then proceeded to his great B-flat Humoresque with only intermittent flashes of inspiration or wit. I sensed a studied constraint in everything she did, right through a generously conceived Chopin group that included his greatest single work, the Barcarolle, played as if by a teacher who had prepared her performances thoroughly but whose goal to play correctly and tastefully was exposed for its timidity. The irony is that when she finally got to Chopin's B Minor scherzo—by far the most hackneyed and familiar repertory item on her list—she let loose with a blisteringly exact yet beautifully organized performance.

While it would have been reductively unfair to say of Davidovich's concert that it was only pianism and disappointingly mindless at times—a performance carried along mainly by the habits and phrases of "tradition" and a style quite brilliantly and dutifully learned at conservatory—there is a good deal of truth, alas, to the argument. For as long as the concert calendar is punctuated with recitals by artists like Schiff, the Davidovich and Horowitz impress will continue to seem insufficiently intelligent, and unmusical.

PART II

The Nineties

CHAPTER 17

Richard Strauss

I N HIS brilliant *New Yorker* profile of Johnny Carson, Kenneth Tynan
came to the conclusion that whatever it was that Carson actually
did, he alone did it, and always did it perfectly. He may be part
stand-up comic, part talk-show host, part Hollywood celebrity, but the
Carson phenomenon, which has endured for longer than two decades, is
more than any one of those things, and more than their sum.

And so it is, *toutes proportions gardées,* with Richard Strauss, whose astonishingly long career (1864–1949) paralleled and in strange ways touched
many of the major changes in twentieth-century music without really participating in them. Glenn Gould described Strauss's serene indifference to
all the trends around him as he unconcernedly did his own thing, much as
Tynan wrote about Carson. Certainly there is a good deal of truth to this
view of Strauss, even if it means forgetting the shattering musical effect of
Salomé (1905) and *Elektra* (1908), operas considered in their time so revolutionary as to be scandalous. Schönberg, Mahler and Debussy were early
devotees of Strauss, but it is the density of literary and cultural associations
surrounding Strauss's career that makes him perhaps the richest, and yet
somehow the most enigmatic, figure in twentieth-century music.

Strauss's long connection with Hugo von Hofmannsthal and his milieu
is alluded to occasionally in Hermann Broch's monograph on the poet, as
it is also in Theodor Adorno's altogether brilliant and little-known study of
Strauss the composer and virtuoso conductor. Almost without significant
exception, all the great names in early twentieth-century Central European music, particularly opera, had something to do with Strauss, from
star conductors like Mahler, Clemens Krauss, Karl Böhm and Herbert von
Karajan to majestically resplendent singers like Lotte Lehmann, Richard

Tauber, Maria Jeritza and Ljuba Welitsch to the most famous impresarios and producers, like Diaghilev and Max Reinhardt.

Perhaps for the post–World War II generation, an early and unexpected exposure to Strauss is required for the mysterious spell to catch on and then, even more mysteriously, to persist. I can recall perfectly that it was in the spring of 1949, when I was 13, that I first heard his music performed, when Krauss brought the Vienna Philharmonic to Cairo. The two concerts I went to were held in the Cinema Rivoli, newly built and boasting a gigantic, somewhat anomalous "theater organ," complete with dancing lights and a charmingly handsome English intermission performer, one Gerald Peal. Krauss's intimate association with Strauss was completely unknown to me (he did the libretto for *Capriccio,* the very last of Strauss's operas), but the *Till Eulen-spiegel* he conducted was overwhelming in its great washes of sound, its virtuosic playfulness and the "advanced" yet lushly compelling chromaticism of its harmonies. Immediately afterward I discovered a recording of "Salomes Tanz"—as the old label had it—in the family collection of 78s, and later that year, on a foggy late August afternoon while spending yet another dreary summer in a lonely Lebanese mountain village, I heard the BBC announcement of his death with an enjoyably mournful regret that I can still recapture.

Strauss's musical output was enormously varied, although it is probably his operatic *oeuvre* that is still most often encountered. Yet he wrote interestingly, and with a professional finish that was idiomatic in each genre and combination, for wind instruments, voice, violin, piano, chamber ensembles and large orchestra. It is generally believed that having gone a step beyond Wagner in *Salomé* and *Elektra,* Strauss thereafter retreated: *Der Rosenkavalier* and *Ariadne auf Naxos,* for example, belong to the less advanced, lusher harmonic idiom of, say, *Lohengrin* or *Hänsel and Gretel,* even though the complexities of Hofmannsthal's texts are much greater and finer than either of the earlier works. But was Strauss's immense later operatic output (it includes, after all, such redoubtable works as *Arabella, Capriccio, Intermezzo, Die ägyptische Helena* and *Daphne*) simply an expert yet reactionary reversion to simplifications of early German Romanticism, or is there some more important modernist achievement threaded through the works as a whole?

Adorno's stunningly biting characterization of Strauss—that he is like a musical traffic agent, pushing through great nervousness and fake serenity without transition; that he is the composer of an illusory music "inasmuch as it is the semblance of a life which does not exist"; that his style is "unfounded," merely the "will of the composing subject alone," unrestrained by the discipline of formal organization and addicted to sudden effects of the sort that remind us how early in this century people delighted in the powers bestowed upon them by turning electric switches on and off—do explain many of the composer's idiosyncrasies and weaknesses (compared with Wagner, for instance). But Adorno writes as Strauss's contemporary, who saw in Strauss an aesthetic practice opposed to that of the second Viennese School, whose cause Adorno served as social champion and philosopher. Nevertheless Strauss's career rests, I think, on altogether more interesting grounds than Adorno allows, and these are revealed almost as often as one of his works is performed today.

First is Strauss's relationship to texts, which are often quite distinguished. Few composers were more interested in the literary, and few developed more working relationships with good writers than Strauss. Yet the music sometimes makes you feel that it is missing the point of the words, or that even if it is beautiful music, it is passing over complexities and allusions in the texts. Conversely, much of Strauss's greatest and most intricate music is set to works or passages in the text that do not warrant such wonderful sound. Thus, for example, his early tone poems *Don Juan* and *Don Quixote* are wonderful compositions for virtuoso orchestra, but they are often laughable illustrations of great literary masterpieces. Strauss set himself up for these losing comparisons by writing out the programs and then illustrating them musically—but in much the way a two-line prose caption might "illustrate" and explain a painting like *Las Meninas.* The whole of *Ariadne,* which in Hofmannsthal's superb text is metatheater at its most precious and refined, is shot through with musical incongruities that give hair-raising coloratura roulades to a trifling text (Zerbinetta's aria) and uninspired strophic repetition to one of the great mystical unions of all time (between Ariadne and Bacchus).

Second, Strauss's capacity for sublime melody and rhapsodic melodic variation, or *Schwung,* is almost always strung together with long patches of dismally skillful (in my opinion) episodic writing, often polyphonic in nature. This is evident in his operas as early as *Salomé,* in which Jokanaan's good qualities (like Chrysothemis's in *Elektra*) are associated with soaring, albeit occasionally banal, major-key tunes. The busy narrative work of the score, however, is given over to the other characters, whose climactic moments—for example, the discussion among the assembled Jews—are overripe, overwritten yet masterful displays of technical skill. This attracts attention to itself and, unfortunately, to the threadbare text. The contrast in Act I of *Rosenkavalier* between the Italian tenor's aria and the chattery passage work of much that surrounds it is stark indeed, as is the same discrepancy between Olivier's sonnet and the very long arguments on the relative importance of music and words that it provokes in *Capriccio.*

In short, Strauss's music is made up of unresolved discrepancies that underline the absence of musical forms (sonata, variation, rondo, etc.) that had guaranteed the continuity and consequence of earlier music. There is a sublime confidence in workmanship that, as Adorno noted, pulls things along at the same time that it unembarrassedly draws attention to itself and to all sorts of missing transitions, sequences and resolutions. And precisely those absences and the abrupt alternation between a sweet melodic strain and a relentlessly competent proclivity for musical working-out make Strauss's work as a whole stand so dramatically apart from the mainstream in twentieth-century classical music. As compared with the rigorous efforts of Stravinsky, Berg or Hindemith to integrate form with content, Strauss's unruffled consistency, which is based at its very worst on heedless inconsistency, partly the tuneful atavism of a *gemütlich* songster and partly the formidable professionalism of a modern expert, seems almost miraculous. So it must have struck his intellectual collaborators, who frequently found themselves trying to supply the missing connections between Strauss's music and its context. Hence, in most of Strauss's middle and later operas, the reliance on a fantasy or fable. The most elaborate, *Die Frau ohne Schatten* (1919), is ornate and complicated enough as it is, but it also depends for its final sense on a much longer narrative prose version written by Hofmannsthal well after the final libretto had been prepared for Strauss's realization.

Considered by some serious critics to be Strauss's greatest stage work, *Frau* has always struck me as his most typical and symptomatic an unsuccessful attempt to bring Die *Zauberflöte* into the twentieth century. Its plot is an utterly unconvincing Orientalist version of "Eastern" parable, involving a childless emperor and empress who must perform an act of selflessness before their union can be made fertile. This gesture occurs in the second scene of the last act, but is prepared for by an immensely long and tedious process through which a dyer's wife, an earthy creature, is cajoled into giving up her shadow (symbolic of fertility) to the empress. The opera is full of miscellaneous quasi-allegorical creatures, including a falcon and a nurse who are messengers from another world (ruled by a mysterious figure called Keikobad), and supporting characters related to Barak (the dyer) and his wife, including a chorus of unborn children.

Frau is the largest of Strauss's operas, and its proliferating but often superfluous action has always reminded me of George Orwell's comment that the profusion of minor characters in Dickens's work testifies to his "weed-like" imagination. Barak turns out to have several deformed brothers, each of whom in Act II is remorselessly given many notes to sing by Strauss. *Frau* seems like an odd choice for the Metropolitan Opera, considering its complicated sets, the large number of characters and its gargantuan, scarcely comprehensible plot. It requires a conductor and performers with immense staying power, who must also be blissfully unaware of the solemn idiocy in which they are involved. But in another sense *Frau* is the perfect opera for the Met: Its unexplained presence in a repertory made up largely of Puccini and Verdi perfectly dramatizes the company's timid planning and unreflective commercialism. *Frau's* verbal and musical texture are so dense as to make any true understanding of the opera totally impossible for an audience already beaten into submission and incomprehension, and the work's unabashed, not to say unreasonable exoticism suits the Met's proclivity for bigness, falseness and coarse spectacle.

On November 13, Christoph Perick conducted the Met's extraordinarily fine orchestra with real drive and eloquence, but his accomplishment in turn underscored the cast's fairly ordinary feats. Only the redoubtable Helga Dernesch, as the connivingly competent nurse, her voice with a mere fraction of its former resonance, did her part with some understanding of what it was all about; so did Bernd Weikl as Barak, a less interesting role. But Marilyn Zschau as the dyer's wife and Ruth Falcon as the empress were barely competent as they negotiated the diabolically demanding music. You felt that they were just trying to make it through to the end with determination rather than passionate conviction; Falcon was substituting for Mechthild Gessendorf, one of last year's Sieglindes, but although her powerful voice has a shrill whiteness in its upper register that could pierce Strauss's often impacted orchestral mass, it remained basically unexpressive. The unfortunate Robert Schunk just barely got through the emperor's part, all too painfully reminding one why Strauss really wrote for sopranos, not for male singers.

There are two transcendentally beautiful (in the imbricated hyper-Brahmsian idiom of Strauss's best "happy" moments) passages in the opera: one, the orchestral transition between the two scenes of Act I; the other, the opera's concluding quartet in which Barak, his wife, the emperor and the empress sing of reconciliation and connubial harmony in a scene that matches the last act of Wagner's *Siegfried* for brilliance and sustained ecstatic inspiration. The Act I interlude illustrates Strauss's seemingly unmotivated capacity for producing music that is never recalled or developed again, but which gestures in an almost Proustian way toward memories of an unspecified earlier idyllic life: urban, cosmopolitan, earnest and somehow good. The music is compellingly European, orderly, melodically tuneful and verging on the kind of sentimentality we associate with handcrafted, rather than mass-produced, objets d'art. In the final quartet Strauss's strenuous wish to climb the highest mountains of human happiness (in the Met's tinselly production the two couples are perched insecurely and hierarchically on two craggy peaks) results in the kind of summarizing yet dutifully skillful music he reserved for his best moments with Hofmannsthal, for example the final trio in *Rosenkavalier* and Ariadne's opening monologue.

Strauss, who outdid himself as he got older (this is the remarkable aspect of his incredibly well-preserved and almost routinely reproduced gift), reverted to this kind of writing in his greatest last period music, mostly written after World War II. Perhaps because his style of ecstatic finality became largely affirmative—unlike the later style of Beethoven, whose mixture of conventionality and soaring sublimity is too unsettling to be comfortable—Strauss's autumnal summational statements in the Oboe Concerto, *Metamorphoses* and the *Four Last Songs* for soprano and orchestra do not point outward, do not suggest what his earlier music under- or misinterprets in the program or text, do not leave one with the impression of a mismatch or incongruity of some sort. On the contrary, the despairing radiance of the music is all under control, stripped of self-conscious flourishes, austere in spirit and, paradoxically, luxurious in effect. The *Songs* are, I think, his most perfect realization of the form, but they are rarely performed because the slightest hesitation in diction, expression or balance between singer and ensemble simply tears the fabric, renders it banal and awkward. On October 28, three weeks before the Met's *Frau,* they were performed in Carnegie Hall by Julia Varady and the Orchestra de la Suisse Romande under Armin Jordan with a professionalism and flat reverence on Varady's part that never really took off, never came up to Jordan's naturalness and expansive ease.

It is strangely fitting that the last of the *Songs,* "Im Abendrot" ("At Dusk"), with text by Joseph von Eichendorff, is *literally* elegiac but in fact opens out at the very end with a quizzical doubt about the actual reality of ending—"Can this perhaps be death?"—as if to suggest that it might not be. The orchestral postlude rests on one of Strauss's favorite devices, a melodic elaboration above a sustained 6/4 pedal chord, that is, a deliberately prolonged and delayed suspension of the conventional ending. Even when he is concluding, Strauss lingers, moves, side steps and asks for a little longer. This is his link to the modernist movement, his own eccentric contribution to it: not to conclude even when there is nothing further to say, not to stop teasing out from "natural" harmony the implications of an already exhausted medium, not to resist ignoring the historical situation of his music while at the same time staging and restaging its anachronistic persistence. Despite the lavishness of his means, the resolutely minute economy of his aesthetic makes Strauss the sovereign as well as the only figure in the genre of post–Romanticism that he created and went on spinning out till his last day.

CHAPTER 18

Wagner and the Met's *Ring*

THIS IS the second spring in a row that the Metropolitan Opera has mounted three cycles of Wagner's *Der Ring des Nibelungen* (the "Nibelungen" in the title is not a plural and does not refer to the tribe of Nibelungs but to one Nibelung, Alberich, who steals the gold in the first scene of the first work in the gigantic tetralogy). It is an odd and certainly an unexpected feature of New York musical life that so large, risky and improbable a venture would be attempted by a house so addicted to the routine and the safe, but the cycles were attempted, and successfully to boot: Most performances were sold out, the crowds were generally enthusiastic, the performances on the whole satisfactory. This year's cycle was, I thought, more notable than last year's, although both times I attended the last, or J.V., cycle, the one in which stars like Jessye Norman and Hildegard Behrens did *not* sing.

Still, the production was the same each time, and the same conductor, James Levine, led all twenty-four performances, which adds up to approximately 432 podium hours, an almost unbelievably long time. Since the *Ring* is scarcely an easy or "natural" work to put across, Levine's sheer staying power and general accomplishment merit an acknowledgment of how serious and considerable an opera conductor he now is. That he has done his work mostly at the Met, unlike the maestros who traipse across innumerable stages with no significant commitment to any, is also a commendable achievement. That few excellent *other* conductors have appeared at the Met in a decade is also a result of Levine's resolute persistence. In any event, Levine's *Ring* has now been almost completely recorded on CD; on June 18, 19, 20 and 21 PBS will broadcast the entire cycle.

The Nation, June 18, 1990.

In every theatrical respect the Met's *Ring* is deliberately, purposefully, studiously "traditional." What this means is, as Donal Henahan, *The New York Times'* chief music critic, noted with undisguised approbation, no austere Wieland Wagner-influenced conception of the kind, with its bare stage and immobile singers, that dominated postwar Bayreuth productions; and no *outré* Peter Sellars or Götz Friedrich-type production either, with the director as total star reinterpreter of Wagner's ideas. The Met's *Ring* was designed scenically by Günther Schneider-Siemssen and based on the uninteresting thesis that if Wagner said the stage was set in forest or river, he meant forest or river, not symbolic allusions to them. As for the over-all production by Otto Schenk, it too was based on a dull faithfulness to what Wagner supposedly planned for the well-heeled German audiences of 1876.

The result is a curiously underdirected and rather half-baked dramatic experience, without real context or clear philosophical statement. You wonder why, in the name of literalism, the Met did produce the bear mentioned in Wagner's stage directions as a companion for the young Siegfried in Act I of the third opera, but not the horse (Grane) to which Brünnhilde actually introduces Siegfried in Act III. By the same token, you ask yourself what dramatic end is served when Wotan cradles the dying Siegmund in his arms *(Die Walkure,* Act II) despite Wagner's specific instructions that Wotan simply stares at the fallen hero from across the stage. Not that the sets themselves were inadequate or threadbare (one set—the falling Gibichung castle in *Die Götterdämmerung*—injured the star Brünnhilde, Hildegard Behrens, and kept her from the whole of the cycle I saw): They were perfectly fine, except that the studied reversion to them in an outdated earlier style called attention not to Wagner but to an ongoing polemic about how the late-twentieth-century opera house should try to stage nineteenth-century masterpieces. As a foray into that debate the Met's *Ring* is rather like the Conan movies serving as the basis for a discussion among anthropologists about the nature of the primitive.

But what one did in fact get *musically* was by no means trivial or inconsiderable, partly because the *Ring* is so huge and rare an undertaking, partly because just to see it in its unfolding is so astonishingly powerful as an aesthetic experience, no matter how simple-minded the production. Wagner began work on the tetralogy in the late 1840s but did not complete work on it until 1874, after a long interruption in the middle of *Siegfried* when he wrote *Tristan und Isolde* and *Die Meistersinger.* The four operas—*Das Rheingold* (a one-act prelude), *Die Walküre, Siegfried* and *Götterdämme-rung* —were given for the first time in 1876 at the Festspielhaus specially built by Wagner for his "music dramas" in the small town of Bayreuth, north of Munich. Everything about Wagner, who by the time of the *Ring's* performance had become one of the most influential figures in European culture, is excessive, contradictory, overwhelmingly powerful and rich. He was a poet and revolutionary whose vocation (after a reading in 1847 of Droysen's translation of the *Oresteia*) was to restore ancient Greek culture and somehow begin the world anew; he was a wonderful musician whose reverence for Beethoven nevertheless spurred him to go beyond Beethoven, to design new harmonic and dramatic structures that shattered most of the musical conventions of his time. He was also an egomaniac for whom an inspiring relationship with Cosima (Liszt's daughter and the wife of Hans von Bülow, a great pianist and conductor who nevertheless remained Wagner's totally dedicated champion) focused his career but did not prevent him from having messily dependent and often sadistic relationships with other people. He was a remarkably prescient psychologist, able to understand the darkest intimacy as well as the largest-scale forces in human history. He was Hitler's favorite composer (partly because, like Hitler, the older Wagner had become a perfervid anti-Semite and German chauvinist) but also the greatest single influence on advanced music in the twentieth century.

Wagner is still almost impossible to comprehend, so untidily does he sprawl across nearly every aspect of the culture of the modern West. As Carl Dahlhaus has suggested, overriding all his theories about race, culture, philosophy, art and history was Wagner's remarkably constant interest in the opera (which he thought had been discredited by the Italians) as reconstructed by him. Onto the music drama he heaped his hopes, talents and interests as a musician, librettist, stage designer, financier, historian, politician and philosophical visionary. Adorno's early book on Wagner attacks him savagely for exactly this mess of ambitions, claiming that notwithstanding his talents Wagner presaged twentieth-century imperialism and terrorism. The *Ring* was Wagner's biggest work by far, requiring not only an unusually competent conductor and large orchestra but also a cast of thirty soloists capable of managing complex, daring music produced not as a series of set arias and recitatives but in the form of what Wagner called "endless melody." At the heart of his scores is a web of interrelated themes or leitmotifs (the sword, the hero, the curse, redemption, etc.) that superseded classic symphonic form. It provided both an overarching musical structure as well as a complete musical language designed to express moods, objects, characters, not only in and of themselves but as they change according to circumstances. So plastic and inventive is Wagner's technique that his 100 or so infinitely varied motifs quite literally constitute the *Ring's* entire musical score: His aim, he once said, was "dramatic perfection above" (on-stage), "a continual symphony below" (in the orchestra pit).

The *Ring* purports to be Wagner's version of history: Spectators cannot merely see or enjoy it the way they might Bellini or Verdi, but must live it over the four days of the cycle. Yet there is no way of really doing this without some fairly close prior knowledge of what is taking place on the stage, much of which, I think, is lost on modern audiences, who can neither follow the German original nor do the research required for full comprehension. The story is in fact an extended decline-and-fall nineteenth-century family chronicle that starts (in *Rheingold*) in the realm of the timeless and ends up (in *Götterdämmerung*) in a shattered, cataclysmic history about whose meaning Wagner himself was uncertain.

The Australian comedian Anna Russell used to do a brilliant sendup of the *Ring*, accentuating (with only some exaggeration) its repetitiveness, its author's propensity to retell the story at each opportunity, its improbabilities and semi-deranged atmosphere. Wagner certainly deserves the spoof. An unstable, remarkably dynamic genius, he saw the entire world as a space filled by his strengths and weaknesses; these are given epic "Wagnerian" scope in the tetralogy. But the *Ring* also contains a mass of inconsistencies whose presence in the score testifies to Wagner's twenty-year struggle to get the thing finished, as well as to his innumerable changes of mind. Thus Wotan, who is one of Wagner's alter egos, is a Zeus-like and yet vacillating and greedy father of the gods. He has had three known marriages, two of them incestuous: with Erda, a primitive earth mother, whose children include the warlike maiden Valkyries, chief among them Brünnhilde; with Fricka (his sister), goddess of marriage; and with an unknown human woman who produced the Wälsung twins, Siegmund and Sieglinde. Much of the *Ring* is an amalgam of Norse and German mythology refashioned to highlight a melancholy late-nineteenth-century theme, man's decreasing supremacy, the consequence of Wotan's tampering with the state of nature over which he and his chosen race of Aryan heroes are supposed to rule.

The great symbolic beginning of the cycle occurs in *Rheingold* when the misshapen Nibelung dwarf Alberich, in an act of original sin, steals the Rheingold, a lump of gold watched over in the river by three Rhinemaidens. He forswears love and gets the gold, which he then fashions into a ring that gives him unlimited power. Wotan's bargain with the giants Fasolt and Fafner had been that in return for their building of the castle Valhalla, Wotan would reward them with Freia, Fricka's sister. When the time for payment comes, Wotan is unable to go through with it; using Loge, the god of trickery and fire, he instead steals the gold from Alberich in order to pacify the giants. Alberich curses the Ring to eternity, and once Wotan reluctantly gives it up to the giants its dreaded power provokes a fraternal quarrel whose first casualty is Fasolt, killed by Fafner. The gods enter

Valhalla at the end of *Rheingold,* their lives and rule now involved in plots and counterplots with humans, dwarfs and giants such as can only end in apocalypse.

During the next three operas we watch the incestuous love story of Wotan's twin children Siegmund (another of Wagner's self-portrayals) and Sieglinde work itself out tragically: Siegmund is killed in battle despite the fact that Nothung, his magic sword, is supposed to protect him, for it is shattered by Wotan. Sieglinde is abandoned, pregnant and unprotected. For trying to save Siegmund from Hunding (Sieglinde's appallingly brutal husband), Brünnhilde is punished by Wotan, left asleep on a rock ringed with Loge's magic fire; the fire will protect her until a hero who knows no fear can walk through the flames and claim her. Wotan is already a considerably reduced god, having in effect sacrificed Siegmund to Fricka, who is miffed at the twins' flouting of customary marital procedure. This is Wagner's sad acknowledgment that conventional society has always exacted a price for his daring genius. Siegmund's death and Wotan's extraordinarily affecting farewell to Brünnhilde, his favorite daughter, both blessed and damned, thus conclude *Walküre,* which is the most accessible of the four works.

In *Siegfried,* opera three, we discover that Mime, Alberich's brother, has been raising Siegfried, Sieglinde's orphaned son (saved by Brünnhilde), and once again, Wagner's idealized self-image. Siegfried hates Mime but stays with him in order that they may together reforge Siegmund's sword. Wotan reappears, this time as "the Wanderer," a one-eyed god who has lost his way and seems doomed to walk the earth without reprieve. Siegfried puts the sword together, rushes off to Fafner's lair (the giant has turned himself into a dragon who sleeps over the gold) and kills him as well as the treacherous Mime. Then, with the gold, he brushes Wotan aside (as Wotan had once brushed aside his father), climbs to the rock where Brünnhilde still sleeps and wakes her with the funniest line in opera: Peering down at the sleeping Amazon, this rough-hewn and bumptious youth exclaims, *"Das ist kein Mann!"* ("This is no man!"). They embrace and immediately become man and wife. End of *Siegfried,* the least regarded but, in my opinion, the most brilliantly composed and complex of the four.

Götterdämmerung, the longest and most conventionally operatic of the cycle, begins as Siegfried leaves Brünnhilde (who is now no longer immortal) in search of adventure. He happens upon the Gibichung palace, and after being given a potion by Hagen (Alberich's son, stepbrother of Gunther and Gutrune, the Gibichung brother and sister rulers) falls in love with Gutrune. He then goes back to Brünnhilde, tricks her into giving him the Ring, and gives her to Gunther as a present. Outraged, she reveals to Hagen that Siegfried, otherwise invulnerable, can be killed by a blow to his back. Hagen does so, Siegfried's death providing Wagner with an occasion for magnificent funeral music. Brünnhilde repents and as a final act of bereaved sacrifice she immolates herself on Siegfried's funeral pyre. The fire spreads everywhere, destroying even Valhalla, which in turn is engulfed by the rising waters of the Rhine. The Ring is returned to the Rhine-maidens, they pull Hagen into the maelstrom, and the cycle ends in one of Wagner's characteristic paradoxes, an enormously destructive catastrophe which is overridden by music that is cathartic and redemptive.

There is no musical experience that matches the *Ring* cycle for sheer, relentless length and single-minded grandeur—Wagner spoke of the deliberate, almost perverse patience with which like a jeweler he set each detail of the gigantic work. In every detail its immense musical fabric shows Wagner's musical genius, capable of sustaining long narrative sequences as well as the wonderful orchestral and choral set pieces that punctuate its tremendous length: the Ride of the Valkyries, the Magic Fire music, the Rhine journey, Siegfried's funeral and the Immolation scene. The *Ring* is gripping as a whole, and continues to be put on, at Bayreuth of course but also elsewhere, where it manages to draw good crowds even though the scarcity of really excellent Wagnerian voices is too critical to be remedied in the near future.

Today there is no Birgit Nilsson to sing Brünnhilde, no Lauritz Melchior to trumpet the heroic tenor part of Siegfried, no Hans Hotter to act and inflect Wotan's combination of majestic power and all-too-human confusion and sorrow (although the Met's James Morris does a credible job). Since Wagner's *Ring* is not only about Wagner but also about the ambivalent cosmic relationship between free will and determinism, between illicit and "normal" passion, you must have dominating performers who can render the difficulties as if on a world scale. Without them, therefore, opera companies that attempt *Ring* cycles seem compelled to accentuate whatever other strengths they possess, for example an eye-catching set designer, a genuinely brooding and menacing Alberich, a first-class orchestra (which along with Morris's Wotan is the Met's special virtue).

Yet for all its inhumanly remorseless forward progress (in which in some ways it resembles a Dickens or Balzac novel), the *Ring* is really a work about slipping and going backward, and was never really fully completed. Proust's idea about it has always seemed the most brilliant of all: Its unity, he said, is provided only by "retrospective illumination." Wagner began with the death of Siegfried, and worked his way back to the origin of all things in the Rhine. Only then did he impose on it the step-by-step march to annihilation, the reassertion of redemptive love, the disappearance of the old order. Unlike the Attic tragedians whom he emulated, however, Wagner had no social or political community on which he could depend for the cathartic rejuvenations of the whole society that take place at the end of the *Oresteia* or the Theban plays; he had to provide everything himself, from out of his ego, his universal artwork, his Kingdom at Bayreuth. Thus he was always *redoing* things, restructuring, repairing, reinterpreting in an effort to get them right and give them stability *as if* from the beginning. That is why the *Ring* is full of characters who, like Wagner himself, tell the story over and over again.

These recitations are direct evidence of how Wagner's central impulse is a sort of desperate narrative that attempts to bring order and rest to a world that is beset, like Emma Bovary's, with creditors and spiteful gossips. Each of the stories told by nearly every character—the Rhinemaidens, Loge, Erda, Siegmund, etc—jostles the others, claiming attention and space, the whole contained by the orchestra, which is the narrative of all narratives. It is this profusion of warring tales and power-driven characters that symbolizes the seething instability lodged at the *Ring's* center, despite the work's outer solidity and imposing bulk. Produce dreams *and* power, hold on to as much as you can, try to dominate others: This is the *Ring's* irreducible core, embodied in the exploits of Alberich, Wotan, Hunding, Hagen, Siegfried and even the dwarf Mime. Each such career, like a line of music, inevitably gives rise to others. Since the contest between them can never be resolved, it can only be re-staged again and again, much as the pursuit of power and capital is an everlasting effort. Wagner fully realized the remarkable parallel between the development of symphonic music and the development of a competitive bourgeois society.

Any seriously considered theatrical and musical conception of the *Ring* today must therefore emphasize the staginess or artificiality of Wagner's attempt to use the opera house as the site where the analogy between the aesthetic and the political could be staged. In addition, an audience should be able to perceive the revolutionary quality of Wagner's musical reach as he brings the two spheres together, employing an alliterative text set to declamatory and melodic utterances of incredible plasticity, inventiveness and personality. When he said of his greatest work that it was "deeds of music made visible" he meant that his was historically the most sustained effort to chart the competitive ethos of his time both psychologically *and* symphonically, in ways scarcely dreamed of by sonata form or classical rondos. In the gripping exchanges in *Rheingold* between Wotan and Alberich, or in *Walküre* between Wotan and Brünnhilde, the double-bindings, scapegoatings and Freudian anticipations are astounding; in their self-consciousness they are manifestly unlike the un-self-conscious tub-thumping bloody-mindedness to be found in Verdi and Puccini, Wagner's contemporaries.

In short, Wagner is uneven, contradictory, wildly improvisatory in style and outlook. He fairly invites not timidity and fidelity but arrogance and panache in order to be produced satisfactorily today. His *Ring* therefore requires, I believe, an eccentric and yet integral vision, of the kind attempted in recent years by Patrice Chéreau and Gotz Friedrich. The Met's solution has to be regarded as on the whole the best of a deferred invitation to do him fully; it is almost like the gathering of guests assembled to wait around before an indefinitely postponed party. Accordingly, the production's weakest aspects can be traced back either to unthinking routine or to a studied pointlessness. Thus Levine's pace for *Rheingold* was impossibly slow, drawn-out, strangely relaxed; the dramatically critical moments (usually involving the thin-voiced and undistinguished Alberich of Julian Patrick) went by without enough emphases. The weak ones simply felt tediously slow. Moreover, since Alberich's music in the *Ring* is unattractively angular and vocally twisted, it demands sharpness of inflection and rhythmic determination, for instance when the horrid dwarf scampers about in pursuit of the mermaids. Levine's rendering was more suited to a stroll on the beach, as was his orchestral work for Siegfried Jerusalem's cleverly sung Loge.

Walküre picked up somewhat, though the unacceptable schmaltz in the cello part accompanying Sieglinde's offer of drink to Siegmund boded ill. As I noted in these pages several years ago ["Music," December 6, 1986], I feel that Levine's involvement with the scores is fitful, as if he still hasn't had enough time to develop a whole reading, and at times the raucous imbalances (e.g., the funeral music of *Götterdämmerung*) argued not only the fatigue of many performances seriatim but also the failure of conception that would allow the brass and wind choirs to bray unrestrainedly. Of the various vocal disappointments the saddest was Christa Ludwig's Fricka in the first two evenings and her Waltraute in the last. A formerly rich and dark soprano who had the voice to do Brünnhilde (I heard her remarkably intelligent Immolation scene with the Chicago Symphony in 1967), she has remained a canny performer with clear enunciation and idiomatic phrasing, but without a voice to speak of. The passionately energetic "Mrs. Wotan" in *Rheingold,* the angry embodiment of aggrieved matronhood in *Walküre,* the tragically beset Waltraute in *Götterdämmerung:* All these suffered Ludwig's thin, often squeaky soprano, with neither volume nor resonance to save the gestures.

James Morris as Wotan has the plush legato nobility of voice and cadenced gravity of demeanor to deliver the part in all its extraordinary richness. I thought his *Rheingold* rendition suffered from Levine's slowness, but by the time of his final appearance in *Siegfried,* confronting the almost totally inadequate Siegfried of William Johns, one knew that his was *the* respectable Wotan of our generation, closely matched by the brilliant (but lesser-voiced) Robert Hale, who performs mainly in Europe. Aside from Gary Lakes, whose all-too-brief but authoritative appearance as Siegmund dramatized the absence of *any* competent Siegfrieds, the heroic tenor part on which the last half of the *Ring* rests was realized with entirely unsatisfying results. Jerusalem did the *Götterdämmerung* Siegfried, sparing us Johns it is true, but provided neither the continuity that Wagner envisioned between the last two operas, nor the heroic volume that the part rigorously demands. But Jerusalem is a skillful and alert artist who at least looks the hero if he doesn't sound it. As Fafner, Hunding and Hagen, Matti Salminen was formidably evil, massive in girth, menacing and dark-voiced in tone. Horst Hiestermann was an excellent Mime—sensible, accurate, intelligent, but without the psychopathic dimensions brought to the role a generation ago by Gerhard Stolze.

Finally, Gudrun Volkert's Brünnhilde. There are no first-rate Brünnhildes around, and anyone who supposes that because she is something of an actress Behrens can do the part excellently is mistaken. Behrens's singing deserves high marks for effort, but the actual sound is basically flawed (some have called it a wreck) and the overall effect, from my point of view, is decidedly poor. She has never struck me as a dramatic singer, and in the Wagnerian roles she does not display the same level of intelligence and inwardness that Gwyneth Jones, her voice now a complete disaster, has occasionally been able to muster. Ute Vinzing and Jeannine Altmeyer are Brünnhildes of some currency but they too fall very short of the desired level. In all these cases insufficient volume and quality of sound (compared with Nilsson or Flagstad) are what disqualifies them from the first rank. So when she entered the breach Volkert was entering a pretty devalued field. Behrens was injured on a Saturday night; a Brünnhilde from somewhere was needed for the following Tuesday (and, as it turned out, for Thursday and Saturday as well).

I was won over by Volkert's heroism, if not by her voice, which is a modest instrument with only average volume; in the middle register (the upper tended to be squeaky and shrill) it has a decent but rather plain expressiveness. To enter an unknown production at a moment's notice, to sing what is in effect the most difficult and the longest soprano part in opera and to do so without a single major mishap—that was pretty impressive. She was both boisterous and tender as the *Walküre* Brünnhilde, rapturously exuberant in *Siegfried* and steady and accurate in *Götterdämmerung,* which was her least convincing evening. On the other hand, the soprano who replaced Jessye Norman as Sieglinde, Hanna Lisowska, was barely adequate, a performance that highlighted Volkert's relatively stellar presence. And indeed, it is apparent that Volkert's unadorned yet reliable delivery of Brünnhilde's part had the special stamp of the Met's *Ring* production as a whole: that in a basic way it puts the tetralogy before New York (and television) audiences and allows them to experience the actual succession of narratives and music by which the cycle is constituted. Even without supertitles and a detailed knowledge of the text it has therefore been possible to understand the extraordinary combativeness and lyrical power of Wagner's genius, to feel the irrational demands he makes on performers and audiences alike and to make some of the musical and intellectual discriminations he requires, as well as the predictions about later music he so startlingly prefigures.

CHAPTER 19

Opera Productions
(Der Rosenkavalier, House of the Dead, Doctor Faust)

A LTHOUGH HE conducted only seven performances of *Der Rosenkavalier* (1911) at New York City's Metropolitan Opera this past fall, Carlos Kleiber nevertheless made a stunning impression. The opera is the best known and most palatable of Richard Strauss's works: Its Viennese setting, its charming waltzes, the bittersweet romance between an older woman and a young man and, above all, the unthreatening, chatty zest of its music and its Hofmannsthal libretto working together brilliantly have kept *Rosenkavalier* near the forefront of the Met's repertory. Yet it is difficult to overstate the extraordinary transformation in the score that was accomplished by Kleiber. Suffice it to say that it is depressingly rare to hear opera conducting of such intelligence and care. Scarcely a phrase in the rather long score came off routinely or passed by unnoticed; Strauss's sinuous lines were inflected and actually led, shaped and rendered without the slightest trace of exaggeration, forcing or fussiness. It was a very Haydnesque effect that Kleiber conveyed, if by Haydnesque we recall Charles Rosen's observation in *The Classical Style* that Haydn's style is one of amiability and conversational exchange. The sense given by Kleiber's work was that it addressed both score and listener, rather than attacking the one or parading itself before the other.

Would that the production showed such qualities. The lead singers—Felicity Lott as the Marschallin, Anne Sofie von Otter as Octavian, Aage Haugland as Ochs, Barbara Bonney as Sophie—ranged from excellent (Otter and Haugland) to good (Lott and Bonney), but there was little brilliance in performance or direction and hardly any emphasis on the combination of perversity and semi-official solemnity that characterized the products of Strauss and Hofmannsthal's long collaboration.

The Nation, January 7, 1991.

Some inkling of how problematic and unusually interesting that extraordinary partnership was is provided by Michael Steinberg in his recent book, *The Meaning of the Salzburg Festival: Austria as Theater and Ideology, 1890–1938* (Cornell University Press). Steinberg makes the case with remarkable scholarship and analysis that summertime Salzburg (with Hoffmannsthal as its spiritual father) was the scene of an attempt to reconstitute Austria as a European cultural center after it had been marginalized by the collapse of the Habsburg empire. This new image of Austria was to be at once nationalist and, in its attachment to ideals taken from the Catholic Baroque, universalist and conservative. The Salzburg Festival can therefore usefully be seen as paralleling Wagner's efforts at Bayreuth to turn music and opera to political and ideological purpose. In Salzburg it was the operas of Mozart and Strauss—worldly, consummately polished, engaging, allegorical and, as they came to be enshrined at the festival, culturally sanctioned—that were to serve a grandiose spiritual mission. Along with Hofmannsthal's *Everyman*, they are still performed annually in Salzburg, although for a period of almost thirty years the festival became the personal stage, as it were, of Herbert von Karajan.

What Kleiber captured in his reading of the score was the significance of Strauss's portrait of late-eighteenth-century Vienna, so often (as in the Met's production) left largely to exquisite posing and cute period comedy. Central to this highly stylized portrait is the waltz, whose antecedents, in the years before it was made famous by Johann Strauss (no relation to the thoroughly German Richard), included the minuets, German dances, ländler and waltzes composed for the aristocracy by Mozart, Haydn, Beethoven and Schubert. Steinberg suggests in an earlier essay that Strauss and Hofmannsthal used dance forms in *Salome, Elektra, and Rosenkavalier* partly because Hofmannsthal believed that only dance could get at the instinctual life hidden beneath-a surface of worldly manners, and partly because words were incapable of saying what the body's physical motions could. Kleiber's conducting underlined the prevalence of the waltz rhythms throughout the score, a prevalence not easily reduced to the mindless oom-pah-pah most conductors settle for; rather, the waltz rhythm was made to speak the inner language of what Steinberg calls a raw core of sexual striving.

But while the music came alive under Kleiber's guidance, the stage work seemed sodden and exhausted. Lott is a beautiful woman but doesn't have either the presence or voice to suggest a powerful 32-year-old aristocrat giving up a young lover (Octavian) and also effecting his marriage to the daughter of a rich bourgeois. The Marschallin is a character genuinely related in drive and vigor to Salome and Elektra, but without their remorseless and basically uninformed frenzy. She remains a perfectly mannered social being; when she expresses sorrow, anger or defiance they are conveyed by a minimum of means—a change in tone here, a gesture or a quickened rhythm there. In Act I, for example, Kleiber varied each recurrence of the underlying dance rhythms as if to register as precisely as possible the changing scene around the Marschallin as she dealt with the various interruptions in her blissful life with Octavian: the appearance of Baron Ochs, her numerous retainers, the dawning sense of some elaborate social transformation and so on. Never too assertive or insistent in the orchestra, these minimal gestures got only an occasional acknowledgment from Lott, who seemed to me trapped in a conventional image of the opera.

For all its period affectations *Rosenkavalier* is in fact a twentieth-century opera, not just a modern imitation of an eighteenth-century court spectacle or comedy of manners. Even later eighteenth-century works (such as the Mozart and Gluck operas) cannot today be given in "authentic performances" but in reconstitutions or reinterpretations of what, also by reinterpretation, is believed to be an eighteenth-century style. This is where the boldly iconoclastic productions of Götz Friedrich or Peter Sellars seem to have it over timid reiterations put forth year after year by the Met and other large establishment houses. Productions should emphasize, I believe, the connections between an operatic work and its immediate context, as well as the self-conscious endeavor of restoring an older work to a late-twentieth-century audience. Both of these approaches contain a good deal more "authenticity" than clumsy naturalistic approximations done with little self-awareness or intelligence.

In effect the Marschallin is connected not only to Salome and Elektra but also to the woman in Schönberg's *Erwartung* and even to Berg's *Lulu*. Moreover, an interesting case can be made for twentieth-century opera—nearly everything between, say, Wagner and Berio, Britten and Henze—as offering performers and audiences alike a complex experience of modernity quite unlike the experience offered by the major nineteenth-century Italian tradition, which sits so stubbornly at the heart of the Met's enterprise. By occasionally bringing in people like the regrettable Franco Zeffirelli to mount productions whose raison d'etre is to abrogate or disguise connections between an opera and its contemporary setting, the Met makes opera a noisy and expensive spectacle, one that draws in the wealthy, the corporate sponsor and the rigidly conservative but that considerably alienates both young and culturally involved people. By also refusing to concede that audiences should understand the action of an opera minute by minute—translations and supertitles are forbidden—the Met further boxes in and eviscerates great works of music drama.

So dominant has this aesthetic become that even when smaller companies in New York try to stage eccentric or difficult work, the result is often disappointing. It was wonderful to have been able to see *From the House of the Dead* (Janáček's rarely performed last opera) at the City Opera this fall, so extraordinarily rich and unusual is this work based on a Dostoyevsky novel (one that Tolstoy considered his contemporary's greatest work). Yet to have seen it in so underdirected, poorly staged and indifferently planned a production was most disappointing. Rhoda Levine's earlier productions for City Opera, notably of Anthony Davis's *The Life and Times of Malcolm X*, were bold and original. For the Janáček, an odd work in that it takes place entirely in a Siberian prison yard and has no real leading characters, she delivered a glumly realistic set, a barely discernible hodgepodge of singers and no action at all—no blocking and only the most rudimentary highlighting. To make matters worse, her singers, although they sang capably enough, poured forth their lines in an almost completely indistinct English. Most of the time the audience could neither understand what was being sung nor see who was singing: This, I think, is an unacceptable price to pay for seeing a work as rich and interesting as Janáček's.

From the House of the Dead is constructed around the confessions of a group of convicts, one of whom, a political prisoner named Alexander Petrovich Goryanshikov, is brought in at the beginning and released at the end. A wounded eagle kept by the prisoners is also set free at the same time, though the opera's overall mood is an unrelieved sadness and desperation. At the center of the opera is an inventive play within a play, which is staged by the convicts for their relief and entertainment. Christopher Keene conducted this scene and much of what succeeded it in the opera with attention and intelligence, if not always with the dramatic flair necessary to carry across the minutely organized merits of Janáček's score from one segment to the other. Only Eugene Perry as Shishkov broke through the encumbrances put on him by the production; his monologue (also a sort of play within a play) about killing his wife is the longest and most sustained piece of the score, and was delivered with an insensate intensity and musical control quite gripping in their effect.

Janáček, however, is one of the few twentieth-century composers whose operatic *oeuvre* is just beginning to be known to a wide late-twentieth-century audience (Strauss is another). And as the work becomes better known in more carefully planned productions than City Opera has mounted for *House of the Dead*, there is a better chance that other, now neglected works from the twentieth-century repertory can be staged. Perhaps these works might even someday displace the massive mid-nineteenth-century emphasis at the Met, along with which has gone poorly directed and sung work of the sort that inhibits the company's artistic growth. Certainly the City Opera, with its recent Ravel, Schönberg and Janáček attempts, has made a start, but New York audiences are still confronted with innumerable *Bohèmes* and *Traviatas* for every *Jenufa* or *Erwartung*.

Few operas are rarer and more deserving of a major New York revival than Ferruccio Busoni's masterpiece *Doktor Faust*, left unfinished at the time of his death in 1924. Busoni is scarcely known today, except perhaps as the transcriber of some of Bach's organ and violin works, still played by many pianists. He was born in Trieste but spent most of his life in Germany, where he was also known as one of the greatest of piano virtuosos. A contemporary of Schönberg, Mahler and Debussy, Busoni was no less a musical revolutionary than they: He wrote a number of highly unusual operas, an immense amount of piano music and a very important treatise on "new music."

The essence of Busoni's style is its complexity and its eclecticism. Most of his major work is both atonal and lyrical, contrapuntal and yet brilliantly dramatic. He was an intellectual and a visionary, someone whose work tried to accomplish syntheses between various styles, world views and techniques. Paradoxically, he often conceived works either on the largest scale (his piano concerto lasts about ninety minutes and requires an enormous orchestra, as well as a male chorus) or on the smallest (many of his finest piano pieces, for instance, are only moments long). In any event Busoni places tremendous demands on performers and, because he seems to have no obvious place in the canon, on audiences.

This is no reason for not performing him, since his work has begun to be available here and there, with usually successful results. In 1986 London's English National Opera staged a production of *Doktor Faust*, and restaged it this year. I happened to be in London at the time of this season's fifth performance in early November. I attended it and was overwhelmed by the work's force, and by the E.N.O.'s perspicacity in engaging a first-class conductor, an excellent cast and an inspired, if occasionally too flamboyant, designer and producer (Stefano Lazaridis and David Pountney, respectively).

Antony Beaumont, the conductor specially brought in for *Faust*, is no ordinary musician; he is an exceptionally fine scholar, the editor of Busoni's letters and the author of a monumental one-volume study, *Busoni the Composer* (Indiana University Press). In addition, Beaumont was the man who actually completed the score of *Faust*, about a decade ago (Schönberg characteristically refused Busoni's widow's request to conclude the work from her husband's sketches). Beaumont discusses his work on the score of *Faust* in a very interesting section of the E.N.O.'s program for the opera, which also includes studies on the Faust legend, on the possible analogies between Faust and Edward Teller (an interesting, if curiously ambiguous notion) and on the late Erich Heller's animadversions upon Mann, Busoni, Goethe and others. All in all Beaumont's appearance was, I thought, a great compliment to both E.N.O. and the work.

Like Janáček, Busoni worked from innumerable small sketches, employing a sort of micrologic of composition, out of which grew the powerfully shaped and designed whole. Unlike Janáček, however, Busoni was haunted (some would say burdened) by his learning and his admiration for Bach, Beethoven and Mozart. A formalist, a scholar and a synthesizer whose commonest gestures were inclusion, complication and incorporation—a lot of *Faust* is constructed like a vast montage—Busoni worked on the opera for almost thirty years and obviously came to identify with its protagonist. He saw the learned adventurer as a composite figure, part Leonardo, part Goethian superman and part Christian heretic; his opera is therefore made of different and often contradictory elements, a mixture of ritual, puppet play and melodrama.

The basic set designed for E.N.O. by Lazaridis is both flexible and highly imaginative: Faust's desk is at stage center, flanked on both sides by immense heaped-up rows of filing cabinets through which run gangplanks, pipes, levers and gauges. To the right and left the stage floor is raised and lowered at sharp angles; the ribbed-rubber slats permit diabolical exits and appearances that, allied with clever lighting effects, communicate not only the hermetic enclosure of an individual scholar (library and laboratory) but also the sense of a world-accumulating power, industry and history (in bureaucratic command center, factory, public archive).

Pountney's production has its quirks, notably the stress on a sort of homosexual partnership between Faust and Mephistopheles and, something only partially in Busoni as I read him, the strictly secular view that finally denies both God and Devil in the interests of a totally (relatively hopeful) human solution for history. (My feeling is that the opera actually communicates an abiding pessimism). Pountney builds on Busoni's own de-emphasis of Marguerite/Helen, who is dissolved and distributed rather lackadaisically by the composer into a series of shadowy female figures (the Duchess of Parma, Helen of Troy and so on). At the end of the opera Faust and the Duchess (plus, it is supposed, the Devil) give birth to a splendid young boy, who redeems Faust in this world from his otherwise sternly arid damnation in the next. Graham Clark as Mephistopheles dominated the proceedings; a Roy Scheider look-alike, he has the physique and the piercing, if not always refined, tenor to render a properly tempting yet macabre and ultimately routed figure. Alan Opie, who does what I have been told is a less successful Faust than Thomas Allen did in the 1986 version, is a fine singer with a fluent baritone. He simply gave out under the role's formidably rigorous duration. Together with the numerous members of the large cast, they gave on the whole a wonderfully agile and interesting ensemble performance of a kind seldom encountered in New York.

There is a commercially available Deutsche Grammophon recording of *Faust,* and it features Fischer-Dieskau in the title role. He dispatches the part's enormous complexities with hair-raising excitement and expression. It was also Fischer-Dieskau who sang the role the only time the opera was performed in New York, a Carnegie Hall concert version in 1964. So far as I have been able to discover, the only fully staged American performance occurred in (of all places) Reno, in 1974. I mention these things because the relative avoidance in New York of difficult but vitally interesting twentieth-century operas like *Doktor Faust* (the same can be said of operas by Henze, Hindemith, Prokofiev, Shostakovich, Britten and others) has further diminished the conventional warhorses that are regularly available. Even though the E.N.O. is not a star-studded company (Opie is no Fischer-Dieskau), the challenge of having to work through and actually realize a contemporary ensemble opera has often meant excellent and challenging productions, carefully rehearsed and directed performances and an innovative use of usually young but eminently willing and gifted artists. It has also meant that the more common repertory items like *Pagliacci* and *Rigoletto* often (but not always) benefit from the same approach. The result is that opera is lifted onto a higher and, in the end, I believe, altogether more profitable (in all senses) level. The timid and self-defeating thesis followed in New York that opera companies should rely on opulent reproductions of a handful of standard favorites, occasional but skimpy efforts to put on unusual operas, overpayment of a few stars and, most of the time, acceptance as a fact of life that opera-going means trudging through months of nondescript evenings is a grotesque mistake. It is additionally compounded by refusing to allow supertitles or operas sung in English (an E.N.O. rule), and also by discouraging, if not actually preventing, a critical and civilized discourse about opera in the late twentieth century from emerging. We now get little more than a scorecard approach to music that is fostered by the minuscule space usually given to reviewers (Andrew Porter in *The New Yorker* being a brilliant exception).

It is worth noting, finally, that many orchestras, visiting or resident, as well as instrumentalists follow a roughly equivalent procedure for their New York appearances. The frequency of safe but grimly uninteresting performances and repertories is thus far too high for a great city like New York.

CHAPTER 20

Style and Stylessness
(*Elektra, Semiramide, Katya Kabanova*)

A MONG THE unending complaints made by critics about opera directors like Peter Sellars who supposedly distort the classical composer's intention, I've never heard any objections to the even greater distortions involved in so-called concert performances of operas. Somehow it is claimed that if you reduce an opera to its alleged musical essence and put it on a concert platform, you serve both work and composer better. But if you let singers wear lavish evening dress and bellow out at the audience with no acting, stylistic principles or dramatic gestures to restrain them, you not only distort, you also mutilate an opera. After all, the composer intended the music to be an integral part of a dramatic construction. And composers, I believe, hear operatic music as bearing within it the stresses, the inflections and even the obstacles imposed on singers by the physical exertions required by acting on a stage with costumes, other singers, and so on. Opera is an extravagant art, as the title of Herbert Lindenberger's excellent book on the subject has it, and it may also be a form mainly allowing excess and superfluity. At any rate, opera is very impure and hybrid. However, as all serious scholars of the genre agree, opera is not unrestrained or formless, nor does it license totally uninhibited modes of display by contemporary performers.

The awful vulgarity, distortion and truly unoperatic excesses of the genre were exemplified as if for all time in a recent Carnegie Hall performance of Richard Strauss's *Elektra* by the Vienna Philharmonic under the direction of Lorin Maazel. To say that it did to operatic style what Operation Desert Storm did to Iraq is only to suggest what bombast and overkill can do. The vast orchestra was stretched out across the stage, over which was built a sort of V-shaped balcony (for victory in the desert?) studded with the cast of soloists. Eva Marton as Elektra stood at the front point; Brigitte Fassbaender as Klytemnestra and Elizabeth Connell as Chrysothemis stood behind her; James King and Franz Grundheber as Aegisth and Orest, respectively, stood behind them. Thus, no singer could address any other singer and roaring forward was the order of battle. To make matters worse, the auditorium was in total darkness (thus making the thoughtfully distributed libretto unreadable) except for garishly colored spotlights of lavender, red and green that shone on the singers when they sang, as well as an artful light playing about on the maestro, who conducted with a brio and brashness that produced a quite literally deafening glob of sound.

Even though the minor roles (handmaidens, knights, etc.) were competently sung, only James King in his tiny part among the principals suggested anything like drama, address or expression. The rest simply produced enormous amounts of sound, as if what Strauss and von Hofmannsthal intended was a two-hour festival of technicolor noise. Nothing remotely like words or phrases came across, especially from Marton, who poured forth sounds of indescribable volume and power to negligible emotional or dramatic effect. Surely Maazel was to blame for so ghastly a rendition of Strauss's last effort at advanced modernity.

First performed in 1909, *Elektra* had an idiom intended to shock by introducing the audience to a harmonic language a step beyond *Tristan* and a stop short of complete atonality. Its libretto was based on Sophocles' play, brought up to date by modern psychotherapy, with decadence as an aesthetic and expressionism as a sort of extreme conveyor of dramatic action. Little of this came through in Maazel's version, which remained fixated on "effects," with scant regard for continuity, persuasiveness or stylistic manners. It was loud, attention-getting, brassy.

Perhaps I read too much into the V-shaped construction that symbolized both the idea that audiences were to be passive recipients of uninterrupted bombast and the moment's all-round triumphalism. But it contrasts starkly with an early February performance by the conductorless Orpheus Chamber Orchestra at Carnegie Hall. This is a remarkable group of mostly young musicians that I've heard in an impressive series of concerts in New York City. Like many other such groups, the core of their repertory is Viennese classicism, with occasional essays in Slavic or twentieth-century tonal works. Unlike some other essentially chamber groups for example, the London Classical Players, Academy of St. Martin-in-the-Fields, Orchestra of the Enlightenment and Orchestra of St. Luke's) they do not make a fetish of authenticity or eccentricity. What gave them particular distinction was revealed, for instance, in the first measures of the Schubert Fifth Symphony, which opened their Carnegie concert. After three chords and a descending scale on the dominant, the movement's main theme (an arpeggiated tonic chord) is announced, usually with considerable fussiness and teasing. Not so by Orpheus: The almost dazzling unobtrusiveness of the motif came across with elegant and simple force, the consequence of a chamber-music attitude that has instrumentalists playing together inward, so to speak, rather than outward to a conductor monopolizing control over them and the audience.

This is striking, perhaps even paradoxical, since public performance is about display, not about inwardness. On the other hand, Orpheus's programs are generally conservative and familiar, and strike one as studiously unadventurous, as if to highlight delicacy of execution and taste rather than dazzlement and virtuosity. Their soloist for the Mozart C Minor Concerto was Radu Lupu, certainly the most fastidious and self-effacing of contemporary pianists, a performer whose pianissimos, rhythmic intelligence and, yes, scales are incredible, but whose strong musical personality is expressed, like Orpheus's, by understatement and an almost stoical reflectiveness. In fine, Orpheus keeps unresolved the paradox between the required extroversion of a really communicative performance and the controlled introversion of musicians playing for and with one another.

It is a pleasure to report that after numerous unsatisfying productions New York's Metropolitan Opera has managed a feat roughly similar to Orpheus's in its recent productions of Rossini's *Semiramide* (1823) and Janáček's *Katya Kabanova* (1921), two relatively rare operas by extravagantly gifted but deeply opposed musical geniuses. It remains the Met's policy not to allow translations or supertitles, the absence of which for *Katya* especially is a real pity, given the compression and complexity of the text as adapted from Ostrovsky's famous play *The Storm*. Jonathan Miller directed the production; Charles Mackerras, today's reigning Janáček interpreter, conducted. Whereas *Semiramide* is the almost parodistic embodiment of display, *Katya* has the manner of a quiet chamber opera, although its material is both generally provocative in a Strindbergian sense and musically as well as dramatically a considerable challenge for orchestra and singers. The core of Janáček's vision is the conflict between Katya and her mother-in-law, Kabanicha, who represents repressive conventionality, albeit with a kind of theatricality that Leonie Rysanek, who sang the role with florid obduracy, was able to project most effectively. Katya is unhappily married to Tichon and betrays him with Boris Grigoryevich, a cultivated young visitor to the provincial Russian town Kalinov, where Katya lives.

Miller's production highlighted the tension between a surface of respectability and conversational exchange on the one hand, and on the other, an uncontainable sexual drive, dark and suicidal in its consequences. (Despite its hysterical atmosphere, *Elektra* does not project as disturbing a world as *Katya Kabanova*.) In conformity with Miller's conception, the barren set designed by Robert Israel allows what appears to be amiable everydayness to go on between various groups of people—until an outburst ruptures the calm. What Miller got out of his mostly excellent cast was a persuasive combination of ordinariness and psychological disturbance; yet nowhere did one feel, except as a fleeting hint, the staginess or melodrama with which Janáček seems occasionally to flirt in this profoundly Russophilic work. There was conviction, suffering and, given the remarkable score, a kind of rapturous concentration from orchestra and singers. Aside from Rysanek, especially good were Susan Quittmeyer as Varvara, Kabanicha's stepdaughter, and Aage Haugland, as a rich and vulgar tradesman who in a compelling Dostoyevskian scene imitates the groveling of a peasant before the redoubtable dowager with terrifying heedlessness.

The one flaw in *Katya* was Katya herself, as sung by the formidable Czechoslovak soprano Gabriela Benackova, the only member of the cast to be singing in her native language. She was also the only member of the group of ten principals rarely to sing to, or play along with, the others. With her face resolutely turned toward the audience, she sang admirably—her voice is a superb instrument—but with little dramatic force or, interestingly, focus. She might have been singing an oratorio, for instance, so little did she seem part of the gripping proceedings around her. Moreover, I sensed no particular appreciation of Janáček's stunning flights of musical inspiration, in which (Act I, Scene 2, for example) Katya suddenly departs her prosaic existence for a narrative of earlier bliss. Miller had set up that particular episode brilliantly: The two women, Katya and Varvara, are at center stage, framed by a toy house (perhaps an allusion to Ibsen's doll's house), itself unframed by anything outside it except an empty stage and one or two distant clouds. Katya's long reverie gradually breaches the silly restriction of daily routine—she is, after all, an *ordinary* person—through a masterly set of repeated and increasingly dense and gradually ecstatic orchestral accompaniments, from shimmering violins and flute to a pizzicato bass and assertive horn; from an impressionistic aural vagueness to an almost sentimental melodic cadence, at which point Katya says that she can see birds and angels singing, and from a great height can also feel an isolated, dispossessed sort of freedom.

The power of this isn't that Katya rises free of her circumstances, but that she obviously can't, and will in effect allow herself to be destroyed by them. Thus what the singer performing Katya needs is a highly provisional, vulnerable and emotionally true rendition of what Janáček's music conveys in its turns and shifts. Miller had it ready to be realized on stage, but Benackova did not. She sang the notes perfectly, but only that. I felt that here was a dutiful, though technically glorious, recitation but not a dramatic reading of this magnificent part, everywhere counterpointed by Mackerras's genuine flexibility and understanding. So the production was somewhat incapacitated by this central flaw, but it was far from unsuccessful nonetheless. The thing about Janáček that Miller grasped so intelligently is that his operatic idiom combines stubbornness and an accommodating delicacy that is musically guided by psychological restlessness and not by theatricality or by the easy conclusiveness provided by conventional harmony. When Katya kills herself despairingly at the end you are meant to feel the sorrow, but you almost immediately experience the unvarying pressures of daily life as Kabanicha accepts the murmured attention of the grieving crowd, whom she still sees as her loyally correct vassals. It is a unique sort of musical and dramatic *aperçu*, gross insensitivity covering itself in convention right after a most unconventional occurrence, that only Janáček in this century seems to have specialized in. But it needs great discipline for an ensemble to manage it; would that it had succeeded somewhat more, although the second time I saw the performance it seemed to me more integrated and therefore satisfying.

If *Katya* is difficult to put on because so much of it stands outside the well-charted operatic and dramatic lanes, *Semiramide* is difficult because it is rooted in very specific early nineteenth-century practice, very remote from late twentieth-century performance styles. I had a much quickened sense of this a short while after I had seen the Met's production, when I heard Philip Gossett of the University of Chicago in a gripping Gauss lecture at Princeton. Along with Alberto Zedda, Gossett has over the years been re-establishing the Rossini texts both with scrupulous scholarship and a very elegant, innately musical style. At Princeton he spoke about what was acceptable and what was not in nineteenth-century styles of singing Rossini's florid and often improvised ornamentation. Since the Met was using his text of *Semiramide,* and since he had worked with the Met on this production as its "stylistic adviser," it is no wonder that this season's *Semiramide* was a great triumph.

What I found interesting in what he said, and what the superb Met principals (primarily Marilyn Horne, June Anderson, Samuel Ramey, John Cheek and Young Ok Shin) actually sang, is that Rossini performances cannot easily be codified into what was and was not acceptable. Instead, Gossett showed that there was a whole range of divergent practices used from which artists could choose, beyond which no one went (or should now go), even though those practices are were like a language learned, passed on and pretty much held to. Unlike *Katya Kabanoya, Semiramide* is built around an impossibly rococo plot involving murder, incest and all kinds of duplicity. Everything about it suggests excess, display, gregariously unself-conscious delight in musical fireworks. Here too (as the lamentable *Elektra* performance inversely proved to its calamitous disadvantage) there are rules and restraints requiring great vocal agility—Horne and Ramey are particularly splendid examples of his—and nothing of the "realism" that so earnestly comes to dominate Italian opera after Rossini.

Rossini was celebrated for his sarcasm and laziness. On being asked which was his favorite among his own operas he snapped, *"Don Giovanni."* Stendhal's admiring memoir of Rossini is inexplicably negative about *Semiramide,* which is actually so full of melody and inventiveness as to be overwhelming, almost impossible to take in. Conducted admirably and efficiently by James Conlon, the Met production spilled itself out tumultu-ously, the music completely mastering and even in the end bypassing the plot altogether. As a comic genius Rossini matched drama and music to each other quite perfectly. In the greatest of his serious works, of which *Tancredi* and *Semiramide* are perhaps the pre-eminent cases, one feels Ros-sini going through expression, dramatic situation and character in order to lay bare the core of his musical inventiveness. The result, I think, is a kind of metamusic, music about music, or music largely detached from its social and historical encumbrances.

Like Stendhal, Rossini was the product of a horrendously disenchanted and reactionary Europe. It is tempting to understand both these great art-ists as using an extremely worldly and knowing fluency in their art to assert a tremendously antithetical vitality against an undeserving and uncompre-hending society. And both artists never relax their grip on rationality, even while on the greatest flights. Theirs is a strange exorbitance, as invigorating as it is refined—particularly in such depressing times as these, when per-formance is as likely to be coercive as it is styleless, and pointless. I know it seems perverse to say that because its excesses are so unrelenting and se-vere *Semiramide* seems more like opera contemplating rather than present-ing itself, but this is how it seemed to me, and thus the connection with the Orpheus Orchestra both in the myth and in the intensity of performance.

CHAPTER 21

Alfred Brendel: Words for Music

ALFRED BRENDEL'S *MUSIC SOUNDED OUT:*
ESSAYS, LECTURES, INTERVIEWS, AFTERTHOUGHTS

MUSICIANS ARE silent on the whole, since audiences are there to witness their virtuosity and interpretive skills, not their ideas or brilliant conversation. There has always been something odd, even comic, therefore, about talking performers. Like the late Leonard Bernstein, for instance, or Vladimir de Pachman, the early 20th-century Polish pianist who would interrupt his recitals with admiring commentaries on his own skill. A silent performer is somehow a guarantee of musical seriousness and commitment, as if only the music counted, only its sound was important. When they have broken the spell in recent years musicians have written either gossipy chronicles or random observations on their own practice (e.g. Gerald Moore and Artur Schnabel). The number of performers who have actually made intellectual contributions in prose is therefore remarkably small and in the nature of things cannot be expected to increase.

Three contemporary pianists stand out in this extremely select company. The first was Glenn Gould, who after he retired from the concert stage in 1964 wrote an immense number of articles, record liners, radio and TV scripts. Gould, who died in 1982, was doubly unusual in that his prose was intended as an adjunct to his playing (it was unusually brilliant and persuasive), as well as the vehicle by which he advanced a comprehensive, if sometimes wacky, world-view. Second is Charles Rosen, less of an all-out virtuoso and eccentric personality than Gould, far more of a scholar and esthetic critic. Also unlike Gould, the various prose works that Rosen produced—his most famous is *The Classical Style*—do not seem directly connected to his style of playing, despite the fact that Rosen the accomplished pianist and Rosen the formidably learned and refined scholar are the same person.

The third is Alfred Brendel, whose most recent miscellany pretty much follows the path of his *Musical Thoughts and Afterthoughts* published in 1976. Brendel is of course a celebrated, frequently appearing pianist. Along with Maurizio Pollini, his remarkable Italian contemporary, Brendel stands near the very top of today's pianism. Although Pollini is, I think, the greater technician and all-round perfectionist, Brendel's reputation rests on his unique and powerfully affecting command of two quite different repertories. The first is the central Austro-Germanic classical tradition from Mozart and Haydn, through Beethoven and Schubert, to Brahms and Schumann. The second is a slightly less central but no less worthwhile music, one that is anchored in the flamboyant yet complex performance practices of Liszt and Busoni, whose work Brendel has championed and performed with great distinction.

Anyone who has been to Brendel's routinely sold-out recitals is just as routinely impressed with his convincingly intellectual *and* virtuosic style. Occasionally he sounds labored or uninspired, dutiful in the bad sense: One sometimes senses in his playing the discrepancy between wanting to program a piece and not being temperamentally at one with it. This is another way of saying that Brendel is not an uncomplicated exhibitionistic showman, since for him as a true musician the interpretation of work includes a great deal of reflection and seasoned preparation. He is—like Schnabel, like his teacher Edwin Fischer, like the recently deceased Wilhelm Kempf—primarily an artist, cultivated, fastidious and, when at his most convincing in the bigger works of Beethoven and Schubert, a superb builder and articulator of structures. One always perceives in his best work a coherence of approach and a refined knowledgeability served perfectly by a redoubtable pianistic technique.

His writing in *Music Sounded Out* is too various (and uneven in quality) to summarize or hold in the mind easily, but it is always compelling when it sheds light directly on what he plays. Thus in his long motivic analysis of Schubert's late sonatas, Brendel illuminates the inner logic of those sublime compositions which, he argues, are not extended rambles but extended and highly organized meditations on a handful of no more than five or six simple formulae that Schubert varies with astonishing skill.

Similar analyses of Beethoven's "new style" in the late works, of Liszt's B minor sonata of Schumann's "Kinderszenen" are wonderfully helpful not only for what Brendel has to say about these pieces, but also for how these analyses inform what he does with the music as a performer whose

Schubert, Liszt, Beethoven and Schumann renditions are in a class by themselves.

Elsewhere in the book there are brilliant, perceptive, but sometimes glib observations on, for example, Mozart's "nervousness," on the humor of Beethoven's "Diabelli" Variations and on the art of building a recital program. One of Brendel's concerns throughout is the comedy of serious music, (the sublime in reverse he calls it), but most of the evidence he gives shows that music is funniest when it isn't meant to be. He cites as an example the 1926 piano recital of a Wilhelm Bund, one of whose pieces—delivered in deadly earnest-carried the following program note: "longing to die in voluptuousness—rearing and sinking back, shimmy-foxtrot as song of destiny, orgiastic dance (disrupted), exclamations of desire, desperate struggle, apoplexy." To which Brendel appropriately responds by asking whether Bund survived the concert.

I do not mean to hint that Brendel is not always intelligent and interesting—he is. But he is too much a performer and practical musician to be as interesting on subjects relatively distant from his own performing concerns—such as Furtwängler or Busoni's opera "Doctor Faust"—as he is when he illuminates passages in Haydn's works or Liszt's "Années de Pèlerinage." I was slightly taken aback at the dryness of his analysis of Schnabel and his curiously flat discussion of playing Bach on the piano (he hasn't got a word to say about Gould's Bach playing, to which *all* interpreters since are extraordinarily indebted). But read mainly as a sort of scrapbook of practical insights into musical performance, Brendel's new collection is very satisfying, especially as it helps us actually to hear and better appreciate what he does in his recitals.

CHAPTER 22

Die Tote Stadt, Fidelio, The Death of Klinghoffer

"THE CENTER cannot hold," Yeats said apprehensively and cosmically in "The Second Coming." When the metaphor of a world falling apart is applied to the rather less grand realm of institutions that have put themselves in charge of performances of Western classical music, it is not entirely so bad a thing as that. Still, there is a much greater likelihood of adventure and exploration at the peripheries. Better the Brooklyn Academy of Music (BAM) than the New York Philharmonic or the Metropolitan Opera; and where choice of repertory, if not always successful realization, is concerned, better the New York City Opera than the many *Don Giovannis* and *Aïdas* across the plaza.

You would therefore actually want to attend (as I did) a rare performance of Korngold's *Die Tote Stadt* at City, though its shamelessly derivative music and the minimal production and stage direction by Frank Corsaro diminished the effort pretty conclusively. I can't help wondering why a good idea has to be left so much to shabby design and lackluster preparation. For most of Act II a sizable group of onstage singers (John Absalom, Stephanie Sundine, Richard Byrne, Charles Huddleston, Fritz Masten) seemed to be standing around, not doing much of anything dramatically except to sing and then stop singing on cue; meanwhile, spectators were forced to endure a dizzying series of slide and film projections supposedly suggesting Bruges and a Freudian story of obsessive love, but in fact making it impossible to distinguish clearly most of what was happening onstage. There is a moderately interesting quasi-Straussian opera lurking within the City Opera's well-conducted (by George Manahan) performances, but it was kept from appearing in all but its most obvious lines—a pity.

The Nation, November 11, 1991.

Or take the Glimmerglass Opera Company in Cooperstown, New York, whose annual monthlong repertory this year was made up of Beethoven's *Fidelio* (directed by Jonathan Miller) and *Il Rè Pastore*, a very infrequently performed Mozart work, which I was told was *the* opera to see. I could only attend *Fidelio*, but I did not regret the trek up to James Fenimore Cooper country for only one performance. The opera house itself is stunning architecturally, and everything about Glimmerglass suggests that the opera is a community affair not overly concerned about being authoritative or "central." Slowly one can discern an emerging predilection for smallish operas intelligently and tastefully done; it would not be hard to imagine Glimmerglass mounting Fauré's *Pénélope* or Rossini's *L'italiana in Algeri* (scheduled for 1992). One can't expect to see the Met try such pieces very often.

Miller's *Fidelio* was an odd, slightly discouraged production, although it is very difficult at this point to do anything particularly new or striking with the piece. *Fidelio* is in many ways not only Beethoven's remorselessly middle-class answer to Mozart's libertine perspectives in the Da Ponte operas but also an attempt to give musical life to a set of abstract ideas about human justice and freedom taken from the French Revolution. An excellent article by Paul Robinson in the March 1991 *Cambridge Opera Journal* argues that so strong was the connection in Beethoven's mind between the events of 1789 and *Fidelio* that the opera's characters and plot are almost completely desexualized and disembodied. You cannot therefore make genuinely believable human beings out of Leonora and Florestan, nor can you do much more than dutifully follow the outlines of a dauntingly austere narrative. I regret that I was unable to grasp Miller's central interpretive point, except that I much commend his wish to give short shrift to the usual affectations and byplay attaching to most productions of *Fidelio*. A ponderously stern and yet streamlined set by John Conklin—bearing an uncanny resemblance to the sort of Benthamite Panopticon memorably described in Foucault's *Discipline and Punish*—left the singers ample opportunity to show off their powers.

This brings us back to the question of opera away from great metropolitan centers like New York and Chicago: The budgets for famous and often theatrically effective singers do not exist. Miller's Leonora was Jeannine Altmeyer, an imposingly handsome woman who first became famous fifteen years ago as the Boulez-Cherau Bayreuth Sieglinde. I gather that she has gone on to do Brünnhilde at Bayreuth and elsewhere, but my general impression is that her star has somewhat faded. She has a huge voice but it does not have much warmth or continuity to it. In Leonora's great "Komm, Hoffnung" aria enormous blasts of sound were followed by sudden dips in volume that were most disconcerting, as if she could only manage short bursts of singing before she needed a rest. But she had a dignity and passion that were moving to me (for all its tremendous weaknesses *Fidelio* has never failed to make its effect, which leads me to wonder whether there can ever be a downright bad performance of it).

Mark W. Baker's Florestan was passable, as was Brian Steele's eccentric portrayal of the usually demonic Pizarro as an unctuous bureaucrat. Neither of them had the voice to dominate a role as, for instance, Jon Vickers or Fischer-Dieskau could, but it's hard to think of heroic tenors and baritones today who would be a real step up from Glimmerglass's. The dearth is everywhere. Rocco, the opportunistic and, I've always thought, unpleasant jailer who is supposed to be fatherly and expansive in his manner, was very well realized by Thomas Paul, who did the best all-round work of the evening. Like Miller's dramatic direction, Stewart Robertson's conducting was intelligently direct, unfussy and antiromantic. But it did not do a great deal to transfigure the proceedings. Beethoven clearly had that effect in mind, especially when Leonora reveals herself and is reunited with Florestan in intoxicating music that presages the Ninth Symphony. His orchestra was not up to such strength, but he did not pace the orchestra enough so as to build inexorably to the massive climaxes.

Nevertheless, Glimmerglass is definitely a place where skill and resourcefulness are at work, largely as a consequence of not being able (and therefore not wanting) to imitate the Met. These are not solely aesthetic decisions but, it is pretty obvious, political ones as well. If artists and institutions concerned with the arts are determined not simply to perform musical works but, in the fashion of *The New York Times*, to produce works for some self-established record, another agenda is at work. I do not think it is at all peculiar that precisely those institutions and their supporters who try to produce work for the record, who think of themselves as preserving tradition, banning outrageous experiments, holding the line and so forth, are also the ones who advance a notion of political correctness that makes some of the posturing of the left in this field look pitiful by comparison.

What is more, such efforts have the budgets, command the spaces and own the organs that can make "tradition" into an orthodoxy. Many of the Met's recent ideas, about Wagner's *Ring* cycle and *Parsifal*—weighty, grave, "realistic," programmatically unexperimental—are the virtual equivalents of political statements that say that the rich and powerful own aesthetic traditions, in which size, lavish verisimilitude and uncritical replications of the past are an acceptable substitute for rethinking, intelligent experiment and daring conceptions. Thus you can overrule the contemporary, and even the modern, in favor of something much more easily salable and far less "controversial" to boot.

I do not mean to say that there is nothing at the center that is worth having. Of course there is, as I've noted in many columns here. But what I am saying is that not enough notice is taken of how the neoconservative attack on the literary and pictorial arts has also taken a significant toll in the world of classical music. One sees it more easily perhaps in the discourse of music journalism, where astonishing corruptions of language and thought have come to be acceptable. The basic idea is that the best thing about music is that it is (the word turns up with some frequency) "nonideological," so that any attempt to interpret music politically or to introduce contemporary concerns into musical practice is considered an intrusion.

How inadequate such a notion is (which has become received dogma at *The New Criterion* and, to a very large degree, *The New York Times*) was best exemplified last spring in a valedictory article by Donal Henahan, the *Times*'s senior critic, who has since been succeeded by Edward Rothstein. Henahan's negative attitude toward nearly every manifestation of the modern was explained in this article as stemming from his regret that twelve-tone music ever happened. Certainly, as Adorno was one of the first to realize, even twelve-tone music could (and very often did) become co-opted and boring, but bewailing its appearance altogether is rather like regretting the discovery of the law of gravity. It is the fact that music, like society, is subject to change and development that maddens neoconservatives; this has made "musical tradition" into one of those unassailable catch phrases serving profoundly regressive ideas about law and order, mechanical realism and rigid and unimaginative performance style.

The paradox is that opera is supposedly the most "nonideological" of all musical genres, yet it is the most manifestly saturated in and directly influenced by politics, history and social movements. Wagner nonideological? Mozart nonideological? Beethoven and Verdi nonideological? Nonsense, of course. But the phrase has been evident in recent discussions and reviews that have bludgeoned BAM's production of *The Death of Klinghoffer*, with score by John Adams, libretto by Alice Goodman and direction by Peter Sellars. A further irony is that the phrase "ideological" indicates politics that the critic happens to disapprove of, whereas a politics that does not trouble *The New York Times* or *The Wall Street Journal* is construed as "nonideological," and consequently never explained or even discussed.

This is not to deny that, as someone with a considerable personal stake both in music and the modern Middle East, I was greatly disturbed at the prospect of an opera on the Klinghoffer murder. I have long been a critic of Abul Abbas, the Iraqi-supported Palestinian whose gang did the dreadful killing, but I have also been a consistent admirer of Sellars's work, which I have discussed here more than once. Thanks to Israeli propaganda and to the criminal idiocy of a small number of Palestinian desperadoes, most Americans tend to apply the terrorist image to the whole Palestinian people, although since the *intifada* began there has been a change for the better in that odious habit. Yet so ugly and gratuitous was Klinghoffer's killing that one would have thought an opera about the incident was in a sense ideologically predetermined, especially for American audiences. The question I asked myself before I saw the opera was whether, without distorting events, there was anything Adams-Goodman-Sellars could do with the episode that might shed new light on it, that would not only heighten our awareness of the appalling background from which Palestinians and Israelis draw so much of their anger and continued suffering but also present an interesting aesthetic experience. How would the three collaborators elude the many traps inherent in the raw history and the incredibly embroiled passions that have fed that history for almost a century?

To say (as Rothstein as well as Raymond Sokolov of *The Wall Street Journal said*) that the opera scants or caricatures or reduces or diminishes the Jewish side of the terrorist incident is, I think, a lapse into automatic thinking, into an easy formula that applies neither to the incident nor to the aesthetic experience of the opera. There is no way of palliating or excusing the violence that killed Klinghoffer, and the opera does not try. What the work attempts instead, I believe, is to imagine a frame, a background, a historical and aesthetic envelope for what, in another context, Thomas Hardy called "the convergence of the twain." Strictly speaking, the frame is an accurate one only in a general sense, because Klinghoffer was an American, not an Israeli, tourist; his assailants were Palestinian refugees whose driven, almost possessed sense of mission can be imagined to contrast strikingly with the innocent Klinghoffer's relatively ordinary background and apparently apolitical character. The background is compellingly established with the opera's opening chorus of Palestinian exiles who sing:

Of that house [in Palestine], not a wall
In which a bird might nest
Was left to stand. Israel
Laid all to waste.

I found this the most musically impassioned and moving sequence in the score, not least because Adams's music unfolds with a majestic calm that in the final strophes of the chorus blossoms into an extraordinary arabesque digression that loops up and down and around a single word with breathtaking continuity, searing the spectator's consciousness with the terrible sadness of it all.

Naturally you would respond to the opera's inaugural sequence (the so-called Prologue, made up of choruses of exiled Palestinians and Jews, plus a sendup of American middle-class life represented by the Rumor family) only if you opened yourself sympathetically to this usually scanted aspect of the Palestinian story. I was certainly prepared for it (since it replicated my own experience), but I do not think my response was entirely an ideological or autobiographical predisposition. The stillness and confidence of Adams's minimalist music was, I believe, at its rarest best in the first chorus, as was Goodman's sober diction. I did not think that level was achieved more than a few times during the evening. To my taste Adams's minimalism makes itself felt best in meditative or lyrical, rather than dramatic, modes; he clearly does not seem to be able to speak in a very assertive or overcoming musical idiom, although his music for *Klinghoffer* is always expertly laid out. The overall impression I got on this one hearing (I listened to it again a month later on the radio) is that he sounds as if he writes *for* occasions and purposes that stand outside and at a distance from the music; the result is music that generally accompanies (often with a kind of defeated pulsating and arpeggiated repetitiveness) the action, or music that frequently sounds strangely retrospective, vague or only partially convinced of where it is going, or music that (in the Achille Lauro Captain's opening soliloquy) is distracted by the words into relatively short bursts of clarity followed by longish passages of un-idiomatically accented recitative. Adams has said that *Klinghoffer* is not a Verdi-style opera but a ceremonial work, rather like the Bach passions: indeed, the three characters played by Janice Felty, a very competent Sellars regular, are commentators on the action, as much as the Evangelist is in the *St. Matthew Passion.*

There is no doubt, however, that Adams is an adept collaborator with the librettist and director, whose vision of the struggle over Palestine resonates more with the Arab than with the American-Jewish side of things. In sticking to the American-Jewish, banal, middle-class aspect of the episode Goodman stacks the deck, thereby letting the inherently more dramatic dimensions of the Palestinian tragedy take precedence over, and somewhat unfairly dominate, the senseless killing of the invalid tourist, whose only crime was that he happened to be on the Achille Lauro when the Palestinians boarded it. But as you sit there watching this vast work unfold, you need to ask yourself how many times you have seen any substantial work of music or dramatic or literary or pictorial art that actually tries to treat the Palestinians as tragically aggrieved, albeit sometimes criminally intent, people. The answer is never, and you must go on to ask Messrs.-the-nonideological-music-and-culture-critics whether they ever complain about works that are skewed the other way, or whether for instance, in the flood of images and words that assert that Israel is a democracy, any of them note that 2 million Palestinians on the West Bank and Gaza have fewer rights than South African blacks had during the worst days of apartheid, and that the paeans and the $77 billion sent to Israel from the United States were keeping the Palestinian people endlessly oppressed? And how many times have we heard people say that Cynthia Ozick's insufferably turgid anti-Palestinian polemics are "one-sided," or that when Joseph Papp canceled a Palestinian theater company's performance in 1989 he was also being one-sided? How could anyone complain that a subject like this opera's was *too* ideological when it is perfectly clear that by the same standard most artistic performances at the center are so often overlaid with stereotypical pieties and justified by a whole chorus of politically correct maintainers of the status quo as to be not openly ideological *enough*?

There can be no obligation laid on any performer or artist to replicate the politics of *The MacNeil-Lehrer NewsHour* when it comes to so-called balance and respectability. That Adams-Goodman-Sellars do not even try is a gigantic plus, I think, and they should be admired for it. But by the same token *Klinghoffer* does in fact require a critical look—albeit one based on having seen only one full theater performance—which quickly reveals striking strengths and weaknesses. There is a studiously antibourgeois quality to the whole that is interesting when the work is powerful and strong and far less so when it is, in my view, insufficiently forceful because capricious or clumsy. The first of these qualities is contained on what completely dominates the entire performance—that is, Sellars's directorial vision: It is lyrical and dramatic at the same time, but also comic (as opposed to tragic) and oddly formal and ceremonial. In his extraordinarily inventive use of space Sellars is superbly abetted by designer George Tsypin, whose gigantic vertical tubular metal structure, with its various levels and gangways, majestically surveys audience and actors alike.

The chorus weaves in and out of the proceedings, as do the Mark Morris dancers, never more beautifully present as an animating human pulse in the drama than in their work here; a couple of years ago Morris's perverse but markedly ineffective version of Purcell's *Dido and Aeneas* (also at BAM) had impressed me through its narcissism and its unjustified assault on Purcell's deeply mournful score and finely calibrated drama. In *Klinghoffer*, Morris's choreography and his dances are used to double the lyrico-dramatic action, and also to bind together the whole performing space in arcs that flow through the fairly static proceedings. Dancers, principal singers and chorus members are dressed alike in simple, pastel-colored street clothes, varied in the case of the terrorists with colored robes and occasional headdresses.

Most impressive of all, Sellars's direction removes the sense of bloody conflict from the drama. There are seven quasi-Aeschylean choruses interspersed throughout, and in their calm reflectiveness, their cosmically placid awareness of the sacred and the profane, these choruses irradiate and to a considerable degree elevate the action to the level of ritual rather than of history. Nowhere is the transformation from violence to ceremonial passion more striking, however, than when Klinghoffer is killed, an action that first takes place offstage and is then transfigured—that is the only word to use here—in an extraordinary "*gymnopédie* of the falling body," as a dancer's body is slowly lowered from the ceiling until it reaches the stage, where baritone Sanford Sylvan, as the already dead Klinghoffer, lies opposite it.

In effect, then, what Sellars has done to the opera is to provide a mesmerizing formal meditation on historical violence, in which one is able to perceive the waste and tragedy tying the characters together in a new ambience. This is not always consistently successful: As part of the Prologue, the easy satire of a New Jersey suburban family—the Rumors—is supposed to define the Klinghoffers' background as a way of limiting or deflating it. Most of the critics found the scene offensive; they alleged that it was anti-Semitic in portraying the Rumors as representative of the worst kind of consumerism and bargain hunting. Actually, there is no conclusive indication that they are in fact Jewish, but I thought the scene was far too long for what it was trying to do, which I also thought was not so important to do in any case. Some of the longer narrative pieces, for example the Captain's opening soliloquy with his face reproduced on a TV monitor upstage, were too drawn out, given that personage's fundamentally unproblematic character. But on the other hand, the chorus about Hagar that opens Act II, with its magnificent pavane for chorus and dancers, distended the action with just the right degree of accented slowness and formality. It was at this point that I also felt something of the same aesthetic dignity that so distinguishes Gillo Pontecorvo's direction in *The Battle of Algiers,* with his stress on the collective identity (what he calls the *personnage choral*) characterizing all sides of the struggle.

In effect, then, *The Death of Klinghoffer* is grossly political and ideological only in its initial attitude toward the historical givens. The work moves almost quietistically well beyond that in its perception of the Jewish-Palestinian agon, and what it achieves thanks to Sellars's daring is considerable, both in what it risks and in what it gains. The dominant *emotions* of the opera are not strictly speaking political but aesthetic ones, similar to those we derive from Yeats's Byzantium poems or Wallace Stevens's great odes. I suspect that *Klinghoffer* will last as an occasional repertory item, the way Messiaen's *Saint François d'Assise* has lasted, although there is something quite special about this version of the piece, which will only attach to this particular group. Sellars has gotten magnificent performances from Sylvan as Klinghoffer, James Maddalena as the Captain, Eugene Perry as Mamoud (misspelled disastrously), Thomas Young as Molqi (and Jonathan Rumor), Stephanie Friedman as Alma Rumor and as Omar, and Thomas Hammons as "Rambo." There was a special heart-rending precision to Sheila Nadler's final soliloquy as Marilyn Klinghoffer that was formidably moving. And Kent Nagano, the remarkably fluent and responsive conductor, held the music together with singular brilliance. But the evening was really Sellars's, rigorously thought through and luminously realized by his remarkable talents.

CHAPTER 23

Uncertainties of Style
(*The Ghosts of Versailles, Die Soldaten*)

T HE RECENT storm of controversy—first over the "West as America" exhibition at the Smithsonian Institution's National Museum of American Art and later over Oliver Stone's *JFK*—suggests an extraordinary public insecurity about the past. This uneasiness is evident in institutions where public representations of the past are supposed to deliver authoritative images not only of what America is (or was) but also of what America should view or listen to. It is a sure sign of imperial ascendancy in crisis, what with the economy a shambles, the official culture under attack and the old formula about American exceptionalism, innocence and patriotism faring very poorly. Hence, I believe, the need individuals and institutions feel to speak for or against an overriding consensus about America, as if what was at stake were not only a performance or an exhibition but American destiny itself. A wearying, humorless business.

Thus when, after decades of performing no new works, the Metropolitan Opera commissions an opera from composer John Corigliano and his librettist, William Hoffman, it bodes ill. So loaded down with expectations and significance was the enterprise, that when it finally came in December and January the opera lumbered in like a mastodon dressed in a pink tutu. Too long in the planning and writing, *The Ghosts of Versailles* was one of the most unsuccessful spectacles I have ever seen at the Met, incoherent and (literally) preposterous as an idea, undistinguished and mostly forgettable as music, bewilderingly opulent and needlessly elaborate as production. (Not surprisingly, it sold out all performances, partly because of media hype, partly because of rave reviews in the daily press.)

It is somewhere said of Wagner's first (and nonextant) opera that in Acts I and II all the characters are killed, only to return as singing ghosts in

The Nation, March 9, 1992.

Act III. It was booed off the stage and has (rightly) never been performed since. Corigliano and Hoffman have not only emulated but have tried to outdo Wagner's conceit: Their opera is entirely populated by ghosts, from Act I, with its Prologue and five scenes, through Act II, with its nine scenes and finale. I very much admired Andrew Porter's dutiful attempt in *The New Yorker* to make sense of this awful mishmash, but even he is finally defeated by the opera's needless involutions. Suffice it to say that *The Ghosts of Versailles* conceives of late-eighteenth-century French history and culture as suspended in a limbo of wraiths and unhoused plot possibilities, in which Beaumarchais's unfinished *La Mère coupable* (after *The Barber of Seville* and *The Marriage of Figaro)* is a pretext for plots and counterplots involving Almaviva, Figaro and Susanna from the world of imagination, and Beaumarchais, Louis XVI and Marie Antoinette from the real world of history.

Already we can see how ludicrous this is when we note that, as the program coyly puts it, "the characters themselves inhabit a world without boundaries" or, for that matter, without sense—to put it mildly. The point of this exercise rests upon a peculiarly American desire to rewrite and reconcile history: Beaumarchais, the radical (who in one scene prosecutes the Queen), and Marie Antoinette, the archreactionary, are in love. In the final moment of the final scene we see the two in an embrace, stage front, while at the back of the stage the "real" Marie is guillotined. But since they are all ghosts anyway, we suddenly realize that even in the land of ghosts there are classes and degrees of acceptability, real revolution being considerably lower in status than Pollyanna and her chums.

As if all this—with an interminable subplot involving Almaviva's illegitimate child and a rascally revolutionary Begearss (sung to no avail by the formidably capable English tenor Graham Clark)—were not enough, there is an interpolated scene near the middle designed to show eighteenth-century "Turkomania." Here we get Marilyn Horne as Samira, the Ottoman pasha's favorite singer, who disports herself in a disgracefully idiotic caricature of not Turkish but Arabic music, with poorly written and pronounced Arabic words as her text. The scene serves no dramatic or musical purpose but that of sanctioned tastelessness: The Arab/Islamic world, quite bad enough in its present morass, is degraded still further by this utterly silly and confusing scene. Why a great singer like Horne should agree to perform such trash is rather bewildering.

Given all this, the real question is whether any music could be good, or bad, enough. Corigliano produced something perfectly suited to it, which I mean as at best an ambiguous compliment. Admittedly, I saw *The Ghosts of Versailles* only once, but the music was broadcast and I have a tape of it to which I have again and again referred. The music seems to me to be an unhappy mixture of three idioms, none of which has imparted a distinctive and successful aural personality to the whole. First, there is a pastiche of eighteenth-century musical style, using Mozart and his contemporaries as the takeoff point; second, there is American musical-comedy plus Viennese operetta style, carried to parodistically brassy and overassertive lengths; then there is a sort of anonymous late- and postserial modernist idiom, overly dominated by Corigliano's impression of what, say, *Lulu* might be like if its techniques could be recycled in the 1990s. This is eclecticism without definition, one symptom of which is a radical uncertainty about when to end individual arias and scenes. The only sizable orchestral interlude occurs in the second act, which suggests that Corigliano was afraid to risk music that wasn't serviceably tied to the action; that interlude is tame stuff indeed, gray and on the whole fairly nondescript.

What makes the opera's weaknesses especially apparent is the enormously lavish scale of the production. It would be hard to fault any of the singers—Teresa Stratas, Hakan Hagegard, Clark, Horne and Gino Quilico, among others—who seemed always to be struggling to find conviction enough to get over the ordeal. But the sets are big and expensive, the production values very much those of Hollywood, and the careening and inane energy of the whole is such as to tug orchestra and cast remorselessly through one hoop after another. I have no doubt that Corigliano, Hoffman and James Levine (the conductor) are gifted and serious artists, but there is something so willfully misconceived and overdone about the enterprise as to beggar even their talents. For in the end we are talking about an operatic production designed to woo the audience not so much with the work itself but with the power of an institution important enough to mount so lavish and expensive a theatrical evening, then to call it a "new opera," all without a hint of irony.

Yet *The Ghosts of Versailles* sits right next to the Met's extraordinary *Idomeneo*, which I saw scarcely a week before. *Idomeneo* is one of Mozart's least tractable works, an *opera seria* of great length, considerable musical complexity and quite impressive vocal difficulty. Levine conducted the performance without a single false moment or imprecise inflection. The plot of *Idomeneo* spins out from the Trojan War and involves an unengaging mix of melodramatic heroics and very stylized situations that out-Glucks Gluck, so to speak. Luciano Pavarotti has made a specialty of the title role, with wonderful results (at least to a non-Pavarotti fan like myself). He did not sing in the performance I attended, the role being taken creditably by the Canadian Ben Heppner, who is a slowly emerging *Heldentenor* with a tendency to be less expressive and various than his excellent voice would otherwise allow. Dawn Upshaw sang Ilia wonderfully, as did the very elegant Susanne Mentzer as Ida-mante. In the third big female role of the opera, Carol Vaness as Elettra got off to a somewhat shrieky start but brought down the house in her big third-act aria, with brilliance and passion combined in rare measure.

What one senses in the striking disparity between *Idomeneo* and *The Ghosts of Versailles* is not only the major discrepancy in the quality of the music but also the Met's institutional commitment to its role not simply as an important opera house but as the opera house of record. When it comes to what are in effect museum pieces—which, for all its grandeur and splendid music, *Idomeneo* is—the mandate is curatorial, and even antiquarian. This has marred the Met's *Ring* productions, as well as last spring's *Parsifal,* which Levine conducted as if he were disinterring, rather than enlivening and animating, the music. Happily for *Idomeneo,* a period piece even in Mozart's time, the Met's approach works. But when it comes to contemporary work, or operas that might be interpreted as having something urgent to say to contemporary audiences, style, decor and production lose the effect of a direct and forceful statement and become instead either parody or a jumble of loose ends. As a whole *The Ghosts of Versailles* is far from being just a screwball effort to redo the French Revolution, to wish publicly that it never happened; it is also an opera meant to be uncontroversial, dealing only with ghosts, lackluster fictions, costumed put-ons who are so distanced and alienating as in the end to be almost completely unaffecting. Thus opera is shoved even further back from relevance or contemporary culture, which has the effect of saying that art ought to be as incoherent and as unchallenging to the status quo as possible. No wonder, therefore, that it was the Met that commissioned *Ghosts* and no wonder that all the opera's much-ado was finally rendered so inoffensive and trivial.

At an almost exactly opposite pole was the City Opera's *Die Soldaten,* an opera completed in the mid-1960s by the German composer Bernd Alois Zimmerman and performed first in this country in Boston by Sarah Caldwell in 1982. City's production last October was, I think, one of its triumphs, not because of the opera itself but because as a sort of junior varsity house, City could devote itself seriously to the work and not worry too much about the politically correct position for a major opera company of record to take. It seems grimly objectionable to mention that *Die Soldaten*'s composer committed suicide shortly after finishing the work, but it really is relevant. My impression is that Zimmerman took seriously Berg's achievements in *Wozzeck* and *Lulu,* and tried to build a work on that achievement. The result is a huge cinematic composition of unrelieved darkness and a kind of unforgiving grandeur that requires not only a large number of extremely skillful singers but an enormous orchestra of more than 100 musicians.

The story is based on a work by Jakob Lenz, an eighteenth-century writer who greatly impressed Büchner (indeed, there's a marvelous story by Büchner called "Lenz"), which Zimmerman turns into a weird combination of both *Lulu* and *Wozzeck*: the degradation of Zimmerman's Marie and her ordeals as enacted in a setting of soldiers' barracks and heartless commercialism. Rhoda Levine's production is brilliantly designed, and so overpoweringly theatrical as to submit the audience to trial by intensity. Among the many superb performers, Lisa Saffer as Marie was in a class by herself: Unfailingly effective, she sang the fearsomely difficult part without a hesitant note or accent—true, direct, lyrical. It is not entirely a coincidence that two of the best male performers—Thomas Young and Eugene Perry—are Peter Sellars regulars, who did remarkable things in *Die Soldaten*.

I said above that the opera was at an exactly opposite pole from *The Ghosts of Versailles.* Except for a couple of very Berg-like moments when he quotes a Bach chorale, Zimmerman, because he is so single-minded and undramatic, is a deeply flawed composer. Doubtless if one were to study the gigantic score there would be niceties and refinements to be discerned. But the general sense it delivers is unmistakably that of a man mirroring his pain and anguish directly onto a musical style uninflected, untempered by anything except anger and despair. In one of the program supplements for City Opera's production a commentator denies this, claiming that far from supplying "overkill" Zimmerman's music provides evidence that the composer was a "master of restraint." This is patently untrue. Were it not for the skill and beauty of Lisa Saffer's presence you would not be able to hear much except heaps upon piles of densely aggressive sonorities; these are immediately expressive, directly, even blatantly, programmatic. The world is horrible, people are shits, innocence cannot, must not survive. Whether this ludicrously reductive *Weltanschauung* is musically boring because we've heard too much twelve-tone expressionism or seen too many horror movies with manipulative soundtracks, it is hard to tell. But *Die Soldaten* tries with all its force and resonances to leap across the proscenium and beat up the audience, a sort of crudely overdone naturalism without enough of a redeeming and clarifying aesthetic. It makes for satisfying a morbid curiosity and then moving on gratefully to performances of other music.

Which brings me at last to two exceptionally satisfying concert performances in recent months, vitally different in most ways, yet sharing a similar coherence of style and conception. I have been listening to the pianist Shura Cherkassky for about thirty years. Oddly enough, however, I have not listened much to his recordings, nor, given his Slavic (as opposed to Central European) pedigree, has he seemed to me to be interestingly at work in the repertory that I am most concerned with: Thus the Chopin, Beethoven and Brahms that often dot his programs seem put there largely to offset the Balakirev and showy Liszt pieces that have been his hallmark. A student of Josef Hofmann—a wonderful piano "great," although in my opinion a mystifyingly sanctified one, since there are only a small number of recordings around—Cherkassky is now 80. He has always been amusing to watch, what with his fussy little gestures, his often cutesy virtuosity, his seemingly unrestricted capacity to amuse and delight his audiences. Yet when he appeared at Carnegie Hall in December there was an effect rather like an epiphany that came from his playing, particularly in works (the Bach-Busoni Chaconne, the Schumann Symphonic Etudes, the Chopin E Major Scherzo) that are now encrusted with the habits and fake traditions of overuse and familiarity. I was reminded of the experience of watching the class clown suddenly turn in an academic performance of such sober mastery as to knock you back.

Part of the surprise was that Cherkassky had lost most of his distracting mannerisms, and with that had gained an unexpected gravity and seriousness of focus. There were moments in the middle variations where I felt that Schumann's obsessive insistence caused Cherkassky to lose his concentration, as if the illogical accents and numbing patterns bothered, or temporarily grounded, him. But in the Busoni, which he took at an unusually slow tempo, there was a robustness and rounded tonal beauty to the whole that made you actually see the stunning elaborations developing out of Bach's formal germ, as well as Busoni's exceptionally intelligent pianistic transformation of what had once been a violin piece. So too in the opening sections of the Schumann, as well as the Chopin Scherzo, where the fantastic lightness of the work, with its ascending and then downward echoing chordal progressions, kept returning with a graceful nonchalance very rarely attempted, much less encountered. Cherkassky returned to his customary repertoire with dashingly entertaining performances of difficult display pieces by Hofmann and Paul Pabst; the latter's paraphrase on themes from Tchaikovsky's *Eugene Onegin* belongs to the category of virtuoso pieces (e.g., the Schulz-Evler *Blue Danube*) that sound as if they could not be learned but have to be elegantly tossed off with a constant apprehension of imminent catastrophe.

You wouldn't want to say that Cherkassky is a Richter or a Michelangeli; he isn't. But when he plays he never seems worried that he might not be making an important statement about history, or that he is only a pianist doing his work. For that, quite without any embarrassment, is what he is, a pianist caught up in his job, without too many irrelevancies or pomposities. Cherkassky is genuine, attractive, persuasive. He shares this talent with the other musician recently in town, Robert Shaw, who at 75 is just as amazingly durable.

Shaw gained prominence in the 1950s, although during that period I attended only one of his performances with the Robert Shaw Chorale. He first came to attention as Toscanini's chorus director for the NBC Symphony, with results in intonation and virtuosity that are still unmatched, particularly in hitherto unperformed or very difficult works. Like Cherkassky he harks back to an earlier, less culturally pretentious time, when music making derived mainly from amateur singing, four-hand piano playing at home and the much awaited weekly broadcasts of the New York Philharmonic and the Metropolitan Opera. This was well before the days of ubiquitous "good music stations," and before the time when it became fashionable to assume that important cultural institutions were vehicles for the nation's identity.

There is something so irrefrangibly modest about Shaw's manner that you think it's all an act, like Rudolf Serkin's way of walking on to the stage somehow plaintively and apologetically. Although Shaw conducted the Atlanta Symphony for a couple of decades the job wasn't *supposed* to be significant, so his achievements were not really noticed. After he retired he started doing more recording and appearing with other orchestras across the country, where I have heard him on several occasions. On January 19 he was at Carnegie Hall leading the Orchestra of St. Luke's, a remarkably fine Robert Shaw Festival Chorus and excellent soloists—soprano Benita Valente, mezzo Florence Quivar, tenor Neil Rosenshein and bass Alistair Miles—in the *Missa Solemnis,* precisely the work for which, under Toscanini, his choral preparation had been the most impressive ever recorded.

It was certainly the finest performance of the piece that I have heard since Toscanini, and yet it could not have been more different. The *Missa* has been brilliantly characterized by Adorno in a famous essay as an "alienated masterpiece," that is, a work whose eccentricity, musical intractability and transcendental conception have never really been accommodated to the musical canon. It is also a very difficult piece to perform, full of abrupt changes in tempo and volume for musicians to negotiate, unfamiliar modal harmonies and, especially in the immense Credo, extremely complex fugal writing characteristic of the Hammerklavier Sonata and the Diabelli Variations, among other late Beethoven pieces. Yet although the *Missa Solemnis* typifies the *Spätstil* or late style, which Adorno says was symbolic of Beethoven's rejection of the ordinary bourgeois world, one can also hear in these forbidding works a search for order and reliability. Maynard Solomon in his *Beethoven Essays* ventures the more personal thesis that the *Missa Solemnis* and the Ninth Symphony reflect Beethoven's declining health, his problems with his nephew and of course his horrific sense of personal loneliness; far from rejecting the world, they are attempts musically to come to new terms with it. "The *Missa Solemnis*," says Solomon, "has the implication of a double question to the deity: Am I merely mortal? Is there hope for eternal life?"

Naturally enough, the interrogatory music of this towering work can be given variously freighted interpretations. What was so impressive about Shaw's was that it was thoroughly, perhaps even insistently, unneurotic. A recent recording of the work by Karajan (EMI) attempts the same feat, with the unintended effect, however, of rendering the music self-satisfied, muddy, sleekly placid. Shaw's energy was focused less on startling detail than on creating a collective personality, that of a traveler perhaps, or of a questing pilgrim. The sounds and tempi were robust, never nervous or querulous. One felt in his conducting something often tried by younger conductors seeking an impression of elevated tranquillity, but rarely achieved. He also gained the illusion of complete naturalness, so that even in perilous spots like the devilish fugue at the end of the Credo, or in the perhaps more difficult Benedictus, whose soaringly serene lines defy normal intonation, Shaw let the music unfold, rather than declaim or announce itself. This is a total illusion, of course, since what goes into such sounds is immense work, manifestly concealed.

He had the soloists sit up near the chorus, at some distance from stage front, which is where they are usually placed. This somewhat took away from the bass's contribution, but it did contribute to the communal and associative effort of the whole. At only one point—in the Benedictus's extended violin obbligato played decently if somewhat monochromatically by Naoko Tanaka—did I feel that what was needed was a bit more striving and less natural-sounding tranquillity; as with much of Beethoven's late music written in a very high register, sublimity and a tense eeriness are its true hallmark, and it sounds merely awkward when it is played too unexcitedly.

Shaw's musical, or rather platform, presence suggests a saintly, incredibly modest man. Accordingly, he takes curtain calls from the back rows of the orchestra, as if to say it's not me, it's all of us, and Beethoven, of course. A bit corny perhaps, but the iron rigor of his performances shouldn't be underestimated either. He is the real thing, a great musician whose avoidance of self-conscious display sets him at odds with the Zubin Mehtas of this world. Perhaps you can do what he does if you are not entrusted with safekeeping a national institution like the Met or the Philharmonic, where you have to take positions about "us" every time you lift your arms or blow your nose. The peculiar thing about Shaw is that, unlike Celibidache, another older conductor of extraordinary attainments and uncompromising standards, he does not communicate marginality or irrelevance. It is as if the music were simply expressing itself. This is the finest aesthetic illusion of all.

CHAPTER 24

Musical Retrospection

ANDRÁS SCHIFF, the remarkable Hungarian pianist, dedicated his February Avery Fisher Hall recital to the memory of Rudolf Serkin, who had died the previous year. Along with the recent passing of Vladimir Horowitz, Claudio Arrau and Wilhelm Kempff, Serkin's death represents the end of a musical era that had gloriously survived World War II. Music and mourning are frequently allied, but it was during the nineteenth century that the art of mortuary music really became an important and independent genre (yet to be studied as such). The difference between Mozart's "Trauermusik" (K.477, composed in 1785) and, two decades later the second movement of Beethoven's "Eroica" Symphony (1806) is dramatic: Whereas Mozart's work is a formally circumscribed piece tied to Masonic ritual, Beethoven's is a long, expressionistic outpouring of grief, disciplined into a demonstration of compositional independence. Out of the Eroica's *marcia funebre* there developed a Romantic music of personal lament à la Werther, with various major composers—Liszt, Berlioz, Wagner, Chopin, Bruckner and Strauss, among others—using the themes of loss, funerary solitude and despair to extravagant lengths, always attesting, ironically enough, to the composer's virtuosity and originality.

This rather strange partnership between sorrow and musical ingenuity heightens the deeper paradox that music is an art of expression without the capacity to say denotatively and concretely what is being expressed. In a sense, therefore, all music is only about music, and this is the inherent tragedy of musical eloquence; no wonder that when we think of Orpheus, the mythical embodiment of music, we see him mourning the death of Eurydice, which he causes by looking back at her. The sadder the music, then, the closer it comes to metamusic, music confined to itself, meditating on itself, mourning the loss of its object.

Schiff's recital demonstrated how this plight needn't necessarily be an occasion for extended breast-beating. On the contrary, it was a stunning exercise in intellectual meditation occasioned not so much by recollections of Serkin's playing but by that Central European pianist's affiliation with a particular kind of learned and even antiquarian music. The two major pieces on the program, both Serkin specialties, were Max Reger's rarely played *Variations and Fugue on a Theme by J. S. Bach* and Brahms's *Variations and Fugue on a Theme by Handel.* By way of contrast, Schiff began the program by playing a Bach French Suite and, just before the Brahms, Handel's variations on the very theme that was to serve Brahms. Schiff's memorial to Serkin therefore emphasized the inner logic by which late-nineteenth-century Western tonal music was condemned to a kind of archaizing, self-referential, overindulgent pleasure, very much like the concert occasion itself. Reger's idiom in 1904 is a step further into this labyrinth than Brahms's in 1861–62: Reger's variations grow successively more complex and outré until the closing fugue, which is scarcely comprehensible harmonically, so rich and cross-referenced has its harmony and rhythmic structure become. Thus everything in the recital referred back to a precedent that it could never quite recover: Schiff to Serkin, Brahms to Handel, Reger to Bach, variations to theme and so forth with a dizzying, extraordinarily pleasurable effect.

Even for such a brilliant performer as Schiff this program was exceptionally rewarding. He follows very much in Glenn Gould's footsteps as a Bach executant, although in adopting Gould's apparently "objective"—that is, staccato, unpianistic—approach, he reveals Bach's keyboard music to be more lyrical and emotive than Gould did. This quite conscious abjuring of lyricism accounts for the underlying tension in Gould's playing, but in Schiff's case the warmth of tone and relative unfussiness of attack are more catholic, more adaptable to different styles even than Gould's. Schiff, in short, is not an eccentric like Gould any more than he is an extroverted pianist in the Rubinstein mold. He is a fundamentally restrained and un-theatrical pianist, despite his formidable technical prowess. What especially moved me about his recital was that he made his points not rhetorically, as if accosting and trying to impress his audience, but very much inside and with the music. Thus the Reger and Brahms works came across as the products of late (even perhaps decadent) polyphonic composers, desperately trying to preserve the German contrapuntal tradition, forced to greater and greater ingenuity in their strettos, running three, four, even five phrases together, which in the end produces a complexity of effect too great for the

tonal system and its conventional rhythmic organization. Played after Re-
ger, Brahms's *Handel Variations* emerged as a true forerunner of twentieth-
century polytonalism. This, after all, is how Schönberg saw Brahms. As for
Reger, a composer who is very much un-listened to and uncared for today,
Schiff's performance restored him to the pianistic canon, as it also recalled
Serkin's presence as an archaic classicist in American concert life.

One other piano recital shared with Schiff's an intellectual and even
metaphysical interest unique in a season afflicted with idiotic bravura
playing that was too often pressed into the service of utterly conventional
programs (how many "safe" Schubert and Beethoven sonatas can one hear
without hating the whole lot?). I heard Russell Sherman for the first time
this March, in a recital given at the Kathryn Bache Miller Theater at Columbia University. As befits a performer with so unusual and compelling
a musical profile, there were a considerable number of pianists in the audience. Sherman apparently specializes in music difficult on technical as
well as stylistic grounds: In this instance he performed not, only Liszt's
"Réminiscences de Don Juan," an impossible waterfall of nervous octaves,
thirds and chromatic runs, but also the First Sonata (1930) by Roger Sessions and, most wonderfully, Book II of Debussy's *Preludes.*

The quality of Sherman's playing is suggested in a long interview he gave
as part of a book about and by Edward Steuermann, the Schönberg pro-
tégé and Busoni student who for years taught piano at Juilliard (I studied
with him for a brief period in the late 1950s). *The Not Quite Innocent By-
stander* (University of Nebraska, 1989) went completely unnoticed by the
press, even though it is not only of significant historical but also musical
interest. Sherman describes Steuermann's pedagogic techniques as stress-
ing the *disabilities* of the piano as a musical instrument and the need for
tactical, presentational and illusionary maneuvers by the pianist in order
to deliver a secret message while playing a piece in concert. This is a pretty
reductive account of a very long and sophisticated exchange about Steuermann between Sherman and Gunther Schuller, but it serves as an index
of Sherman's own style as a pianist: immense skill in playing *and* thought
about the work, not as enhancements or distractions of the virtuoso's role
but as a way of getting the work across like a series of thoughts—that is,
intelligently, consistently, organically. At the same time one felt with his
performance of the Liszt and Debussy (the Sessions was, I thought, mercilessly exposed as an unsuccessful period piece) that there might have
been such a message had the music been able to speak directly. Without
that faculty the largely commemorative and re-creative techniques of the
pianist were what one was left with: a reaching out, and then a kind of wise
despondency.

The effect of Sherman's playing furnishes an exact contrast with Maurizio Pollini's, once the most prodigiously enjoyable of performers but now, as demonstrated by the first of his two March Carnegie Hall recitals, a painfully unenjoyable, even downright nasty, version of his earlier self. The program was simple but substantial: the Schubert opus posthumous late B-flat sonata, followed by the twelve Chopin Études, Opus 10. It would be hard to imagine that often clumsy and uneven sonata played worse. Slow, gigantically portentous, repetitive and pedantic in his playing, Pollini produced a rendition of almost frightening boredom, as if to say, "I can play even more soberly and seriously than Brendel and Schnabel." Whereupon he turned on the Chopin Études with an appalling display of bad-tempered virtuosity, in which each of these astonishing pieces was mercilessly skewered, hammered, stomped on. Nearly everything was too loud and too fast; flurries of muffed passages alternated with inexplicably obtrusive, poorly conceived bursts of real bravura. As in his recital last year, Pollini now gives the impression of someone uninvolved in his playing, his extraordinary gifts adrift in an aimless wash of clangorous sound.

I say this with considerable sadness and perplexity. Pollini was one of the great pianists of the age, yet he is now strangely unpleasant to listen to; one senses boredom, anger and frustration at the routine of playing endless recitals, plus an overall loss of purpose that is quite depressing. The difference between him and Sherman (or Schiff) is that he seems unable to inform his playing with a *project*, a reflective and partly extra-musical rationale for what is at bottom only a form of muscular prowess. Both Schiff and Sherman put together programs with a narrative purpose in mind—commemorative, philosophical or historical, broadly referential—so that even the relatively anodyne procedures of the concert platform can seem invested with ideas beyond the plainly evident procedure of traipsing through a set of very well-known musical masterpieces. Such rare pianists as Schiff and Sherman are dramatic without being theatrical in their interpretations, which is to say that between the inescapably physical art of mastering the keyboard and the audience, they interpose a body of tempering, self-conscious thought that frames the concert interestingly, thereby presenting it as something more than a feat of freakish acrobatics.

It is Joseph Horowitz's argument in his recent books on Toscanini and piano competitions that the requirements of the marketplace have a direct effect on musical performance. For, he argues, not only do musicians answer to the demands of sponsors, managers and record companies, they also adapt their playing in conformity with what is perceived as acceptable (or safe) styles, repertories and careers. Following on his books, Horowitz had the witty idea of scheduling a series of recitals by competition losers at

New York's 92nd Street Y. I was able to make only the one by Van Cliburn Competition nonwinner Pedro Burmester, a Portuguese pianist of considerable talent, whose main work was the *Goldberg Variations*. I found his playing extremely convincing, with a quirky, highly individualistic intelligence that gives one the impression of a style of performance depending on his own (as opposed to received) ideas. Whereas most performances of the *Goldberg* attempt a unifying conception of the whole, Burmester's emphasized the atomistic quality of the work, each of the thirty variations remaining a monad that implied, but was not explicitly connected with, all the others. One hopes that Burmester will soon be back.

Market requirements of course bring to mind that citadel of unresolved corporate and aesthetic interest, the Metropolitan Opera, whose spring 1992 season saw a return of James Levine's musical realization of *Parsifal,* Wagner's last and arguably his most problematic opera. I saw, but did not write about, Levine's 1991 *Parsifal,* which had the disadvantage of Jessye Norman as Kundry, a role for which, as actress and stage presence, she is most unsuited. Norman is a marvelous singer and musician whose prodigious talent is now so bogged down in a confusion of wrong styles, wrong parts, wrong personae (her ghastly and almost totally unnecessary affectations are by now seriously getting in the way of her remarkable voice) as to make her presence on the operatic stage sometimes painful to watch. This year Levine had the compelling Waltraud Meier, an artist of great cultivation and sensually dark-hued voice. In a sense Meier had two things to battle besides the role's impossible difficulties (Kundry, after all, is both saint and whore, and those who play her have to switch back and forth between the two as well as manage a great deal of mysterious stillness)—first, Levine's exaggeratedly slow tempo, and second, a production of almost laughable vulgarity. She acquitted herself brilliantly, I thought, although then she appeared at Carnegie Hall in May with Levine and the Met Orchestra in Mahler's *Das Lied von der Erde,* she was unable to do the same, so poorly did Levine's nonchalant and unbalanced conducting serve her.

Parsifal belongs to a genre that can be (and has been by Adorno in a fine essay) called Late, that is, recapitulatory, autumnal, given to great simplicity and confounding complexity at the same time. Wagner's harmonic style is both archaic and very advanced, a sort of uneasy compromise between *Die Meistersinger* and *Tristan,* with a lot of maddening Holy-Grail-and-Christ religiosity and not always convincing pseudoprofundity going along with the music. The trouble with Levine as a Wagnerian conductor has always been his tendency to confuse ponderousness with seriousness, so that during the Vorspiel or Prologue to *Parsifal* his extreme deliberation virtually pulled the music out of shape, leveling Wagner's carefully written dotted rhythms in the melody so badly as to give them no profile at all.

Levine's cast had a hard time of it. Last year's Robert Lloyd was more affecting as Gurnemanz than this year's Kurt Moll, a good singer whose sodden and muffled accents in the part were evidence of falling prey to Levine's heaviness. Both productions were fortunate in their brave tenor heads: Domingo last year, Siegfried Jerusalem this year. Domingo's is the better, if more flashy, voice; Jerusalem's is the more fully comprehended dramatic realization. What one missed more than anything else about this set of *Parsifals* was some glimmering of self-consciousness, which is certainly there in the work to be teased out, but cannot be seen if mawkish reverence is all you want a production to communicate. *Parsifal's* concern with the miraculous (and with magic) is all-pervasive, in Klingsor's lair as well as in the weird subtlety of Wagner's retrospective meditation on his own successes and power (much as Yeats does it in "The Circus Animal's Desertion"), but the work also expresses a tinge of self-deflation best rendered in modern productions that employ some parody and a bit of deliberate hokiness in staging. All this was lost in the suffocating absence of even a glimpse of theatrical intelligence.

There was a good deal of that in the John Dexter production of Benjamin Britten's *Billy Budd,* with libretto (courtesy of Melville) by E. M. Forster. The performance was conducted by Charles Mackerras, the itinerant Australian whose work one is normally at least grateful to have, but which I have always found curiously unsatisfying (I've written about him here as a Mozart and Janáček specialist). The overall problem with this otherwise creditable production was its evenness, the absence in it of great heights, gripping drama, brilliantly crafted moments. Thomas Hampson, who sang Billy, is one of the hottest baritones around, much in demand as a Rossini and lieder singer; he is accomplished, reliable, ingratiating. Neither he nor the usually powerful Graham Clark, as Captain Vere, seemed in Act II (the killing of Claggart, Billy's sentencing and execution) to be about the problems of good and evil, moral responsibility and, above all, death. Here competence and sheer professionalism kept things going, not—as Britten's penetratingly psychological music intended—a probingly passionate experience of these momentous problems. As for Claggart, James Morris, he was his usual monochromatic self, a singer with an undoubtedly interesting voice but whose dramatic understanding (to say nothing of his delivery) of major roles, including Wagner's Wotan, is depressingly subpar, with poor diction and wooden gestures undermining even the massive nobility of his voice.

The retrospective and commemorative aspects inherent in much music and therefore in any musical season were compounded by the Rossini and

Mozart celebrations that dragged on, I thought, unreasonably. I exclude from the general complaint an amusing omnibus concert of Rossini arias designed by Philip Gossett and well executed by a cast of the usual suspects (Hampson, Marilyn Horne, Samuel Ramey, June Anderson, et al.) at Avery Fisher Hall. With the exception of the fourteen-part "Gran Pezzo Concertato" from Rossini's masterpiece, *Il Viaggio a Reims,* the program featured a series of snippets very difficult to concentrate on, unless I turned my faculties off and listened to what in effect was a Rossini hit parade, hardly a commemoration of the great man's almost unbelievably prolific melodic and dramatic genius.

A more fitting occasion for celebrating his gifts was afforded New York by Riccardo Muti's final Carnegie Hall concert with the Philadelphia Orchestra, in which Rossini's *Stabat Mater* was performed along with Cherubini's Symphony in D major. Clever idea, to put the two great Italian Parisians next to each other on a program conducted by another expatriate Italian; in addition, it allowed me to gauge the vast improvement in Muti's skills since he conducted the Philadelphia in the Mozart C minor mass during its first Carnegie Hall season a decade ago. Slick, operatic and showy Muti still is, but he has become a fastidious disciplinarian, and an expert shaper of orchestral and choral sound. The *Stabat Mater* is a direct antecedent of Verdi's *Requiem;* like the *Requiem* it requires tremendous power and dark brilliance of execution which only Carol Vaness, of the four soloists, was able to give.

Lastly, in an often melancholy season of retrospection, commemoration and mourning, it was particularly fitting that William Christie's company, Les Arts Florissants, reperformed its revival of Jean-Baptiste Lully's *Atys* at the Brooklyn Academy of Music last March. Like Rossini and Cherubini a century and a half later, Lully was a French-Italian composer celebrated in Louis XIV's court as an early master of opera, but he has largely remained unperformed (except for some instrumental music) until Christie undertook this *Atys.* I am not an early-and-authentic-performance fan myself, but I found this occasion irresistible. After a steady diet of overly emotive late-nineteenth- and early-twentieth-century operas, the finicky, mannered and comically overdressed style adopted by Christie provided many pleasures. Not the least of these was a sustained contrast between the drama's violent passion—Atys is loved by the jealous goddess Cybele, who instead of presiding over his marriage to Sangaride renders him so mad as to kill the poor girl unwittingly—and Lully's perversely subdued and restrained music. All artifice and decorum, Christie's fine company is of course restricted in scope by works like *Atys,* but the remorselessly hierarchical and elitist conception of opera that *Atys* embodies does remind one that the social origins of opera were decidedly unpopular, and forbiddingly stylized to boot. Christie himself is an accomplished harpsichordist, abetted by some first-rate singers—in particular Howard Cook as Atys, Monique Zanetti as Sangaride and Guillemette Laurens as Cybele—plus a flawless group of dancers and instrumentalists. All in all it was the unashamed aesthetic preciosity of the piece that one responded to, not its vision of things. And, like András Schiff's pianism, it proves that great effects can be made by understatement.

CHAPTER 25

The Bard Festival

MOST SUMMER music festivals originate in celebration and commemoration that later harden into routine and become unashamed touristic promotion. This has certainly been true of Salzburg, which began (as Michael Steinberg's book on its origins amply shows) as a Mozart festival whose aim in the post-World War I period was to revitalize the idea of Austria as the home of a Catholic Baroque world view and to give Austria a new sense of international mission. The works of Mozart, von Hofmannsthal and Richard Strauss were the core of its repertory and, until World War II, it succeeded quite brilliantly albeit not on the grandiose scale imagined by its founder. After the war it was hijacked by Herbert von Karajan for his self-glorification. As a student I attended the Salzburg Festival once (in 1958), and although impressed with the remarkable level of performances—in the course of a week I heard Karajan do *Fidelio* and the Verdi *Requiem*, Karl Böhm do *Così fan tutte* with Elisabeth Schwarzkopf and Christa Ludwig, Dimitri Mitropoulos conduct Barber's *Vanessa* and a superb Brahms concert with the Vienna Philharmonic and Zino Francescatti, plus recitals by Glenn Gould and Dietrich Fischer-Dieskau—I could already sense the degree of alienating opulence and reactionary as well as pointless display toward which it was tending. Thereafter, unless you were a corporate C.E.O. or a German banker, Salzburg was simply out of reach, dominated entirely by Karajan's imperiousness and cold arrogance. Reports about the new regime started this year by Gérard Mortier suggest a different although unclear tack, with a healthy dose of avant-garde works (e.g., Peter Sellars's 1992 production of Messiaen's opera *St. Francis*) played there for the first time.

The Nation, January 25, 1993.

Six years ago I reported here about the Santa Fe Opera, where I heard an interesting performance of Strauss's basically unperformed opera *Die ägyptische Helena* and (for me at least) the altogether less interesting Monteverdi *L'Incoronazione di Poppea.* I returned in 1992 for Gay and Pepusch's *The Beggar's Opera* (1728) and Strauss's *Der Rosenkavalier,* both of which received competent if uninspiring realizations. *The Beggar's Opera* is rarely encountered these days, largely because its music consists of arias and ensembles that are either too slight and unsustained, or because in some way they are only orchestrated folk songs, neither category of which is considered to be interesting enough for conventional opera companies; besides, Gay's plot is deliberately provocative and even insulting to middle-class audiences since it treats thieves, pimps, corrupt politicians with a jolly naturalness completely devoid of either cant or hypocrisy. Brecht and Weill constructed *The Threepenny Opera* out of the eighteenth-century work, and that isn't accorded many performances nowadays either. Benjamin Britten did a fascinating modern version of *The Beggar's Opera,* but like the others it is scarcely ever performed; it was given one of its rare realizations last summer at the Aldeburgh Festival, which Britten himself founded.

Santa Fe entrusted the musical end of things to Nicholas McGegan, who conducted, played continuo and edited the score with elegance and economy. The problem, however, lay elsewhere. When you try to put on an early-eighteenth-century opera you really have only two options: to do it in straight period style with its eighteenth-century qualities and limitations emphasized with preciosity and in as mannered a way as possible; or the reverse, to do it as a twentieth-century, up-to-date work that just happens to have been written by an eighteenth-century composer. Peter Sellars has mastered the latter option, Nicholas Hytner the former (in, for example, his recent English National Opera production of Handel's *Xerxes).* To try to mix them up, to take a little from this and a little from that, is to have the worst of both worlds, achieving little more than an occasional archness of tone, or a quick gag or two. This in effect was what was wrong with Christopher Aiden's direction of *The Beggar's Opera* at Santa Fe. The characters wore eighteenth-century costumes on which twentieth-century additions had been imposed (sneakers, for instance, or Gloria Swanson cigarette holders; the writer-narrator pecked at a typewriter wearing an eyeshade straight out of *The Front Page).* They made twentieth-century gestures, their accents covered the spectrum from Alabama to Queens, and all in all they seemed too self-conscious to pull off the trick. Thus do actors flounder, when they are not wallowing, in that state of nondescript in-betweenness that passes for stylish comedy on far too many U.S. stages. And to make matters even more incoherent, Macheath (James Michael

McGuire) belonged to one school of acting, the excellent Lisa Saffer as Jenny Diver to quite another.

It isn't that I am against contradictory or even confusing impulses in an opera production, but one has to feel that they are about something, or that they contribute to an overall effect or series of effects. While it is true that Paul Steinberg's scene design was ingenious—the set was divided by a diagonal that gave a long corridor-like slant to entrances and exits and also focused the action on a fraction of the stage—it was difficult to know what the production intended. From being a satire on the middle classes in its original form, *The Beggar's Opera* became an inconsequential and basically inoffensive spectacle, neither politically engaging nor particularly memorable. As for *Rosenkavalier*, that was both conventional and soporific in the extreme: I did not stay past Act II.

Santa Fe proves that summer festivals can all too easily lose their intellectual and aesthetic purpose and become occasions for a routine display of wares, without much in the way of audience satisfaction except for an evening's show. All festivals, in short, should require something more from their audiences besides the price of a ticket and stupefied silence. The only summer festival I know of that consciously tries to do more both for and with an audience is the one that has been put on for the past three years at Bard College, with its events concentrated into two August weekends. It was begun in 1990 by Leon Botstein, the president of Bard, working with Sarah Rothenberg, a fine pianist and member of the Bard faculty. Each year's festival is devoted to one composer (Brahms in 1990, Mendelssohn in 1991), and participants are drawn from the New York City musical world, mostly young musicians who play in the Metropolitan and City Opera orchestras, as well as a handful of young pianists and vocalists who have made a career of playing unusual repertory, chamber music and of course the standard classics. The key to the Bard Festival is the conviction that audiences want to listen to a lot of music (ten of twelve concerts over four or five days), but also want to interact with it intelligently. Thus each concert is preceded by a lecture; there are numerous panel discussions with accredited experts and musicians; and performers, panelists and audience have many opportunities to talk with one another during the festival. The result is quite unique. There is a sense of continuity throughout; the distance between performers and listeners is pretty much broken down; above all, one has an experience of having lived through a composer's work not as an alienated consumer but as a directly involved and constantly informed contemporary.

This year's composer was Richard Strauss (1864–1949), a highly problematic and extremely complex instance of an artist who not only lived through most musical innovations of the period, roughly speaking, from

Brahms and Wagner to Boulez and Cage, but also kept his idiom tonal and his style high-Romantic, as if oblivious to everything around him; Glenn Gould called him the greatest musical personality of the twentieth century precisely for that reason, although an estimable segment of the musical intelligentsia still considers Strauss an overrated, uninspired throwback, an opportunist and a lifeless imitator of real musical thought. Nor is this the only controversy surrounding Strauss. He was one of the leading musical figures under the Third Reich (Wilhelm Furtwängler was another) who remained in Germany right through its ugliest period and somehow managed to survive, although not without recriminations and accusations that characterize him as collaborator, accomplice, immoral spectator. Furtwängler was apparently more honorable when it came to helping Jewish musicians than Strauss, but the controversy still rages and in Strauss's case—unlike Furtwängler's, about whose tremendous conducting talents there is no significant doubt—involves the complaisance, so to speak, of his music as well. Can one argue, for instance, that Strauss's refusal of twelve-tone music was morally equivalent to hanging in with the old order, whose symbols were of course Hitler and Wagner? Or, following current modes of inquiry regarding the pristine detachment of the artwork, are we to think of Strauss only as a musician, whose sordid ties with the Nazi musical establishment are relevant to operas like *Capriccio*, written in 1942?

These questions came up here and there throughout the festival but nothing conclusive can be reported. Strauss, I think, is an enigma whose music as Gould argued, seems to express an ecstatic indifference to everything around him, both in music and society. That is one definitely problematic point. Another slightly more invidious, is that cultural and musical criticism at present have nothing like the instruments adequate for considerations of complicity, collaboration or involvement as between art and politics. During the Bard Festival, the most sustained efforts at such an investigation were Michael Steinberg's interventions in print and viva voce as participant in panels and as lecturer. The festival produced a volume of critical essays as a companion to the music, and in that context Steinberg's contribution was quite disappointing. I have extravagant admiration for his talents as cultural historian and as critic (witness my numerous comments here and elsewhere in regard to his book about the Salzburg Festival), but I felt curiously let down by his essay, which seemed to me to try unconvincingly to link Strauss's music directly if not to Nazism then to questions about it. He tried the same task during his spoken comments. The main difficulty is that unless we take on the whole question of the partnership between politics and art as a universal issue—for example, what about American art during the Vietnam period, or novels and essays and stories and music written during the Gulf War?—we rarely get beyond hortatory testimonials to the horror of German fascism, raised eyebrows and finger pointing. Strauss's music as such is studiously impervious to "the question," and no amount of even very intelligent and informed suggestion is going to make the remarkable string sextet (played at Bard) that opens *Capriccio* or the unbelievable polyphonic invention of *Metamorphosen* (1946) with its twenty-three solo voices or the plangent eloquence of the *Four Last Songs* (1948) yield up their secret vice.

The thing about Strauss is that whether you like him or not he was a consummate (some would say *the* consummate) musical technician, moving from the bombast and neo-Wagnerian extravagance of the youthful tone poems, through the decadent expressionist adventurism of *Salomé* (1905) and *Elektra* (1909), to the sugary complexities of his long collaboration with Hugo von Hofmannsthal (*Rosenkavalier, Ariadne, Arabella,* etc.) and the sumptuous yet strangely attenuated style of his late works, which include a remarkable series of orchestrated and chamber pieces (the oboe concerto, the three sonatinas, and so on). Botstein and Rothenberg arranged the performances to cover most of the genres he excelled in (except opera, for understandable logistic reasons) and, more resourcefully, set the works among the music written by his most interesting contemporaries. So in addition to the Mozart G Minor Quintet, his favorite piece by his favorite composer, Strauss's work rubbed shoulders with an astonishing range of often unheard and extremely distinguished music by Schönberg, Brahms, Hindemith, Busoni, Max Reger, Ernst Krenek, Kurt Weill, Franz Shreker, Hans Pfitzner, Hanns Eisler, Gustav Mahler, Ernst Toch and even the Waltzing Josef and Johann Strauss (unrelated to Richard except by historical period). In addition, Botstein unearthed music by once well-known and even influential contemporaries, whose music I have never heard performed before—people like Alexander Ritter, Max von Schillings, Siegmund von Hausegger, nowhere near as gifted as Strauss and somewhat overblown and anxious, but perfect as a foil for him and, curiously, interesting as progenitors of 1930s to 1950s Hollywood movie music of the kind produced by Miklos Rosza, Dimitri Tiomkin and the redoubtable Erich Korngold.

All this plus acres of Strauss, including works that are literally never performed, most notably the astoundingly complicated, fiendishly difficult (even unplayable) 1927 "Panathenäenzug" (Panathenian Procession) for piano left hand and orchestra. Ludwig Wittgenstein's brother Paul, a pianist who lost his right hand in World War I, had commissioned the piece from Strauss (as he had the Left Hand Concerto from Ravel), and with characteristic prodigality Strauss unfurled this grotesque thirty-five-minute piece in the form of a passacaglia—a series of variations on a recurring bass theme.

Ian Hobson played it with daunting aplomb, though it is the kind of work you remember and appreciate in a limited way for the pianist's having gone through it at all, rather than for any particular beauty in the music. Another unusual item was a decent but far from transcendent performance of the *Last Songs* by Ashley Putnam, with the inclusion of "Ruhe, meine Seele," a song originally written in 1894 but not orchestrated by Strauss until 1948. Timothy Jackson, a young musicologist, made a rather laborious (not to say comic) case for calling them the *Five Last Songs*, with, in my, opinion, dubious results in performance, much like sticking an undoubtedly authentic Greek hand on the Venus de Milo and calling it newly complete. As I said, Putnam (called in as a last-minute substitute for Helen Donath) did a decent job under the circumstances, but although her voice is clear and direct in intonation, she is so free of any eccentricities or personal inflection in performance as to seem more routine than inspired.

On the other hand, most of the recital and chamber ensemble performances were effective, mainly because they contributed to an overall informative and pleasurable purpose, i.e., an extended experience with the world of Strauss's music. This was the particular distinction of the Bard Strauss Festival—that rather than replicating the exhibitionistic and hopelessly atomized character of routine concerts on the one hand, or on the other using the festival format as an excuse for gouging patrons for expensive versions of what they get anyway, it made Strauss accessible as a working, living composer. There were a lot of different pieces performed, and they were performed not by stars who limousined in and out but by highly accomplished, often brilliant young performers whom one could hear several times over the course of several days. We're talking here of a cast of dozens, too many to mention one by one, but a few performances and works stand out: a rich, brooding work by Ernst Toch, his String Quartet (1919), Op. 18, performed marvelously by Erica Kiesewetter, Annamae Goldstein, Vincent Lionti and Peter Wyrick (all of whom also played in the festival orchestra); a spiritedly brilliant reading of the Kurt Weill cello and piano sonata by the exceptionally fine pianist Diane Walsh, and cellist Jerry Grossman (with Grossman, Laurie Smulker and Ira Welter, Walsh also performed Strauss's early piano quartet, and then with Eugene Drucker, one of the finest young violinists around, she played the Pfitzner sonata: an extraordinary feat, but also a consistent pleasure for the fluency, musicianship and unforced naturalness of her pianism throughout); the pianist Todd Crow in three stunning performances—Strauss's piano sonata (one of only three), a selection from Reger's *Tagebuch* and Krenek's *Five Piano Pieces* (Op. 39)—that make one wonder why he isn't seen more on New York platforms, so void of unusual programs and pianists of imagination and taste; a superb performance of Busoni's Second Sonatina (1912) by Anton Nel, who brought to this completely original and hair-raising work a pianism of true refinement and conviction.

It should be clear that performances at this level are satisfying for two reasons: the overall context, that is, a program with overall purpose and sense, and second, musicians participating together in an undertaking not *principally* defined by the exigencies of careers and professional advancement. Rothenberg and Botstein obviously deserve most of the credit for this, so a word or two are in order about their contribution. Rothenberg is a very fluent pianist, as her performances of the Brahms C Minor Piano Quartet and Strauss's *Stimmungsbilder* amply testify. But like Botstein she is also articulate and intellectually searching, qualities that permeate her playing, which is self-aware and engaging. The virtues of actually connecting performance with historical and cultural realities not just of its but also of our world are very rare, but one sensed that convincingly in Rothenberg's playing and in her comments about the works. Perhaps the single fact of enclosing performances within rubrics like "The Chamber Music Tradition: Brahms and the Young Richard Strauss" or "Modernism and Repression: Music by Strauss's Avant-Garde Contemporaries (1914–1918)" elevated music-making to the level not of consumption but of practice: This too helped the performers, as well of course as the audience, a great deal.

Although he had many estimable people helping him, I must suppose that Botstein was the key figure in all this. There is no point here in going over his many remarkable accomplishments as probably the only college president in history to be so directly involved in cultural work (as opposed to management and fundraising, both of which he is apparently quite good at). The level of enterprise and intelligence revealed at the Bard Festival in the end must be derived from his example and leadership: On that score he is quite amazing.

But he is also a conductor, and over four very big (and very long) afternoons and evenings he led what in effect was a pickup orchestra, suitably inflated for some of Strauss's largest numbers, with always interesting, if not always perfect, results. Just to get through so much complicated and difficult and unfamiliar music was a feat; there is no gainsaying that. But there are aspects of his orchestral leadership that must be noted, alas, critically. One is that, perhaps because of the large, acoustically very unflattering tent used for his concerts, Botstein was not always a master of balances. In the first program, for instance, subsidiary choirs played at a sound level equal to that of the principals. Too often the result was muddy, and phrases either emerged or disappeared as if struggling unsuccessfully for their all-too-brief lives. Second, Botstein's conducting was not plastic enough in the opening concerts, but in the later two—particularly his re-alization of *Tod und Verklärung*—there was marked improvement. Third, because of his essential modesty, when it came to one of Strauss's greatest works, *Metamorphosen*, Botstein seems insufficiently to have organized, and even not enough to have imposed on the piece, an overarching drama, theme, message. Conducting involves a good deal of playacting, a measure of histrionic charlatanry, operatic narcissism; Botstein is often far too sober and straightforward. *Metamorphosen* is an elegy, a recapitulation of early work, an amazing metamusical reflection, and needs conducting that soars and mourns and emotes incessantly. Botstein took the piece a shade on the fast side and then marched through it briskly, not bending and peering and pointing (figuratively speaking) as the work really requires. There is a stunning version of *Metamorphosen* performed by Furtwängler and the Berlin Philharmonic in 1947 that is now available on disc; listen to that and you get an indication of what intensities and overwhelming acuteness the work *can* communicate.

I do not want to end on a carping note. Rarely have I attended so sat-isfying and so purely enjoyable a musical event, as consistently intelligent and well executed as Bard's Strauss Festival. For this, in the analysis, Leon Botstein deserves the major credit. He has produced what is really a model of musical life, something hinted at only very intermittently in big-city concerts, never so lovingly and compellingly realized as under Botstein's supremely intelligent guidance.

For me, there was one particularly jolting work that stood out over all the others. Performed with rapt concentration by The William Appling Singers under Appling, a remarkable choral conductor, it was heard for the first time in the United States: Strauss's *Deutsche Motette*, Op. 62, composed in 1913, revised in 1943. As Timothy Jackson's program note suggests, the work's revision belongs, with *Metamorphosen*, to a period in Strauss's life when refashioning and essentially rewriting early works (as opposed to producing new ones) formed his main occupation. The *Motette* climaxes with perhaps the longest and most complicated fugue I have ever heard, whose text ("O show me, to revive me in dream the work finished/That I had begun") and idiom suggest the later style, and Strauss's concern with transfigured nature as an alternative to orthodox religion.

But the memory of its extended contrapuntal dexterity (and not any "nat-ural" imagery) has remained with me for a long time partly because it will not be performed (or recorded) again any time soon, partly because it dra-matizes the Straussian conundrum particularly well. As the Bard Festival showed, few composers other than Strauss have lived so undistractedly through so many conflicting upheavals in musical style and conception, and at the same time remained so ostensibly unaffected by them.

The *Motette*'s fugue and *Metamorphosen,* however, provide a somewhat different view of this by now commonly held idea about Strauss. In my opinion, we should think of the late Straussian style as the key to his music, a hyper-mature, infinitely recapitulatory and yet weirdly antique thing, studiously taking note of formal and harmonic developments all around him and then stepping back from them into musical styles perfected by seventeenth- and eighteenth-century antecedents. In short, both the *Motette* and *Metamorphosen,* with their almost unthinkable polyphonic complexity, are Strauss's response to the equally demanding rigors of Schönberg's and Webern's innovations, whose key of course is the polychromatic and infinitely contrapuntal and transformable tone row. Strauss's feat in the late style is to provide answers to the multivoiced compositional challenge posed by the second Viennese School, and to deliver his answer from within a tonal and formal tradition supposedly left behind after Brahms and Wagner. Far from being a sentimental throwback, Strauss appears in this light to be reanimating the history of tonal music, showing that what the great modernists (Schönberg, Berg, Bartók, Stravinsky and Webern) did by way of renouncing the tonal world could be responded to by re-excavating that history again and again.

This is a thesis to be developed elsewhere, but its broad lines as I have stated them underline the importance of Strauss's late work to the whole enterprise of concertgoing and contemporary performance. He embodies the spirit of what it means in a world as far removed as ours from the classical period of the eighteenth century (to which in his late works Strauss kept coming back) to perform classical music with an awareness of later developments in style and genre. Strauss clarifies the canon without in any way diminishing the force of the contemporary; on the contrary, I think by remaining within the tonal world he strengthens the force of atonal and polytonal music. And that was the singular achievement of the Bard Strauss Festival: to enable musicians and audiences alike to make that discovery. Drenched in the evil of the Third Reich, Strauss's music and biography offer a formidable challenge to humanistic understanding.

The composer for the 1993 Bard Festival will be Dvořák.

CHAPTER 26

The Importance of Being Unfaithful to Wagner

'THE BEWILDERING variety of interests and standards in Wagner scholarship (or what passes for it) is congenitally resistant to study'. Thus John Deathridge, the leading Wagner scholar of the English-speaking world, at the beginning of his chapter on Wagner research in the *Wagner Handbook*. If so learned and *au courant* a scholar as Deathridge is daunted by trying to make sense of Wagner research and interpretation, what about the rest of us? For not only was Wagner both contemptuous of history in general and constant re-maker of his own history, but the enormous range of materials that have survived him (including, of course, his 15 operas) has made almost any relatively straightforward approach to him impossible. Deathridge deepens the problem by saying that even a *Gesamtforscher* ('a versatile scholar who can do everything') would probably fail to adjudicate or negotiate the discrepancies: between the fantastic quantity of sources and Wagner's shifting ideologies, for example, or between Wagner and Wagnerism, or between the music and the texts. The difficulties are dizzying and appear limitless. 'A viable view of Wagner research', Deathridge concludes, 'has more to do with the dynamics of history than with an absolute vision of how it should be'.

Hence the appearance of the *Wagner Handbook* and *Wagner in Performance*, handsome, amply-stocked volumes by many hands, surveying the Wagner phenomenon from numerous, not altogether co-ordinated contemporary perspectives. Most of the contributions on set design of musical styles (those of singers as well as conductors) are fascinating as a compendium of scholarly uncertainties allied with confident, sometimes overbearing brashness. Crucial to all this is Bayreuth itself, where Wagner believed he could control his work: in the case of *Parsifal* he was able to prevent its

The London Review of Books, February 11, 1993.

performance elsewhere. Bayreuth, however, was as much a centre of social authority and power as it was a trend-setter in aesthetics, with its hidden orchestra and conductor, its innovations in singing style, and its unusually uncomfortable seats. Deathridge correctly refers to Wahnfried (Wagner's specially built house in Bayreuth) as often as he refers to Festspielhaus, because it was here that Wagner and later Cosima were able to keep the Wagner production engine on track; at Wahnfried after Wagner's death Cosima and then her daughter-in-law Winifred all too effectively held court alone, as Syberberg's chilling cinematic portrait of her attests. Hitler and Richard Strauss, Toscanini and Houston Stewart Chamberlain came there, as well as a whole host of lesser figures, sycophants, geniuses, philosophers, charlatans, and professional Wagnerians of every stripe and calibre.

One says all this about the bewildering richness of Wagner's legacy with an eye of Paul Lawrence Rose's *Wagner: Race and Revolution,* a book whose single-minded—albeit forceful and historically well-informed—account of the Wagner phenomenon renders the man and his operas pretty much as violent, revolutionary anti-semitism. Reading Rose, on the one hand, and, on the other, one of the chapters of the *Wagner Handbook* or *Wagner in Performance,* you would not realize that they are talking about he same thing, so different in tone and intent is Rose from the other two. Take as an instance Matthias Theodor Vogt's brilliantly original essay 'Taking the Waters at Bayreuth' in the Millington/Spencer collection. Vogt's ingenious point is that Wagner was obsessed with hydropathy, and that for him hydrotherapy, or a water cure, was as necessary for human beings as fire therapy was for gods: think of how *Götterdämmerung* ends, with its fiery destruction of Valhalla and the rising flood waters of the Rhine reclaiming the earth as well as the *Ring* itself. That this was not an airy theoretical vision but something profoundly felt as well as a matter of necessary quotidian practice is shown by Vogt in passages like the following, written by Wagner in 1851, while at work on 'Young Siegfried', the germ from which *The Ring of the Nibelung* gradually emerged:

> My daily routine is now as follows, 1st, half-past-five in the morning wet pack until 7 o'clock; then a cold bath and a walk. 8 o'clock breakfast: dry bread and milk or water. 2nd, immediately afterwards a first and then a second clyster; another short walk; then a cold compress on my abdomen. 3rd, around 12 o'clock: wet rub-down; short walk; fresh compress. Then lunch in my room with Karl [Ritter], to prevent insubordination. Then an hour spent in idleness: brisk two-hour walk—alone, 4th, around 4 o'clock: another wet rub-down and a short walk. 5th, hip-bath for a quarter of an hour around 6 o'clock, followed by a walk to warm me up. Fresh compress. Around 7 o'clock dinner: dry bread

and water. 6th, immediately followed by a first and then a second clyster; then a game of whist until after 9 o'clock, after which another compress, and then around 10 o'clock we all retire to bed.—I am now bearing up quite well under this regimen: I may even intensify it.

That Wagner managed to do any work at all (apart from quelling insubordination) is a miracle. His obsession with water dominates all his operas—*Tristan,* the *Ring,* the *Dutchman* and *Parsifal* especially—and has to be considered as much a part of his work as his appalling anti-semitic tirades, or his attacks on conventional, particularly Italian and French opera (Rossini's excepted, as the charming Michotte work makes clear), or his absurdly grandiose revolutionary proclamations. The question therefore isn't so much finding the one thing about Wagner that commands all the others, but of learning somehow to discriminate, make judgments, and criticize him intelligently and, above all, imaginatively and unreductively. The various surveys of singing, conducting, and set design provided by both the Deathridge and Millington/Spencer books give one the material on which composite interpretations of Wagner's work could be built, ranging from the vibrato and rubato employed respectively by singers and conductors to the stodgy naturalistic productions put on by companies like New York's Metropolitan or the revisionist stagings originally mounted by Wieland Wagner, the composer's grandson, during the post–war years at Bayreuth and followed variously there and elsewhere by Patrice Chéreau, Götz Friedrich, Ruth Berghaus, Harry Kupfer, and Robert Wilson.

As Adorno argued in an autumnal and even conciliatory reflection on Wagner published several years after his savage book on the composer, 'Wagner is the first case of uncompromising musical nominalism . . . the first in which the primacy of the individual work of art, and within the work the primacy of figure, in its concrete elaborated reality, is established fundamentally over any kind of scheme or externally imposed form'. This by no means lets Wagner off the hook; he is still hopelessly involved in dreadful ideologies, in a morass of uncertainty and irresolution that produces his greatest failures as well as his finest achievements. Adorno then adds:

If it is true about Wagner that no matter what one does, it is wrong, the thing that is still most likely to help is to force what is false, flawed, antinomical out into the open, rather than glossing over it and generating a kind of harmony to which the most profound element in Wagner is antithetical. For that reason, only experimental solutions [Adorno means productions, but he could be read as proposing also the need for experimental, i.e. self-conscious and ironic and non-literal, interpretations] are justified today; only what injures the Wagner orthodoxy is true. The defenders of the grail shouldn't get so worked up about it; Wagner's precise instructions exist and will continue to be handed down for historians. But the rage that is unleashed by such interventions proves that they strike a nerve, precisely that layer where the question of Wagner's relevance for today is decided. One should also intervene without question in conspicuously nationalistic passages like Hans Sach's final speech. In the same way, one should liberate the musical dramas from the stigma of the disgraceful Jewish caricatures Mime and Beckmesser—at least through the accents set by the production. If Wagner's work is truly ambivalent and fractured, then it can be done justice only by a performance practice that takes this into account and realizes the fractures, instead of closing them cosmetically.[1]

Few people who are professionally involved with Wagner are capable of this kind of attitude, and even fewer can realize it in their interpretative work, intellectual or theatrical. For what Adorno describes is deeply ironical and almost Brechtian: accentuating the discrepancies in Wagner, and doing it both by deliberate anachronism (not being true to his explicit stage-directions, for instance) and with a sense of freedom about what must remain unresolved, antinomian, bewildering in his work. This in the end leaves the music pretty much as it is, since for all his endless posturing about being a revolutionary in all things, the musical style of his operas (even *Tristan* and *Parsifal*) grows naturally out of the music of his favourite antecedents, Bach, Mozart and Beethoven especially. To liberate Wagner from his anti-semitism may seem impossible to critics like Paul Rose, but it is in fact relatively easy, since Beckmesser and Mime are not explicitly Jewish characters at all: both parts can be played without the offensively caricatural traits so often heaped on them. A few nights ago I saw Hermann Prey do Beckmesser in an otherwise dreary *Meistersinger* at the Met. Rather than the neurotic, black-suited Shylock figure regularly trundled out, someone who barks more often than he sings, Prey's Beckmesser was a pouty, vaguely adolescent, and extremely vulnerable middle-aged man, using his insecure learning as a shield for his sexual uncertainties. But the revelation was Prey's singing, which *was* singing first of all, and in addition expressive, rhetorically very precise and (to be a bit tautological) authentically Wagnerian in style, rather than an imitation of that style's clichés.

---

[1]From 'Wagners Aktualität' (1965), which will appear as 'Wagner's Relevance for Today' in *Grand Street*, 44.

Although there has been a spate of writing on Wagner, only one musicologist to my knowledge has attempted a full-scale interpretation based not only on the 'fractured and ambivalent work' but also on the idea that interpretation itself is subject to the dynamics of history. I refer to Jean-Jacques Nattiez, a French musicologist now teaching in Montreal, and the author of a remarkable pair of books, *Tétralogies: Essai sur l'infidélité* (1983) and *Wagner Androgyne* (1991). *Tétralogies* was written in conjunction with the famous Boulez-Chéreau Bayreuth *Ring* of 1976; strangely the book hasn't been translated into English, although an elaborated précis of the argument is included in the Millington/Spencer volume. An English translation of *Wagner Androgyne* is, I gather, about to appear. There is a curious, though compelling reductionism in the later work, which argues that Wagner's music is about the history of music, and that his imagination was in the grip of a long-standing obsession with uniting man and woman prophetically in a single androgynous figure (rather like Plato's fable in the *Symposium*).

It is, however, Nattiez's brilliant analysis of the notion of 'fidelity' to Wagner's operas that is particularly relevant here. Using Boulez and Chéreau as his reference points, Nattiez argues that Wagner's music is not about return and repetition, but about transition. 'In order to be faithful to Wagner', he says, 'one has to de-Wagnerise him'. Wagner's 'exuberant anarchy' encourages this sort of volatility and flair in his interpreters. Not everything that Wagner thought found its way into the scores of his works; what a director like Chéreau attempts to do therefore is to accentuate those aspects of Wagner that encourage re-interpretation, new constructions, re-animation of the work in contemporary terms. Similarly, Boulez argues that 'anyone who claims to be safeguarding a work within its initial tradition soon finds himself standing guard over a tomb'. What Nattiez suggests is that to be unfaithful to Wagner is to be faithful to him: 'Every producer, every conductor proposes a *possible* Wagner'. All this is not unlike Harold Bloom's theory of misreading.

In the end, however, Wagner survives not only because interpreters are imaginative or reverent, but because the sheer beauty and force of his music give coherence to the experience of seeing the music dramas staged. This is clearly what moved and impressed exceptional Wagnerians like Proust, Thomas Mann and Mallarmé. It is precisely Wagner's extremely varied legacy–a legacy which includes Toscanini, Boulez, Schoenberg, and critical critics like Deathridge, Nattiez and Adorno—that Paul Rose's book attempts to refute. Not that his book wants either for telling points or for historical evidence. That Wagner was an anti-semite in the tradition of Fichte, Kant, Bakunin, Marx, the young Hegelians and Gobineau, Rose more than adequately proves. That Wagner's 'revolutionary ideals' rather than mere atavism were the source of the *Ring* is also amply researched and confirmed. That Wagner was obsessed with the figure of the Wandering Jew (who is embodied in the Flying Dutchman and Kundry) is certainly the case, as Rose shows. Finally Rose suggests that 'the crucial characteristic of Wagner's, and indeed the prevailing German concept of "Jews", is that it is a plastic fluid notion that can often change its meaning seamlessly without the consciousness or intention of a writer or thinker. In German revolutionary thought, the revolution and the Jews are thus nebulous, almost mystical symbols. They are not the precise, practical conceptions of Western liberalism'.

At this point we might demur—but only until we remember that Wagner's ideas about water were equally nebulous, obsessive, overstated, impractical and imprecise. Yet what Rose is saying over and over again is much less frivolous. In his view, Wagner, as one of the chief authors of anti-semitic ideology, should be accorded a kind of attention not ordinarily given to those other musicians or artists who have inflicted their overweening egos and monstrous passions on the world (like de Sade, for example, an author not mentioned by Rose). The crux of the claim against Wagner is advanced, I think injudiciously, in an appendix originally written for the New York *Forward* in January 1992. Here Rose proposes the novel thesis that Wagner's music contains

> a distillate of Wagner's own personality, above all, his violent hatreds. His personal viciousness happened to be directed against Jews, but any target would do—the French, personal friends who somehow offended, supporters who did not grasp the purity of his ideas, unobliging husbands . . . Listen, for example, to the ferocity of Siegfried's funeral music–breath-taking in its violence as well as its grandeur. One might claim that it's worth paying the price of emotional shame to hear such music. But then compare it with its model, Beethoven's *Eroica* funeral march. Here one has the same magnificence, but without the shameful cruelty and hatred which permeate Wagner's work.

Therefore, Rose concludes, Wagner should not be played in Israel since in listening to his music there is a danger of forgetting the Holocaust: 'the Israeli ban on Wagner is a pre-eminent rite for warding off the dissolution of one of the core experiences of Jewish history and memory'. There is of course a serious contradiction here. For if it is true that Wagner's music is a distillate of his hatreds, playing it, far from dissolving memory, should actively remind listeners of what those hatreds were. Besides, if 'any target would do' how can we be sure that only Jews were intended; surely a case could be made for not performing his work in France, or warning husbands

not to listen, and so on. Yet Rose's comparison of Beethoven and Wagner shouldn't go unnoticed: four ounces of ennoblement in Beethoven as
against two in Wagner. It's like a drunk-driving test. And how, listening to
Wagner, does one pay that price in 'emotional shame'? Is it like going to a
peep show? And what if in fact no such *specific* content—hatred, violence,
cruelty—is ascertainable in the music? The fact is that Rose's claims about
music are ludicrous. How can he on the one hand insist on the indiscrimi-
nate nebulousness of Wagner's ideas, and on the other confidently assert
that they are distillable into specific ideas of hatred in the music?

Wagner has not lacked for critics of his vile ideas: Robert Gutman's
Richard Wagner: The Man, his Mind and his Music (1968), while perhaps
not as thoroughgoing as Rose in connecting Wagner's anti-semitism with
revolutionary ideas, is unsparing in its excoriations of the man's despicable
pronouncements and behaviour. But Gutman stops well short of banning
Wagner's music altogether. Rose's simplistic approach has it that art is, in
effect, only a repetition—perhaps cunningly disguised–of the artist's political and moral beliefs, as if style, form, idiom, irony, play no role whatever.
Unwittingly perhaps, with his suggestion that every measure of the music
contains specific political directives, he accords Wagner an even greater
power than Wagner himself might have hoped for. To experience Wagner
is only (or mainly), he says, to experience anti-semitism. As for the various
Jewish musicians who have conducted, sung, played, directed or designed
the operas, from Hermann Levi to Barenboim, Levine and Solti, they are by
implication either dupes or complicit scoundrels. 'The questions of Wagner's
anti-semitism and Hitler's exploitation of it are fundamental', Rose writes,
'but what is ultimately at stake in banning Wagner is the sustaining of the
memory of the Holocaust itself. There was a Holocaust, and Wagner's self-
righteous ravings, sublimated in his music, were one of the most potent elements in creating the mentality that made such an enormity thinkable—and
performable'. Here we have Wagner as Hitler's enabler—the final straw.

The crucial word is 'fundamental'. Rose—currently Hecht Professor at
Haifa University—is a fundamentalist, a Khomeini of the arts, who might,
like the frequently, and justly, criticized Iranian mullahs, ask for books to
be banned or burnt as an instrument of state authority. Rose can scarcely
bear to allow for the possibility that people can listen to Wagner's music or
see his music-dramas without forgetting either the man's deplorable ideas
or their horrific extension into the public policy of the Third Reich. He
makes no provision for counter-interpretations of Wagner's music (such
as those recommended by Boulez and Nattiez), nor does he consider it a
possibility that Wagner's work might (as Adorno suggests) contradict itself

or that there are other ways of reading Wagner beside Rose's own literalist canons.

This is distressingly sad as well as impoverishing. Rose by implication endorses both the Iranian (and other Muslim) authorities who wish to ban *The Satanic Verses,* and those many historical victims of Western culture who advocate expunging Dead White Males and their views from academic curricula. Relationships between art and evil ideas (and practices too) should of course be elucidated, but ought we to ban Edmund Spencer for his genocidal views of the Irish, or Carlyle for his theses on the 'nigger question', or Renan for his ideas about the 'semitic mind'? Some years ago Chinua Achebe attacked Conrad's racism in *Heart of Darkness,* and found direct links between that work and the dehumanisation and exploitation of Africa. What he was trying to do was not prevent Africans from reading Conrad, but rather to show them that it wasn't necessary to see Conrad as a 'classic' or great writer. That is a view one can argue with, however much one may agree or disagree with Achebe's critique of Conrad's reactionary and racist politics. But to equate Wagner proleptically with the Holocaust is to go much further than Achebe, and further even than Walter Benjamin, for whom every document of civilization was also a document of barbarism. It is to amputate unseemly and horrible experiences altogether from the realm of the human, and as such a view incapable of development, argument or reconciliation.

I realise that Rose writes as an Israeli whose tragic legacy as a survivor of the Holocaust may include the impossibility of ever coming to terms with the German tradition that produced not only Wagner but also Heidegger and others who were complicit with Nazism. Yet, as a Palestinian, I would venture to suggest that an additional yet routinely overlooked consequence of European anti-semitism was what happened to the native Palestinian people. A recent book by the Israeli-Palestinian scholar Nur Massalha documents the concept of 'transfer' in Zionist thinking from Herzl, Weizmann, Ben Gurion to their heirs, Shamir and Rabin.[2] Going over mountains of Hebrew-language documents Massalha shows that every Zionist leader of the Left, Right or Centre, with no significant exceptions, was in favour of ridding Palestine of Palestinians, by all means necessary, force and bribery included. The expulsion took place, as we know, in 1948. A month ago 415 more Palestinians were thrown out by the Rabin Government.

---

[2]*Expulsion of the Palestinians: The Concept of 'Transfer' in Zionist Political Thought, 1882-1948,* Institute for Palestinian Studies, Washington DC, 1992.

There are troubling continuities and analogies here, most of them too obvious to point out. The epistemology of Rose's arguments about Wagner is seriously flawed, since it all too easily collapses art, history, genocide into each other, and seems by extension to validate excision, book-banning and avoidance as tools not only of analytic research but also of state policy. In 1948 Israel was established as a state for the Jewish people, but—with the kind of viewpoint that Rose excoriates in Wagner—it projected a state that was Arab-free. In my opinion there are better ways to deal with others—even hated and feared others—than to wish they were not there, and expend a great deal of intellectual, political and military effort to get rid of them. The Palestinian people have recognized Israel since 1988: there has been no comparable recognition of Palestinian nationalism by any responsible figure in the Israeli Government, despite the fact that it is the Palestinians who originally lost their land and society and who have lived under military occupation since 1967. Rose's book on Wagner is as unyielding in its intellectual politics as Israeli governments have been, with results that are hardly more satisfactory than the anti-semitism against which these politics are defending. Wagner's music deserves to be treated with less defensiveness and retrospective bitterness.

CHAPTER 27

Music as Gesture (on Solti)

F OR AN audience, watching as opposed to only hearing a musical performance is very much part of the whole experience. What we see can either enhance such qualities as elegance and clarity or it can startlingly dramatize faults inherent in the performance. This is especially true of conductors, at least half of whose effort is bodily gesture as well as baton waving. I have seen and heard Georg Solti for at least twenty-five years, but it wasn't until his Carnegie Hall appearances last February with the Vienna Philharmonic—in a bewilderingly spotty and even incoherent performance of the Bruckner Eighth Symphony—that I could at last *see* how much his gestures and overall podium behavior undermine, and ultimately cripple, the best of his musical intentions.

Bruckner's slow, carefully plotted and elongated compositional lines are intended to produce a deliberate unfolding effect, leading to massed climaxes whose *raison d'etre* is that they are immense conclusions to what led up to them so inexorably. After thousands of concerts and TV appearances and reams of adulatory encomia, Solti has now acquired a podium persona that is one-third busy maître d', a third circus lion-tamer, another third "maestro" (e.g., Kostelanetz or Iturbi) as imagined by Hollywood musicals of the forties and fifties. All his swishing, bobbing, weaving, thrusting, lunging and, alas, posing, made it impossible even for the venerable Vienna Philharmonic to play the gigantic work with the requisite unfolding effect. Instead one got what seemed to be a rather boring pattern of inconsequential passage work punctured (not punctuated) by either an occasional passage of exaggerated inflection, or—Solti's specialty—a tremendous, apparently gratuitous explosion of sound. You could admire the huge sonority

The Nation, January 17, 1994.

or the orchestra's responsiveness, but there was neither a whole symphony nor, finally, anything resembling a musical line.

I've always rather liked Solti, however, even his vanity and extraordinary air of self-satisfied, uncomplicated accomplishment. He made his name with the first postwar *Ring* recording, done with great drama and an unsurpassed cast. Compared with Pierre Boulez's Bayreuth *Ring* (recently released on video and disc) it is bombastic and, cast aside, primitive; where Boulez is sinuous and lyrical, Solti is lumbering and exaggerated. Solti's specialty has always been late romantic music—his Mozart, for instance, is often extremely pedestrian—especially big operatic works like the *Ring, Moses und Aaron* or *Die Frau Ohne Schatten,* whose coherence is both odd and hard to grasp. In a sense the complicated vocal and dramatic goings on have shielded audiences and performers from the man's peculiar physical jerkiness; plus of course his age and knighthood have given him added aura and prestige. Unlike George Szell and Toscanini (or Fritz Reiner for that matter), Solti has neither the severity nor the composed maturity of the virtuoso conductor, partly because in the end he cannot seem to blend in physically with the music or the orchestra. A second Vienna Philharmonic program, of Mendelssohn and Shostakovich symphonies, was intermittently interesting, but it never rose beyond that.

By contrast, a Tanglewood appearance this past August by the English musician Simon Rattle conducting the Boston Symphony in a performance of Haydn's *Creation* supplied a remarkable confluence of physical gesture and supple sound that few conductors today can match. Rattle is only in his 30s but ranks among the finest conductors, although he has given me the superficial impression of someone perhaps too carefully husbanding his resources and tending his career. The impression has to do not with nurturing a public image but rather with consolidating and rather too gingerly tending an enormous gift. He has refused offers to move from Birmingham, whose orchestra he has built into a fine instrument, and he has confined himself to a repertory that is (almost too) perfectly suited to his predilections: Sibelius, Mahler, Britten, an occasional Janáček opera, some Haydn and a few other mainly twentieth-century composers. There has been some attention paid to composers, from the first half of the nineteenth century, but (again superficially) Rattle seems much more likely to do a piece over and over than to attempt a constantly expanded range. Similarly with his guest conducting, which by Zubin Mehta standards is almost nonexistent. Three years ago I heard him conduct a spirited performance of Janáček's *Cunning Little Vixen* at Covent Garden; otherwise he does much more symphonic than operatic work.

Haydn's *Creation* has almost the status of the *Messiah* but is performed far less often. Like *Messiah* its pleasures are immediately accessible, its writing always inspired, its structure elegant and supremely effective, its ensembles of an extraordinary mastery. In other words, it's hard to go wrong with it. Rattle's reading was exceptional first of all for the lithe and generally economical shape he gave the piece, with its occasional naïve distentions (Haydn's self-indulgent addiction to animal pictures—worms, whales and elephants, for example—can be silly) held in check, its sheer charm subdued by Rattle's highlighting of the work's contrapuntal virtuosity. In fact the novelty of Rattle's approach was his minute attention to choruses rather than to soloists, of whom only one, the soprano Barbara Bonney, had the voice and technique to perform as an instrumentalist. Thus his carefully regulated gestures cued each part; these were kept musically in place by Rattle's flexible beat, his eyes, torso and head. So rather than getting a series of disconnected stage effects supplied independently by orchestra, soloists, chorus and conductor, the overall impression consolidated the unity of the work, the audience's eye connected to its ear and mind.

Rattle is an intriguing conductor for those abilities of course, but also because of the lurking doubt that is hastened by his superbly plotted performances: Is everything contrived and planned, and is there no room for spontaneity, fantasy, improvisation? Certainly because it is a dramatized version of Genesis, *The Creation* encourages a kind of theatrical outwardness, on which Rattle capitalized nobly. Everything seems to converge from different parts of the stage toward the conductor, who is the work's focal point and its supremely observant eye. Rattle therefore wasn't so much in the work as drawing it out according to some well-established plan (in the manner of Pope, say, rather than of Wordsworth). Yet so satisfying an effect does he produce, that you ask whether he hadn't also consumed the music so completely as to have subdued and perhaps even domesticated it. Much as I admired and enjoyed the performance, I was left wishing for some uncertainty and tentative exploration, whereas most of what I sensed was a superb professionalism carried very far indeed.

Nevertheless I prefer Rattle's sense of definiteness and hard work to the still curiously unsatisfying conduct of his slightly older contemporary James Levine. Not that Levine is not interesting: He most certainly is. One of the most profitable ways of negotiating the Metropolitan Opera's immense schedule is (barring the occasional Verdi performance) to pick out Levine's appearances and then go to see them. Last season he did an extraordinary *Contes d'Hoffmann*—muscular, searingly dramatic, unfailingly intense and even overwhelming—thanks to an impressive cast and his own completely involved leadership. In the orchestra pit, a conductor is nowhere as visible as on the symphonic podium; in addition, operas deliver a much greater amount of both visual and aural material for an audience to process than a symphonic concert. Still, Levine's performance in the Offenbach work, surely one of the most complex and challenging of all nineteenth-century operas, was visually evident in the musical responsiveness of Carol Vaness in the three female leads, Susanne Mentzer as the Muse and (most of the time) Placido Domingo as Hoffmann. Levine conducted the ceaselessly restless and elaborate score with sinuous elegance, as if he had in fact become the inventive E. T. A. Hoffmann himself.

But the problem with Levine is what he tries to do with the purely German repertory. For *Les Contes d'Hoffmann* is a hybrid Franco-German work. By contrast, Wagner's *Meistersinger,* which Levine also conducted last season, openly claims to be a work about the supremacy of German musical art, embodied in the final scene by Hans Sachs's peroration to the holiness of German art as it might be threatened by foreigners. Set in medieval Nuremberg, the opera is a paradoxical mix of sublime music, second-rate humor and simplifying fable. Of all Wagner's mature works it is the one that most embarrasses, not to say puts off, his admirers: Wagner's lampooning of Sixtus Beckmesser, the town pedant, is merciless and, it has been argued without sufficient proof, anti-Semitic. Added to the hortatory paeans to German art, and the often needlessly complicated story of youthful passion tamed into artistic competence, *Meistersinger* comes up either as one of Wagner's most challenging or least interesting music dramas.

I myself think it belongs in the former category, a work of the most inventive musical imagination at odds with its own plot, ideological intentions, and characters. Hans Sachs, the great singer (and shoemaker!), is both a coarse bully and a humane philosopher; Walther, the young knight, is both a callow and heedless youth as well as a gifted artist; Eva, his love, is at once a tokenized female chattel and a domestic counterpart of Brunnehilde. The story focuses on an idealized brotherhood of medieval mastersingers—men who have qualified for the title by learning how to sing according to a prescribed code of musical ethics; they comprise a healthy, sunny equivalent of the gloomy Grail brotherhood in Parsifal—who are burghers at the same time as they are subtle artists, bound to their art not as professionals but as keepers of a tradition and a craft. So on the one hand Wagner is a patent chauvinist appealing to his aristocratic patrons in the most nationalistic and self-aggrandizing way, and on the other he celebrates the art he practices by actually staging the passage from apprenticeship to mastery.

The plot is simple. It is midsummer, and one of the Meistersingers, Veit Pogner, offers his daughter Eva as a prize to the winner of a singing contest.

She and the visiting knight Walther von Stolzing love each other, but he must learn to channel his lyrical gifts into acceptable aesthetic form, which has to be passed communally by the Meistersingers as the result of a test. Walther fails the test in Act I but passes it triumphantly in Act III. Beckmesser is both his severest critic and his rival for Eva's love. Commonly portrayed as a black-suited caricature of all of Wagner's enemies, he was played brilliantly in the Met production by Hermann Prey, who presented him as an awkward, almost adolescent figure, rather like an overachieving and obsessive college freshman confronted by an apparently willing Marilyn Monroe. In all this, Hans Sachs plays the role of friend and confidant of Walther, stymying Beckmesser and maintaining *real* artistic standards, even though it is revealed to us that he too is secretly (albeit passively) in love with Eva.

There are two basic styles for interpreting Wagner's music dramas. One is to abide by a spurious sense of tradition and realism and to assume that Wagner has resolved all his problems. This results in a ponderously literal reading, with characters, setting and music compelled into prefabricated, superficially German designs supposedly originated by Wagner himself at Bayreuth in the period 1876-83. The other style is revisionist. It assumes (what in effect is, I believe, true) that Wagner did not have his ideological schemes under control, and that rather than being a straightforward realization of them, the operas are churningly mobile, even volatile records of unsuccessful attempts at resolution. To interpret Wagner authentically is to expose and highlight the inconsistencies, not to try to flatten them all into a naturalistic, and therefore misleading, conception. There have been successful interpretations of this second kind that go all the way from Robert Wilson's *Parsifal* to Patrice Chereau's Bayreuth *Ring* cycle in the mid-1970s, to all sorts of attempts at wild psychoanalytical, expressionist and "ethnographic" readings that stress Wagner's struggle and not his triumphalist extra-musical proclamations.

Levine has always had a predilection for the first of these two interpretative styles, with musical results (to say nothing of quite unsatisfactory quasi-realistic scenic and dramatic effects) that are mystifyingly retrograde. Wagner for Levine as conductor evidently means heavy, over-deliberate, stodgy, assertive. Levine's beat distends the music, seizing on Wagner's superficial self-confidence to produce a declarative, ultimately monotonous sound rather than the kind of sensuous wash of colors and supple rhythms that Pierre Boulez seems alone to have been able to get from orchestra and singers (Boulez is the great Wagnerian of our time). Perhaps Levine is too impressed by Wagner's postures of swaggering authority. But one should never forget Adorno's shrewd insight, that the louder and squarer Wagner gets, the less he knows what he is doing.

Except for Prey, the cast of Levine's *Meistersinger* played the characters as stock opera strutters, the men bluff and bold, the women clinging and fluttery. The Finnish soprano Karita Matilla as Eva revealed a wonderful lyrical soprano tone far too often undermined visually by her flapping arms and her painfully comic gestures that seemed (only) to express surprise, shock and ecstasy. The greatest disappointment was Donald McIntyre as Sachs. As much as (perhaps even more than) Wotan, Sachs is Wagner's greatest baritone conception, a man torn between lawfulness and rebellion, benevolence and nastiness, resignation and passion. Partly because he was constrained by the unsupple and far too unmodulated orchestral sound—Levine didn't even seem to *enter* the music and seek out its rebellious cross-purposes—McIntyre sounded tired and matter-of-fact; his famous third act monologue, which describes the world's craziness, had all the flair of an Avis lease.

But I think Levine's mistake was to think of Sachs in the first place as someone who had a fully fashioned philosophy of life rather than as a partially confused and skillful operator (like Wagner himself) who can rise to a public occasion and dominate it without any real justification. Nowhere is this more apparent than in the final scene, in which a huge crowd of choristers and soloists stand as if transfixed by Sachs's offensive baloney about German art. Why not stage the scene either as a kind of mock Nuremberg rally, or comic-style, as if the pretentious orator gets little attention from the loitering Nurembergers, who by their disrespectful behavior have demonstrated that they have no time for such antics?

I noticed the same kind of problem with Levine's performance of Mahler's *Das Lied von der Erde* (with the Met orchestra and the great Waltraud Meier as mezzo soloist) at Carnegie Hall in May of 1992. Levine has a fantastic musical gift for actually trying in his conducting to represent the music's shifting late-Romantic uncertainties, Mahler's extraordinary amalgams of different genres and usually discordant kinds of timbres, as well as his elaborate off-beat rhythms. But when Levine gets to music like the long and serene final song ("Der Abschied") in the cycle, he seems to lose his ingenuity and resourcefulness altogether. Granted that even by Mahler's very high standards and by the composer's own admission, the song is almost impossible to conduct: Its enormously drawn-out lines, which signify an ecstatic acceptance of mortality, stupefy the ordinary time-beater, for whom phrases stretching out for pages on end defy bar lines and steady beat. As Donald Mitchell puts it in Volume III of his Mahler studies, the only way to do it is to ignore the conventions of routine beats and let the music carry you beyond lines and strict patterns into a heightened form of ritual.

This Levine did not do at all. Instead he communicated a most discouraging sense of winding down as if a gigantic instrument had simply given out, with the strangest and emptiest slowness trying to stand in for poetic resignation. Poor Meier seemed to have been rendered perplexed, even disconsolate by the elaborate, but ultimately empty, heaviness and deliberateness of what Levine appeared to be doing. Here too one could see the conductor standing outside the music, seeming to fuss with it from above, so to speak.

This was in stark contrast with Claudio Abbado's overwhelming performance of the Mahler Ninth in Carnegie Hall with the Berlin Philharmonic this past October. Most of the local critics concerned themselves only with the rather banal task of comparing Abbado's orchestra with Karajan's, generally finding Karajan more brilliant. Nothing could be further from the truth. Abbado must be the most complete and satisfying conductor now before the public. He commands an awesome range of musical literature, and does even the less interesting works in it with a remarkable combination of consummate professionalism and humility. The Berlin played faultlessly and quite without the tiresome sheen of glossy perfection evidently so prized by Karajan's admirers, among whom I counted myself twenty years ago. Watching Abbado perform the Ninth, one could both see and hear him fetch out the sound physically, as if what he was doing recapitulated the composer's intellectual gestures in composing it. I was especially struck by the work's slow final pages, which unfurl in an amazingly drawn-out D flat, with dozens of little ritards, accents and diminuendos producing an even more supernal effect than "Der Abschied." What was so compelling about Abbado is that he never let the music flag or just sit there; you could witness the physical effort of getting the sound to come out, but you never lost sight either of pulse or of internal stress. And for a series of instants Abbado *was* the music.

CHAPTER 28

Les Troyens

F OR SHEER grandeur of scale, elevation of style and audacity of conception, Berlioz's last opera, *Les Troyens* (1863), is *The Ring of the Nibelung*'s only nineteenth-century competitor. Yet whereas Wagner actually lived to see his tetralogy staged and indeed canonized in his own specially built opera house in Bayreuth, Berlioz saw only the second part of his great two-pan adaptation of Books I, II and IV of Virgil's *Aeneid* realized in a shoddy, skimpy condensation at Paris's Théâtre Lyrique. Indeed, it wasn't really until the late nineteenth and early twentieth century in Germany, not France, that the complete *Troyens* was given; and still France lags behind Germany, Britain and the United States in number of performances, as well as in appreciation of Berlioz's extraordinary (and deeply eccentric) genius. As has been often said, Wagner was completely of his time and culture, bringing to a remarkable if often problematic culmination trends already present in German philological speculation, music, philosophy and poetry; Berlioz on the other hand was less at one with his time and place. A visionary cosmopolitan, he was more comfortable with Shakespeare, Virgil and Goethe than with French writers. And as for music, he was more German, a follower of Beethoven and Gluck, than French, given that France then as now underestimated and mistreated its musicians. French audiences were the least understanding in Europe, the musical establishment and institutions more conventional, stuffy and reactionary than any other.

Still, *Les Troyens* is profoundly French in its genius. Its rhetoric and vocabulary are nineteenth-century transformations of seventeenth-century classical drama and eighteenth-century neoclassicism; so too are its depic-

The Nation, June 27, 1994.

tions of Cassandra and Dido, the opera's two magnificent heroines. Berlioz's innovative ideas about grand opera—a principally Parisian phenomenon— are indebted not only to Auber and Meyerbeer but also to Gluck, whose operas were originally intended and also staged for Paris (in 1862 Berlioz himself mounted a celebrated production of *Orfeo*). And, I would argue, Berlioz's daring theatrical imagination used *Les Troyens* as an artistic ve- hicle for paralleling in music the contemporary expansion of the French empire in North Africa, which is where the second half of the work is set.

Because of its almost five-hour length and the enormous demands it places on directors and opera houses' resources, *Les Troyens is* only infre- quently encountered. It was last performed at the Metropolitan ten years ago, but returned this winter for a handful of performances, three of which I attended. The paradox is that even though both production and perfor- mances were quite flawed, the experience of actually attending the piece was deeply moving, even thrilling. Like *Fidelio, Les Troyens*'s sincerity and intensity seem to survive either botched or misconceived stagings. Unlike *Fidelio*, however, Berlioz's masterpiece is difficult to see and hear complete; to make matters worse, there is only one complete commercial recording now available, Colin Davis's still fresh-sounding 1969 Covent Garden read- ing with Jon Vickers as Aeneas towering over the rest of the generally good cast. In early December I happened to be in London when Davis led an integral concert performance of the work, with overwhelmingly powerful results that necessarily stopped short of the dazzling monumentality the staged opera can achieve.

The Met is perhaps the one house where *Les Troyens* should get definitive performances, but does not. There is first the highly imperfect, not to say slapdash, underrehearsed and non-directed half-baked production itself, partly "Roman" in style, partly modernist-suggestive. Berlioz divided the opera into two parts: Acts I and II, the fall of Troy; Acts III and IV, the Tro- jans at Carthage. The Met followed this procedure. Cassandra dominates part one, Dido part two: Both women kill themselves, the former to escape Greek servitude, the latter because Aeneas deserts her. For such extreme situations, Berlioz's dramatic idiom is comparably idiosyncratic. Deliber- ately grand in the effects he tries to achieve, he nevertheless composes scenes in fiery bursts, and is never held in by cautious reliance on a logical or even plausible plot. Yet his directions and notations are (we are begin- ning to discover) extremely precise, disproving all the clichés about Roman- ticism as vague and simply grandiose. Everything is calculated by him to achieve the maximum in expressivity, melancholy and political statement, although he had no illusions that his directions were going to be followed.

In 1857 he wrote his sister Adele prophetically that of a dozen specific effects he planned for *Les Troyens,* he knew opera houses would give him at most two or three.

So to mention a few of the lapses he foresaw: While Berlioz stresses that Cassandra should first appear amid a crowd of celebrating Trojans (as the opera opens, the Trojans have suddenly left, leaving behind the wooden horse), at the Met she is perceived after the crowd has exited, thus robbing the audience of a calculated contrast between her lonely dread and the crowd's festive exultancy. Andromache is supposed to be in white robes of mourning when she and Astyanax appear in pantomime before the assembled Trojans. Costume designer Peter Wexler had her wrapped in a nondescript stripe. The wrestler's dance in Act I was transmuted into an acrobat's dance; in Act IV the dances of courtesans, Carthaginian slaves and Nubian slaves (Berlioz specifies each) were inexplicably staged by choreographer Gray Veredon as ballets performed by men and women in tutus. For the splendid Royal Hunt and Storm music that open Act IV Berlioz asks for an elaborate pantomime, which the Met simply ignored. In the final scene Berlioz specifies that the distraught Dido, having been abandoned by Aeneas, come out in readiness for her suicide with her left foot bare. This nice touch was scratched by the Met, as was also an even more important authorial indication, the appearance of the word ROMA above the Carthaginian chorus cursing Aeneas and his descendants. Set designer Wexler treated us instead to an effigy of three wolves, a clever touch, perhaps, but added on gratuitously. If you are going to give audiences a partially realistic late-nineteenth-century performance, you must do it either with attention to all of Berlioz's specifically requested directions or not follow them at all.

Cassandra as rendered by the French soprano Francoise Pollet has the shorter and more concentrated of the two female leads. Pollet has impeccable diction and style, though she isn't much of an actor. Yet she can successfully project the great dignity and passion of a woman gradually losing her lover, her family and most of her people as she struggles to remain true to her searingly catastrophic vision. Pollet's voice has authority and richness in the lower registers, a smooth yet not very potent sound in the upper. Her excellent (and somewhat slow-moving) Alice Tully recital of works by Mozart, Duparc, Debussy and Schubert confirmed her remarkable musical self-confidence, her dominating serenity as an artist.

In what for me is the greatest ensemble scene in opera, the finale to the fall of Troy, Pollet's presence gave the number its one authentically tragic, almost demonic note: Cassandra provoking a large chorus of Trojan women into mass suicide as an alternative to Greek servitude. Berlioz's blazingly taut conception is massively scored for soprano soloist, the main chorus of women, a smaller chorus of timorous maidens, a Greek captain looking for the Trojan treasure and a chorus of Greek soldiers bursting on the scene as Cassandra plunges a sword into her belly. The orchestra is by turns menacing, jubilant, hysterical and triumphant; harps, clarinets, strings, tympani, horns and trumpets move through double and triple times with gathering effects, the whole culminating in great D-flat chords to the chorus's cries of "Italie."

Berlioz's intention here and at several points in the opera is to keep reminding his audience that despite the Trojan travails, a new Troy will be created in Italy from which, of course, will come the Roman Empire. This is a more insistent motif in *Les Troyens* than it is in the early books of the *Aeneid*. True, Berlioz's Virgilian passion, as he called it, was perhaps the dominating aesthetic idea in his life, but it received added consolation from his no less consistent admiration for French imperial expansion. Napoleon pioneered the first great successes of the empire with his celebrated Egyptian campaign in 1798. In the 1830s France occupied Algeria, and for decades thereafter was engaged both in putting down one rebellion after another, and in gradually incorporating the territory into its imperial system. Morocco was attacked in 1844, Guinea made into a protectorate in 1849. There were French expeditions in the 1860s to Madagascar and Indochina. All this was part of Berlioz's world, not least his extraordinary admiration for Bonaparte and his heirs; indeed, one of his lesser compositions was an "Emperor" cantata for Napoleon III. Jacques Barzun is right to suggest that Berlioz's political ideas were not really codified as between democracy and aristocracy; but as others have noted, there is nothing in Berlioz to suggest an interest in democracy. His first work was "The Arab Mourning His Steed," and from beginning to end he was, like so many of his contemporaries (Hugo, Châteaubriand, Delacroix), fascinated with the Orient. Barzun also speculates that Berlioz's Italian journey in 1830 informs many of his greatest works, including *Les Troyens*, not only because it infused him with that sunny dash and romance we also find in Goethe and Stendhal but also because Italy was the site of Europe's first southern empire.

I do not want to suggest that Berlioz was an imperialist in a reductive sense, any more than I want to argue that *Les Troyens* is a crudely ideological opera. Nevertheless, I believe that it is incomprehensible as a great work of art without some account of the heady grandeur it shares both with Virgil as the poet of empire and with the imperial France in and for which it was written. Carthage's Queen Dido in the opera is at first a contested, if somewhat emotionally scarred, North African monarch. She is initially seen languidly surveying her subjects, her military triumphs and her lush fields. From the moment that Aeneas and the wandering Trojans enter her life, however, she experiences great passion and an ever-growing sorrow. After a sublimely beautiful duet with Aeneas (based not on Virgil but on some lines from *The Merchant of Venice*), she experiences an abrupt end to her happiness when, without any warning, Aeneas is summoned back to resume his imperial mission to Italy. Berlioz intersperses the love scenes with ballets and vignettes of Trojan sentinels comparing the pleasures of Carthaginian women with the rigors of sea life, or anxious exchanges between Dido and her sister Anna. The overall theme is the obligation to serve the idea of imperial destiny, no matter the terrible human costs.

But it is clear that here, as in the Troy section of the opera, Berlioz is mostly concerned with the tragedies of royalty, of great historical personages, of national destiny. However, even more than the somewhat one-dimensional Aeneas, Dido is required to go back and forth between her official and private selves; it is a less taxing role than Cassandra, but also allows the soprano a wider range of expression. Maria Ewing sang the part in two performances I saw, Carol Yahr the third. Ewing has great dramatic style and, like Pollet, secure musicianship. The first time her not overly large voice was marred by the remnants of a cold, so there was some holding back, a bit too much scooping and unfocused bellowing, all of which disappeared the second time I saw her. Her voice doesn't have the ample richness of Janet Baker or Regine Crespin, although she is impressive enough in the middle register. I thought she made the best of a tough situation, and was especially convincing as Dido abandoned and filled with desire for revenge. Yahr did creditably, given her somewhat more lyrical and light instrument: She didn't have the compelling tragic majesty of Ewing's portrayal, but was affecting as a younger, more vulnerable Dido nonetheless. This could not be said of Gary Lakes as Aeneas, whose imposing physical presence is betrayed by a voice that sounds strained, misses notes and shouts rather inexpressively when the going gets rough.

Les Troyens above all demands orchestral and stage organization, both fairly intermittent in Fabrizio Melano's staging and James Levine's conducting. Berlioz can be ponderous and overwhelming, but those qualities are not best served by an enormous phalanx of choristers trudging on and off the stage, standing around idly or looking lost the rest of the time. Berlioz is not Cecil B. De Mille after all, and if one is going to try to do him well then there should be some sense of purpose, some idea to the production. I found this completely missing in the Met's half-abstract, half-realistic concept. And yet there was a sense of Berlioz struggling to get through the Met's strictures and Levine's often distracted leadership, which was better in Carthage than in Troy. Levine now seems to me more prone than ever to the inflated and distended line; this tendency made Cassandra's final scene rather diffuse (by contrast, Colin Davis kept things taut and even explosive), whereas Dido's essentially broad music through the love duet with Aeneas was beautifully rendered. Her final scenes, however, sagged dreadfully, as did the orchestra's playing, thanks to Levine.

The irony is that although as director of the Met Levine is probably responsible for the generally poor dramatic quality of the productions— surely he must be the one to choose directors as well as designers—he doesn't seem to be aware that if what is occurring on stage is incoherent or sloppy, it must have a negative effect on his conducting. And although the orchestra remains superlative (thanks to Levine), one can't help noticing how out of sync stage, orchestra and singers so often seem to be. I also think that sticking to the absurd principle that everything should be sung in the original language without supertitles contributes to the basically unintelligent and mystifying quality of the whole.

A major casualty of this odd approach (perhaps approach isn't the right word here, since absence of approach is really what I am trying to describe) was Strauss's *Elektra*. The night I went Hildegard Behrens was replaced by Penelope Daner, who performed bravely enough, but neither her thin voice nor her dreadfully awkward stage presence helped her case. The much celebrated Brigitte Fassbaender gesticulated and grimaced her way through Klytemnestra's music with results that were quite simply disastrous. Deborah Voigt saved the evening as Chrysothemis only because (no actor she) she has a wonderful voice and fine musicianship. But what a mishmash was made of this twentieth-century re-creation of another episode of the same story that gripped Berlioz. For reasons known only to himself, director Otto Schenk placed the toppled statue of a gigantic metallic horse near the entrance to Agamemnon's palace. It was there that Elektra burrowed frantically for the ax she used to kill her mother. She never found it, though she kept referring to it and actually waved it around like an absent wand. Once again, Levine's conducting stressed the broad, the massive, the ponderous elements in a score that is nothing if not dazzlingly varied and mercurial, as is of course von Hofmannsthal's libretto.

There was a hint of something different in the performance of Verdi's *Otello* that I attended in which Placido Domingo and Carol Vaness played Otello and Desdemona. It certainly didn't come from the abominable production by Elijah Moshinsky, nor from the senseless opulence of Michael Yeargan's sets. Rather it came from the revelation to be had in Valery Gergiev's conducting, which was amazingly plastic, intelligent, dramatic and paced. I cannot recall a performance of the opera so extraordinarily effective as his, even though the stage proceedings were on the whole dull and even stupid. One example will serve for the whole: As he sings about kissing Desdemona in the final scene, Domingo stands about ten yards away from Vaness. I'm not at all a Verdi fan, but even I know that this makes the old boy seem more vulgar and illogical than he really is. Domingo did his thing to great crowd-pleasing effect, but I was struck by how strained and generally harsh his singing seemed. Vaness was fine, but perhaps due to the production, distant and even at moments cold.

The question remains as to why Met performances seem designed to be less communicative and intelligent than most orchestral and/or instrumental concerts. Compare the Met's *Les Troyens* with the Philharmonic's recent *Harold in Italy,* a remarkable Berlioz composition for viola and orchestra, and you are almost dumbfounded by the gap between them. Charles Dutoit's conducting, Cynthia Phelps's playing, the orchestra's ensemble—all conveyed an overwhelming impression of coherence and intelligence, skill and planning. Another striking contrast with the Met was afforded me in early February when I was in Amsterdam and attended a shattering performance of Berg's *Wozzeck* directed by Willy Decker at the Netherlands Opera. This is a house with far fewer resources than those of the Met, but its *Wozzeck* produced an evening of great power and distinction because it was clear that Decker had a conception of the work that transfigured every part of it. Why do so many people accept such low standards at the premier American opera house when it is not the lack of money or of talent that is to blame? The mystery is that having taken a curatorial rather than an avant-garde position toward the canon, the Met persists in violating the masterpieces in its care instead of doing them carefully and attentively.

I am happy to conclude with a salute to one exception in this season's roster, Benjamin Britten's *Death in Venice* (1974), his last and most difficult opera, based on the Mann novella. Perhaps because it could never have competed with either the expensive blockbusters like *Otello* or resurrected mediocrities like *Stiffelio* that pass for the Met's contribution to innovation, *Death in Venice* was directed with almost sublime competence by Colin Graham, conducted superbly by David Atherton, sung and acted with mesmerizing effect by Anthony Rolfe Johnson as Aschenbach and Thomas Allen as the devil's various incarnations. Unfortunately, performances of this opera do not seem scheduled again anytime soon.

CHAPTER 29

Child's Play

"T HE CHILD Mozart," as Maynard Solomon, his latest biographer, aptly calls him, is the image of the composer that has entered Western civilization: no one was more precocious than he, no one more able from infancy to produce music with such extraordinary ease and of such astonishing quality. Solomon quotes Daines Barrington, the English scholar who witnessed the wunderkind's talents and then reported on them to the Royal Society: "Suppose then a capital speech in Shakespeare never seen before, and yet read by a child of eight years old, with all the pathetic energy of a Garrick. Let it be conceived likewise, that the same child is reading, with a glance of his eye, three different comments on this speech tending to its illustration; and that one comment is written in Greek, the second in Hebrew, and the third in Etruscan characters. . . . When all this is conceived, it will convey some idea of what this boy was capable of." Sight-reading, extended improvisation, transposing, playing blindfolded, writing down—note perfect—music that he had heard only once, identifying the pitch of any sound, all in addition to composing sonatas, chamber pieces, concertos, and even a couple of operas from the age of about five: Mozart's gifts bordered on the supernatural, and have remained unequalled.

Yet a mere recital of his feats brings us no closer to Mozart the human being. The language of music is both expressive and mysteriously elusive: a piano concerto by Mozart *says* nothing at all, and is only incidentally tied to the moment in his life when it was composed. Musicological analysis can describe changes in style, illustrate features of form and of the tonal palette, characterize the logic and the harmonic language of a work. The problem remains of connecting, in some meaningful way, the experiences of Mozart's life with the actual music he produced, revealing how the former somehow sustained and—to some degree, at least—can explain the latter. The great virtue of Maynard Solomon's massively documented "Mozart: A Life" (HarperCollins; $35) is that he has brought together Mozart's life and musical accomplishments more skillfully and intelligently than most of his predecessors in a compelling—indeed, often harrowing—synthesis. He begins not with the picture of consummate grace and supernal achievement to which Mozart's works have surely entitled him but with a curious absence in the record: the fact that Salzburg's most famous son seems to have been written out of both its collective and its official memory a decade before he died, in 1791, presumably as a punishment for his "voluntary migration" from the city's oppressive subjugation. Disinheritance becomes Solomon's clue to understanding Mozart, even "a precondition of his creativity." And, as Solomon develops his insight, the inner core of the composer's identity is shown to be bound up in his painfully complex relationship with his father, Leopold—who was himself a disinherited son with "an erotically tinged drive to dominate and a penchant for an almost Jamesian vicarious creativity." Solomon focuses on this father-son partnership and shows how it imprisoned the young Wolfgang Mozart creatively and personally in the older man's sphere as rebel and—here Solomon's ingenuity gives an audacious edge to his interpretation—as willing captive. Even after Mozart had begun his own family, the internalized relationship remained a constant in Wolfgang's psyche.

Were this partnership simply one of exploitative parent and clever child, it would not have endured so long, and so profitably, for both. It was predicated on love and admiration, not merely on venality and greed; in contrast, the boy's relationship with his mother was much less rich. Leopold was, of course, the organizer of his son and daughter's huge European tours; Solomon provides a staggeringly detailed portrait of the seven-year-old Wolfgang and the twelve-year-old Marianne, his pianist sister, as they trekked across the Continent "for three years, five months, and twenty days, and . . . traveled several thousand miles by coach, stopped in eighty-eight cities and towns (including repeat visits), and performed for audiences totaling many thousands." But if Leopold instigated his son's discovery of the world, he also instigated the boy's stunningly fluent gifts as a composer in the current neoclassical style—courtly, Italianate, conventional. Wolfgang's childhood, Solomon says, was a joint venture between the son and the father. It gave both of them visibility and wealth, and it freed Leopold to live away from duties, both familial and professional, to which his modest attainments might have condemned him. The words "magical" and "miraculous" recur frequently as the prodigy (who seemed to enjoy the arduous performing schedule imposed on him) revealed more and more of his talents.

Inevitably, the boy wonder grew into a brilliant adolescent, and began to forge on his own an aesthetic voice through which to express his concerns and his inventiveness. Solomon, in his classic 1977 study of Beethoven, interrupted his narrative to note significant developments in the artist's style; he does this for Mozart with a singular discernment in a series of chapters that delineate the essential features of style, form, and rhetoric which give Mozart's sound its strikingly inimitable qualities—elegance, formal perfection, idiosyncratic inflections. What stamps these chapters with rare cogency is that they not only characterize with tact and skill the works of a given period but also ingeniously reveal the music's sources in Mozart's life at that time. The teen-ager's growing sense of independence, his explorations of Paris and Vienna prior to leaving Salzburg for good, his fidelity to the past combined with "a subversive cast of mind so subtly concealed in convention": all these color his Salzburg serenades and divertimenti, written for the archbishop's court between 1772 and 1776, and, to a lesser extent, his more traditional concertos and chamber works of the time.

Solomon lets us see Mozart establishing his creative individuality in these "social" works that "simultaneously represented the composer's ties to his community and his powerful attachment to feelings associated with pastoral and idyllic states of being." Idyllic and ironic at the same time, these relatively undiscussed compositions reflect the young man's attachment to his father (and thus tradition) and his own "anxiety of originality," which now allow him only the first venturings into "a deepened world of feeling." And as Mozart writes more of this music, with its courtly dances and lute simulations, he moves beyond aristocratic self-congratulation into "representations of an ideal pastoral world, even of the classical image of Arcadia itself, and what had been a readily consumable festive music linked to a particular celebration now becomes a stylistic resource of extraordinary affective range, celebrating broad areas of human experience, centering on nature, love, and play."

Yet even after Mozart married Constanze Weber, in 1782, and moved to Vienna, he remained in bondage to his father, torn by dualities that had him vacillating between enjoyment and "a need to be dominated"—between the pleasures of adult freedom with a new family of his own and "the performance principle," which his father sternly supervised. Leopold was never resigned to his son's marriage, and took no interest in his son's children. (He was, however, able to pry Marianne's son little Leopold loose, and rear him, in a futile effort to re-create his original family.)

According to Solomon, the music of Mozart's maturity provides a record of the composer's gradually achieved sense of artistic sovereignty. This is magnificently evident in the C-Minor Mass (K. 427/417a), which he wrote in 1782–1783 in part as a testimonial to his love for Constanze, and in which he at last sheds the "neo-classicist aesthetic" so dear to his father. Whereas his music had once reflected his being caught between "opposed effects" (Solomon provides a particularly informative analysis of the andante/ adagio movements of the middle seventeen-seventies, works that convey the sorrow he felt at his mother's death and the disintegration of the family structure), during the middle seventeen-eighties he used music to place himself in a new line of succession, with Haydn his conscriptive father substitute. He has moved away from piano works by around 1786, and embarked on a still more heightened Viennese career, as impresario and opera composer. His father dies in 1787; and his music takes on a new dimension of beauty, one laced through with a feeling for mortality that is "shockingly voluptuous," as the musician Charles Rosen called it, a mastery rather than a yielding. Intermittently, Solomon affords us persuasive descriptions of the mature works, where "the chaste, sublimated surface of Mozart's music conceals turbulent, potentially eruptive currents of feeling." Of the B-flat concerto (K.595) and the G-minor symphony (K. 550), he writes:

> It perhaps is only when we feel the power of Mozart's music to bruise us that we can discover its enchanted healing powers as well. . . . We may follow the joyous path pursued by Mozart's play impulse, delighting in his antic disposition, marveling at his capacity for turning things inside out, for finding carnivalesque juxtapositions and endless possibilities, at every turn affirming the sheer vitality that inhabits the universes of sound inscribed on a state of silence that he brought into being.

Solomon points out a few other areas of relative freedom that Mozart was able to explore both in music and out of it: his frequently indulged penchant for luxury, for punning and often scatological language games; and for the Masonic order, which he looked to as a fulfillment of his desire for justice and rationality (and which informs "Die Zauberflöte," his penultimate opera). But the horizons of his life as a harried, money-short musician gradually darkened around him. Wolfgang was written out of his father's will, even though for most of his life he had been the family's mainstay and source of financial security. Marianne had chosen Leopold over Wolfgang in the continuing unravelling of the family romance, and Wolfgang's intimate connection with her, too, frayed over time. He suffered a serious depression in the late seventeen-eighties, accompanied by what appeared to be a diminishment of his creative powers. He was restored to almost miraculous productivity in 1789, though, with "Così Fan Tutte," the last—and, in my opinion, the greatest—of the operatic masterpieces he wrote with the librettist Lorenzo da Ponte.

Only two of Mozart's six children survived infancy, and he, too, was always in precarious health. He died, in his thirty-sixth year—an exhausted, and even a pathetic, man—in December, 1791, of acute rheumatic fever. Solomon definitively disposes of the notion that Mozart may have been the victim of a conspiracy; in addition, he provides adequate evidence that Mozart's humble funeral was the result neither of extreme penury nor of general neglect. Most Viennese citizens opted for what were then called "3rd class" burials, and, besides, it is likely, Solomon suggests, that Mozart actually wanted burial without a coffin as an "emblem of his beliefs"—a way of asserting "the brotherhood of souls, equal in death as they should have been in life."

I do not know a musician's biography as satisfying and as moving as this one. True, Solomon's obsession with getting all the details down leaves the reader dizzy after uninterrupted infusions of long, sometimes tedious, lists of ducats and florins, of cities and people, and of Köchel numbers. He occasionally has a tendency to overinterpret, as in his fanciful speculations on Mozart's invention of "Adam" as one of his wedding-document names, and to overreact, as when for far too many pages he rummages excitedly through Mozart's not particularly interesting "Excerpts from the Fragments of Zoroaster," a set of verbal riddles and proverbs written in 1786. Such lapses, however, are offset by fascinating anecdotes: Mozart often spoke in recitative; he loved sumptuous and sometimes gaudy clothing (in particular a bright-red coat with gold buttons); he had "a marked antipathy to France"; his letters to his cousin Maria Anna Thekla are like "a thesaurus gone mad"; until he was nine, he had an irrational fear of trumpets.

There is an unfailingly humane and generous spirit at work in this long and absorbing volume. Rarely have social and political analyses been so effectively joined to psychoanalytic probings (inspired by Freud, Melanie Klein, D. W. Winnicott, and Paul Ricoeur) as they are in Solomon's hands; and I have encountered nothing that is quite like the detailed charting of so profound a genius as Mozart's, especially as that genius interacts with the nourishing, and psychologically debilitating, relationship with Leopold. Far from being presented as a relentless list of wounds and complexes, the familial bond is seen as a condition of both men's humanity. "In the end," Solomon says of their attempts to break loose from each other, "a father and a son, trembling within a conflicting welter of disquieting emotions, weighed the compensations of their respective rebellions, wondered if they could have acted otherwise, tried to conceal their wounds, and were powerless to change course."

The real tests of a composer's biography, however, are whether the music is somehow made more clear by it and whether a narrative life actually helps us to interpret the music in a new way. Solomon succeeds handsomely in both respects. Although he has obviously benefitted from previous scrutinies of Mozart's work (most notably Charles Rosen's "The Classical Style"), he shows us the music as emerging from the deepest recesses of the man's spirit, its formal and stylistic characteristics the result both of a highly disciplined and institutionalized "classical" aesthetic and of personal impulses, psychological stresses. It is impossible now to listen to the "Haffner Serenade," say, and not recall the idea of Mozart's trying to use a hackneyed form to pull away from his father's orbit and create a choreography of ironic, albeit "correct," pastoral gestures; or to the C-Major Piano Concerto (K.415) and not note that the "military style boldly moves to annex Viennese classicism as part of its theater of operations." Moreover, no one before Solomon has explained the haunting, often surprising alternation of major and minor modes in even a "simple" piece like the C-Major Piano Sonata (the bane of every beginning piano student) and the way in which Mozart undermines "the rococo surface as though to subvert not only the vision of tranquillity, but the aristocratic order it is customarily intended to validate." In reading Solomon, we come to know not so much a transformed as an *inevitable* Mozart, ever the miraculous creator but also the considerable human being, unsurpassably impressive and somehow closer at hand.

CHAPTER 30

32 Short Films About Glenn Gould

T HE FILM you are about to see tonight is quite unusual, beginning with its title *32 Short Films About Glenn Gould*. It was directed by François Girard, a French-Canadian director and is about the remarkable Anglo-Canadian pianist Glenn Gould who died in the fall of 1982 aged almost exactly 50. Gould first came to prominence with a couple of recitals in New York and Washington in 1955: I was an undergraduate at the time and although I didn't attend either recital I did read about both of them and then a year later bought the record that Columbia Records made of the recital, the *Goldberg Variations* by Bach. I don't think it is an exaggeration that the whole course of musical performance, and especially Bach on the piano, was changed as a result of recital and record. Gould immediately became a major international star and, uniquely in the history of recorded piano performance, he inaugurated an entire territory of repertory and performing style of his own. No one sounded like him at all, no one could come close to him in playing complicated contrapuntal music whose clarity and precision was almost supernatural, and no one had the gifts that he had. The soundtrack of Girard's film is entirely made up of Gould's playing, a lot of it music by Bach, a composer with whom he became particularly identified. Bach's *Goldberg Variations* was the first record he made, and just a month before he died Gould re-recorded it: the two performances are completely different, yet both are unmistakably by Gould. Now the *Goldberg* is one of Bach's last, most complex yet strangely energetic scores, an elaborate series of 30 meditations on a simple theme, which is played at the beginning and then again at the very end of the piece: hence the theme stated twice, plus 30 variations, equals 32 — 32 short films because each variation is both quite short and always about the theme,

Miller Theatre, May 11, 1995.

just as the film is shot as a series of variations on the same figure, namely Glenn Gould.

One thing Girard doesn't attempt in the film is to show you Gould—who is impersonated in the film by a young actor Colm Feore, who does bear a slight physical resemblance to Gould but who often catches his extremely unmistakable manner quite well—Girard doesn't attempt to show you Gould actually playing the piano. There are several possible reasons for this. In the first place Gould had absolutely extraordinary mannerisms at the piano that were quite incredible to behold: many critics and concert-goers commented, or complained about them. He sat at a very, very low chair so that his fingers and eyes were at about the same level. He sang, often quite loudly when he played, and—more disconcerting—he waved his arms around like a conductor conducting himself playing the piano. I once saw him perform Strauss's *Burlesk*—a fiendishly difficult piece—with the Detroit Symphony under Paul Paray: Gould not only played the piece with immense flourish but he also conducted the orchestra from the piano, which drove poor Paray quite mad. Another perhaps more urgent reason for not showing us Gould at the piano is that although Gould suddenly quit playing recitals in public in 1964—he was 31—and never played in public again, he was probably the most televised, filmed, and recorded musician who ever lived. Gould was deeply-influenced by another Canadian, Marshall McLuhan, and believed that music was essentially communication. He was enamored of radio and wrote several radio scripts, but he also believed that listening or watching a performer was, or rather could be, a creative act, if the audience was given enough to listen to and watch. There are literally hundreds of hours of Gould seen playing on the BBC, or the CBC; Sony has reissued these as laser discs and videos; to ask an actor to imitate what has already been given so much filmic time would have been to risk caricature or ungainly and unprofitable repetition. So in the film you always see Gould either before or after he played, not while playing.

What the film does portray with great skill is Gould's apartness, his solitary eccentric ways, and his ecstatic—a word he used often in John Donne's sense of standing outside of—attitude as far as music and life were concerned. He could memorize a piece of music just by looking at it, and his sight-reading skills were astounding: he could play whole operas, symphonies, choral works at the piano with unbelievable ease. He didn't seem to need to practice, and according to many pianists today he had perhaps the most stupendous technique in music, beyond those even of Horowitz and Hoffman. Each of his fingers seemed to have an intelligence of its own. He was a control freak and hypochondriac who spent long hours driving alone in his car, lived in a hotel room rather than a house, and saw no one socially, although he liked to call people up in the middle of the night. No pianist that I can think of had as interesting and as wide-ranging a repertory, from Bach, the Elizabethan and Dutch 16th and 17th century keyboard composers, to Handel, Haydn, Mozart, Beethoven, Grieg, Bizet, Brahms, Wagner, Strauss and all the major modernists—Schoenberg, Berg, Webern. He seemed to hate the standard 19th century romantics like Chopin and Schuman, yet he recorded Liszt transcriptions and his own versions of Wagner with stunning results. He thought Mozart was a second-rate composer, and preferred Petula Clark, though he recorded all the Mozart sonatas in such a way as to make you believe that he disliked them. He conducted, played the organ and harpsichord and composed, all with the same dazzling intensity and brilliance that make most other pianists seem both tame and quite dull. Above all, he *controlled* himself and his life.

Perhaps the single dominating idea of his life and work (which by the way included a huge amount of interesting, if sometimes over-written prose) was the idea of not belonging to one's own time and place. He thought that nothing could be worse than simply following the *Zeitgeist* or being modish. He was therefore not just an eccentric but also an original, someone who believed it was his task as an artist and performer to originate everything he did, including himself. He sounded and talked like no one else, and no one could sound like him. Luckily he had the genius to do this. The challenge of making a film about this man is therefore to find a form and style that renders him faithfully without at the same time trying to imitate or copy him: in this I think Girard succeeds quite brilliantly. What you are left with is an impression of someone who created his own way without regard for convention or precedent. In the end of course it comes back to the way he played the piano, the way when he played the music you felt that the music was actually opening its mouth and speaking to you as if for the very first time.

CHAPTER 31

Bach's Genius, Schumann's Eccentricity, Chopin's Ruthlessness, Rosen's Gift

CHARLES ROSEN'S *THE ROMANTIC GENERATION*

CHARLES ROSEN's new book is about the group of composers who succeeded the great Viennese Classicists Mozart, Beethoven, and Haydn, and the aesthetic movement they represented. The Post-Classicists emerged for the most part during the period from the death of Beethoven (1827) to the death of Chopin (1849). A substantially expanded version of the Charles Eliot Norton Lectures given at Harvard during 1980–81, *The Romantic Generation*, which follows in the path of its distinguished predecessor *The Classical Style*, is a remarkable amalgam of precise, brilliantly illuminating analysis, audacious generalization, and not always satisfying—but always interesting—synthesis, scattered over more than seven hundred pages of serviceable but occasionally patronizing prose that takes Rosen through a generous amount of mainly instrumental and vocal music at very close range indeed.

What must be said immediately is how well, how enviably well, Rosen knows this music, its secrets, its astonishing harmonic and structural innovations, and the problems and pleasures of its performance: he writes not as a musicologist but as an extremely literate pianist (the book is accompanied by a CD of illustrative extracts played by Rosen) for whom a lifetime of study and public rendition has given the music its very life. Although the book does have its longueurs it is often grippingly, even excitably, readable. Yet the reader must keep *hearing* the music, since all of Rosen's interesting points relate finally to a revolution of audible effects intended by his three major examples, Chopin, Schumann, and Liszt.

Running through the work is an underlying concentration (*cantus firmus* would be a more appropriate phrase) on the polyphonic genius of Johann Sebastian Bach, and the power of his genius at work in Romantic music

---

that was supposed to be at odds with his learned rigor and fugal mastery. No, it was not, as is often said, Mendelssohn who 'discovered' Bach for the nineteenth century, but Chopin, Schumann, Liszt, and well before them Beethoven and Mozart, all of whom grew up on the *Well-Tempered Clavier.* Chopin 'idolized' Bach; Beethoven was inspired in his third-period works by the preludes and fugues; Liszt and Schumann returned to Bach's work for pointers on how to redistribute piano music contrapuntally in various registers.

Rosen's interest in Bach's presence in Romantic music is an implicit refutation of Glenn Gould's charge that all those composers, like Chopin and Schumann, whose work forms the core of the contemporary pianist's repertoire (which Gould of course both avoided and excoriated), were interested only in *vertical* composition. In perhaps the most interesting section of his book Rosen shows that Chopin—routinely thought of as a swooning, 'inspired', small-scale salon composer whose music is basically 'effeminate'—is in fact an ingenious contrapuntalist of the most extreme sort, a musician whose affecting surfaces conceal a discipline in planning, polyphony, and sheer harmonic creativity, a composer whose only real rival in the end was someone as different and as grand as Wagner. As Rosen says,

> there is a paradox at the heart of Chopin's style, in its unlikely combination of a rich chromatic web of polyphony, based on a profound experience of J.S. Bach, with a sense of melody and a way of sustaining the melodic line derived directly from Italian opera. The paradox is only apparent and is only felt as such when one hears the music. The two influences are perfectly synthesised, and they give each other a new kind of power.

According to Rosen, Bach is important in another respect. Although one can analyse the scores of such late contrapuntal masterpieces as the *Art of Fugue* or the *Musical Offering,* it is impossible to hear all the polyphonic effects, which are intended as theoretical, rather than actual, sounds. Eighteenth-century composers like Bach, Mozart and Handel conceived and annotated their music, Rosen says, to produce 'a particular beauty that is only partially related to any imagined performance—an irreducibly inaudible beauty, so to speak'. With Beethoven, however, there is an inevitable quality to the sound, which suggests that he 'has reached the ideal fusion of conception and realisation'. But for the Romantics, Schumann in particular, the inaudible, the unplayable, the unimaginable can be incorporated into performance: 'it is an essentially Romantic paradox that the primacy of sound in Romantic music should be accompanied, and even announced, by a sonority that is not only unrealisable but unimaginable'.

What the core Romantics did therefore was to extend the range of musical composition so as to include not only the inaudible, but also harmonic overtones, new sonorities produced by the pedal, tone colour, timbre, register and spacing, thereby 'permanently enlarging the role of sound in the composition of music'. At another level their conception of music itself took on new meanings and made possible the invention of distinctive forms influenced by such Romantic literary concerns as the fragment, ruins and landscape. Precisely because it was imprecise and general (as opposed to discursive language, which was both concrete and exact) music came to be considered the Romantic art par excellence. Rosen makes a number of connections between various Romantic compositions and the ideas of Schlegel, Vico, the physicist Ritter, Senancour, and the traveler and naturalist Ramond de Carbonnières, who in his descriptions of landscapes and glaciers is presented as a major (and completely unknown) anticipator of twentieth-century thought.

There is, alas, a sloppy garrulousness about some of Rosen's exposition: not in his analysis of individual musical pieces, but in his relentless paraphrasing of, and haughty quotation from, intellectual and poetic authorities. All the material will be familiar to readers, say, of M. H. Abrams and Frank Manuel, or, on particular Romantic subjects like ruins, Tom McFarland and others. Rosen rambles on and on, quoting not only translation but even the French and German originals, in displays of erudition that make one extremely impatient. Very rarely are direct inferences drawn from all this cultural background—which is itself unnervingly disconnected from social, economic and political realities such as the French Revolution, or the advent of industrialization, or the developing interest in economics, as informatively discussed by Albert Hirschmann and Michel Foucault. It is as if, in the best of all possible worlds, Ritter had interesting notions about music and speech, as did Vico, as did Sterne, and Tiech, as finally did Schumann. It is very hard to doubt a community of interest here, but Rosen's method is too casual, too delighted with its own capacity for ferreting out aperçus from diverse writers, for the reader to be left with more than a sense that all those ideas were in the air and somehow made their influence felt in composers' predilections for song cycles, or for the depiction of landscape in their music, or—as Rosen brilliantly shows in the case of Schumann—for the use of fragments as compositional style, giving works like the *Dichterliebe* that sense of half-finished, forlorn desuetude which is uniquely theirs.

Rosen's procedures for the analysis of a cultural period may be too little thought through, too entertained by free-wheeling analogies and 'look-at-this' correspondences, too scanting of the immense and very useful scholarship on the material, but they are often stunningly effective for looking at aspects of the Romantic piano and voice literature. He goes much beyond anyone else in revealing the sources of Schumann's amazing eccentricity, which was well-anchored in a whole series of formal practices, and marvelously shows them at work in all the major compositions of the 1830s, the only truly creative decade of Schumann's life. In particular, Rosen does a spectacular job of reading the C major *Fantasie* in terms of Schumann's use of Beethoven's *An die ferne Geliebte,* the great song cycle that bridges his second and late-period styles. No other writer on music has his gift for walking and playing through pieces, pointing out how memory, quotation, observation are giving concrete musical realisation that extends from the printed score, to the hand on the keyboard, to the pedal, and then is received by the listener's ear.

No wonder then that Rosen can demonstrate that 'the song cycle is the most original form created in the first half of the 19th century'. And when he shows in detail how such episodic piano works as Schumann's *Davidsbündlertänze* are elaborations of 'a musical structure experienced progressively as one moves through it: the disparity of the individual dances reveals the sense of a larger unity only little by little as the series continues', he gets to the heart of a major aesthetic achievement:

> The reappearance of the melancholy second dance is not only a return but more specifically a looking back, as the Romantic travelers delighted to look back to perceive the different appearance of what they had seen before, a meaning altered and transfigured by distance and a new perspective. In Beethoven's instrumental works the return of an initial theme had often been transformed and radically altered by rescoring and rewriting: but in the *Davidsbündlertänze* the *Ländler* [or dance] is apparently unaltered, transformed simply by distance in time and space, by the preceding sonorities, by everything that has taken place since the opening. An age that began with the attempt to realize landscape as music was finally able, in the most radical and eccentric productions of Schumann, to experience music as landscape.

The equation of Schumann's best work with his eccentricity is a matter returned to in the book's final pages. The composer's obsessive sense of detail, Rosen believes, deprived his work of great breadth but made up for it in 'hypnotic intensity'. I would not myself be so dismissive, not even by implication, of Schumann's symphonies, in particular the superb Second, nor would I scant *Das Paradies und die Peri,* but Rosen's scheme for Schumann is quite inflexible and leaves the chamber music out almost entirely. He argues, for example, that when, after that fruitful decade, Schumann went back to his works to revise them, he always made them worse, not better. But carving out of the oeuvre its most quixotic and certainly its most incandescently eccentric moments Rosen has found a draconian way of dealing with Schumann's peculiar inconsistency of approach and, in the years before his final insanity, the quieting down of his musical ardor. But this is just too schematic and reductive, I think, too impatient with the perceivable outlines of a more various and integrated achievement than Rosen allows.

There are no such intermittences in his account of Chopin: three large chapters on him amounting to two hundred pages are the core of *The Romantic Generation.* Even though there has been some crucial new work on Chopin on the last decade (which Rosen acknowledges), no one has been as disciplined, as well-informed, as discerning, as Rosen, for whom Chopin embodies the paradox of being 'the most conservative and most radical composer of his generation'. The great thing about these Chopin chapters for a Chopin fanatic like myself is that they can inform and perhaps even change the way he is played. This is particularly true of what Rosen has to say about Chopin's counterpoint (he 'was the greatest master of counterpoint since Mozart') and the way an energetic polyphonic strategy that implies three- or four-part writing is at work even mainly single-line works like the entirely unison, high-velocity last movement of the B flat minor Sonata.

Rosen then proceeds to a truly inspired reading of the Third Ballade in terms of Chopin's adaptation of narrative forms for use in instrumental writing: this allows him to look at the other Ballades as well as the late-period Polonaise-Fantasie and to elucidate them not only according to their amazingly resourceful use of harmonic devices neglected by other composers (the alternation of major and minor modes, the use of related tonalities for coloristic purposes), but also in terms of a heterophony that is as skillful as it is 'secret', concealing itself in what may appear to be 'soft' or even 'sugary' music.

Chopin, Rosen argues extremely persuasively, is in reality not just superbly organized and skilled as few composers have been, but

> ruthless, capable of asking the pianist to try for the unrealizable in delicacy as well as violence. The unrealizable in Chopin, however, is always perfectly imagined as sound. His structures are rarely beautiful or interesting in themselves on paper, as are those of Bach or Mozart (to name his favorite composers): they are conceived for their effect, even if the intended public was a small and very private one in some cases. That is why his long works have been underestimated: forms like the Third Ballade or the Polonaise-Fantasie appear lopsided on the page. They are justified by performance, although

Chopin is among the most difficult of all composers to interpret. His music, never calculated like much of Bach, for solitary meditation, works directly on the nerves of the listener, sometimes by the most delicate and fleeting suggestion, sometimes with an obsessive hammered violence

as in the concluding pages of the B minor Scherzo.

The theme of Chopin's ruthlessness and 'sadism' is developed through a marvelous consideration of the pedagogical techniques embodied (and to some degree derived from Bach) in the *Etudes*. Here as elsewhere Rosen delivers himself of casual observations—on the decline of writing music for the young, on the nature of virtuosity and the pianist's need to bear pain, Chopin's 'irony and wit but not a trace of humor'—that sparkle with worldly cleverness and long experience. He is just right, I think, in his account of the Romantic tendency to 'morbid intensity', and, in Chopin's case, the ability to transform sentimental clichés of illness or deep, if conventional, feeling into 'fierce concentration' rendered more imposing, as in the Nocturnes, 'with a profusion of ornamental and contrapuntal detail'. A final chapter on what Rosen considers Chopin's 'most original and eccentric works'—the Mazurkas—consolidates the main claims for Chopin as 'the only composer of his generation who never, after the age of 21, displayed the slightest awkwardness with longer works', or for that matter with short ones. All those features of Chopin's idiom, which include his sources in Polish dance rhythms and Italian opera, as well as his formal and harmonic genius for blurring frontiers between sections, constructing the most inventive thematic transfigurations and returns, are taken by Rosen to constitute a truly distinctive Romantic *style*—the greatest single realization of which is the Barcarolle, a late composition and, in my opinion, Chopin's most magnificent.

It would be difficult to follow the dense, inspired chapters on Chopin with the same level of detail and genuinely turbulent insight, and Rosen doesn't manage it. Not that he isn't full of perspicacious observations on Liszt and Mendelssohn, whom in a backhanded compliment he calls 'the inventor of religious Kitsch' in music. (I had always thought of Vivaldi that way!) In fact, he has a great deal to say that is interesting, but the episodic quality of his writing suggests that weariness may have set in. Besides, the categories he has invented for describing Romantic style in Schumann and Chopin seem to have been much harder to apply to others. This is a case of definitions and formulations getting the better of analysis and even taste. Thus the desultory, rather witless chapter on Berlioz, whose work is encapsulated by Rosen in the maddeningly inconsequential one-liner, 'it is not Berlioz's oddity but his normality, his ordinariness that makes him great', which produces little more than a series of reluctant admissions that Berlioz may not have been *that* interesting but he could manipulate chord inversions and root positions with surprising skill. It's perhaps relevant that Berlioz was the one member of the Romantic generation who never studied or wrote for the piano; this sets him even further apart for Rosen, who is similarly patronizing about music after 1850.

Except for some unconvincing animadversions on Bellini and Donizetti, both of them composers of a cloying inadequacy, plus a few sound pages on the more gifted Meyerbeer, Rosen doesn't show much interest in Romantic opera: Weber, for instance, isn't mentioned, neither is there much about Rossini's historical music dramas. Early Wagner is left out entirely along with the emergence of the Romantic orchestra, not only in the work of Weber and Berlioz, but also in Mendelssohn (a fleeting reference there) and, more important, Beethoven. Rosen doesn't have to mention everyone and everything—his book is already substantial enough—but it is at the edges and at the beginning of his story that the capriciousness, and the unreflecting closedness of his scheme, make themselves felt. Why, for example, is Beethoven not looked at in his middle and third-period works as an important source of Romanticism rather than a mere indictment of it by virtue of his oeuvre's monumentality? His enabling presence is certainly to be found in Schumann, Mendelssohn, Berlioz, Liszt, and of course Schubert. Only Chopin seems not to have felt his powerful example, but even that resistance highlights the fact that Beethoven was as much a part of Romanticism as in his early period he was of the classical style.

And in his understandable reluctance to get involved either with the society of which Romanticism was a part, or with cultural theory, Rosen disallows himself insights and concepts exactly where and when in his own argument he might have benefited from them. The Romantic composer's isolation is one of Rosen's themes, yet he does not (at sufficient length) investigate why that isolation should have existed, and the bearing that both the onset of secularism and the end of aristocratic privilege may have had on it.

Rosen is too intelligent not to notice these things (he notes, for example, that Romanticism did not produce religious music, although many composers wrote Requiems), but his rapid allusions simply shut off discussion. Take the extremely vexed question of the relationship between a composer's life and work. He advances the thesis that 'the most interesting composers have arranged their lives and their personalities in order to realize their projects and their conceptions most effectively and convincingly', then follows with the unexamined claim that 'a purely musical experience is as powerful a sensation as anything outside music'. But what is 'inside' and 'outside' here, and where do lives and personalities end and musical experiences begin? These plonking declarations aren't much of a substitute for a conception, or indeed a theory, of such relationships.

It is hard to disagree completely with the book's summary proposition that Romantic music developed out of an exasperation with rational systems and the Classical hierarchies of genre, but the notion has nowhere near the force contained in Rosen's account of the consequent unpredictability of Romantic composition, of the Romantic attempt 'to attain the sublime through the trivial', through the carefully exploited detail, and the eccentric, personal structure. It is the lucidity and resourcefulness of Rosen's remarkably fine analytic examples that will carry readers, not his attempt to legislate general ideas about art and life. On the other hand, the book will certainly change most minds about what Chopin's and Schumann's achievements really were: more important, readers will listen to and play Romantic music with a much more alert understanding than before.

CHAPTER 32

Why Listen to Boulez?

P IERRE BOULEZ is 70 this year, and is now the only major composer-performer of Western music appearing in public. Earlier in this century there were several such figures—Rachmaninov, Bartók, Messiaen, Prokofiev, Britten, Strauss and others. The split between the platform star and the serious composer has become almost complete, the result of the economics of record production and virtuoso careers, as well as the difficulty for the average concertgoer of understanding much less liking, most contemporary music as it is usually represented (misrepresented is the more accurate word). Aside from a few "postmodern," not to say reactionary, composers like Arvo Pärt and Henryk Górecki who have made it big with the record-buying crowd, there is supposed to be no real audience for the kind of music composed by Boulez and Stockhausen, music that is neither tuneful nor in any ready-made way accessible to ears that have been sated with recordings of Mozart, Brahms and Beethoven. As a result, musical audiences today are the first in history not principally exposed to the music of their own time.

Give them what they want, say the impresarios and managers of, for instance, the Metropolitan Opera and the New York Philharmonic; if what "they" want is an unending repetition of late-eighteenth- to late-nineteenth-century classics, "they" shall get them, especially if ticket sales keep up. A glance at recent repertory performed at the Met or Carnegie or Avery Fisher Hall reveals an extraordinarily conservative policy of Austro-Germanic symphonies and sonatas and Italian operas, with a tiny hypo-critical sprinkling of one Elliott Carter and a few Shostakovich or Messiaen works thrown in. The Met has yet to perform Messiaen's St. *François d'Assise* or Ligeti's *Le grand macabre*, or anything like an adequate sampling of works by Henze, Busoni or Hindemith. For this season Carnegie has announced an all-Beethoven-sonata seven-concert series by Maurizio Pollini, who this past summer at Salzburg did a remarkable five-concert program of Schubert songs for male chorus; pieces by Schönberg, Gesualdo, Nono and Ligeti; solo and chamber pieces by Boulez, Brahms and Berg; as well as the last three Beethoven sonatas. "Why does he not do the same thing in New York?" I asked Hans Landesmann, one of the Salzburg Festival's directors. "Pollini did want to," he replied, "but Carnegie only requested him for the Beethoven series," Not to be outdone, Alfred Brendel is performing the five Beethoven concertos next season with Kurt Masur and the Philharmonic.

Boulez stands out against so dreary a background not only because (except for his tenure with the New York Philharmonic) he has paced his conducting appearances so as not to seem too regular or routine a presence, but also because more than any other twentieth-century composer (Schönberg is his closest rival) he has been performer, composer *and* critic, a man whose collected prose, numbering thousands of dense, acutely intelligent pages, has constituted for him and an ideal audience a complete discursive intellectual framework for his work as conductor and composer. Aside from Wagner, there has been nothing like this all-front campaign by a musician to create his own stage, tradition and critical vocabulary. The French publisher Christian Bourgois has just released the first part *(Points de repére, tôme I)* of a collected edition of Boulez's writings, which opens with a 1954 essay, "Probabilités critiques du compositeur." arguing forcefully for understanding the composer's function as including his work as critic. With characteristic sarcasm Boulez advances the notion as a way of scandalizing the French predilection for "spontaneous" creativity.

Nor is this all. Again like Wagner, Boulez has succeeded in establishing a domain comprising a research institute (Institut de Recherche et Coordination Acoustique/Musique, or IRCAM) and a performing group, the Ensemble Inter-Contemporain, both of them based in Paris, where Boulez is also a professor at the Collège de France. Boulez is certainly the most powerful presence in contemporary music, radiating a unique authority (an authoritarian Modernism might be one way to characterize it) that compels attention and even awe.

No one has as much access to every corner of the music world as Boulez. He can perform wherever and whatever he chooses. Consider the evidence: During the seventies he did a distinguished stint at Bayreuth, and less of one with the New York Philharmonic, which he led from 1971 to 1977. He has regularly recorded concerts with the London, Chicago, Cleveland and Vienna orchestras. His operatic forays across Europe (a recent *Pelléas et Mélisande* with Welsh National, and a *Moses und Aron* in Amsterdam, neither of which will ever be seen in New York) will long be remembered. In short, Boulez is in the process of trying to reshape concert life, to bring it more in line with his ideas about the great music of the past century as well as to make it more amenable to his own music.

Messiaen was Boulez's teacher, and an illuminating account of Messiaen's teaching methods and influence in Paris in the forties (Jean Boivin, *La Classe de Messiaen*) records the temperamental divergence between master and student that occurred in 1948. Although their relationship was a rich and largely positive one, the contentious Boulez (he had already begun his outspoken frontal assault on the traditions and practices of contemporary music) implicitly contrasted his method with his eclectic teacher's. Messiaen *juxtaposes*, he said, whereas I try to *compose;* in Messiaen this led to musical canvases covered with sonorities not connected to one another by necessity but by harmonic adjacence governed by pleasure and intuition. Reading through Boulez's critical writings of the forties and fifties, one is struck by the acutely demanding rigors of his requirements, according to which such masters as Schönberg, Berg, Bartók and Stravinsky were found wanting in logic, rhythmic organization, coherences of various kinds.

In April, Boulez conducted three sold-out concerts of twentieth-century music with the London Symphony Orchestra in Carnegie Hall; each concert featured one work by him, in addition to classics from the twentieth-century repertory. The concerts—intellectual, sensuous, inventive, critical and articulated—were organized along thematic and argumentative lines that focused attention on common elements in the works. In this way Boulez transformed the *juxtapositions* of normal concerts into *compositions* according to a considered plan. Program One comprised memorial and retrospective compositions: Ravel's *Tombeau de Couperin*, a twentieth-century ironic celebration of the eighteenth-century master—*gallant*, decorative, ceremonial. Boulez's *Pli selon pli, improvisation III*, was a stunning contrast in scale and power, based on one of the most difficult of Mallarmé's sonnets, "A la nue accablante," whose suggestion of apocalyptic devastation and sepulchral compression is met with a vast, unsettling score set for soprano (brilliantly realized by Laura Aikin) and orchestra. Webern's *Six Pieces*, which record the death of the composer's mother, and Berg's *Violin Concerto*, whose occasion is the death of Alma Gropius's daughter and is subtitled "to the memory of an angel," concluded the program.

Program Two presented *Le Sacre du printemps*, Messiaen's *Poèmes pour Mi* (sung by Maria Ewing, a dedicated performer of compelling honesty and high interpretive competence) and Boulez's *Livre pour Cordes*, all of them early works of technical exploration and unique expressive force, the former competing with but not entirely mastering the latter. Program Two shone a light on how twentieth-century Modernists derived music from what Mann in *Dr. Faustus* called "speculating the elements," elements musical and emotional: Messiaen's partially static, partially ecstatic love poetry intended for his first wife is informed by the sacrament of Christian marriage, against which Stravinsky's *Sacre*, with its pagan ritual, is counterpointed.

The last program seemed the most miscellaneous, an amalgam of works like Ravel's *Ma Mère l'oye* suite and Stravinsky's *Chant du Rossignol*, in addition to Boulez's *Notations I–IV*, his most accessible and romantic piece, and two song cycles by Berg, the *Seven Early Songs* and Op. 4, the *Alternberg Lieder*, both sung by Jessye Norman with such affected posing and nonstop mannerism as to undermine her musical attainments in the works. The works on the program were ones of return and recapitulation—the Ravel an early composition for piano orchestrated five years after the two-piano version was written, Berg's *Early Songs* composed in 1905–8 and orchestrated twenty years after, *Chant du Rossignol* originally a fragment of an opera, redone as a ballet for Diaghilev after Stravinsky had already scored the *Sacre* and *Petrouchka* for the company. The *Notations I–IV* grew out of Boulez's first piano pieces, which he expanded and orchestrated years later, with the aim, as yet unfulfilled, of adding eight more works to be performed in groups of four as musicians choose.

With the exception of Daniel Barenboim, whom I heard with the Chicago Symphony in Tokyo doing a spectacularly warm and winning rendition of *Notations*, more attractively shaped than Boulez's in New York, it is hard to imagine any conductor today planning and executing a series such as this. Every recent review of Boulez's conducting speaks of the unprecedented clarity and precision of his beat, the marvelous control he exerts over orchestras, as well as the exquisite refinement of his ear. This is all true. But he is not the best builder of balances, as shown by his tendency to overpower soloists and to produce climaxes out of proportion to the overall effect. In the Berg concerto Anne-Sophie Mutter was frequently drowned out, as was Ewing in *Poèmes pour Mi*. In the second, and in my opinion least successful part of the *Sacre*, I felt Boulez to be struggling against the music, straightening out its occasionally underwritten sections, propping up its more striking episodes with very loud, if summary, explosions. Nevertheless, Boulez is extremely instructive to watch. He does not use a baton, and can be seen actually counting and conducting through every measure of even the most complicated rhythmic patterns in Stravinsky, his own music and Messiaen's works, in which the percussive possibilities of the orchestra are exploited with an exhilarating brilliance and wit.

Each program had a rationale that held the various items together in such a way as to illuminate the compositions and elaborate a context. Boulez's concentration on our century's music gives the lie to the notion that "modern" music is so difficult and rebarbative as to defy either comprehension or pleasure. Boulez's idea is to present the music as constituting a single cultural and aesthetic enterprise, with a number of different phases and styles, many of them still in evolution. This is very far from what most performers trot out before audiences who are reduced to Milton's "blind mouths," consumers who might just as well be gazing idly at one shop window after another on Madison Avenue.

Boulez has been trying for decades to extend the function of the concert hall from its almost restaurant-like status (you're in there at eight to consume only one item on the menu, you eat and you're out by ten) to something resembling a museum in the best sense, where over a longer period of time you experience works of art interacting with one another; you can browse, listen to lectures and so on. Moreover, Boulez is right to consider classical music today more isolated and restricted in its scope than any other art. With that isolation has come what a generation ago Adorno referred to as "the regression of listening," which has eliminated "structural" or integral listening in favor of listening sporadically, in which signature tunes, commercialized classics and debased norms of performance have taken over the act of apprehending classical music.

Boulez's enterprise is to restore the experience of music to the realm of intelligent critical reception by placing his own music as well as that of his contemporaries in an expanded context. No longer is twentieth-century music either a nasty pill that audiences can easily avoid, or an esoteric activity confined to academics and to small, isolated concerts attended only by other composers. There is no question that whether or not one likes or understands works like *Pli selon pli,* they gain in power and intelligibility when experienced in the presence of other twentieth-century works that are reactions not only to various Modernist literary texts but to other attempts to render terror, sorrow and awe. And performances such as Boulez's force open the self-satisfied little boxes in which lazy audiences and unenterprising concert organizers have placed classical music, the better perhaps to restrict its genuine force and often disturbing eruptions. For Boulez, music can be a form of resistance to the crassness and superficiality of mass culture; in this view he follows Schönberg, Adorno, Webern and other High Modernists who have tried to counteract prevailing musical practice with an articulate and intellectually aware sense of the bigger picture. Decidedly not like John Cage, on the one hand, or minimalists like Philip Glass and John Adams, on the other, Boulez is a composer interested in the past as something requiring constant revision, and in constructing the cultural present. This project demands the effort of not only poets and philosophers but also musicians. That the project extracts from audiences a comparable effort at interpretation and understanding makes the whole process of composition, performance and reception a difficult one simply to sit back and "enjoy."

But it is tremendously interesting for, and entirely within the capacity of, most concertgoers today. We need more efforts like Boulez's, not just more performances of twentieth-century music. Recent efforts to construct "thematic" weekend programs for orchestra and instrumentalists are definitely a step in the right direction, as are intelligently crafted festivals as different from one another as those of Bard College, Aldeburgh and Bayreuth. But Boulez's single-handed attempts to do for music—his own and that of his contemporaries—what hardly anyone else has done since World War II constitute a heroic and genuinely affecting milestone in the history of modern culture. That is why he should be listened to and why despite the temptations to dominate and "star" he has been so impressive. No one is less the preening, temperamental personality paraded before worshipful audiences than Boulez, who remains a figure of sober melancholy and meditative abstraction in pursuit of authentically coherent aesthetic goals.

CHAPTER 33

Hindemith and Mozart

PAUL HINDEMITH began working on *Mathis der Maler* (*Mathis the Painter*), his finest opera, in his early 50s. How he actually arrived at the finished work, which was banned by the Nazis and subsequently premiered in Zurich in May 1938, is a complicated and tangled story, although it is apparent that he had no very clear idea of what he was trying to do until two or three years into the work's composition. Hindemith was attracted to the figure of Matthias Grünewald, sixteenth-century painter of the Isenheim altar triptych, partly because of his solitary, somewhat obscure artistic eminence, and partly because Matthias worked during and seemed involved in a turbulent period in German history, the Peasants' War (1524–5), which reflected a period of extreme tension between Catholics and Protestants.

With the onset of National Socialism in Germany, Hindemith began almost immediately to feel the pressures of the party in conflict with his own proclivities—innovative, but decidedly unrevolutionary—as a composer; Hindemith never abandoned tonality as had Schoenberg and his disciples, and always believed himself to be continuing, as opposed to breaking with, the great Austro-Germanic tradition that included Bach, Beethoven, Brahms and Wagner. Hindemith first produced a *Mathis der Maler* symphony, written for Wilhelm Furtwängler and the Berlin Philharmonic, and then after a fallow period expanded his ideas and the structure of the work into what became the opera's final form, a massive seven-scene work, compelling in its music and themes, probingly evocative in its exploration of the relationship between the artist and society.

By that time, however, Hindemith was an outcast in his native country, his music banned for its decadence and un-Aryan character, his friends and champions (preeminently Furtwängler) at odds with the Nazis and his future uncertain. Hindemith later came to the United States and taught at Yale, although his interests and attachments remained European. Yet despite its honorable pedigree as a testament to artistic integrity, *Mathis der Maler* has always been a marginal work in the operatic repertoire: It is a long, relentlessly challenging and intellectual piece, whose demands on audience, singers, orchestra, conductor and stage director far exceed those of most twentieth-century operas, including those by Richard Strauss, Berg, Stravinsky and Britten. With a cast of a dozen soloists and a score that lasts about four hours, *Mathis* is no soothing bonbon. It was given a performance of distinction in New York by the Hamburg Opera in 1967, and an undistinguished one by the New York City Opera last fall. Hearing that Peter Sellars would be staging it at London's Covent Garden last November, I made it a point to attend.

As with every Sellars production that I have seen, this one was compelling and brilliant in conception, deliberately uncompromising in its appeal to a late-twentieth-century audience, Mathis feels himself attracted to the peasants' cause, but he is also a confidant of the arrogant and powerful Cardinal Albrecht, whose favorite painter Mathis is. Torn by the attractions of worldliness, art and social engagement, the painter becomes for Sellars a symbolic figure drawn into contemporary social struggle (Schwalb, the peasant insurgent, has become a black urban guerrilla). Businessmen, political bosses and thuggish policemen populate the stage. The basic set by George Tsypin is a postmodern abstraction in steel and plastic with one steep ramp diagonally cutting across a stage surrounded by catwalks, fragmented skyscrapers and parapets. Into this inhospitable environment march emissaries from the established authorities (church, government, business), as well as militiamen, insurrectionary workers and of course Mathis, beset by claims on his loyalty and attention. Sellars further multiplies his set's signifying power by running a line of print plus two monitors—his libretto in English—against the backdrop, to emphasize that what we witness in *Mathis der Maler* is a struggle for clarity and definition in a world literally full of clamorous alternatives, battles for ascendancy, processes of authority.

Sellars seizes on what is particularly interesting about the opera—its profoundly unsettled inner core—and opens it up, destabilizing all the possibilities with which Hindemith (using Matthias as an autobiographical surrogate) was trying to come to terms. Thus the opera's climax is the sixth tableau, Mathis as St. Anthony submitting to the display of one temptation after another, each of them played by a leading character from the worlds of religion, finance, politics and art that the painter inhabits. And each of those figures in the opera is shown to vacillate between possibilities:

Cardinal Albrecht, who returns in the scene as St. Paul, and was sung superbly by the Danish Heldentenor Stig Andersen, is an arrogant prince of the church, an ascetic and an ardent lover of the arts. Far from resolving the story's tensions, Sellars uses the stage to show Mathis working through them finally to come to provisional rest by simultaneously acknowledging what he has done well, what he strove for, what he made, what troubled him and what he loved.

Less a conventional opera than an extended passion play set to music (perhaps modeled on Bach's *St. Matthew Passion*) whose scenes in the Covent Garden production were dramatized by Sellars in order to sustain, rather than purge, extraordinarily complex emotions, *Mathis der Maler* radiates doubt and insecurity rather than redemptive faith. Perhaps this is what at bottom the Nazis, like any authoritarian party, hated about Hindemith, that strangely winning amalgam of a completely secure craftsman whose music is designed to communicate ideas and emotions, and at the same time does not provide answers or a blueprint for loyalties and attachments of the kind most politics require. For Sellars and his well-rehearsed cast, *Mathis* is an intense musical and dramatic exploration of collective predicaments, aiming to plunge the audience into a turmoil of affecting, albeit unresolved, situations, each of which posits its own demands and partial settlements. For all his great gifts, Mathis is a contemporary Everyman, and ably portrayed as such by the American baritone Alan Titus—an unheroic man of conscience singing of how what is in his heart as an artist stands in hopeless contradiction with what he must live through existentially.

Sellars was well supported throughout by the young Finnish conductor Esa-Pekka Salonen, whose taut yet urgently expressive style produced an orchestral sound of rare power and leanness. This *Mathis* was, I think, Sellars's finest operatic achievement: More's the pity then that a U.S. production is unlikely for obvious commercial and political reasons. Sellars is a radical, yes, yet he has a real nobility and generosity of vision that neither condescends to nor tries to overwhelm the audience. What his *Mathis der Maler* conveys is what of all opera directors today he is best at doing: making you feel that opera is a unique way of involving audiences at many levels—dramatic, visual, musical and political—in the collective pathos of contemporary life. For him, opera embodies that complex of frustrated hopes, loneliness and striving, which its music, drama and visual elements can embody and also elevate to the level of argument. This is very far of course from the alienating, curatorial vision of most other directors, and it is possibly what opera managers and many critics resent about him.

Sellars is one of the only U.S. directors trying to do what a host of European counterparts do more easily—connect opera to an ongoing social and political debate. That such a practice already exists as a tradition for European directors like Chéreau, Kupfer, Muller, Berghaus, among others, has made their job easier to do, and conversely much harder for Sellars, who has to fight (often exaggeratedly) against the prevailing belief here that operas are essentially harmless, if not completely antiseptic, works like *Bohème* and *Chenier*, to be looked at for their gigantic, realistic sets, costly stars and humanly meaningless plots. Thus Sellars's choice of *Mathis der Maler* hooks him directly into a substantial debate about music and society in Germany that begins with Hans Pfitzner and Busoni, and continues through the thirties and forties with Hindemith, Adorno, Thomas Mann; there's an excellent account of this in Marc Werner's book *Undertones of Insurrection: Music, Politics, and the Social Sphere in the Modern German Narrative* (1993). As it happens, Sellars's production of *Mathis* ran concurrently in London with a play by the South African playwright Ronald Harwood, *Taking Sides*, a confrontational, not always very subtle representation of Furtwängler's investigation as a supposed Nazi collaborator by a harsh, sometimes vulgar U.S. colonel. This gave more of a context for the opera, since it was of course Furtwängler who had championed Hindemith. Inadvertently perhaps, play and opera reminded one of the contentiousness of debate about opera's social and philosophical meaning, now almost totally lacking in U.S. productions dependent on corporate sponsors, who will have none of it.

An unfortunate case in point was provided by the Met's new winter production of *Così fan tutte*, Mozart's most difficult and beautiful work. For a while I was impressed with Lesley Koenig's no-nonsense approach and her unaffected way of letting this quasi-Sadean piece unfold. She was superbly abetted by a first-rate cast of singers: Thomas Allen as Don Alfonso, Carol Vaness as Fiordiligi, Susanne Mentzer as Dorabella, Dwayne Croft as Guglielmo and Cecilia Bartoli as Despina. Only tenor Jerry Hadley seemed unable to match the others, his excessively mannered singing and incessant scooping spoiling Mozart's lines. After the two swains return disguised as "Albanian" visitors dressed in Arab clothes (the audience tittered appropriately) the whole thing began to seem like a road movie without a director. And when the lovers were made to return to each other at the end, clinking champagne glasses in the most dispiriting and Buchanan-like assertion of "family" values, one felt again the sheer weight of unthinking convention and resolute mindlessness so often the case in recent New York opera performances. Mozart's opera is nothing if not an excoriating attack on amorous constancy and stability of character: To turn it into a silly moralizing fable of love restored is to disembowel and empty it of its vitality.

CHAPTER 34

Review of Michael Tanner's *Wagner*

MICHAEL TANNER'S *Wagner* is a very curious performance indeed. It isn't just a chip that Tanner carries on his shoulder but a large bundle of resentments and petulant dislikes, with which he proceeds to a laborious reinterpretation of Wagner's life and work. This is surely the first book that suggests that Wagner was not such a bad fellow after all, his anti-semitism, egregious narcissism, stupendously demanding character and remarkably irregular, even abnormal, life notwithstanding. In effect Tanner manages to downplay all that, accommodating what is still unassimilable and difficult about Wagner to a string of resourceful, sometimes ingenious, interpretations of the operas and the prose works. His interpretations are marred, however, by gratuitous tilting at critics and scholars.

The most immediate problem for the reader is that Tanner cannot get his tone right. Is this a book for a general audience? Is it meant to be a contribution to the already very impressive literature on Wagner as philosopher and music-dramatist? Is it supposed to be a refutation of what a lot of people now think about Wagner? Or is the book intended mainly as a sort of middle-level account of Wagner for people who do not know much about music? Tanner wobbles around between all these alternatives, none of which he explores in any depth. What we end up with is a book that gallops through each of the main works in a descriptive style that often does justice to Tanner's own rather attractive passion for Wagner, but is not compelling enough to make an all-round case.

Tanner is preoccupied by a whole series of imagined enemies—scholars who are too priggish, producers, conductors and directors who, like Boulez, Chéreau and Wieland Wagner, don't have the right ideas, historians who are too concerned with Wagner's many foibles and obsessions. This preoccupation produces in his prose an unpleasantly disapproving sarcasm that adds nothing to his argument. For instance, he seems to be not generally in favour of contemporary productions of Wagner, but often leaves us only to assume which offenders he has in mind during his rather telegraphic attack (the dismissive phrase 'styles which sometimes employ the catch-all title "post-modern" to hide their nakedness' cannot possibly account for all the modern directors—some of them extremely interesting ones—who have had a go at making Wagner topical).

What we are left with is a sense of Tanner's sour disapproval rather than argument or demonstration, while we remain uninformed about what style of production he actually prefers.

Perhaps this peculiar feature of the book derives from his understandable anxiety to be different given that Wagner has provoked a vast amount of commentary and scholarship, a great deal, but by no means all of it, silly or wrong. Still to have something new to say about Wagner's operas is very difficult.

Tanner's best points are in the form of shrewd local observations. *Lohengrin*, he says with reason, is sometimes a very prosaic work, well endowed with gorgeous music, but is fundamentally an opera in which Wagner is evidently stalling. Or, to put it more charitably, Wagner is composing a work which will give him the possibility of discovering what might satisfy him as an artist. After *Lohengrin* Wagner wrote little for five years—perhaps, Tanner says, because he discovered the dangers of his considerable dramatic and musical gifts growing apart from each other. In the two other early works (*Der fliegende Holländer* and *Tannhäuser*), Tanner sees numerous flaws that show the young composer unable to find the proper material for his enormous gifts. Only when Wagner gets to *Der Ring des Nibelungen* does the whole thing come together in what is by any standard one of the great monuments of modern Western art.

A convincing part of Tanner's argument about the *Ring* is that modern realisations of the work have not stressed enough the universal, larger-than-life aspect of its characters—Wotan especially—who are too often reduced to caricatures of capitalist greed or fascist ideology. Wotan, he says, is a corrupt politician yes, but he is also a real visionary. The other part of what Tanner does is to show us how in the unfolding tetralogy Wagner was determined to reveal the complexities of human life without somehow being able to reconcile them all: 'a promise of wholeness is held out by one part of it, and denied by another'. This is scarcely an original point, but here and there Tanner does very well with individual sections of the *Ring*. I found his explanation of why it is that Wagner abandoned the writing of

Siegfried (opera three in the cycle) at the end of Act Two, and several years later came back to Act Three after he had composed *Tristan und Isolde* and *Die Meistersinger von Nürnberg* most persuasive. He speculates that Wagner had first to discover whether a profound human love as embodied in the relationship between Siegfried and Brünnhilde would be thwarted by society or whether it would die of its own internal logic.

However, Tanner unaccountably omits any mention of the startling burst of German nationalism emitted at the end of *Die Meistersinger* by Sachs and his Nuremberg compatriots. Along with Tanner's somewhat circumspect, not to say cavalier, defusing of the quite reasonable charges against Wagner (that much of his work is imbued with xenophobia and anti-semitism) this is really quite the weakest part of Tanner's attempt at understanding Wagner. He is right, I think, to give Barry Millington (who has made anti-semitism into an obsession at the core of Wagner's music) very short shrift, but he is wrong in believing that the difficult interpretive problem posed by the connection between Wagner's relentlessly insistent social, racial and political views and his aesthetic works can be dealt with in a few school-boyishly clever sentences. Wagner deserves to be taken more seriously than that. This is emphatically not a matter of collapsing Wagner's ideas into a number of ideological themes, nor of taking the related view, that his art was too lofty and complex to be saddled with mere anti-semitism, or un-savoury proto-fascist ideas.

As Mark Weiner has shown, Wagner is incomprehensible outside the extremely peculiar and radically anti-semitic culture that produced him. He was an unreconciled, highly unstable combination of German nationalism, extreme insecurity, borrowed Schopenhauerian pessimism, tremendous musical inventiveness, and grandiose dramatic aesthetic conceptions.

As Tanner rightly says, he was gripped by the dialectic between love and power, as well as the whole complex of religious and psychological suffer-ing, redemption and transfiguring death, which is well observed by Tanner in his analysis of *Parsifal*. To make matters even more difficult, Wagner was also a genius at creating new sounds—indeed he was a technician of the aural and the verbal like no one before him.

The system of motifs that Wagner perfected for the *Ring* and the three later works is crucial here, although Tanner says scarcely a word about it. In addition, Wagner's overweening sense of self was such that he in-dulged his peculiar personality no matter the cost. It therefore seems logical to approach his works as, in various ways, embodying most, if not all, of these things, rather than trying to turn him into a figure whose appallingly unattractive character and hugely powerful expressivity could be seen as somehow regular, acceptable, belonging to one of us. Each age must try to achieve that synthesis of Wagner's dizzying capacities and deformations again and again; the effort must a least be made.

Tanner, alas, flattens him out too much, interprets him both too comfortably and in too smug and proprietary a fashion. Though there are valuable insights scattered throughout this book, the overall effect is unsatisfyingly thin.

CHAPTER 35

In the Chair

PETER OSTWALD'S *GLENN GOULD*
AND THE TRAGEDY OF GENIUS

O NE OF the most talked and written about musicians after
World War Two, Glenn Gould quite consciously set about
making himself interesting and eccentric. Most performers
do, but Gould went beyond anyone. It helped a great deal that he had a
phenomenal digital gift, a perfect memory, a very high intelligence, but in
addition he was self-conscious and self-observant to an extent most other
performers would scarcely be able to imagine. This was not just a matter of
takes and re-takes of everything he played, but also of imagining and thinking about himself playing in the greatest detail. In 1964, when he was 34, he
deserted the concert stage and retired into an appallingly claustrophobic
world of his own making: he never woke up before three in the afternoon,
rarely left his hotel room in Toronto, worked all night with his own tape-
recorders and splicing-machines, and with a few exceptions, confined his
social life to long phone calls after midnight. He was very secretive, despite
his loquacity and hated any criticism, even though his playing was so original and compelling that he became a cult figure among other musicians and
the general public when he was still in his twenties.

His reputation outside Canada was made with his first recording, the
fabulous *Goldberg Variations* issued in 1955 by Columbia Records. The first
in a long series of Bach recordings that he made all through his life, Gould's
first *Goldberg* (he re-recorded it in 1981) is still his best known, still his
most astonishingly vibrant and fluent recorded performance. Part of its
impact came from the fact that it had no competitors or predecessors (only
Wanda Landowska had done it on harpsichord and Rosalyn Tureck, little
known outside New York, on piano): the piano music of Beethoven. Chopin, Rachmaninoff dominated the landscape. Gould instantly transformed

the geography of pianism and with his capacity to deploy an almost verbal intelligence through his fingers—each knowing how to act independently of the rest—set standards that no one has been able to emulate or match. The art of the piano was thus redefined; romanticism was displaced by a lean, preternaturally clear contrapuntal skill in which the alliance of Gould's extraordinary gifts with Bach's great keyboard masterpieces—the Partitas, Toccatas, French and English Suites, Inventions, both books of the *Well-Tempered Clavier,* most of the *Art of Fugue*—became almost the core of the repertoire. Brendel, Pollini, Barenboim and Martha Ageriach were consolidating their presence at the same time but none of them had a common border with Gould's Bach. It was as if he had re-invented the idea of what it meant to be a pianist, but had done it in such a way as to become the idea's only representative.

Testimony to Gould's genius is the growing literature about him. Early studies like Geoffrey Payzant's *Glenn Gould: Musik and Mind* focused on the aesthetic views which Gould had expressed in all sorts of writings, but which Payzant, a professor of philosophy at the University of Toronto, pulled together for the first time into coherent, if not entirely complete form. Later books and studies were first-person accounts of knowing, working and conversing with Gould, which revealed a good deal about his attitudes to various composers, to recording, aspects of his life and so forth. Not until Otto Friedrich's *Glenn Gould: A Life and Variations* (reviewed in the LRB, 26 March 1992) was published with the co-operation of Gould's estate was there enough raw information about the details of the pianist's quite amazing eccentricities. Friedrich had the tact to present the material in all its often puzzling, and even sordid, detail without trying to make too much of Gould's psychology. Clearly, however, Gould was severely hypochondriac and, given his addiction to all sorts of medicines, spent most of his adult life more or less poisoning himself with the assistance of his various doctors. Friedrich puts it this way:

> And the doctors kept prescribing drugs. Aldomet for the high blood pressure, Nembutal for sleep, tetracyline and Chloromycetin for his constant colds and infections. And Serpasil and Largostil and Stelazine and Resteclin and Librax and Clonidine and Fiorinal and Inderal and Inocid and Atistocort cream and Neocortez and Zyloprim and Butazolidin and Bactra and Septra and phenylbutazone and methyldopa and allopurinal and hydrochlorothiazide. And always, in addition to everything else, lots and lots of Valium.

He was also a control fanatic who tried (often successfully) to dominate every situation. Friedrich again:

Control—the word kept reappearing in almost everyone's recollections of Gould. He had always wanted to control all the circumstances of his life and over the years it became a passion, an obsession. It was the need to be in control, really, that drove him from the concert stage to the recording studio. And in the recording studio, he had to control all the engineering, where the mikes were placed and how they were used, to make the recording companies come to his native city, to his own studio, where his own equipment would be the only equipment, with everything under his control.

A few years ago I asked Yehudi Menuhin what it was like to work with Gould. They had made a television programme together consisting of a Bach sonata, Beethoven's Op. 96 and the Schoenberg *Fantasie,* interspersed with discussion between the two of them. Menuhin said that Gould was a truly fantastic musician but when it came to the filming of their discussion the pianist had insisted on writing not only his own part but his partner's as well. 'That way nothing can go wrong', he said by way of explanation to the equally adamant Menuhin. Gould gave way but it took a fair amount of time to persuade him to cede 'control' to someone else. He did the same kind of thing with the pieces and composers he played: only he knew what he was going to play, how it would sound, how fast (or slow) it would be taken. He confounded his public when, after a steady diet of Bach and Beethoven, he turned to composers like Richard Strauss, Sibelius, Grieg and Bizet, praising them to the skies and certainly above the pianistic romantics whom everyone else played. Even with Bach and Mozart, he chose tempi that defied convention and, since he played the same work differently on different occasions, it was as if to say: 'I control this work and can render it the way I please'. I heard him several times in the late Fifties and early Sixties before he quit playing concerts, and I believe I have heard nearly all of the dozens of recordings he made: he has never failed to grip me with his inventiveness and rhythmic vitality, although everything he played had an element of interpretative wilfulness in it. No wonder first-rate pianists like Alfred Brendel still cannot fully accept the liberties and often unmusical sounds that Gould forced on the classical compositions he favoured.

The latest biographical and interpretative analysis of Gould is by the psychiatrist Peter Ostwald, the author of interesting psycho-biographies of Nijinsky and Robert Schumann; a good amateur violinist, and a friend of the pianist, Ostwald died of cancer before his book was published, but was apparently able to finish his manuscript despite the travails of his final weeks. Ostwald's is the first study that tries not only to account for Gould's egregious behaviour as pianist and human being, but also to tie that behaviour specifically to the tragic personal cost of being the genius he was. Much of the anecdotal material in the book is also in Friedrich's biography, though Ostwald has additional stories and insights of his own. The central theme in Gould's life, according to Ostwald, was his unstilled anxiety, a narcissistic pattern of self-concern and self-immersion that was fed and accentuated by the life of the performer continuously under scrutiny. Gould's peculiar antics on stage—playing with legs crossed, conducting himself and the orchestra, humming and singing, using a very low chair that brought his eyes and fingers to roughly the same level—were exhibitionistic, but they were also indications of his need for personal transfiguration -the 'fusing of bodily display with musical intelligence'—in the course of performing. Ostwald's novel approach to Gould is premised on the notion that performers are subject to special stresses and that these are compounded (not relieved) by the unusual capacities a great musician like Gould possesses. Along with a group of doctors in Berkeley, Ostwald worked in the Health Group for Performing Artists, a relatively new medical sub-specialty devoted to the unique problems of musicians who spend most of their lives preparing and then displaying their accomplishments for an avid public.

Some years ago I described the rarefied and terrifying world of the concert artist by referring to the public ordeal that Gould tried to escape from as 'an extreme occasion'. Quite apart from the sheer nervousness induced by exposure to a large number of people who have paid good money to watch a pianist, violinist or singer do things that almost by definition no one else can do, the performer's isolation on stage dramatises the precariousness of a situation in which all kinds of dismaying things can happen—memory slips, fumbled passages, complete confusion, missed concentration, finger trouble and so on. Then there is the sense that the audience is waiting for you to fail, waiting for you *not* to come through; in this respect concert-going has an element of the blood sport. Lastly, as Gould felt, giving concerts involves the performer in a world of intense competition, a world filled with other musicians who are crying to get ahead at your expense, who have a stake in your decline or disastrous performance, who want your dates, your recording deal, your fee, your manager, your fame. To maintain a high level of polish and brilliance, which is what the business demands, is to live at an impossible pitch of intensity; one concert performed or record completed, and you must start thinking about the next. No wonder that a fair number of Gould's contemporaries—Vladimir Horowitz, Gary Grafman, Leon Fleisher, John Ogdon, to mention a few of the most gifted—succumbed to mysterious illnesses and had to curtail appearances and whole careers. The extremity of being out there alone, day after day, sooner or later catches up with one, especially if, as in Gould's case, the innate will to control life and body was constantly challenged—not just by the rigours of a performing life, but by mortality.

So delicate and refined is the great musical performer's playing mechanism that it is difficult for an outsider to understand what goes on; the line separating even the gifted amateur from a pianist like Gould is a matter of total difference, not degree. To be able to sight-read and memorise anything, to translate one's reading of notes on a page into an immediate sound on the instrument, using one's fingers in mostly unnatural ways, to have the confidence (this is of capital importance) to know that one can do this at any time: these were all capacities that Gould possessed in the highest degree. Only someone like Barenboim—who conducts dozens of opera and symphonic works from memory, plays the piano and conducts at the same time, and seems never to practice—has comparable talents, although he does what he does as a matter of course, without the mad energies expended by Gould. Ostwald describes how Gould was nurtured into becoming an unusual musician by his mother, a dourly Protestant Toronto piano teacher, who thought she could induce musicality in her unborn child by constantly playing music on the gramophone and radio during her pregnancy and his infancy. By the time baby Glenn could sit, she would put him on her lap, sit at the piano, encourage him to press down on the keys, all the while singing hymns, chorales, Canadian folk tunes. 'Mother, child and the piano quickly became a unity', Ostwald writes, adding that this may be 'the origin of Glenn's future posture while playing. His need to be very close to the piano would recall the warm feelings and earlier proximity of both mother and instrument'. Soon the child had perfect pitch, but he also developed peculiar aversions—to round objects like marbles, for example, to a red fire-truck—and ecstatic responses to some of the music he listened to: *Tristan und Isolde* brought him to tears at a very early age. Ostwald suggests that 'a marked fear of certain physical objects, disturbances in empathy, social withdrawal, self-isolation and obsessive attention to ritualised behaviour', all of which continued through his childhood and adolescence (and even later), 'does resemble a condition called Asperger Disease, which is a variant of autism', and is often found in unusually gifted people (Wittgenstein and Bartók are the examples Ostwald cites).

The virtue of Ostwald's intelligently sympathetic account is that he does not reduce Gould's phenomenal gifts and accomplishments to a set of psycho-pathological symptoms. There is joy and exultation in the descriptions of his Bach performances, and an almost circumspect admiration for his ability to elude the embrace of teachers and senior pianists (like Schnabel) whom he admired. His mother's role in his life remained central and may have been the source of his obsessive drive for perfection; it was her habit of finding fault with him that he projected onto every audience. Which in turn was part of the reason he came to prefer the sterile atmosphere of the studio to the anxiety-filled excitement of the concert hall; the studio became 'almost like retreating to those peaceful, isolated organ lofts where he liked practising as a child'. Mrs. Gould saw a future Mozart in her son, though she very much guarded against his exploitation as a child prodigy. Strangely, however, Gould's father—a prosperous, but not artistically inclined Toronto furrier—was never close to his son, although a special chair he made for the boy was the only one the pianist ever used. When its padded cushion was worn through, Gould continued to sit on it.

This meant that Glenn was now sitting directly on the wooden H-frame, which could only have been uncomfortable if not painful, since support had to come from a centrally placed board running the entire length of his crotch. The board was attached to the front and back of the frame, leaving two large empty spaces on either side where his buttocks were unsupported. Thus the weight of his body had to come down on his perineum and genitals . . . He treated this chair, built by his father, almost as a sacred object and never complained about it.

It is strange that Ostwald says very little about Gould's masochism in a context like this, since much of his later life, with its relentless self-observation and punishing routines of self-correction (many of them based on a frighteningly imperfect knowledge of how the human body works), suggests a musician disciplining himself for his supposed imperfections and imagined faults. Reams of his diaries contain blood-pressure and temperature readings taken on an hourly basis, plus endless comments on his dissatisfactions with his playing, speculations on which fingers, joints, knuckles, muscles were functioning badly, and descriptions of his volatile state of mind. Ostwald never treated Gould himself but he did put him in touch with a number of psychiatrists and neurologists whom he saw intermittently without conclusive results. He seemed not to tell one doctor what another physician had either suggested or prescribed for him. His mortal fear of infection and illness deepened over time, and because of it he never visited his mother as she lay dying in hospital. He consistently over-dressed, wearing heavy coats and woollen sweaters and hats in the warmest weather; he never exercised, and seems to have subsisted on one daily meal of scrambled eggs. When he visited Felicia and Leonard Bernstein at their house he was persuaded finally to take off his woollen cap; and

Felicia somehow managed to wash his hair, which because of the cap and his wholly indoor life seemed never to have been washed before.

Despite the startling joy and pleasure that many of his recordings convey, Gould appears to have suffered constantly. He was sexually inhibited, even puritanical; his relationships with women were, with one exception (the wife of a well-known pianist, conductor and composer), short and for the most part abruptly terminated; he had an aversion to physical contact and seemed to have derived no solace or nourishment from the various friends whom he used opportunistically and then dropped. Ostwald's book characterises his life after his mother's death in 1975 as hell; neither his piano-playing nor the radio and TV documentaries that he appeared to make with enthusiasm gave him much satisfaction. In part this was the result of 'overuse disorder' and 'repetitive strain injury', but surely the psychological strain of trying to achieve the highest standards of performance must have played a central role in his protracted misery. Only one other (equally troubled) musician seems to have earned Gould's jealousy and perhaps envy—Horowitz. Gould was apparently convinced that he was a better pianist than the demonic Russian, that his octaves were more virtuosic, and that he was deserving of greater fame and attention; mostly it was the impossible desire to make his musical ambitions cohere that drove him to insane exertions. He never achieved much distinction as a composer, and at the age of 50 had only just begun to take up conducting seriously (hiring an orchestra miles away from Toronto in order to practise his baton technique in secret) before he died of a stroke in October 1982.

Still, the sheer productivity of his career is breathtaking: Friedrich lists 100 closely printed pages of concerts, recordings, radio documentaries, and many hours of television films. Listening to him over the years, seeing his films, reading his essays, one is struck by his undiminished capacity for a remarkably contrapuntal, many-voiced self-articulation. Ostwald is right to say that for Gould music and speech were two versions of the same thing; even when he was perverse and contrary ('Mozart', he would say, 'died too late, not too early') you could at least argue with his views and challenge his readings. For him every performance was a reading in the literal sense: the work he played seemed to be advancing an argument, making points, creating a percipient form that unfolded deliberately and self-consciously before the listener. There is always a sense of superb organisation in Gould's performances, an organisation that completely eschews 'pianistic' effects, colour, rubato, great washes of sound, but relies instead on articulation, clarity of voice, mastery and control of each sound, down to the lowliest bass. I have heard a few major pianists disparage Gould's lack of 'musicality' or 'phrasing' without at the time realising that he was in effect opposed to the traditional rhetoric that every amateur or professional pianist has had to learn. He was never allied either to a pedagogical tradition or to a national school (Polish, Austrian, Russian or French). Without ever saying it explicitly, he was, I think, interested in creating himself anew with each performance of a Bach fugue or Wagner transcription. And yet the effect of his playing is that it always recalls something, whether a harpsichord, or a pianoforte, or the human voice, in the process of telling itself (as Gerard Manley Hopkins put it) with originality and inventiveness.

From his survey of Gould's later diaries and notebooks Ostwald surmises that he was a musician in trouble, his hunger for control unappeasable, his loneliness and unsupported efforts making greater and greater claims on him, his health deteriorating and his body abused beyond resistance as a result. In his last years, Gould's search for perfection intensified as a result of

> the recent loss of his mother, who in his conscious and unconscious memory was the incessant corrector of mistakes and prodder toward improved perfection. Now that she was gone, these critical functions were entirely within himself. Disconnected from the balancing influence of his mother, he was tackling the problems of his keyboard performances with the same compulsive fury that he applied to everything else he ever touched: his conversations, his writings, his recordings, his radio programmes and television shows.

Another difficulty was his inability to bring together his identities as pianist, intellectual, composer, conductor; inevitably it was the pianist in him who dominated the others, but that role alone did not give him the fulfilment his polymorphous drives demanded. Ostwald wonders whether the sense of diffusion that assailed him, compounded by his cloistral isolation, dissipated the primary image of himself as pianist which 'has been built up in childhood under his mother's guidance'. He consulted a great many doctors but never exposed himself to a full psychoanalysis. Ostwald is too discreet to imply that there was something wrong with that reluctance, but some such charge hangs over the book.

Clearly the costly distortions of personality and behaviour in the man were directly connected to his sense of purpose as a performing interpreter of classical music. Does this make him typical and somehow exemplary, or eccentric and merely solitary? He was scathing about the competitiveness, superficiality, greed and show business aspects of the concert scene (exposed remorselessly by Norman Lebrecht) but he was a prosperous man who made considerable amounts of money. (In a Swiftian touch, he left most of his estate to the Salvation Army and to the Toronto Humane

Society for animal welfare; the most interesting photograph in Ostwald's book is of Gould singing to a group of Canadian cows.) His skilfully manipulated alliance with Columbia Records indicates a worldliness we do not often associate with him. After all, say his biographers, his first phone call of the day was always to his stockbroker, so on one level at least he was a good manager of his own affairs. But Gould's tragedy was that of the performer divorced from music-making as a matter of contemporary social and cultural practice. Even so stupendously endowed a talent as Liszt played his own music and that of his friends; today's pianists play the music of the past, despite Gould's fanciful belief that every performer and every listener could be 'creative' by jiggling the dials of an amplifier.

The trouble with Lebrecht's laborious jeremiad against the classical music business is that he attacks its excesses without being sufficiently aware that it is itself an excess. Once playing the piano or violin, or singing, become professional, i.e. paying activities, it is hard to fault exceptionally gifted individuals for demanding a lot for their performances. Gould knew all that perfectly well, but tried always to give the impression that he was really all about something else—an ideal of perfected articulation regardless of cost, a self-awareness that defied convention, a manner of life premised not on healthy well-being but on unnatural self-projection. His saving virtue wasn't just his incredible talent but also his irony, a very rare quality in today's music world, with its overpaid stars, fawning public relations flacks, monomaniacal impresarios all picking over an inert, hopelessly unimaginative repertoire. Gould took himself seriously, but was always ready to mock himself in impersonations of the boxer Dominico Patrono, the actor Myron Chianti, the musicologist Sir Humphrey Price-Davies, the conductor Sir Nigel Twitt-Thornwaite. Part of his very expensive self-consciousness was a way of keeping an eye on his own tics and foibles and somehow indulging the volatility of his usually contradictory impulses. Everything about him was disturbingly antithetical and perverse in some way, but what a rich experience he provides.

CHAPTER 36

On *Fidelio*

IDELIO IS the one opera in the repertory that has the power to
sway audiences even when it is indifferently performed. Yet it is
a highly problematic work whose triumphant conclusion and
the impression it is designed to convey of goodness winning out over evil
do not go to the heart of what Beethoven was grappling with. Not that its
plot is complex, or that, like many of the French operas of the day which
influenced Beethoven and whose brilliance he admired, it is a long and
complicated work: *Fidelio*'s success in the theatre derives in part from its
compactness and intensity—in the course of two extremely taut acts, a
devoted wife rescues her unjustly imprisoned husband, foils a tyrannically
cruel Spanish grandee, and manages to release all the other prisoners arbitrarily imprisoned in his dungeons. Unlike most other operas, however,
Fidelio is burdened with the complexities of its own past as well as the huge
effort it cost its composer before he was able to present it in its 'final' form
in Vienna on 23 May 1814. It is the only work of its kind he ever completed;
it caused him a great deal of pain; yet despite the attention he lavished on
it, he failed to get the satisfaction from it, in terms either of popular success
or of aesthetic conviction, that his efforts entitled him to.

What we know today as *Fidelio* is the third version of a three-act opera
originally produced as *Leonore* in 1805 and again, in a somewhat truncated
two-act version, in 1806, and finally, in an even more edited and reconfig-
ured two-act version, in 1814 and 1815, as *Fidelio*. And that isn't all. *Fidelio*
must be the only opera whose composer wrote no fewer than four overtures
for it (three to *Leonore* and one to *Fidelio*, composed for the 1814 version):
these works are still played in the concert hall, although, of the four, only the
overture to *Fidelio* makes no musical reference to the opera itself. Thanks

to musicologists and musicians there now exists a fairly accurate composite version of the 1805–6 *Leonore,* which in recent years has been performed and recorded. Indeed, I know of two important performances of *Leonore* in 1996, one in New York and the other some weeks later in Salzburg, in a lean, semi-staged concert rendition by John Eliot Gardiner and his period-instrument Orchestre Romantique et Révolutionnaire. This was followed, again in Salzburg, by Georg Solti conducting several staged performances of *Fidelio,* and in New York by Kurt Masur and the NY Philharmonic doing one extremely loud and stodgy concert version which highlighted Gardiner's much more dynamic conception and execution.

Gardiner's commitment to *Leonore* as a more interesting work than *Fidelio* was buttressed by a spirited essay he wrote for the New York pro-gramme booklet. 'With the *Leonore* of 1805', Gardiner suggests, 'Beethoven was struggling to recover the fiery revolutionary fervour and idealism of his Bonn years after the relatively cosy time he had been having in Vienna. If *Leonore* could be said to spring from that self which continually searches for the ideal in the face of fear, *Fidelio,* by contrast, represents Beethoven's more settled, static response to tyranny and injustice, freedom and self-sacrifice'. *Leonore*'s effectiveness, Gardiner continued, comes from the 'power and purity of its emotion'. Gardiner is very harsh about *Fidelio,* which he claims reinforces 'its abstract collective and philosophical message' at the expense of 'personal and human complexity'. It was *Fidelio* and not *Leonore* that was, he says, 'hijacked to honour Hitler's birthday' because of its 'unfortunate nationalistic baggage', and *Fidelio* again that, along with *Germania* and the *Battle Symphony,* put the remains of Beethoven's heroic style at the service of the reactionary impulse in Europe. But he is certainly right to suggest that the 1815 *Fidelio,* whose associations with the Congress of Vienna lent weight to its authoritative density, never satisfied Beethoven, who often complained that the work needed rewriting from the beginning, despite the inordinate labour he had already expended on it over a period of ten or eleven years. Thus Gardiner in conclusion: 'it is a fallacy to claim that in *Fidelio* Beethoven in every case refined and strengthened his first idea'. And this leads him to add that there is 'no final version that subsumes all that is good in the others'.

Whether or not we agree with Gardiner's judgment in favour of *Leonore* over *Fidelio,* it is important to consider the later version as a continuation of developments that occur in *Leonore,* as a later opera, therefore, rather self-consciously encumbered with its own past—a past that persists as a central theme in all three versions of the work, that won't settle down and co-operate, that keeps coming back to dislocate the certainties of the 'res-cue opera' form that Beethoven was using. My reading of *Fidelio* sees the later version as extending and deepening rather than ending the work, or struggle, in progress that Gardiner discerns in *Leonore*.

Maynard Solomon notes that 1813 was an unproductive year for Beethoven, immediately after which he resorted to an 'ideological/heroic' manner which yielded a series of noisily inferior works 'filled with bombastic rhetoric and "patriotic" excesses' that 'mark the nadir of his artistic career'. Such works as *Wellington's Victory* and several compositions written for the Congress of Vienna belong to the same period as the revisions to *Leonore* that resulted in the 1814 *Fidelio*. Solomon suggests that this 'ideological/heroic style' can be traced back to the 1790s in such works as the Joseph and Leopold Cantatas, as well as the Friedelberg war songs, yet in central works—Solomon cites the Third and Fifth Symphonies, *Fidelio* and the Incidental Music to *Egmont*—this aggressive, quasi-militaristic style 'was sublimated into a subtle and profound form of expression'. It is not surprising that, as the last work in this series, *Fidelio* explicitly recalls some of its predecessors, perhaps as part of its own obsession with the past. A well-known example occurs in the second scene of Act Two: given permission by Don Fernando to release her husband from his chains, Leonore steps forward to perform the task of liberation. The music modulates from A major to F major, and proceeds to a moving oboe solo and chorus borrowed almost literally from the Joseph Cantata. In the opera, the episode bestows a majestic calm on what has so far been a turbulent and confused scene. Again, it would be hard to miss the echoes of the finale of the Fifth Symphony in the opera's last scene; however animating the words and voices, there is in both a similar, pounding use of C major to possess the tonic and thereby dispel any lingering shadows.

Fidelio can also be interpreted as a terrific counter-blow to *Così fan tutte*, an important antecedent and part of the past that Beethoven is working with. On the one hand, he incorporates the disguises, if not the malice of *Così:* on the other, he uses unmasking to assert the bourgeois ideal of matrimonial fidelity. Memory in *Così fan tutte* is a faculty to be done away with in the pursuit of pleasure: in *Fidelio* it is a vital part of character. Yet at the heart of what Beethoven is arguing for—persistence, constancy, personal character as a source of continuity—there seems to be a contradiction that will not disappear. Every affirmation, every instance of truth carries with it its own negation, just as every memory of love and conjugal fidelity brings with it the danger, and usually the actuality, of something that will obliterate it. Most critics who have written about Beethoven's heroic middle period—most recently, Scott Burnham, but also Paul Robinson, for whom *Fidelio* is a relatively uncomplicated enactment of the French Revolution—can see nothing except the triumphalism with which he appears to end these works. If we look a bit more closely at *Fidelio*, however, keeping its incorporated and cancelled versions in mind, we will see a more gripping, much more ambiguous and self-conscious struggle going on—one which makes *Fidelio* a more challenging opera than it often appears to be.

This struggle is evident from the beginning, although most commentators tend to treat as frivolous the opening scene, in which Jaquino and Marzelline spar over their future together (which Marzelline dreads because she has already fallen in love with her father's assistant, Fidelio—i.e. the disguised Leonore). Like most things in opera, however, it is a hybrid, made up of elements that do not, because they cannot, blend; this produces a volatility and tension that Beethoven is trying to represent throughout the opera. It derives at the outset from the incompatibility of desires and hopes: Jaquino wanting at last to be alone with Marzelline, she pushing him away, Fidelio interrupting their spat with insistent knocking. Each has a different conception of time: time as urgency for the eager young swain; as hope for Marzelline; as anticipation and waiting for Fidelio. *Fidelio's* first appearance bears most of the scene's symbolic freight—and it is meticulously described by Beethoven: dressed as a young man, she carries a box of provisions on her back, a box of letters on one arm and, on the other, a collection of chains. We are immediately to see the character as furnishing nourishment in the present, but also, like her husband and perhaps the other prisoners, loaded down with punishments brought on by past behaviour.

Rocco's appearance gives Beethoven an opportunity to tie together the four characters of the opening sequence using a canon at the octave—again inspired by the canon in Act Two of *Così*. The idea of the canon is very similar in both works, a sort of *discordia concors* in which the characters express their incompatible sentiments in a rigorous, even scholastic, but at the same meditative, form. 'Mir ist so wunderbar' is significant for another reason, which takes us to Beethoven's problematic of representation in the opera and the kind of irreconcilability I mentioned earlier as hampering, and certainly complicating, the affirmations he seems to be trying to make. Bouilly's *L'Amour conjugale*, which Gaveaux had already set to music in 1798, provided him with an entirely predictable rescue plot, in which wrongs are righted, and the prisoners freed. One of the things we respond to in *Fidelio* especially is the authority with which one form of power is dislodged and a new, or at least much more acceptable one, established in its place: Pizarro, the bloody-minded, tempestuous tyrant, is replaced by Don Fernando, emissary of light and truth. No reason is given for this salutary change—it emanates from an off-stage source of goodness and justice inaccessible to Florestan, Leonore, Pizarro and the rest. Fernando makes clear to us that he has been despatched by the monarch, and is therefore a deputy, or substitute.

It is far too easy—and, I think, inaccurate to describe this rather slen-
derised politics as Beethoven's attempt to embody in dramatic form the
enormous liberation he had once discerned in the French Revolution. There
is something far too swift and almost magical about the opera for it to
represent a political process. Unlike Wagner or even Mozart, Beethoven
was neither particularly well-read nor philosophically inclined. He read
the great contemporary poets like Schiller and Goethe, but when it came
to philosophical ideas or how to think about history, he was more or less a
beginner. The striving and pathos of *Fidelio* have more to do with the actual
business of putting words and music together for the stage than with any
historical event or general idea about humanity. The ready-made story offered by Bouilly and Gaveaux was the starting-point for an endeavour to
translate what had been wholly musical exertions into visual, verbal and
plastic terms and this he found strange and difficult to do, especially when
strong emotions about a woman were involved. As all his biographers af-
firm, Beethoven was routinely moved by passions for unattainable women,
but at the time when he began to work on *Leonore* he was especially vulnerable. A fragment of a letter to Countess Josephine Deym, a woman for
whom he evinced the most powerful feelings but who did not reciprocate
his advances, shows what this did to him:

> why is there no language which can express what far above all mere regard—
> far above everything—that we can describe—Oh, who can name *you*—and
> not feel that however much he could speak about *you*—that would never
> attain—to *you*—only in music—Alas, am I not too proud when I believe
> that music is more at my command than words—*You, you,* my all, my hap-
> piness—alas, no—even in *my music* I cannot do so, although in this respect
> thou, Nature, has not stinted me with thy gifts. Yet there is too little for *you*.

Without wishing to read too much of this turbulent letter into Joseph
Sonnleithner's ungainly libretto For *Fidelio*, I still think we can see in it
something of the travail experienced by Beethoven as he tried to transfer
his musical impulses into the words and actions of the opera, a sense of the
disparity between his musical competence and the consternation he felt as
he articulated his feelings in melodic language. The purest instance occurs
in the powerful, yet strangely tongue-tied duet in the second act between
Florestan and Leonore, 'O namenlose Freude'. Until this point, Florestan
has been a hidden prisoner and Leonore has been disguised as a young
man, both Rocco's helper and the illicit object of Marzelline's affection.
Neither has been able to speak openly to the other. Then in the tempestuous
dungeon quartet 'Er sterbe' Leonore reveals herself, the 'magical' trumpet

call is heard twice, and it becomes clear to Pizarro that he and his evil plans have been defeated: finally, the husband and wife face each other and pour out their love for one another. In *Leonore* Beethoven had inserted a long-ish spoken interchange between husband and wife, each discovering the other, assuring the other of their presence, making the transition from a state of solitude to one of blissful union; in *Fidelio* this is almost completely eliminated, and although the sung duet in both versions is similar, the later music is more agitated and astringent.

There is no doubt that this moment has a greater psychological truth in the earlier version of the opera. But as with so much of the later version, the dialogue is eliminated as a way of intensifying the present at the expense not only of a hindering past, but of dramatic verisimilitude. It is as if Beethoven were snatching the characters up from the dreary prison—so laboriously explored and described earlier on in Act Two—into another, higher, even metaphysical realm where language and ordinary communication are im-possible. One of the most striking characteristics of the duet is the amount of hyperbole and exaggeration in it—joy is nameless, sorrows are untellable (*unnennbar*) and happiness is overwhelming (*übergross*). These expressions are repeated several times, giving the music of the duet the breathlessly stammering, excited, elevated quality of the letter to Countess Deym. In addition, the duet involves a relentlessly ascending, aspiring, striving motif which is almost unique in the opera. It makes a striking contrast with the generally plaintive quality of the preceding music—in the dungeon trio, for instance, in which Rocco and Fidelio, who are there to dig Florestan's grave, take pity on the starving man and offer him food and drink. The trio is melodically shaped by the descending figures, usually seconds and thirds, that give the music its pathos.

Then, too, there is the main theme of Florestan's aria at the beginning of Act Two: when recollecting his early life in the desolate tranquillity of Pizarro's dungeon, he is given that basic descending figure which is triply fa-miliar because it is a motif in all three of the *Leonore* overtures. The passage is especially worth looking at because it is the first time Beethoven gives us at least a glimmering of an idea of the nature of Florestan's crime. In Act One, Rocco, his altogether too accommodating and servile jailer, informs us only that the man is in prison because he has powerful enemies. Now the prisoner himself avers that in his youth, 'Wahrheit wagt' ich kühn zu sagen, / und die Ketten sind mein Lohn' ('i boldly dared to speak the truth, and these chains are my reward'). Beethoven offers us no indication at all of what that truth is, except that it contained a denunciation of Pizarro's 'treason', (which is unspecified), but it is clear that Florestan's entombment, his death-in-life has distanced him permanently from some irrecoverable, unrepeatable utterance in the past. So rare and (to his worldly enemies) so threatening is that truth that, having once spoken it, he cannot do so again. We must assume that what Florestan said is political to some degree—and eloquent and dangerously effective: in the final scene Don Fernando describes Florestan as a noble soul 'der für Wahrheit stritt', 'who struggled for the truth'. What exactly that truth is, however, is not disclosed, either in *Fidelio* or in its earlier versions. In all three Florestan consoles himself for having done his duty ('meine Pflichten hab ich getan') in uttering that elusive truth, which nevertheless remains very much a political liability—an indescribable but deeply felt encumbrance.

Until his fall in Act Two, only one character in the opera, Pizarro, fully inhabits the action. It is his jail, his castle, his will; his servitors and prisoners are under his control; he is vengeful and cruel, and even though he is a one-dimensional figure, he is clearly someone to be taken seriously. In his well-known study of *Fidelio*, Carl Dahlhaus notes that whereas the lesser characters of the opera—Rocco, Marzelline and Jaquino—try to create an idyll suited to their class-based tastes and predilections, Florestan and Leonore, who seem to belong to a higher class, strive on behalf of a utopia based on brotherhood and freedom. Pizarro is the foil to both schemes. He breaks up the idyll by forcing the venal and temporising Rocco into service as an accomplice to murder; and so far as a political utopia is concerned, he is the embodiment of everything dystopic. He has an almost sensual feeling for the present moment: he will, for example, be able to have his revenge on Florestan, and at the same time revel in the act of killing itself.

Like so much else in the opera that is emphatically, indeed feverishly, gestured at, none of this will come to pass. At the climactic moment of Act Two, as Leonore and Rocco ready the grave, and Pizarro prepares himself for his long-awaited moment of self-realisation, Beethoven rather ingenuously engineers not only Leonore's brave interposition between her husband and Pizarro's bullet but also the magically-timed trumpet call. More has been written about this episode than any other passage in *Fidelio*, and the providential trumpet call has been interpreted as a symbol not only of freedom, but of hope, the new bourgeois world, the end of humanism and so on. Characteristically, Adorno has one of the shrewder insights in his 1955 Darmstadt Lecture, 'Theater-Oper-Bürgerturn'. I will not try to summarise the whole of his argument, but his main intention is to identify opera as a specifically bourgeois form. Thus the relevant passage on *Fidelio*:

> The fanfare of *Fidelio* ... consummates almost ritualistically the moment of protest that breaks open the eternal hell of the prison cell and puts an end to the rule of force. This interlocking of myth and enlightenment defines the

bourgeois essence of opera: namely, the interlocking of imprisonment in a blind and un-selfconscious system and the idea of freedom, which arises in its midst.

This seems to me to grasp very accurately the singular abruptness that characterises *Fidelio*'s style, and is very different from the more flowing, more humanly acceptable procedures of the opera's two earlier versions. John Eliot Gardiner's description of *Leonore* as a work in progress catches the sense of labour, development and process that makes the earlier version so compelling; above all, Beethoven seems much more interested in developing a set of relationships in *Leonore* rather than a set of positions. This is very evident in the quasi-domestic scenes of Act One in which, for instance, Beethoven allows for a little foreplay—excised from *Fidelio*—between the love-struck Marzelline and her father's ever so coy and evasive young assistant. The abruptness of *Fidelio* has less to do with the unmediated amalgam of enlightenment and magic that Adorno speaks about than with a strange, almost two-tiered style. At one level, various numbers are used to advance the action: the trio sung by Fidelio, Rocco and Marzelline ('Gut Söhnchen, gut') in Act One, for example, which prepares Fidelio and Rocco to go down into the forbidden areas of the prison, and—a sort of continuation of the trio—the Rocco-Pizarro duet a few moments later in which 'der Gouverneur', as Rocco calls him, presses Rocco into quick action in order that Florestan might be killed before Fernando arrives. At another level, sudden spaces or moments of opportunity are created so that one or more characters can stand outside the action and reflect, calmly or passionately, as the case may be, on their sentiments. 'Mir ist so wunderbar' is a perfect example of the latter device, as is the superb Prisoners' Chorus, which for a brief moment is allowed to take place outside Pizarro's dark prison cells.

All this produces a highly eccentric kind of continuity in *Fidelio*: perhaps 'discontinuity' is a better word for it. If a listener were first to hear *Leonore* and to follow that with a hearing of *Fidelio,* there is every likelihood that the 1814–15 version of the work would sound disjointed and forced, despite the linking dialogue (retained by Beethoven from *Singspiel*), but powerfully effective even so, precisely because the composer has forged a discontinuous style carried forward not by considerations of plot or psychology but, on the contrary, by the sudden intensifications I have been trying to describe. Yet even with Don Fernando's magical appearance late in the opera, we experience Beethoven's world in most of *Fidelio* as somehow natural and, more important, secular. Leonore and Florestan are ordinary citizens without any apparent hereditary rights. They both have an acute sense of injustice which is not shared by Rocco, or his daughter or Jaquino. But it is very likely, given what Florestan tells us so sketchily about his past, that he and his wife belong to a better class, though one which is less protected and privileged than either Pizarro's or Don Fenando's. Dahlhaus tries to explain the social distinctions in the work with reference to French aesthetic classifications said to have been borrowed by Beethoven from the Encyclopaedists (there is not, alas, much evidence to support this ingenious theory). He suggests that the early scenes between Rocco, his daughter, Jaquino and the disguised Fidelio are taken from the *comédie larmoyante*, whereas the interplay between Pizarro, Florestan and Leonore is based on the *tragédie bourgeoise*; finally, according to Dahlhaus, the tableau and pathetic scenes that give the opera its unique emotional quality are indebted to what Diderot and Lessing considered to be a wider category than the first two, and which in fact included them, that of the *genres intermédiaires*, which allowed dramatists to assign convincing and moving attributes to characters who are not noble or of high civil rank.

Plausible enough, but is that the only way to explain *Fidelio*'s extraordinary political and visionary power, given the work's abruptness, its lapses and strange ellipses as well as its passionate discontinuities? I think not. There are two strong undercurrents in *Fidelio*, one political, the other quasi-metaphysical: neither has played a prominent role in analyses of the opera, most of which accept its explicit themes of freedom and constancy as defining, if not exhausting, its meaning. It is taken to be internally consistent and to accomplish, in its conclusion, a complete synthesis of its various elements. Borrowing from Adorno, Rose Subotnik formulates the distinctive feature of Beethoven's second-period style as the 'apparent ability' of its structures and movements

> to derive the principle of formal organisation not from any outside source, but from within themselves, and thus to establish as a reality the musical analogue of the free individual, the 'musical subject', which has mastered external constraint and dissent and determined its own destiny . . . [In fact] the recapitulation [or conclusion] seems to confirm the rational irresistibility of the subject's return to itself, since it nearly always seems to emerge as the logical outcome and resolution of what has preceded.

What I have been trying to suggest is that *Fidelio* is a work riven by different pressures and counterforces, partly the result of its own complicated history as a collaborative, much fussed-over work whose irregularities of style, disruptive energies and unstilled, problematic nature were often beyond Beethoven's control. Certainly it is wrong to interpret the opera as reconciling all its elements as if by a creative miracle, though naturally enough the work pre-eminently bears the mark of Beethoven's genius. Steeped though he was in French and Viennese opera, Beethoven's only attempt to produce one himself also bears the marks of the enormous problems he faced in trying to get it right. *Fidelio* highlights not only its own peculiar features but also those of opera in general, a cultural form that is thoroughly hybrid and wonderfully overstated. But because opera as spectacle has become so routinised and unthinking, we don't find it in ourselves to do much more than venerate this cultural form and reproduce a set of clichés about it—clichés that are no less unthinkingly reinforced by modern producers and directors. That there might be something invisible (faultlines and unresolved antitheses, for instance) and transgressive about most interesting operas eludes the spectator for whom opera is out there, the bigger and more lavish the better: at the Metropolitan Opera in New York there is no shortage of applause for a typically overstuffed and under-directed Zeffirelli production of a bad Verdi and worse Puccini—and apparently no sense of what an appallingly vulgar mess the whole business is.

It is all the more important to recognise that the creative subject behind *Fidelio* is a fractured and only partially coherent thing, surrounded by uncertainties and incapacities, facing problems it cannot resolve and solutions it cannot fully pull off. *Fidelio*'s political undercurrent is a perfect case in point. Tyranny and benevolence operate more or less as equivalents in *Fidelio*; they can be substituted for each other by the miracle, or myth as Adorno calls it, of prompt arrival: Pizarro's police and Fernando's trumpet are interchangeable. Florestan's explanation for his plight is that the state has moved against him, but we never learn—nor can we—what sort of state it is. Who are the other prisoners? Are they also unjustly punished intellectuals, or do they include thieves and murderers? All strive for freedom and light, but is it clear that they are all moved by principles (like Florestan) or fidelity to a loved one (like Leonore)? Yes, it is the case, as Maynard Solomon and others have pointed out, that the opera moves in Act One from Rocco's quarters in the castle to the underground gloom of the prison, and in Act Two from the darkness of Florestan's dungeon to the sunny, liberating atmosphere of the yard, but what can the composer do to guarantee that the story of tyranny will not repeat itself?

The fact is, as he well knew, that the source of real power in his society lay outside anything that *Fidelio*, as a relatively compressed theatrical work, was able to represent. Beethoven's audience, his patrons in effect, were aristocrats, not ordinary middle-class citizens. He lived at the heart of an empire during a period of violent change and counter-revolution: the opera's audience was presumably made up principally of delegates to the Congress of Vienna. In a seminal article published in 1971, well before his

Beethoven biography appeared, Maynard Solomon argues that to the Viennese and Prussian aristocrats who nurtured Beethoven's early career, the Enlightenment was welcome not only as the creation of French aristocrats or of men like Rousseau who had been adopted by the aristocracy, but as representing

> a philosophy of duty, service and rationality, in part as a means of avoiding the painful reality of social existence and national fragmentation, in part as the false consciousness of a dying class . . . and if it was one of the means by which absolutism co-opted the radical intellectual and neutralised the mood of its most advanced sections, it simultaneously was one of the means by which absolutism was ultimately destroyed . . . Separated from the degraded sources of their immense revenues [their vast landed estates] by distance and generations of myopia, the nobility nurtured the arts, and especially music, with a lavishness equalled only by its vast expenditures on food and dress.

There was a 'disharmony' between someone like Beethoven and the sources of patronage and this, Solomon goes on to say, was 'a spur to the breaking of existent moulds, to the expansion of the means of musical expression'—and this in turn supplied new utopian images which permitted the composer to disengage from the old style of patronage altogether, to write pieces of his own choosing, not for gifted aristocrats but for professional musicians like himself. If the aristocracy saw a possibility of utopian affirmation in music and elaborate operatic entertainment despite war, the revolution and the fading of the old order, then it was possible for a few great musicians to find for themselves a new mode of utopian affirmation—and this, Solomon daringly proposes, was sonata form. 'The sonata distinguished itself from all other fantasy forms by its containment of its own fantasy-content, its moulding of the improvisational, its suppression of the extemporaneous, its rationalisation of the irrational. It was with this development that the sonata became a closed, rational, musical system, a "principle" of composition rather than just another musical form'.

The problem with sonata form, however, is that although it furnished a rigorous system of order, tonality, contrast, development and recapitulation in instrumental music—symphonies, sonatas, quartets—it could scarcely serve the same totalising function in opera, which is too long and various to be confined in that way. Individual numbers within the opera may employ sonata form, but what drives the work as a whole is the plot, a narrative sequence with its own dynamic of beginning, development and conclusion. A century after Beethoven, Alban Berg, faced with the same problem in *Wozzeck,* felt that he had to seek a separate principle of musical organisation to give the opera a sense of 'dramatic unity', and for this devised a remarkably complex series of forms, often archaic—classical suite, passacaglia, fugue. *Fidelio* belongs to the same tonal and compositional world as the *Eroica* and Fifth Symphonies, but the narrative complexities of opera required a more flexible system of organising sound.

What Beethoven retained from his experiences with sonata form was the need for closure, for achieved stability after a long and turbulent struggle. Hence the crucial status of the final scene in which punishments and rewards are handed out. In *Fidelio*, the last part of the last chorus is a mighty ensemble led by Leonore and Florestan for all the main characters (except Pizarro) plus the entire chorus. Full of anticipations of the choral movement of the Ninth Symphony, the ensemble concludes with a terrifyingly accented presto section, the last few moments of which settle into an anxiously strident dominant-tonic pattern similar to the last measures of the Fifth. Ostensibly, the much-repeated words of this section inform us that Leonore cannot be praised too highly and so 'hail to her who saved his life'; they are also a tribute, by implication, to the new freedom that seems to have been established thanks to her heroic fidelity.

There were plenty of indications in preceding scenes that Pizarro's castle is not a temporary, makeshift structure, but a dominating feature of the actual world. Yet the chorus which sings away enthusiastically in Fernando's commanding presence represents townspeople who have lived in close proximity to Pizarro's dungeons and seem never to have heard of him before. And alas, the genial Rocco reveals himself to have been a collaborator, blaming others for his role as jailer and becoming, in spite of his protestations, Pizarro's virtual accomplice. So the final cadences are much more provisional than they sound—a temporary union of Beethoven's romantic and Utopian impulses with the sordid world he and his librettists have been representing throughout the opera. And then there is the silence which confirms the precariousness of the affirmative cadence, which cannot be extended beyond the last C major chord. Solomon puts the general point well, and though he only mentions *Fidelio* in passing, I think his remarks apply to that work, too:

> In Beethoven no affirmation is complete: the finale of the *Eroica* is a prelude to the struggles of the Fifth; the brittle affirmations of the Fifth's finale in turn do not result in harmony or resolution. There are no ultimate reconciliations in Beethoven: there are a series of utopian reconfirmations, but all are conditional, one-sided, temporary. Each work in Beethoven's total output is part of a larger entity and each affirmation, each happy ending looks forward to a new struggle, to further agonies of introspection, to winter, death and

towards a new victorious conclusion. . . . The works are a perpetual cycle of struggle, death and rebirth. Each work looks both backward and forward—Janus-like—for within the work, the happy ending acknowledges the pain which preceded it.

The metaphysical current in *Fidelio* is part of a contemporary cultural pattern, well described by M. H. Abrams in *Natural Supernaturalism.* The age of the French Revolution is one of 'apocalyptic expectation', which impresses a whole generation of poets and philosophers, and the composer himself. Yet most of them lose 'confidence in a millennium brought about by means of violent revolution', though 'they did not abandon the form at their earlier vision. In many important philosophers and poets, Romantic thinking and imagination remained apocalyptic thinking and imagination though with varied changes in explicit content'. In *Fidelio* as well as in, say, the Ninth Symphony, Beethoven is very much of this disenchanted, yet still apocalyptic, cast of mind; one finds in both works the kind of reconstituted theology that Abrams speaks about, but in a radically problematic musical and dramatic form which, almost in spite of itself, highlights a lack of confidence in millennial change while retaining aspects of its enthusiasm and sense of triumph.

Finally, it would seem that *Fidelio*'s internal wrestling with its own past, its attempt to transcend its early earthbound versions, and its own dramatic setting in the actual, with an intensely elevated lunge at utopian brotherhood, points towards Beethoven's so-called late style and to the torments of his last years. He never stopped looking for another opera libretto to set, but because of his deafness and the anomalies of his fame and isolation, he retreated further and further into the abstruse style announced in 1816 by Opus 101, the A major Piano Sonata, and in 1817–18 by Opus 106 the Hammerklavier Sonata. What in *Fidelio*'s last scene is left unarticulated beneath the resounding final C major chords is uncovered once and for all in the late style where, as Adorno has said, Beethoven attempts no reconciliation between sections: 'the caesuras, the sudden discontinuities that more than anything else characterise the very late Beethoven, are . . . moments of breaking away; the work is silent at the instant when it is left behind, and turns its emptiness outward'. And, he also says, 'that sets the mere phrase as monument to what has been making a subjectivity turned to stone'. The uniqueness of *Fidelio* is that it arises, so to speak, in the heroic element of his middle period but ends up as herald of last works. No final synthesis here, but rather testimony to what Adorno calls Beethoven's 'power of dissociation', his ability to tear the works 'apart in time, in order, perhaps, to preserve them for the eternal'.

CHAPTER 37

Music and Spectacle
(*La Cenerentola* and *The Rake's Progress*)

S TAGINGS OF opera are made out of a set of compromises among performers, directors, conductors and, especially now, the economics of audiences, sponsors and ticket sales. There seems to be a general consensus that the classical music business is in a bad way because of corporate greed, a declining audience for the musical canon, increasingly overpaid stars (like the Three Tenors) and an unimaginative, not to say downright reactionary, attitude on the part of performers and impresarios who prefer a diet of safe masterpieces to contemporary or out-of-the-way repertory.

And yet opera continues to draw in young people, experts in fields like literature, painting and philosophy, and the general public in a way that is quite unlike any other. Even with its fairly uninteresting repertory, the Metropolitan Opera generates the kind of attention that Carnegie Hall, with its wonderful array of well-known performers, does not. The very extravagance of opera, its improbable mixture of drama, set design and music, is partly the reason, as is the likelihood of novelty and unusual entertainment, all of it subject to the compromises that have to be worked in no matter how lavish the production. Still, a great deal more information traverses the distance between stage and auditorium in opera than between recitalist and audience, and that gives the spectator a complex pleasure unavailable elsewhere.

With so enormous a stage, however, the Met faces a tremendous task in trying so animate and fill it interestingly, especially when producing small-scale or chamber works ill suited to a gigantic 4,000-person seating capacity and mammoth stage area. Last year's *Carmen* utilized a typically overwrought Zefirelli conception merely to stuff every empty space

The Nation, January 12, 1998.

with animals, innumerable humans and a few leading characters who were completely lost in the teeming mass. It was impossible to do that with this year's first-ever production of Rosini's *La Cenerentola,* except when the chorus appeared and more or less passively sang for (rather than with) the small-scale Cinderella story unfolding at the center. Increasingly the Met's problem is that it cannot, or will not, spend enough time or directorial energy to do something really gripping about a vast, empty center that is seized momentarily by a singer and then left inanimate until the next one steps in. Clearly Cecilia Bartoli as Cenerentola was supposed to be the focus of the production, and with her capable hectic voice and cutesy gestures she did a decent enough job. But if you sat beyond the first five rows she appeared to be a tiny doll strutting through an immense emptiness with a large orchestra to accompany her.

Theatrically, however, the Met's *Cenerentola* was a less than satisfying experience, since for all Rossini's merriment and comic exuberance, his genius invariably suffers when his almost uncontrollable inventiveness and consummate stylishness are subordinated to humdrum farce or the formulas of slapstick and jolly, unthinking banter. James Levine's orchestra is now so virtuosic, his conducting so assured and emphatic, that the discrepancy between orchestra and stage is quite stark. Stendhal, who virtually worshiped Rossini and wrote a book about him, never much cared for *Cenerentola* because, he said, there was no idealism in it. Not that its music is lacking in verve, "that brisk and impetuous style," which for Stendhal was Rossini's main characteristic, but that there is something too prosaic, too shoplike and mundane for the opera to succeed as fantasy, unless an ingenious director or highly gifted set of actors can introduce a new element into its all-too-familiar story. Not knowing how (or perhaps not daring) to lift the proceedings from one level to another, director Cesare Lievi resorted to busy comings and goings, not enough to bringing out, for example, the eccentric elements in the character of Dandini, the Prince's valet who spends most of the time disguised as his master.

Simone Alaimo as Don Magnifico, Cinderella's step father and one of the great *buffo* bass parts in the repertory, started out brilliantly in his first number, but only fitfully recaptured that early panache as the opera wore on. Bartoli remains a captivating singer, of course, though she seems to be doing less with her considerable musical gifts than when she first appeared in New York several years ago. Unlike that other great mezzo, Anne Sofie von Otter, who as Sesto in the Met's revival of Jean-Pierre Ponnelle's 1984 production of Mozart's *La Clemenza di Tito* dominated the stage with her extraordinarily crafted, musically compelling performance. Bartoli seems to be getting through less on phrasing and shaping than on often glib, albeit skillful, technique, as if having sung the role 900 times, she can toss it off with banal assurance.

Stravinsky's *The Rake's Progress* was the other new Met production of note this fall, conducted once again by the remarkable Levine and directed by Jonathan Miller, the gifted British intellectual, scientist and theatrical all-rounder whose stagings are regularly intelligent, humane and interesting. I very much admire Miller, who happens also to be a friend, although I don't always agree with his productions, which often strike me as interesting but not completely successful. He has often said that unlike more fashionable experimental directors, like Harry Kupfer and Peter Sellars, he does not saddle an opera with some directorial "concept" that is supposed to deliver a completely coherent vision of the work that compels and transforms every detail in it. This is the hedgehog notion that Miller thinks violates the work's integrity with as imposed solution; his view is that of the fox who realizes an opera as a series of uninteresting episodes, full of telling detail and carefully worked-out stage directions.

Stravinsky's *Rake*, however, is itself a sort of hedgehog, in which a twentieth-century artist returns self-consciously to Hogarth's eighteenth-century world so as to render it as part ironic imitation, part tour de force of neoclassical style, a step back and away from twelve-tone dissonance and avant-garde experimentation. Mozart's *Don Giovanni* is one obvious model (Stravinsky's score is dotted with echoes of that work), as of course is Hogarth's famous series of pictures. W. H. Auden and Chester Kallman's libretto is exceptionally sophisticated (often perversely so) and required from Stravinsky an unusual effort in trying to match the complex rhythmic and syllabic play of the words with the tonal effects provided by the timbres and combinations of a twentieth-century orchestra.

Stravinsky's conception of the opera includes a level of self-consciousness that both accentuates and undercuts the plot's parable-like structure. An exceptional density of superimposed elements makes of Act III the finest part of the opera, which is no longer simply the story of a young country boy who comes to town (under the wing of the devilish Nick Shadow) and is corrupted there by money and sinful pleasures. He also meets a fabulous creature straight out of circus and fairy-tale fantasy, Baba the Turk, a bearded courtesan, whom he marries as a way of escaping the drudgery of reason and the senses. By the third act Tom is already tired of Baba and along with Nick becomes a ruined con man subject to the depredations of an auction, and is later confined to Bedlam, pathetically convinced that he is Adonis waiting for his Venus. From being the story of a prodigal son corrupted by the city, *Rake* is transformed into a story of modern capitalist fraud and romantic madness, which Stravinsky's music renders with a taut poignancy and appeal missing from earlier scenes. But even that mood is overturned in the opera's coda, when all the main characters reappear to comment discordantly on what each sees in the story that has just unfolded.

Miller had an excellent cast to work with, and in Levine's conducting an inspired transparent sound that sustained the work's musical interest to the end. Dawn Upshaw as Tom's country girlfriend, Anne Trulove, and Samuel Ramey as Nick Shadow were superbly in form both musical and dramatic, but despite his fine voice Jerry Hadley's Tom was partly disabled by a kind of dispirited flaccidity. Denyce Graves as Baba had intermittent moments of brilliance but one sensed that the difficult part eluded her. Yet the Met's gigantic maw was not kind to Miller's essentially small-scale, rather modest interpretation of the work, which for reasons not immediately evident he set in between-the-wars England.

What I missed were extravagant gestures that exploited Stravinsky's arch knowingness as well as the capricious digressions that Auden provided as a way of staving off the predictable boredom inherent in all moralistic parables. Too much of the stage action was taken up with domestic business that brought the work down to a drama of personal dimensions but was contrary to the opera's protean and all too obvious self-transformations. What was really lacking was a concept flexible and audacious enough to encompass the Stravinsky-Auden genius and perhaps even go beyond it in large-scale, overstated gestures closer to the circus or a sprawling nineteenth-centry novel than to *Brideshead*. Stravinsky's irony pollutes even the sincerity of Anne's true love for Tom, but I thought, alas, that Miller took it too seriously, made of it too much the core of his idea for the opera. Still it is rare enough to have this masterpiece performed, so even in this flawed realization it makes for a rich evening.

Two other events of note were baritone José van Dam's Carnegie Hall recital in early November and a two-piano concert by András Schiff and Peter Serkin. Van Dam is one of a shrinking number of actor-singers whose superb musicianship gives unique merit to everything he does. Not a young man anymore, he usually makes up for diminished resources in parts like Berlioz's Méphistophélès and Wagner's Hans Sachs with an extraordinary capacity to bring alive what he sings with total conviction and a consummate technique. The only trouble with his November recital was that except for a handful of Ravel songs at the end, which he sang with wit and intelligence, there was a monochromatically somber, often lugubrously restrained tone to the Brahms, Fauré and Duparc selections that dominated the program.

Only in an ecstatically rendered encore of Schumann's "Ich grölle nicht" was there the dynamism missing from rather too carefully husbanded cadences of what went before. In their Metropolitan Museum of Art recital of Mozart's *Sonata for Two Piano,* Reger's *Variations and Fugue on a Theme of Beethoven* and Busoni's far too seldom performed *Fantasia Contrappuntistica,* Serkin and Schiff demonstrated the technique and adventurous programming that have made each of them so eminent. Unfortunately, Schiff's remarkably expansive and imaginative musicality overwhelmed poor Serkin, whose narrow tone and constricted phrasing were no match for his partner's gorgeous tone and virtuosic audacity. Would that Schiff and Radu Lupu were to pair up for a series of two-piano and four-hand works: The repertory is a rich and much neglected one, and deserves the kind of exposure that so many humdrum solo recitals (of the same canonical works over and over again) have denied us.

CHAPTER 38

Review of Gottfried Wagner's *He Who Does Not Howl with the Wolf: The Wagner Legacy—An Autobiography*

OTTFRIED WAGNER is Richard Wagner's great-grandson, and an extraordinarily unhappy fellow. So unhappy in fact that his book is an unrelieved jeremiad against his family, especially his father Wolfgang, now the head of the Wagner establishment in Bayreuth, as well as his great-grandfather the composer, a loathsome anti-semite; Gottfried's English grandmother Winifred, an arch-reactionary pro-Nazi admirer of Hitler, and pretty much everyone who has had anything to do with the performance of Wagner's operas in the twentieth century.

No one seems to sympathise with or understand poor Gottfried, whose wish somehow to atone for his family's ghastly history leads him from one disastrous excess of groveling or aggressive assertion to another, most of them the result of his uncertain talent as *régisseur,* musicologist, and intellectual historian. He, of course, blames his unsuccessful career as opera director, polemicist, and public scold on his father's malign influence and the man's apparent omnipotence. Every production of Gottfried's that fails (and most of them do), every nasty critique of his work, every personal misfortune, is blamed on Wolfgang's baleful reach, his amazing power as the head of Germany's most important cultural institution, the Wagner festival at Bayreuth from which he has banished his son, and blighted his future. *He Who Does Not Howl* is unsparing both in its messy details and in the aggrieved tone with which they are remorselessly delivered. It makes for decidedly unpleasurable reading.

It cannot have been easy to have been the neglected youngest son of a driven, unpleasant man who seemed to have carried the weight of the Wagner legacy, including his affinity for fascism, on his shoulders. First there was Wolfgang's competition with his gifted brother, Wieland, who almost single-handedly scrubbed the great music-dramas clean of their dreadful past in symbolic, spare, modernist productions in Bayreuth after the war. At first Gottfried admired his uncle, but when he discovers a box of films, papers, and photographs that show how close the Wagner family was to Hitler, and how willingly its members participated in that unholy mix of Nazi anti-semitism and German xenophobia which characterized the Thirties and the Forties, he realizes that neither Wieland nor Wolfgang is worthy of his regard.

Then, after Wieland's untimely death in 1966, the Festival is directed by Wolfgang who, according to his aggrieved son, undid Wieland's achievements and returned Bayreuth to a basically reactionary state, its conventional designs and productions essentially appealing to the German establishment for whom the Festspielhaus, with Arno Breker's outlandish quasi-Nazi bust of Richard decorating the entrance, would remain an unreconstructed temple of racist ideology.

Very few people associated with the performance of Wagner's operas come off well, according to Gottfried. He accuses most of them either of concealed pro-Nazi sentiments or of unalloyed sycophancy and opportunism. When his father hires two distinguished Jewish conductors for Bayreuth—Daniel Barenboim and James Levine—they earn the young man's excoriation as 'alibi-Jews', imported into the Wagner shrine as a token of appeasement for an unsavory past. None of the great Bayreuth *Ring* productions meets with young Gottfried's approval and because he is so stingy in his accounts of their work we are not given an opportunity to understand why. On one occasion, for instance, he enjoys listening to *Tristan* in the Festspielhaus 'although' Barenboim was conducting. This is neither criticism nor analysis: it is slanderous insult. And so for page after page.

One wishes that his domestic life were more interesting, but it isn't. He goes from one marriage to another, he adopts a disadvantaged Rumanian boy, he makes new friends and, of course, many many new enemies, and works fitfully as a shoe salesman, bank employee, assistant director, itinerant lecturer. He is accorded a period of redemption when, sanctimoniously but entirely predictably, he travels to Israel to lecture and atone in public for his family's manifold sins. He gives lectures on his great-grandfather's anti-semitism, on Nietzsche and Liszt (who is his great-grandmother Cosima's father) and endlessly pursues his research on Kurt Weill whom he elevates to the status of Wagner's great aesthetic antagonist.

Trapped between his famous name and the need to do something original with it, he oscillates between self-pity and insult, hurling generalizations—most of them unexamined and unacceptably vast—in all directions. 'Richard Wagner himself', he says grandiosely at one point 'had already contributed his part to the indissoluble link between Bayreuth, Theresienstadt, and Auschwitz'. Jammed together here are the Nazi, and specifically Hitlerian infatuation with Wagner, Wagner's own anti-semitism, and the Holocaust, with scarcely a thought given, say, to the music, to Wagner's extraordinary genius, or to the many anti-Nazi Wagnerians who have kept the works alive by re-interpreting them, and so on.

The real problem with this dreadfully translated book is not only its unrelieved stridency and complaint, its catalogue of woes and often trivial anecdotes, its insults and tiresomely long maudlin recitations of Gottfried's misadventures, but the fact that young Wagner himself has so little of substance to say about Richard Wagner, his works and their relevance for our time. I searched in vain for some alternative account of what the *Ring*, or *Tristan*, *Parsifal*, and *Meistersinger* really mean to Gottfried, but kept coming up with unaffecting one-liners. The *Ring*, he tells us at one point, leads to apocalyptic nuclear disaster. And how would one translate this searing insight into an actual production of the colossal tetrology? We are never informed. Even if we accept that Wolfgang Wagner's Bayreuth productions are not works of genius, we need to have them analysed more carefully, and substitute accounts provided, before we can be intellectually satisfied with Gottfried's across-the-board denunciations. Complaint and dismissal do not carry one very far, and so the fiftyish, no longer so young Turk is high and dry.

I cannot resist saying that as an instance of Gottfried Wagner's inadequate view of things his attitude towards Israel is particularly telling. For while it is certainly fair to connect the country's establishment with anti-semitism and genocide, it is also true that in the process of its creation Israel caused the destruction of another society. And the dispossession and denial of Palestinians as a nation continues to the present moment. Gottfried makes no mention of any of this, as if his mission is just to connect some things with others, but to simply leave out or ignore equally impressive connections.

There is a great deal to be said about the consequences of Wagner's music and vision, but why arbitrarily curtail one's understanding of them? So intent is the plaintive Gottfried with exposing his difficulties and sorrows that he is incapable of seeing beyond his warm tears. This is a book to be flipped through, perhaps, but not for a moment taken seriously as a contribution to understanding Richard Wagner, his work, or even his almost wantonly unattractive family.

CHAPTER 39

Bach for the Masses

F OR A little over an hour a day in two consecutive weeks recently,
British artist Christopher Herrick sat at the Tully Hall organ and
played through Bach's staggeringly vast output for what his contemporaries considered his main instrument. (The fourteen-concert series
of Bach's complete organ works was a noteworthy presentation in the otherwise haphazard confection of events that constituted this summer's Lincoln Center Festival, which seems to be shrinking in quality and quantity.
This year the cancellation of a much-touted Shanghai opera left a ragged
program of New York Philharmonic concerts, a lamentably uninteresting
Leonard Bernstein series, assorted undistinguished plays and new music
events, leaving us to make do with the occasional surprise, such as Herrick.) As organ builder, technician, composer and virtuoso performer, Bach
consolidated Italian and North German styles and then transformed them
into a new, complex idiom for organ-playing that has remained the basis of
all subsequent composition for the instrument.

The novelty and importance of Herrick's achievement in providing so
comprehensive a panorama of this great musician's *oeuvre* was not only
that such a marathon is rarely attempted but that it allows one to hear the
sheer inventiveness and prodigious intelligence at work in every phrase of
a highly complex and intellectual style that is capable nevertheless of pathos, drama, exuberance and other forms of considerable expressivity. Most
of us first encounter Bach's keyboard works as students. His inventions,
suites, preludes and fugues are the necessary pedagogic phases in building
a keyboard, usually piano, technique. Memories of that difficult experience
alas crowd out the musical pleasures available in Bach, with the result that
many people think of his keyboard works as exercises, and damn difficult

The Nation, September 7, 1998.

ones at that. The technical problems he presents derive mainly from a con-trapuntal style in which every voice (every finger) must be independent, so that what one hears is not a melody and simple accompaniment but a flowing, constantly transformed texture comprising two, three, four, five or six voices, each of them imitating the others with minute differences in rhythm, inflection, melodic variation. Most players end up by strug-gling through this, with the result that Bach's amazing harmonic audacity, ingenious rhythmical flexibility and constant melodic inventiveness (many performers can scarcely manage two voices, whereas Bach requires the capacity to play several strands simultaneously, each with complex clarity) are ignored.

It is also true that to hear Bach's entire output for organ as Herrick presented it is in a sense to hear something stripped of its context. All Bach's organ work was intended for and originally heard only in Protestant churches; as choirmaster, organist and court composer Bach spent much of his musical life in Leipzig's St. Thomas Church. There were no organs out-side the church, neither were there concerts as we know them today. Bach's audience was a congregation, the essence of whose experience during the service was of course worship. Yet what one discovers in listening to the numerous types of work that Bach devised for the service is how varied was its musical part—with its chorales, motets, preludes and fugues, antiphonal choruses, instrumental interludes—and how over the years that he served, Bach's indefatigability kept him producing one extraordinary work after another, each geared for use during particular Sundays at particular seasons like Lent and Easter, at specific dramatic and liturgical moments in the ser-vice. Bach's church music generally and his organ work in particular (all of it located at extremely specific points in the communal life of his church) deserve, I think, to be considered the core of his immense effort as perhaps the most industrious great composer of all. More's the wonder, then, when it is taken out of that place and strung through fourteen concerts, that each piece reveals such mastery of technical and spiritual means. Playing them as Herrick did seriatim revealed their amazing quality and allowed one to contemplate them as musical, rather than church, works.

The organ itself is a dominating instrument, designed to fill the church with its sound, as well as make emotional impressions on the congregation that would include veneration, awe, jubilation, meditation and contempla-tion. The very fine but dry-sounding modern Tully Hall instrument that Herrick used so compellingly doesn't have the resonance or range of a large church instrument, but it served the purpose nevertheless of exposing each work in optimal performance and (albeit dry) acoustical circumstances. Perhaps I should explain a bit more about organ sound. Unlike the piano, the organ cannot be made to sound louder or more lyrical by how one *strikes* the keys; since its sound derives from air being pushed through pipes of varying sizes and shapes, it does not matter whether the organ's keys are struck or touched forcefully or gently. The volume of sound is the same. The distinguishing marks of the organ are that it not only has keyboard manuals (four in this case) to be played by the fingers but also pedals, notes to be played by the feet. The sound is made richer and more varied as a result.

In addition, the sound of the organ is transformed according to registration, that is, the particular combination of pipes—which resemble instruments like strings, woodwinds, etc.—chosen by the performer to deliver the piece. Given the large number of registration stops, or possible sounds, the combinations available to the organist are nearly infinite; once chosen, however, the piece is stamped by that selection, which determines the character of the performance. Such things as constantly varied volume, dynamics and tonal color, which a pianist can manipulate at will, thus have no role in the act of organ playing. Herrick's registrations were remarkable and furnished the audience with a wide range of sounds to seduce the ear as well as control the work's effect, considering that so many of the pieces were based on chorales whose textual meaning Herrick's registration illuminated. Thus, for example, a somber phrase such as "Valet will ich dir geben" (I shall say farewell to you O world) is conveyed in a dark registration of bassoon and bourdon, whereas "Ein feste Burg" (Luther's mighty fortress hymn) gets a bright, brassy sound, in which trumpets and treble woodwinds predominate.

Bach's religious vision is Protestant Lutheranism, of course, but its method of expression in music is thoroughly contrapuntal, or polyphonic—the art of combining musical lines ingeniously without ever violating the rules of counterpoint or letting the academic, technical side of things get the upper hand. This is the paradox of his organ works: that each illustrates a specific contrapuntal technique—fugue, variation, chorale, prelude, fantasy, passacaglia—but does not let the skill of the technique (never before or again achieved at so high a level) overshadow the expressive, liturgical or emotional aim of the piece. Herrick played a handful of pieces, such as the Canonic Variations on "Von Himmel hoch," the C Minor Passacaglia and Fugue, the "Ricercare" from the *Musical Offering*, whose elaborateness and astonishing contrapuntal outpouring are overwhelming. Such pieces are dazzlingly virtuosic and, I think, show Bach using his unparalleled powers to rival the fecundity and multiplicity of the natural world. But they are also pieces that are virtual encyclopedias of polyphonic technique, useful to students as they must have been to Bach himself as a compendium of all that can be done with a given technique, a sort of work defining the absolute limits of that kind of counterpoint. The same is true of his display pieces, such as the toccatas, whose intention is to show the performer as outstripping the ordinary organ player in such matters as brilliant runs, rapid passages for pedal and repeated intricate patterns for two, three or four manuals.

Counterpoint is a learned, almost academic style of composing since it is rule-bound in a very rigorous way. Certain note combinations, for example parallel fifths, are generally forbidden, whereas variations on the main theme, such as inversions (playing the theme backwards), strettos (introducing a counter theme before the whole theme has been articulated), modulations and transpositions are required. Bach's death in 1750 sent his work into eclipse during the classical period that followed, partly because the erudition of his technique was felt to have been superseded by more melodically and formally based music (e.g., the sonata form of Haydn, Beethoven and Mozart); but one of the most moving things in the history of music is the way later composers rediscover and are inspired by Bach's awesome contrapuntal genius. Beethoven turned to him in the *Missa Solemnis* and some of the last piano sonatas; Mozart also revered him and incorporated fugal writing into his late operas and symphonies in homage. Romantics like Chopin, Mendelssohn and Schumann learned how to use Bach's music as a way of imparting complexity to their own. And when Wagner came to the composition of *Die Meistersinger von Nürnberg,* Cosima's diaries record his complete immersion in the works of Bach, since it was that particular chorale-based style that animated Wagner's vision of an ideal Germany in his only comic opera.

One of the virtues of Herrick's marathon series was that with only an occasional overtheatricality he dramatized what Bach was best known as to his contemporaries—being an overpowering virtuoso, someone for whom all the keyboard instruments, but specially the organ, posed no problem that he could not dispose of with extraordinary skill. A recent book by the American musicologist Lawrence Dreyfus, *Bach and the Patterns of Invention* (Harvard), does a great deal to "illuminate the special nature of Bach's compositional technique by showing how he fully assumed and understood the conventions of his time. Bach was no revolutionary or iconoclast, but used conventions in such a way as to give them entirely new meanings, far proceeding anything other composers had dreamed of. Invention is not creating out of nothing but rather—as the literal meaning the world suggests—*finding* in a phrase the possibilities for development that are there to be found. Thus Dreyfus shows Bach's uncanny ability to divine in advance that any musical phrase might be capable of in the way of contrapuntal development, and then produce the result almost as a matter of natural logic.

He did this by remaining within the musical environment of his time, but so conscious and so rigorous was his power of working on a piece of music that, Dreyfus says, his works are kind of musical map, a meditation on those conventions that highlights or elevates them into occasions for new reflection and analysis, thereby transforming them totally. Thus, Dreyfus writes, his patterns of invention are

> the web of compositional thoughts and actions that Bach brings to his works, patterns that not only govern the creation of a single piece of music but, what is far more important, disclose a musical experience in which music plays a privileged role.... What the piece ... embodies is a neat paradox embracing freedom and necessity, showing how one is inextricably linked to the other, how the exhilarating discovery of new thoughts brings with it severe responsibilities—in short, showing how one assumes risks and draws the appropriate consequences. This inherent respect for music demonstrates nothing less than a respect for the inherent meaningfulness of the world and every manner of *res severa* [in Bach's case, a rigorously worked out composition] found in it.

I thought the best opportunity for observing Bach's organ composition in this perspective came at the midpoint in Herrick's traversal of the work, when he gave a complete performance of the *Orgelbüchlein* (*Little Organ Book*). This is a collection of forty-five short (i.e., one- to three-minute) pieces spanning the liturgical year, each of them based on a chorale tune and each of them refashioned by Bach into a chorale melody surrounded or embellished by contrapuntal lines that highlight a tune or sometimes only a phrase in it. Herrick (himself a former church organist) played them superbly, with total concentration, so that one could uninterruptedly hear an example of the aesthetic imagination elaborating—inventing—occasions out of basically quite humble, even banal, material, delivering them instead as highly wrought compositions designed to reveal the whole range of possibilities available to a working musical intelligence. It put me in mind of Keats's marvelously suggestive phrase in the *Ode to Psyche,* "the wreath'd trellis of a working brain." That the music happened also to be devotional in character added to the intensity of Herrick's rendition, since he recalled for us in his playing (as did the excellent program notes by Malcolm Boyd) that these pieces were addressed by Bach "to the highest God to praise him, and to my neighbor for his self-instruction."

I think finally that Herrick's idea of the enormously rich material he presented conveyed two things never far apart in Bach's work: the religious and the pedagogical. Each work, from the most extroverted toccata and fugue to the most inward-looking and mournful of the Passion pieces, seems to have been thought of as an act of worship and also a kind of standing lesson in solving a very particular compositional problem. In the sheer profusion of pieces and the admirable consistency with which Herrick performed them, there was rarely an ordinary moment (although at times the organist's energies flagged and once or twice his digital technique failed him, humanly so). Bach was never meant to be played that way, over so relentless a daily course. Rare are concert experiences of this sort, for despite the pressure and the strain, and as Herrick moved inexorably toward the end of his performance, contrapuntal necessity and inventive freedom illuminated each other with magisterial beauty.

PART III
2000 & Beyond

CHAPTER 40

Daniel Barenboim
(Bonding Across Cultural Boundaries)

S TANDING BEHIND me in a London hotel lobby was an unmistakably familiar figure who had bobbed up to ask for something at the
reception desk. June 1993: I was there to give the BBC Reith Lectures but had coincidentally bought a ticket to hear Daniel Barenboim play
the First Bartók Concerto with Pierre Boulez and the London Symphony
Orchestra. And suddenly there was Daniel himself in the same queue. I'm
not one for importuning celebrities and, to be honest, he was so identified as an Israeli musician that the barrier for me as an Arab was hard to
overcome—but there he was, and overcome it I very quickly did. Some immediate but forcefully profound recognition passed from one to the other
of us, as it so fortunately but only rarely does in life. Between that Friday
noon and Sunday evening, the time of his concert, we spent the time we
could fitted around his rehearsals and my lecture-writing. A nearby Arab
restaurant kept a table for us when we were able to eat together. Mostly
there was incessant talk: music and politics of course, art, life, the whole
bit. I felt that something was waiting to come forth, and by heavens, it did.
Backstage to congratulate him and be introduced to Boulez I glimpsed my
book *The Question of Palestine* propped open on the practice piano stand.

One of the great musicians of the century, Barenboim up close is also an
enormously animated and prodigiously articulate intellectual energy. This
is completely unusual in general of course, but dispiritingly infrequent in
the musical world, where the solitude and precariousness of the profession,
an often depleted sense of self expended in music-making, the murderous demands of a career, the psychological uncertainties of a touring life
tend often to cow most virtuosos into an all-too-careful parsimony and
personal reticence. Barenboim is exactly the opposite, with the result in

New York Times, February 27, 2000.

our remarkably rich and deep friendship that it has transformed my life. He's on the go non-stop and I, crippled by illness and my own commitments as a teacher and writer, am not often even on the same continent with him, literally as well as figuratively. Yet he's ever present somehow, he always has time, never seems particularly rushed though he may be recording Albeniz's *Iberia*, directing the Berlin State Opera and the Chicago Symphony, planning concerts, soloists and productions five years away, meeting innumerable dignitaries, musicians, managers, agents, friends, reading scores and books, conducting and playing the piano, all somehow simultaneously. During difficult periods of treatment and illness for me he's regularly on the phone. Once in early 1996 I had done an "Orientalism in Music" weekend with Daniel and the Chicago Symphony. Turning pages for the Sunday afternoon four-hand recital that he and Radu Lupu were playing I was overcome with shaking chills, then was taken to hospital with pneumonia for ten days. Thereafter he constantly came to see me, always encouraging and concerned, brimming over with jokes, polyglot ideas, and pluri-cultural projects. Complexity is all with him.

We've spent time together in Berlin and Tokyo, Paris and Tel Aviv, New York and maybe Cairo next, as a happy result of the fascinating itineraries of the glamorous conceit and the more prosaic lecturing and teaching lives. What also sustains our friendship, I think, are the intertwined geography and history of our early years, in Palestine for me, and later Israel for him (the Saids were out of there in 1947–8, two years before the Barenboims arrived from Argentina), and this silently enjoins us to feel the inevitability of music, coexistence, friendship and ideas as playing a role there now and in the future. Of course we don't necessarily agree about 1948, and neither of us for different reasons actually lives there, but the place draws us back all the time and we do know that separation between our peoples isn't the answer either. How then to do things together, considering that neither of us has or wants any kind of official position or role?

It's hard to imagine anyone more willing to try than Barenboim. We've held (and will continue to hold) exhilarating public as well as private recorded conversations which constitute a book in progress. Each of us draws on the experiences of the other, as well as his own, not just music and literature, but the politics of culture, Zionism and Arab nationalism, the importance of Furtwängler (with whom he had studied as a boy and whom I had heard in Cairo in 1951) and many related subjects. The fertility and the direct translation into action of his ideas is irrepressible, whether he's describing how to produce a specific sound in a Bruckner symphony, or cajoling someone to invite this Arab or Israeli musician here, calling Yo-Yo Ma to join us, inviting Zubin Mehta to attend a recital in Ramallah, setting up workshops, colloquia, masterclasses, discussions. An endless series of episodes in what must be the busiest career in music, but here are two specially striking examples.

One: in March 1998 Daniel was playing a recital in Jerusalem, I was making a BBC film about Palestinian life on the West Bank. We had a family dinner at the home of the President of Birzeit University, Hana Nasir, who had recently returned after a twenty-year deportation. Hana and Tanya, his vivacious wife, hit it off brilliantly with Daniel, who was the first Israeli to be entertained in that house (the point of course is that Barenboim is never just that, but also Argentinian, French, German, Italian, generically Middle Eastern, Russian, multiplying identities and perfect accents in all the languages, real or faked, like a spinning metaphor). Less than a year later, as the family's dear friend and honored guest, he came back to play the first ever recital at the University (and the first by an Israeli in Palestine), concluded by a four-handed Schubert encore with a talented young Israeli-Palestinian pianist. There is no containing him by routine formats, and everything that evening was utterly transformed, as all of us, Daniel included, mentally scrambled to grasp what new and unprecedented thing had quite amazingly just transpired.

Two: in August 1999 he, Yo-Yo Ma, and I convened a carefully selected group of seventy-eight Arab and Israeli musicians aged eighteen to twenty-five in Weimar, that year's European cultural capital. Even eight young Syrians turned up, plus Palestinians, Egyptians, Israeli Arabs and Jews, Lebanese, etc. complemented by twelve Germans. For three weeks there were master classes with Daniel and Yo-Yo, plus first desk players from Chicago and Berlin, plus chamber music, plus seven hours of daily orchestra rehearsals, plus evening discussions led by the two of us. No days off. About three afternoons a week Barenboim drove off to conduct (by memory naturally) *Tristan* and *Meistersinger* at Bayreuth, then would return at 2:00 in the morning ready to start rehearsals at 9:30. By the end, after rivettingly intense, humorous, profoundly instructive and inventive measure-by-measure drills without a score anywhere near him, Daniel's orchestra emerged, tackling the Schumann Cello Concerto with a superb Yo-Yo, the Beethoven Seventh, Mozart's Two Piano Concerto (an Israeli and Palestinian pianist as elegant soloists), and even an overture for the final concert, played to a sold out spellbound audience in Weimar's main hall. We had spoken of Goethe's magnificent *West-östlicher Diwan* with the sometimes fractious kids, but this last evening topped it all.

During those three weeks all sorts of surprising things happened: an Israeli soldier-cellist and a lissome Syrian violinist seemed to have fallen for each other, heated arguments about identity and politics dissolved into incredible ensemble playing, and everyone was struck dumb with horror during an afternoon's visit to nearby Buchenwald, the pall broken when Daniel irritatingly heckled the humorlessly dutiful German guide. That particular night, after our discussion, he and Yo-Yo played Brahms and Beethoven memorably and at midnight, to huge acclaim, he delivered Opus 109 as an encore. No sleep afterwards. "This guy is stupendous," a mild-mannered Egyptian oboist said to me. I recalled the look of surprise on the Israeli musicians' faces as Daniel drew a super-refined A major scale out of him in the Beethoven.

"Nervous?" I once asked him in Paris while en route to a performance of *Wozzeck* that he was conducting, a day after he had conducted two Beethoven symphonies and a concerto whose soloist he had been. "No," he said, "why should I be nervous? Let them be nervous!" Strictly speaking there is no "them" in the oppositional sense for him. He has the uncanny instinctive gift for direct, unpremeditated engagement—with the score, the instrument, an orchestra or singer or instrumentalist, the audience, its ears, mind, and heart. This is by no means only facility or genius, which he possesses abundantly. It is total self-application and confidence not so much in himself as in the situation to which he is single-mindedly devoted. Pomposity and posturing are thoroughly foreign to him as a result (he doesn't seem to have time for either), just as after ending even the most searing, tautly articulated performance he can spin out side-splittingly funny Jewish or musicians' stories as if nothing had happened. He is so concentrated on what is at hand that what he does is reassuringly precise, concrete, and luminously clear, and neither fussy nor precious.

All of the arts are in a sense silent: they express themselves in different media of course but even though they belong to history and human reality they ultimately say no more than themselves. Proust calls the work of art the child of silence. Yet literature uses words that have everyday meaning; the figurative arts also reflect reality in forms such as cinema, sculpture, photography. Aristotle defines art as mimesis, imitation. Of all the arts, however, music which depends on and is sound, is the most silent, the most inaccessible to the kind of mimetic meaning we can get for example from a poem, or a novel or film. Of music it is right to say with Keats: Thou still unravish'd bride of quietness, Thou foster-child of silence and slow time. For the performer therefore the task is nothing less than to make music speak in ways, alas, that are too esoteric and difficult for most of us to grasp. In a Weimar rehearsal Barenboim explained the orchestra's waffling as follows: "Until now we have been insinuating—now we have to actually say it." Yes, you can assume that Beethoven's Pastoral symphony is about nature, or that Siegfried's Funeral March is about mourning the death of a hero, but beyond those rather obvious and plainly insufficient labels where is one to go for the understanding and meaning of a piece of music? The performer is principally an interpreter, someone who gives the realization of statement to music, even though most interpreters take their task to be a technical one, getting through the music in whatever way seems most efficient or effective, and usually those seem pretty banal when one encounters a great interpreter like Barenboim. The hallmark of his interpretations as pianist, conductor, and teacher, is this extraordinary capacity he has for first finding the note, giving it birth, then shaping into a life with as many of its inflections, pauses, climaxes, and episodes, and then finally allowing it to sink back into the silence from whence it came.

This whole intense and elevated process of drawing music out of its silence, so to speak, is the supreme interpretive gift not just of realization and articulation, but of something else, that I call *elaboration*. We all articulate words, ideas, emotions when we speak of course, but that is something quite natural, like the act of speaking itself or using language, which is innately given to all human beings. The great interpreter does more, when he makes music speak, gives it statement, and this is what distinguishes Barenboim so finely, so subtly from other musicians: I refer to his seemingly infinite capacity for taking the material of music and giving it the density and complexity of life itself, life elaborating itself into pattern, structure, order, energy and, not least, surprise and joy.

You feel that this remarkable musician brings a quasi-biological drive to the aesthetic project, gathering together so many strands, experiences, voices and urges in a contrapuntal web whose purpose in the end is to give all this diversity, all this utterance, all this complexity of sound and life the clarity and immediacy of a deeply human, yet transcendental presence. This is neither domination nor manipulation. It is elaboration as the ultimate form of expression and meaning. He does it in his playing, as he sculpts sounds from the piano with his fingers, in his conducting, as he pulls sounds from his orchestra that even its finest instrumentalists didn't know could be emitted. There is nothing of the icy perfection or inhuman display of the supreme virtuoso—which of course he is—in what he does. There is rather the sense finally that he makes one feel one's humanity and, yes, one's love and mortality as well, through an aesthetic experience that by means of a marvelously well-wrought sound connects the listeners to others, other selves, other musics, other utterances and experiences.

What it comes to mainly is Barenboim's actual sound itself, whether he creates it from and at the piano, or as a conductor from his orchestra. Twenty or so years ago I recall saying about his conducting that it sought a middle road, something too cautious, in his interpretations and his characteristic sound. Over time this search has deepened as Barenboim seemed to be absorbing more, and at the same time modifying and transforming more and more noticeably the things he admired in Artur Rubinstein, Claudio Arrau, Edwin Fischer, Sergiu Celibadache, and Furtwängler, artists whose culture and life informed, rather than were excluded by, their performances. These aspects of Daniel's music sound to me like extensions or expansions of the tone produced, so that instead of a line or chord being self-consciously in the middle with visible and audible room around it, the sound has grown to occupy the whole of one's auditory attention: it is more affirmative, mature, satisfying, complex, and doesn't allow you to look off nervously to the fringes for what might still be said. This kind of satisfaction is achieved through highly plastic and unostentatiously inflected tempi that convey the music on a path of pulses and transitions carrying the line forward into what one senses as full declamation. Inevitable, life-enhancing, unneurotically offered. In all senses of the phrase, Barenboim's music is for our time. .

CHAPTER 41

Glenn Gould, the Virtuoso as Intellectual

ONLY A few figures in the history of music, and only a small handful of performers, have had as rich and complex a reputation outside the musical world as the Canadian pianist, composer, intellectual Glenn Gould, who died of a stroke in 1982 at the age of fifty. The small numbers may have something to do with a growing gap between the world of music itself (excluding "the music business" of course) and the larger cultural environment, a gap that is much wider than, for example, the fairly close proximity of literature to painting, film, photography, and dance. Very likely, today's literary or general intellectual has little practical knowledge of music as an art, little experience of playing an instrument or studying solfège or theory, and except perhaps for buying records or collecting a few names like Karajan or Callas, any sustained familiarity— whether that concerns being able to relate performance, interpretation, and style to each other, or recognizing the difference between harmonic or rhythmical characteristics in Mozart, Berg, and Messiaen—with the actual practice of music. This gap is the probable result of many factors, including the decreasing prominence of music as a subject in the curriculum of liberal education, the decline of amateur performance (which once included piano or violin lessons as a routine part of growing up), and the difficulty of access to the world of contemporary music. Given all these things then, a few names that have important currency spring to mind: Beethoven of course, Mozart (mostly as a result of Salzburg and *Amadeus*), Rubenstein (partly because of film, partly because of his hands and hair), Liszt and Paganini, Wagner naturally, and more recently Herbert von Karajan, Pierre Boulez, and Leonard Bernstein. There may be a few others, like the three tenors who have mostly to do with opera and publicity, but even such remarkable musicians as Elliott Carter, Daniel Barenboim, Maurizio Pollini, Harrison Birtwistle, György Ligeti, and Oliver Knussen may seem exceptions that prove the rule rather than central figures in our cultural life.

The point about Gould is that he seems to have entered the general imagination and stayed there until now, almost two decades after his death. He was the subject of an intelligent feature film, for example, and he keeps turning up in essays and fiction in quite unusual ways, as in Joy Williams's "Hawk" and Thomas Bernhard's *The Loser* (*Der Untergeher*). Records and videos by and about him still appear and sell, his first record of the Goldberg Variations was recently included in *Gramophone* magazine's list of the century's ten best recordings, and new biographies, studies, and analyses of him as pianist, composer, theoretician are given noticeable attention in the mainstream, as opposed to specialized, media. To most people he almost stands for Bach, more so even than extraordinary performers like Casals, Schweitzer, Landowska, Karl Richter, and Ton Koopman. As we are now commemorating the 250th anniversary of Bach's death, it is worth our while, I think, to explore Gould's connection with Bach, and its pertinence to the matter of virtuosity, asking how Gould's lifelong association with the great contrapuntal genius establishes a unique and interestingly plastic aesthetic space essentially created by Gould himself as intellectual and virtuoso.

What I don't want to lose sight of in these reflections, however, is that first and foremost Gould was always able to communicate a very high degree of pleasure not only in what he did as performer and personality but in the kind of intellectual activity his life and oeuvre seem endlessly capable of stimulating. As we shall see, this is in part a direct function of his unique virtuosity, which I shall try to elucidate, in part also the result of its effects. Unlike the digital wizardry of most others of his class, Gould's virtuosity was not designed simply to impress and ultimately alienate the listener/spectator but rather to draw the audience in by provocation, the dislocation of expectation, and the creation of new kinds of thinking based in large measure on his reading of Bach's music. I adapt the phrase "new kinds of thinking" from Maynard Solomon's reflection on what Beethoven inaugurated in composing the Ninth Symphony; that is, not only a search for order but a search for new modes of apprehension, and even a new system of mythology in Northrop Frye's sense of the term. Gould's distinction as a late twentieth-century phenomenon (his years of activity, including the period after he left the concert platform in 1964, begin in the mid-fifties and end with his death in 1982) was in almost single-handedly inventing a genuinely challenging and complex intellectual content, what I have just called new modes of apprehension, for the activities of the virtuoso performer, which I believe he remained all of his adult life. I do not think it is necessary to know all this about what Gould was up to in order to enjoy him, as so many people still do: yet the better one can comprehend the general nature of his overall achievement and mission as an altogether unusual type of intellectual virtuoso, the more interestingly rich that achievement will appear.

Recall that the virtuoso emerges in European musical life as an independent force after and as a result of the exemplary careers of Paganini and Liszt, both of them composers and demonic instrumentalists who played a major role in the mid-nineteenth-century cultural imagination. Their major forerunners, contemporaries, and successors, Mozart, Chopin, Schumann, and even Brahms, had themselves been important performers but always secondarily to their fame as composers. Liszt, though a significant composer, was known principally as an astonishingly compelling figure on the recital platform, to be looked at, admired, and marveled at by a worshipful, sometimes incredulous crowd. The virtuoso after all is a creation of the bourgeoisie and of the new autonomous, secular, and civic performing spaces (concert and recital halls, parks, palaces of art built to accommodate precisely the recently emergent performer and not the composer) that had replaced the churches, courts, and private estates which had once nurtured Mozart, Haydn, Bach, and, in his early years, Beethoven. What Liszt pioneered was the idea of the performer as a specialized object of wonderment for a middle-class paying public.

A great deal of this history is contained in a fascinating compilation of essays about the history of the piano and pianists, *Piano Roles,* edited by James Parakilas. And as I have written elsewhere, the modern concert hall where we go to hear prodigies of technical skill is in effect a sort of precipice, a place of danger and excitement at the edge, where the noncomposing performer is greeted by an audience attending the event as what I have called an extreme occasion, something neither ordinary nor repeatable, a perilous experience full of constant risk and potential disaster albeit in a confined space. At the same time, by the mid-twentieth century the concert experience was refined and specialized at a profound distance from ordinary life, discontinuous with the activity of playing an instrument for personal pleasure and satisfaction, entirely connected to the competitive world of other performers, ticket-sellers, agents, intendants, and impresarios, as well the even more controlling record and media company executives. Gould was both product of and reaction to this world. He could never have attained his degree of eminence had he not had the services of Columbia Records and the Steinway piano corporation at his disposal at crucial moments in his career, to say nothing of the telephone company, concert house managers, intelligent recording producers and engineers, and medical networks he worked with all of his adult life. But he also had a phenomenal gift that functioned brilliantly in that environment and yet moved beyond it at the same time.

There isn't much point here in going over the characteristics that made Gould the extraordinary eccentric that he was: the low bench, his humming, gesticulating, untoward grimacing and conducting as he played, the strange liberties he took with composers like Mozart whom he disliked, and indeed, the odd choice of repertory that would include the Bach that he made uniquely his, plus composers like Bizet, Wagner, Sibelius, Webern, and Richard Strauss, who were not widely known for using the keyboard as their medium. But there is no way of denying that from the moment Gould's recording of the Goldberg Variations appeared, a genuinely new phase in the history of virtuosity began: he lifted the sheer mastery of playing before the public to an elevation, or call it a side-road or deviation, of an unprecedented kind. What made his appearance a more pronouncedly original event was that he had no known precedents in the history of music. (Busoni comes to mind, but seeing or hearing Gould at work makes any serious comparison with the Italian-German thinker and pianist unthinkable.) Gould belonged to no dynasty of teachers or national schools, and he played repertory (for example, Byrd, Sweelinck, and Gibbons) that had never been thought before as furnishing staples for a piano recital program. Add to this his remarkably fleet, rhythmically tense method of playing well-known pieces, plus his core attachment to fugue and chaconne forms that are perfectly embodied in the sarabande aria and thirty variations of the Goldberg Variations, and, initially at least, you have a totally unanticipated talent aggressively challenging the placid and passive audience that has learned to sit back and wait to be served up a short evening's fare—like diners in a good restaurant.

A few measures of Gould's 1957 recording of the Beethoven Third Piano Concerto with Karajan, or a scene or two from his video performances of fugues, tell us immediately that something beyond concert virtuosity is being attempted here. It should be added that Gould's basic pianist capacities were indeed quite awesome, certainly on a par with Horowitz's, who seems to have been the one pianist Gould considered his (overrated) rival. When it came to rapidity and clarity of execution, a phenomenal gift for double thirds, octaves, sixths, and chromatic sequences, a magnificently sculpted portamento sound that resembled the piano being played like a harpsichord, and amazing power for sheer transparency of line in contrapuntal textures, an unparalleled ability to sight-read, memorize, and play complex contemporary, classical orchestral, and operatic scores on the piano (see for instance his renderings on Strauss operas, voice parts and all), Gould was easily the technical equal of artists like Michelangeli, Horowitz, Barenboim, Pollini, and Argerich. So one could listen to Gould for some of the same pleasures afforded by the old-fashioned or modern virtuoso, even though there was always something more that he did that made him so thoroughly unusual.

I don't want to recapitulate here the many interesting accounts and analyses of Gould's playing: we have an updated version of Geoffrey Payzant's pioneering study, for instance; we have Peter Ostwald's sensitive psychiatric account of the sadomasochistic component in Gould's performing as well as affective life; we have most recently a fully fledged philosophic and cultural study by Kevin Bazzana, Glenn Gould: *The Performer in the Work*. All of these, along with Otto Friedrich's excellent biography, are fastidiously intelligent and faithful renderings of Gould's practice as something more than a performing virtuoso. What I shall propose, though, is an account of Gould's work that places him in a particular intellectual critical tradition, in which his quite conscious reformulations and restatements of virtuosity reach toward conclusions that are not normally sought out by performers but rather by intellectuals using language only. That is, Gould's work in its entirety—one mustn't forget that he wrote prolifically, produced radio documentaries, and stage-managed his own video recordings—furnishes an example of the virtuoso purposefully going beyond the narrow confines of performance and demonstration constitute an argument about intellectual liberation and critique that is quite impressive, and radically at odds with the aesthetics of performance as understood and accepted by the modern concert audience.

Adorno's studies of the regression of hearing amply showed how impoverished those circumstances were, but in particular he anatomized the kind of *Meisterschaft* and domination associated in contemporary performance practice with the cult of virtuoso musician. Adorno finds this typified in the figure of Toscanini, a conductor, he argues, who was created by a modern corporation to compress, control, streamline musical performance into sound that would grip the listener against his will. I quote the following short extract from "The Mastery of the Maestro" published in *Klangfiguren:*

> Behind his confident manner lurks the anxiety that if he relinquishes control for a single second, the listener might tire of the show and flee. This is an institutionalized box office ideal detached from people, which mistakenly sees in itself an unwavering capacity for inspiring the audience. It frustrates any of the dialectic between the parts and the whole that operates in great music and

that is realized in great interpretations. Instead we have an abstract conception of the whole right from the start, almost like the sketch for a painting,
which then is, as it were, painted in with a volume of sound whose momentary sensuous splendour overwhelms the listener's ears such that the details
are stripped of their own proper impulses. Toscanini's musicality is in a way
hostile to time, visual. The bare form of the whole is adorned with isolated
stimuli that shape it for the kind of atomistic listening associated more readily
with the Culture Industry.

Certainly Gould's desertion of the concert platform in 1964 at the height
of his career was, as he said many times, his way of escaping precisely
the kind of artificiality and distortion Adorno describes so trenchantly and
ironically. At its best, Gould's playing style communicated the opposite
of the atomized and desiccated musicality that Adorno ascribes however
unfairly to Toscanini, the best of whose Verdi and Beethoven performances
had the clarity and lean interconnectedness of Gould's Bach. In any event,
Gould eschewed distorted effects that he thought typified the requirements
of a stage presence, where one has to catch and retain the attention of listeners in the fifth balcony. So he escaped into the stage altogether. But what
was this an escape into, and where did Gould think he was going? And why
was Bach's music so specifically central to Gould's intellectual trajectory as
virtuoso?

We can begin to answer these questions by looking at an address Gould
gave in November 1964 to the graduating class of the University of Toronto.
His speech was couched in terms of advice that, I think, really outlined
his own program as performing musician. He spoke to the young graduates of the need to realize that music "is the product of the purely artificial
construction of systematic thought," the word "artificial" signifying not a
negative but a positive thing, "that it does relate to an obverse," and is not
at all an "analyzable commodity," but rather that "it is hewn from negation,
that it is but very small security against the void of negation that surrounds
it." He goes on to say that we must be respectful, take proper account, that
is, of how impressive negation is when compared to system, and that only
by keeping that in mind will the new graduates be able to profit from "that
replenishment of invention upon which creative ideas depend, because invention is, in fact, a cautious dipping into the negation that lies outside
system from a position firmly ensconced in the system."

Even allowing for a certain confusion between various imperfectly deployed metaphors, it is possible to decipher the sense of what Gould is trying to articulate here. Music is a rational, constructed system; it is artificial
because humanly constructed, not natural; it is an assertion against the

"negation" or senselessness of what everywhere surrounds us; and, most important, music depends on invention as something that involves venturing beyond system into the negation (which is Gould's way of describing the world outside music) and then coming back into system as represented by music. Whatever else this description is, it is not the expected kind of professional counsel volunteered by virtuoso instrumentalists who perhaps would more likely be dishing out advice about practicing hard, being faithful to the score, and things of that sort. Gould is addressing the difficult and surprisingly ambitious task of stating a credo about striving for coherence, system, and invention in thinking about music as an art of expression and interpretation. Moreover, we should remember that he says these things after years of association with a particular kind of music, Bach's, along with which he had undertaken a longstanding, volubly stated and restated rejection of what he called "vertical" romantic music that by the time he began his career as a musician had already become the highly commercialized and accepted staple of the piano repertory, featuring the kind of manneristic pianistic effects that most of his performances (especially of Bach) avoided strenuously. In addition, his dislike of being in close touch with the march of time, his appreciation of out-of-time composers like Richard Strauss, his interest in producing a state of ecstatic freedom by and in his performance, his complete retirement from the ordinary routine of concretizing—all these added substance to Gould's unusual virtuosic enterprise offstage so to speak.

And indeed the hallmark of his playing style, as he continued to produce it in the complete privacy of the recording studios that he inhabited late at night, was first of all that it communicated a sense of rational coherence and systematic sense, and second, that for that purpose it focused on performing Bach's polyphonic music as embodying that ideal. Now it is not as easy as one may think to have seized on Bach (and dodecaphonic music strongly influenced by Bachian rationalism) and then made him the cornerstone of a pianistic career in the mid-1950s; after all, quite formidable pianists like Van Cliburn and Vladimir Ashkenazy skyrocketed to fame at the very same moment, and the music they performed with éclat was furnished out of the standard romantic repertory of Liszt, Chopin, and Rachmaninoff. That material was a lot for a young and in effect provincial Canadian pianist to have given up at the very outset, the more so when we remember that not only were the Goldberg Variations unfamiliar music, but Bach piano performance itself was extremely rare and very much associated in the public domain either with antiquarianism or with the school exercises so disliked by unwilling piano students, who thought of Bach as a difficult and "dry" composer imposed by their teachers as discipline not as pleasure. Gould went much further in his writing and in his playing of Bach, asserting that an "ultimate joy" was contained in the effort to produce an "exuberant and expansive effort at re-creation" in performance. So we had better pause here and try to understand the implicit assumptions behind Gould's statements in 1964 and the kind of pianistic idea he articulated in his playing of Bach, and the reasons for choosing Bach in the first place.

There is first of all the polyphonic web itself that radiates outwards in several voices. Early on in his work Gould emphasizes that Bach's keyboard works were not principally written for any one instrument but rather for several—organ, harpsichord, piano, etc.—or for none, as in the *Art of Fugue*. Bach's music therefore could be performed as if in marked isolation from the rituals, conventions, and political correctness of the Zeitgeist, which of course Gould dismissed at every opportunity. Second, there is the fact of Bach's reputation in his own time as a composer and performer who was both anachronistic in his return to the old church forms and the rules of strict counterpoint, and daringly modern in his sometimes excessively demanding compositional procedures and chromatic audacity. Gould builds on these things quite deliberately by setting himself very much against the grain of normal recital practice: his stage manners were anything but conformist, his playing went back to a preromantic Bach, and in his unadorned, unidiomatic, unpianistic tone he attempted in a completely contemporary way to make musical sound the material not of consumerism but of rigorous analysis.

A justly celebrated essay published by Adorno in 1951—"Bach Defended against his Devotees"—formulates some of what I have been suggesting about Gould in terms of a contradiction lodged at the very heart of Bach's technique: the connection or link between counterpoint, that is, "the decomposition of the given thematic material through subjective reflections on the motivic work contained therein," and, on the other hand,

> the emergence of manufacturing, which consisted essentially in breaking down the old craft operations into its smaller component acts. If this resulted in the rationalization of material production, then Bach was the first to crystallize the idea of the rationally constituted work . . . it was no accident that he named his major instrumental work after the most important technical achievement of music rationalization. Perhaps Bach's innermost truth is that in him the social trend which has dominated the bourgeois era to this very day is not merely preserved but, by being reflected in images, is reconciled with the voice of humanity which in reality was stifled by the trend at the moment of its inception.

I doubt that Gould had read Adorno or at that point had even heard of him, but the coincidence between their views is quite striking. Gould's Bach playing bears the inflections of a profound—and often objected to—idiosyncratic subjectivity, and yet it is presented in such a way as to sound clear, didactically insistent, contrapuntally severe, with no frills. The two extremes are united in Gould as, Adorno, says, they were in Bach himself. "Bach, as the most advanced master of basso continuo, at the same time renounced his obedience, as antiquated polyphonist, to the trend of the times [*gaudium*, or style gallant, as in Mozart], a trend he himself had shaped in order to help [music] reach its innermost truth, the emancipation of the subject to objectivity in a coherent whole of which subjectivity itself was the origin."

The core of Bach is anachronistic, a union of antiquated contrapuntal devices with a modern rational subject, and this fusion produces what Adorno calls "the utopia of the musical subject-object." So to realize Bach's work in performance means the following: "the entire richness of the musical texture, the integration of which was the source of Bach's power, must be placed in prominence by the performance instead of being sacrificed to a rigid, immobile monotony, the spurious semblance of unity that ignores the multiplicity it should embody and surmount." Adorno's attack on fraudulent period instrument authenticity is not to everyone's taste of course, but he is absolutely right to insist that what in Bach is inventive and powerful should not be squandered or sent back to the sphere of "resentment and obscurantism"; Adorno adds that the "true interpretation" of Bach's work is "an X ray of the work: its task is to illuminate in the sensuous phenomenon the totality of all the characteristics and interrelations which have been realized through intensive study of score. . . . The musical score is never identical with the work; devotion to the text means the constant effort to grasp that which it hides."

In this definition, Bach performance becomes both disclosure and heightening, in which a particular kind of inventiveness in Back is taken up by the performer and reformulated dialectically in modern terms. An example is the last fugal movement of the G major partita, where Gould's playing shows an amazingly prescient and almost instinctive understanding of Bach's creativity as manifested in a king of polyphonic writing that is at the same time both virtuosic and intellectual in the discursive sense. For a brief explanation of what I mean I have relied on a recent study entitled *Bach and the Patterns of Invention* written and published in 1996 by Laurence Dreyfus. In my opinion Dreyfus pioneers a new level of understanding of Bach's basic creative achievement, and in so doing transforms our appreciation of what it is that Gould himself as performer was able to do. It is a pity that Dreyfus nowhere mentions Gould because the common element for both of them is the word "invention," which Bach himself used and which Dreyfus correctly relates to a rhetorical tradition going back to Quintilian and Cicero. *Inventio* has the sense of rediscovering and returning to, not of inventing as it is used now, e.g., the creation of something new, like a light bulb or transistor tube. Invention in this older rhetorical meaning of the word is the finding and elaboration of arguments, which in the musical realm means the finding of a theme and elaborating it contrapuntally so that all of its possibilities are articulated, expressed, and elaborated. Much used by Vico, for example, *inventio* is a key term for his *New Science.* He uses it to describe a capacity of the human mind, the *ingenium,* for being able to see human history as something made by the unfolding capacity of the working human mind; for Vico, therefore, Homer's poetry should be interpreted not as the sage wisdom of a rationalist philosopher but as the inventive outpourings of a necessarily fertile mind, which the later interpreter is able to recover inventively by putting herself back into the mists and myths of Homer's very early time. Invention is therefore a form of creative repetition and reliving.

This idea of both interpretation and poetry as invention can be given a musical extension by looking at the special quality of Bach's polyphonic composition. His remarkable gift for invention in his fugal writing was evident in his ability to draw out of a theme all the possible permutations and combinations implicit in it which, through skillful practice, he could make it undergo as a theme presented to the composing mind, like the material of Homer's poems, for a skillful performance and invention. Here is how Dreyfus puts it:

> Rather that conceiving musical structure as unconscious growth—an aesthetic model that presumes a spontaneous invention beyond the grasp of the intentional human actions—I prefer to highlight the predictable and historically determined ways in which the music was "worked on" by the composer [Bach]. This intention to speculate on Bach's willfulness invites us to imagine a piece of music not as *inevitably* the way it is, but rather as the result of a musicality that devises and revises thoughts against a resilient backdrop of conventions and constraints. . . . While it is true that parts and whole in Bach cohere in a way that is often just short of miraculous . . . I find it more profitable to chip away at musical "miracles" . . . pursuing instead Bach's inclination to regard certain laws as binding and others as breakable, to accept certain limits as inviolate and others as restrictive, to judge certain techniques productive and others fruitless, and to admire some ideas as venerable while

regarding others as outmoded. In brief, . . . analyses that capture Bach as a thinking composer.

Thus Bach's gift translated itself into a capacity for inventing, creating a new aesthetic structure out of a preexisting set of notes and an *ars combinatoria* which no one else had the skill to use so outstandingly. Let me again quote Dreyfus here in connection with what Bach was doing in the *Art of Fugue:*

> Examining these pieces from the vantage point of the many different kinds of fugal invention, it is striking how, within the context of a monothematic work, Bach was never concerned with providing "textbook" examples of the subgenres, which might conceivably have laid out in the disposition of each piece in an exemplary and justifiable order. Typically, he crafted instead a set of highly idiosyncratic pieces that show how very far fugal invention can be pursued in the quest for harmonic insights. . . . This is why the *Art of Fugue* pieces so often go out of their way to frustrate pedagogically oriented definitions of fugal procedures at the same time that they assert the preternatural status of fugal procedures as a source of the most inspired inventions.

To put it simply, this is exactly the kind of Bach that Gould chose to play: a composer whose thinking compositions provided an opportunity for the thinking, intellectual virtuoso to try to interpret and invent or revise and rethink in his own way, each performance becoming an occasion for decisions in terms of tempo, timbre, rhythm, color, tone, phrasing, voice leading, and inflection that never mindlessly or automatically repeat earlier such decisions but instead go to great lengths to communicate a sense of reinvention, of reworking Bach's own contrapuntal works. The sight of Gould on stage or on videotape actually doing this, acting it out, gives an added dimension to his piano playing. Most important, as one can hear in the early and late Goldberg performances that eerily frame his career, one at the very beginning, the other at the very end, Gould excavated the highly refined contrapuntal as well as chaconne structure of the work to announce an ongoing exploration of Bach's inventiveness through and by way of his own virtuosic realizations.

So what Gould seems to be attempting at such moments is a full realization of a protracted and sustained contrapuntal invention, disclosed, argued, and elaborated, rather than simply presented, through performance. Hence his insistence throughout his career that the very act of performance itself had to be taken out of the concert hall, where it was limited to the implacable chronological sequence and set program of the recital order, and planted in the studio where the essential "take-twoness" of recording technique—one of Gould's favorite terms—could be submitted to the art of invention—repeated invention, repeated takes—in the fullest rhetorical sense of "invention."

Among other things, then, what Gould did with Bach anticipates what we are only now beginning to realize about the latter's enormous and singular gift, a gift which 250 years after his death in 1750 can be seen to have sired a whole generation of aesthetic children, from Mozart, through Chopin, to Wagner, Schoenberg, and beyond. Gould's performing style, his writing, his many videos and recordings testify to how well he understood the deep structure of Bach's creativity, and show also his consciousness of how his own career as virtuoso had a serious intellectual and dramatic component as well—which was to carry on that kind of work in performances of Bach and other composers who were, in a sense, invented by Bach.

I find it particularly dramatic and even poignant that on some important occasions (i.e., his liner notes to the Goldberg Variations recording) he would refer to Bach's major work, the one he chose to make his own, as having a generative root, an "aptitude for parental responsibility," in spawning the great exfoliation of thirty variation-children. Gould himself struck everyone who knew him, as well as his listeners and posthumous audience, as being a singularly isolated figure, celibate, hypochondriacal, extremely odd in his habits, undomesticated in every sense of the word, cerebral, and unfamiliar. In almost every way, Gould did not belong, whether as son, citizen, member of the community of pianists, musician, or thinker: everything about him bespoke the alienated detachment of a man making his abode, if he had one, in his performances rather that in a conventional dwelling. The discrepancy between his feelings about Bach's music as fecund and regenerative, on the one hand, and his own unreproductive isolation, on the other, is, I think, more than mitigated, and indeed overcome by his performing style and what he performed, both of which were resolutely self-created as well as anachronistic, the way Bach's were. Thus, the drama of Gould's virtuosic achievement is that his performances were conveyed not only with an unmistakably rhetorical style but as an argument for a particular type of statement, which most musical performers do not, and perhaps cannot, attempt. This was, I believe, nothing less than an argument about continuity, rational intelligence, and aesthetic beauty in an age of specialized, antihuman atomization. In his own semi-improvised way, therefore, Gould's virtuosity first of all expanded the confines of performance to allow the music being rendered to show, present, reveal its essential motivic mobility, its creative energies, as well as the processes of thought that constructed it by composer and performer equally. In other words, Bach's music was for Gould an archetype for the emergence of a rational system whose intrinsic power was that it was, as it were, crafted resolutely against the negation and disorder that surrounds us on all sides. In enacting it on piano, the performer aligns himself with the composer, not the consuming public, which is impelled by the performer's virtuosity to pay attention to the performance not so much as a passively looked at and heard presentation but instead as a rational activity being intellectually as well as aurally and visually transmitted to others.

The tension in Gould's virtuosity remains unresolved. By virtue of their eccentricity, his performances make no attempt to ingratiate themselves with his listeners or reduce the distance between their lonely ecstatic brilliance and the confusion of the everyday world. What they consciously try to present, however, is a critical model for a type of art that is rational and pleasurable at the same time, an art that tries to show us its composition as an activity still being undertaken in its performance. This achieves the purpose of expanding the framework inside which performers are compelled to work, and also—as the intellectual must do—it elaborates an alternative argument to the prevailing conventions that so deaden and dehumanize and derationalize the human spirit. This is not only an intellectual achievement, but also a humanistic one. And this, much more than the kind of electronic fiddling Gould often spoke about misleadingly as providing listeners of the future with a creative opportunity, is why Gould continues to grip and activate his audience.

CHAPTER 42

Cosmic Ambition

CHRISTOPH WOLFF'S *JOHANN SEBASTIAN BACH:*
THE LEARNED MUSICIAN

T HE CORE repertory of Western classical music is dominated by
a small number of composers, mostly German and Austrian,
mostly of the 18th and 19th centuries. In their work, perfection—
of form, melody, harmony and rhythm—is common; in fact it occurs in
their music with a frequency unimaginable in painting (except perhaps for
Raphael) or literature. Yet even in such extraordinary company Johann Sebastian Bach (1685–1750) stands in solitary eminence, at the very pinnacle
of the art. A large number of his works are still quite regularly performed
and, since last year marked the 250th anniversary of his death, he is guaranteed to feature on every hall and church programme. There is also a vast
outpouring of Bach recordings, which, until DGG curtailed the series, included John Eliot Gardiner's amazing cantata performances. One of these
took place every week for a year all over Europe and North America—the
intention was to match the composer's own Sunday series for the churches
he served as choirmaster and organist. Yet even this enormous quantity of
work is not the totality of Bach's output. According to Christoph Wolff, his
most recent and thorough biographer, at least half of Bach's church oeuvre
has been lost, along with many instrumental and ensemble pieces. The
sheer density and quality of what remains is all the more staggering.

Like Handel, his contemporary, and Mozart, born nine years after his
death, Bach had an aural as well as dextral facility that made people gasp.
At the keyboard, whether performing a work of his own, sight-reading or
improvising, Bach also had a gift for polyphony unequalled before or since.
With the striking exception of Berlioz, who refused to allow Bach to impress him, every major composer has been stunned by his fertility, by the
ingenious combining, shaping and weaving of voices that constituted his

style and which he brought to a refinement far exceeding that of earlier German polyphonists such as Pachelbel and Buxtehude, from whom he had learned the basic elements. No composer after Bach was so thoroughly the 'learned' musician that Wolff describes. The works he composed (and very often performed) were so beautifully and so intelligently worked out and elaborated that they exhausted the resources of tonal sound. In Bach's counterpoint, the listener is aware of a remarkable complexity but never a laborious or academic one. Its authority is absolute. For both listener and performer, the result is an aesthetic pleasure based equally on immediate accessibility and the greatest technical prowess.

Because it is a highly specialised and even esoteric art, classical music must be studied in a highly organised and structured manner. For the non-musician, to attempt more than just humming or coaxing the single line of a tune out of an instrument is practically impossible. The science of sound-production, the rigours of the well-tempered harmonic system, the formalities of composition, the physical discipline of learning how to play and then perform on an instrument (or to sing an aria or lied)—all these require years of practice and study, especially in the perfecting of mind-ear-hand (or voice) co-ordination and the ability to deploy it unerringly, without hesitation, that lies at the heart of virtuoso performing. Many pretenders to musical proficiency have seen their ambitions for a successful career collapse after discovering that musicality or a love of music isn't enough, that what one really needs is an inborn capacity to translate what is seen on a page of music or heard in the ear directly into the muscles of hand or throat. All great musicians were and are endowed with this gift, which involves a dexterity, as well as perfect memory and pitch, that one either has or doesn't have. Age allows one to develop a set of skills, but not to acquire the gift. Musical lore is filled with examples: Mozart's ability to hear a piece once and then write it all down perfectly; Beethoven's seemingly unending power to improvise pieces at the keyboard that many witnesses swear were finer than the ones he wrote down; or—one of my favourites—the young Saint-Saëns visiting Wagner and Liszt at Bayreuth, sitting at the piano and giving a perfect rendition of *Siegfried,* the unfinished full orchestral score of which Wagner had left at the keyboard as he chatted with his father-in-law. Both Wagner and Liszt were staggered by Saint-Saëns's ability first to decipher a hugely complicated and totally unfamiliar text in one medium and then somehow to reduce it all instantaneously to ten fluent fingers and a keyboard in another.

In the past hundred years, virtuoso performers who are also major composers, figures like Britten and Rachmaninov, have become increasingly rare. There is no one like that today, unless one considers extraordinary conductors—Pierre Boulez, for example, who is also a great composer—to be virtuoso performers akin to pianists and organists. Today's concerts are extreme events, something quite apart from everyday life. Pollini or Barenboim or Yo-Yo Ma are individuals with unusual musical talent who perform a programme of music in a way that is at the same time risky and challenging for them and enjoyable and exciting for listeners: they don't need to have the ability to do anything other than play extremely well. The musicians who teach or compose in addition to virtuoso playing are much more the exception than the layman thinks. Musical proficiency is a talent in and of itself, and that, I believe, is related to music's nature as an esoteric art. Unlike the words of a great poem, which have all sorts of specific meanings and possibilities beyond those made use of by the poet, the notes in a piece of music in the end either refer back to themselves or to other music, and are uncorrupted by references or connotations that stand outside the actual sound. Programme music proves rather than contradicts this, since nine times out of ten it is the music which, by means of a few vaguely mimetic sounds (fifths played by 'hunting' horns, growls in the double basses meant to sound like a dragon, a march in a minor key that stands for an army's defeat etc), confirms the programme rather than the other way round.

Until the mid-19th century, the sense and the intention, if not the meaning, of music derived to a considerable degree from the church (Protestant or Catholic) and the court. It is a cliché in musical history that Beethoven's distinction as a musician was to have broken the submissive connection between the composer-performer such as Haydn (and many lesser others) and the great patrons, such as the Esterhazy family. Mozart was scarcely more than a lackey in imperial Vienna and a servitor in the Archbishop of Salzburg's entourage, though our analysis isn't yet sophisticated enough to allow us to tell whether, in their work, composers like Haydn and Mozart were really acting for, or against, the values and interests of their aristocratic patrons. Maybe one day a case will be made for seeing the Mozart operas with librettos by Da Ponte and some of his grander piano concertos—as well as Haydn's Creation—as gestures of rebellion and adumbrations of alternative social forms. My own impression is that so much of the music of these two great court musicians is additionally challenging because it seems to express a chafing, in form and content, against the restraint and servility imposed on them by their social superiors. No one has doubted the personal anguish in, say, Mozart's C minor and D minor piano concertos or the quiet, although triumphal, self-satisfaction in *The Creation* (Haydn showing himself to be in direct contact with natural generation as opposed to the requirements of his patron): what if those works were also, internally, an expression of impatient self-assertion, of pushing against the form, stretching it beyond the limits of Charles Rosen's rather too reconciliatory idea of 'the classical style'?

One of the great strengths of Wolff's biography is the detail he provides about Bach's education and self-education and how, in practical terms, they dictated the kind of music—traditional, yet constantly pushing at the limits of what was acceptable—he would go on to write. Bach was born in 1685 to a family of musicians in the town of Eisenach, a newly independent principality, 'well positioned on the so-called Hohe or Ober-Strasse—at the time a major trade and post route east-west in Germany—between Leipzig and Frankfort-on-the-Main'. His father Ambrosius was a piper and the director of the town's music company, a position that required him to perform both in the town hall and in St. George's Church. Immersed in music from a very early age, Johann Sebastian carried on a family tradition that stretched back for generations and remained for the rest of his life a creature of the four institutions that 'formed the foundation of 17th-century musical culture in Germany: town, court, school and church'.

Throughout the book, Wolff makes it clear that Bach was always reacquainting himself with the basics of his Latin and German education, the premise of which was that religious faith and the science of 'real things' were compatible and could be systematised together. The analogy between Bach and Newton that Wolff goes on to make (rather fitfully, but provocatively) is daring but, I think, plausible so long as we accept first that 'belief in God as creator and the perfection of God's creation' were 'central' and, second, that the language of music and the language of science are commensurable. I'm not at all sure about the second assumption, although the first was common enough in the 17th and the earlier part of the 18th century.

I can, however, understand the attractiveness of this analogical argument to an assiduous biographer such as Wolff. The magnificence of Bach's music, its polyphonic ingenuity, and its amazing way with the Lutheran as well as Latin liturgy do not square with the woefully inadequate terms of his unpleasantly hectic employment. Why did such a talent have to put up with the grinding routine and the genteel poverty and servility of his social role? Wolff speaks at one point of Bach's desire for emancipation and autonomy, linking it (rather timidly) to a wish, in the composer's early life, to explore the organs of North Germany, thereby eluding his chores for a little while. But this is scarcely enough to satisfy what must have been a genuine wish to break out of his lowly role as chorister-apprentice and, at a later time, loyal retainer in various courts, churches and schools.

He seems to have had a voracious appetite for musical knowledge throughout his school years, copying out scores, walking long distances to listen to other musicians, working long hours day and night. All this in addition to being locked into a rigorous schedule at his school, St. Michael's, in Lüneberg near Hamburg. There he had at his disposal both the harpsichord and the organ, which he studied under Georg Böhm, one of his most influential teachers, who introduced him 'to the genre of stylised dance in general, and to French music and performance practices in particular . . . he also provided Bach with compositional models—preludes and fugues of his own and of other Northern composers as well as chorale variations, a genre in which he excelled'. The wonder of it was that Bach took in everything that was available to him, made it his own, and then pressed on into new territory, even though the circumstances of his life and career were at a further and further remove from his creative energy.

The outlines of his post-school career are unsurprising for someone of his class and background, except in two respects. One is that, as Wolff shows, he was always open to musical experimentation and novelty, even though in all major respects he remained a dutiful Christian and traditionalist. From Italian composers such as Corelli, Albinoni and Legrenzi, he learned how to be proficient in 'consistent and logical part writing, the design of closed and rounded movements, the differentiation between thematic expositions and related yet non-thematic episodes, and the integrated use and expansion of sequential patterns'. He also soon acquired an understanding of the 'genuine French musical style and manner of performance'—i.e. the courtly grace and *galanterie* prized by his aristocratic patrons. From Buxtehude and Pachelbel (known today only as the author of the lamentably ubiquitous canon) he took the magnificent contrapuntal modes and gave them an unprecedented grandeur. But all of this and more has to do exclusively with Bach's music. The narrative of his life, except for his last years when, along with his exact contemporary Handel, he was the most celebrated musician in Germany, has so far been buried in the detail of acquiring, keeping and eventually leaving one or another job as organist and choirmaster.

Wolff records examples of Bach's stubbornness, irascibility and quarrelsome nature. These episodes of unseemly or unexpected behaviour, like others illustrating Bach's capacity for innovation, stand out from the dense fabric of dates, places, names, financial transactions, job descriptions, patrons, schedules, programmes and hypothetical situations that Wolff revels in. Suddenly, Bach leaps out at us, an animated, seething man whose musical reasoning sometimes overcomes or circumvents the trivial obstacles that make up his life.

In nearly every position that he occupied after completing his education, something of his intransigence may be glimpsed. Several of his students are on record as having been the butt of his arrogance and impatience. His relationships with the various feudal patrons and clerical higher-ups to whom he reports invariably reach a point of sometimes violent exasperation; in Weimar, for instance, he is jailed for almost a month because of his insubordination. He is always dissatisfied with his pay and shrewdly on the lookout for better employment while pretending to be happy where he is. He always wants more recognition and more freedom for himself, despite the fawning letters he writes to his providers. He is an eager combatant when it comes to other musicians, ever willing to accept duels in keyboard improvisation and virtuosity. During his early years of employment as a court musician, church choirmaster and schoolteacher in provincial towns like Arnstadt, Mühlhausen and Weimar, so long as he has what Wolff calls 'opportunities for exploration, experimentation and training', he exploits them; once they are exhausted he begins to chafe and stirs up his situation so that he will be forced to leave.

According to Wolff, Bach had reached the peak of his keyboard mastery in 1710, at the age of 25; by 1714 he had already explored everything that was available in the harpsichord and organ literature. When the music he was asked to perform or teach seemed too affected and perhaps beneath consideration, he would become agitated and inventive—hence his revolutionary fingering ideas, devised to produce smooth playing and transform the thumb from an obstacle into an equal partner of the other fingers.

Wolff has amassed so much in the way of facts and quasi-facts about Bach's life as a working musician that one begins to feel he is not so much trying to understand Bach from within (in the memorable phrase Ortega y Gasset applied to a study of Goethe), as compiling a book designed to pre-empt any other biography any time soon. No one else need try, you feel, when, for example, he informs us that we do not have the facts about the guest list or the music performed for Bach's wedding (he married his first wife on 17 October 1707, 'a Monday', he adds helpfully) but then reels off a list of people who might have been there, and another list of pieces that might have been played. Certainly we need to know what Bach's jobs were, how much he made, and what sort of duties he performed, but the much more valuable detail about the development of his musical mind, his compositional method and the overall structure of his work, is often drowned in lists of thalers, household duties and the like. It is as if Wolff hadn't thought through or constructed a model in the Adornian sense for what might have been the role of the everyday in Bach's life as well as its relationship to his deeper concerns about music.

There is no easy or ready-made method for discussing the life and work of a musician whose art in its essence is so different, so remote from his everyday chores or even his career. Yes, the occasions for Bach's cantatas and organ music are plainly connected to the Biblical texts for a given Sunday in the liturgical calendar, as well as to the titles of Lutheran chorales, and Wolff is superbly complete in his descriptions of these. But when it comes to such long-term projects as the *Clavier-Übung,* the keyboard partitas and suites, the orchestral works, the chorales, the great contrapuntal studies, and even the choral works, which together form a mighty ensemble, he is disappointingly episodic (what little he says is nevertheless full of insight). Why, for example, was Bach so fascinated by the harmonic possibilities afforded by chorales that he kept producing and reharmonising them up to his last waking minute? What was that all about?

Wolff would have done better to talk about these matters separately, instead of interspersing comments here and there. A more fruitful approach would have been less positivistic, less relentlessly sequential, more reflective, in the manner of Maynard Solomon in his Beethoven and Mozart biographies, which present the known facts and then go on to talk imaginatively and at length about groups of works like Mozart's serenades or Beethoven's late quartets and sonatas. When Wolff refers in his preface to Bach's life as 'a highly fragmented mosaic' and his biography as an attempt 'to walk the bridge between two poles, the down-to-earth backdrop of Bach's life and the intellectual framework of his artistry', he underestimates the dissipating effect of that fragmentation. Indeed it's almost impossible for the reader to see the overarching design of this complex oeuvre even though it is clear from listening to a handful of pieces that there was such a design and that it is worth trying to reconstruct speculatively in a biography as opulent and generous as this one. Better than telling us who the guests might have been at the composer's wedding.

Wolff's unwillingness to provide a really imaginative aesthetic construction of Bach is further underlined by what he says at the end of his book about the splitting up of the composer's estate after his death in 1750. He argues that because many manuscripts were lost or went to different heirs, it became impossible to establish Bach's musical legacy in its totality for another fifty years. He draws a comparison with Newton: 'the main ideas for which their work stood were clearly present, even already at work' in what was recovered or already accomplished before they died.

What then is this stubborn totality that survived, this musical paradigm, which Wolff goes on to characterise summarily as 'principled yet moving, scientific, yet human'? Isn't it possible to say more about it from our vantage point? Wolff's reticence on this matter is all the more poignant for the fact that Bach himself tried to deal with the matter—unsuccessfully or incompletely, as it turns out. In 1735, at the peak of his success—he was soon to be made Electoral Saxon and Polish Court *compositeur* while still employed at St. Thomas's School in Leipzig—Bach is described by Wolff as attempting to recapitulate the main outlines of his life in a genealogical sketch and family tree. In so doing he

> was opening a broad historical spectrum that induced him to look in two directions: the musical past of his family and its future—ancestors on one side and his own children on the other—with himself in the middle. The past, present and future of the family tangibly mirrored the past, present and future of music within his realm and reach. . . . So he embarked on a journey of reflection to critically survey his major works and set the stage for such large-scale projects as *The Art of Fugue* and the B minor Mass.

Bach seems to have been trying for more and more inclusiveness in his compositions: not just one partita or one prelude and fugue, but a whole slew of them, pushing at the limits of composition and, apparently, at the limits of the daily round, with a string of posts at Arnstadt (1703–7) Mühlhausen (1707–8) Weimar (1708–17), Cöthen (1717–23) and finally Leipzig (1723–50), where he spent the best part of his working life as Cantor et Director Musices. His first wife had died in 1720; the following year he married Anna Magdalena Wilcke and produced several children to add to those he had had with his first wife (some of whom died in infancy).

An endless schedule of teaching, composing, performing, drilling, quarrelling (with musicians or students or anyone else), worshipping and serving seems to have impelled Bach to rectify this time of dissipated effort aesthetically, not just in the composition of more and more abstruse pieces, but in works whose core identity was a compendium of elaborations which encircled, regrouped and reformed sequences of notes and themes into prodigiously detailed structures of contrapuntal sound. In such structures no individual note or even work has a merely ornamental or digressive function: everything—melody, harmony, rhythm, tonality, genre—plays a role. One can get a sense of this extraordinary animation of every last detail from the vast collection of harmonised chorales that Bach produced to the *Passions*, the B minor Mass and the cantatas, over two hundred of which have survived the loss and destruction of as many again.

The pity of it is that from time to time Wolff has much that is penetrating to say about the work itself—his scattered comments about Bach's status as learned musician, an adept at 'musical science', are just one instance. To my mind, the theme of music being an intermediary between God and the reality of this world suggests not just a servile adulation of God and his work, but also an unconscious desire to rival it, which grows more apparent in massive late works like *The Art of Fugue*, the B minor Mass and the *Goldberg Variations*. Unfortunately, because he takes Bach's almost tiresome piety at face value, Wolff doesn't even entertain the possibility of rebellious-ness. Bach would have been well aware of his power to generate what one contemporary called 'strange, new, expressive and beautiful ideas' that must have seemed now and then to have escaped God's dominion entirely, and to have assumed the outlines of a separate world altogether.

He remains one of the few composers—late Beethoven, Wagner and Schoenberg come to mind—who spent a great deal of time exploring tonality, modality, harmony, the various combinatorial possibilities of themes, rhythm and variation. In *Doktor Faustus,* Thomas Mann speaks of Adrien Leverkuhn's (and his father's) inclination 'to speculate the ele-ments' (*die elementa spekulieren*)—that ultimately dangerous pursuit of dabbling not just in nature's oddities (inanimate crystals that behave like animate forms for instance) but in alchemy, necromancy and magic, arts not unrelated to music, which put the speculator in the position of cre-ator. In fact, Mann associates the practice of music itself with theology, with Leverkuhn's demonic pact, and with Germany's modern perdition. These associations are even more suggestive in the retrospective case of Bach because it is his polyphonic music in particular that makes Adrien an original composer.

I'd like to take Wolff further for a moment or two than he is willing to go, although the analogy with a great scientist is his not mine. All the evidence we have about Bach the performer and Bach the contrapuntal genius-composer is that he had an uncanny power with individual phrases or themes whose combinatorial potential he could understand at a glance. *Bach and the Patterns of invention* (1996), a brilliant study by Laurence Dreyfus, reveals how his creative powers derive from a capacity for finding (*inventio*), fetching out and knowing how to use all the combinations of which a given phrase was capable. Like a mathematician with a rare in-sight into the heart of natural numbers, what their basic properties are, the way they cohere, combine and behave in groups, Bach saw into the tonal system, discerning its potential for concentration, expansion, expression and elaboration, its harmonic as well as melodic capacities, the rhythmical and logical compatibilities of groups of notes, as well as the articulation of inherently beautiful phrases taken from a huge number of possibilities. No one else in musical history has had that power to such a degree. This meant, as Dreyfus has been by far the most perceptive in arguing, that, taking an almost random selection of notes such as the King's Theme in *The Musical Offering,* Bach was able on the spot to put it through every permutation and also to keep those combinations occurring together according to a rigorous set of rules over which he had complete mastery. And on top of all that, he had the digital skill and the instant mind-to-hand power to perform such work at the keyboard, without preparation.

The sheer quantity of Bach's work adds to one's amazement. He went from job and job, from Mühlhausen, to Weimar, to Cöthen where, as Wolff points out, he managed to produce 'the *Brandenburg Concertos*, the *French Suites*, The *Well-Tempered Clavier*, the sonatas and partitas for solo violin, and the suites for solo cello'. Any of these might be considered a monument, but Bach's compositional energies seemed habitually to express themselves in groups of pieces, as if to use Wolff's phrase—he resolved 'to leave nothing untried'. Once started on a work, he let it grow, from an often humdrum or undistinguished core (and in one of his most astonishingly complex late pieces, the Canonic Variations for organ on the chorale melody 'Von Himmel hoch', from an almost childish figure), to far-reaching structures, unimaginable to even the most practised musical mind. The little D minor theme in *The Art of Fugue* is one such example, as is the bassline of the aria of the *Goldberg Variations* (essentially a descending G major scale), or the King's Theme in perhaps the greatest of his contrapuntal masterpieces, the ricercare of *The Musical Offering*. Wolff is particularly fine on the word-generated music of the cantatas, as rich and complex as anything Bach wrote.

In the deliberate, patient, overwhelmingly plotted and elaborated texture of his work, Bach is Beethoven's exact opposite. Even in those late compositions that show the direct influence of Bach's counterpoint (the fugues of Opus 106, 110 or 130, the Missa solemnis and others) Beethoven's mode is dramatic, pulsing forward in phrases of irrepressible energy, conquering territory and moving on rather than consolidating and encircling in an ever-widening arc as Bach does. Every one of Beethoven's works contains a different set of methods for this attack, whether in the statement, development or recapitulation, very often via tiny themelets that are scarcely more than broken triads (as in the first movement of the *Eroica*) or thematic patterns fashioned out of repeated notes (the first and second movements of the Seventh Symphony). Bach is epic; Beethoven drama. What I find so compelling about Bach's last works (the B minor Mass, the *Goldberg Variations*, *The Art of Fugue*, *The Musical Offering*) is that, unlike Beethoven, whose third-period works tear apart the genre and leave a set of broken, unfinished, fragmentary forms. Bach seems intent on incorporating every nuance, every twist, every harmony and rhythm.

Steeped as he was in Protestant belief, drilled in its practices, immersed in its music and lore, Bach remains the pious-seeming Christian, which is how all of his interpretive biographers, especially Albert Schweitzer, have persuaded themselves to see him. Yet there is something unmistakably demonic and frightening about his fervour. Of course, he worked on his study of technique and on his scores, but in almost all of them he achieved feats of creativity that must have left him deeply impressed by his own gifts. One can't help wondering whether all the piety and expressions of humility before God weren't also Bach's way of keeping something considerably darker—more exuberant, more hubristic, verging on the blasphemous—at bay, something within himself, which his music with its contrapuntal wizardry also communicates. Surely Wolff must have glimpsed something of that.

Despite its problematic reticence and structure, Wolff's biography is an invaluable achievement. Not only does it present all the facts clearly and unambiguously, it allows the reader to appreciate the immense labours that filled Bach's life. There is scarcely a moment of leisure that stands out, even though he seems to have lived a more or less contented domestic life. The heights and depths of emotion are there in his music, however, along with the tremendous range of expression and ravenous articulation of emotion. Beyond the bursts of irascibility and impatience, and the ghostly outlines of a cosmic musical ambition, the great Kapellmeister is convincingly a true believer, a devout Lutheran whose ostensible mission was the glory of God and, to a lesser extent, the fulfilment of his worldly duties. Whatever else he may have felt (his letters provide few clues) we can only intuit from the rare moments when his life and music come together unexpectedly. Wolff offers one such scene from July 1750, as Bach lay on his deathbed, his illness having prevented him from concluding the last piece in *The Art of Fugue*. This piece still stands, and is performed, as a great torso of a fugue, suddenly broken off after the letters BACH are sounded in the music (in German nomenclature, B is what we would call B flat and H is B natural).

> Bach asked 'a friend' . . . to play for him, on his pedal harpsichord, the chorale Wenn wir in höchsten Nöten sein' ('When we are in the greatest distress'), BWV 668, now hearing it as a setting of 'Vor deinen Thron tret ich hiermit' ('Before your throne I now appear'). Listening to the piece, he realised that it could benefit from some improvements in a number of contrapuntal, melodic and rhythmic details. He then asked the friend to change the heading of the chorale to 'Vor deinen Thron tret ich hiermit' and dictated the changes deemed necessary in order for him to be ready to appear before his Creator's throne . . . The extant sources for this extraordinary organ chorale . . . indisputably verify the composer's involvement, both spiritual and artistic, with the larger setting close to his end. They offer a true glimpse at Bach's deep-cooled devoutness . . . At the same time, the emendations that elevate the

final version, 'Vor deinen Thron tret ich hiermit', from the earlier 'Wenn wir in höchsten Nöten sein' represent a final instance of a lifelong striving for musical perfection.

Bach's unappeased creative energy is so powerfully clear in this vignette that we demur at Wolff's use of the words 'involvement' and 'devoutness'. Much more is at work here, and this is why Wolff is correct to add that last, slightly dissonant observation. Unappeasable.

CHAPTER 43

Barenboim and the Wagner Taboo

A FUROR HAS erupted in Israel which deserves very close attention. I refer to the case of the remarkable pianist and conductor Daniel Barenboim—a close personal friend of mine I should say at the outset—and a performance he gave on July 7 in Israel of an orchestral extract from one of Richard Wagner's operas. Since that time, he has been subjected to vast amounts of commentary, abuse, and amazed expostulation, all of it because Richard Wagner (1813–1883) was both a very great composer and a notorious (and indeed deeply repulsive) anti-semite, who well after his death was known publicly as Hitler's favorite composer and commonly associated, with considerable justification, with the Nazi regime and the terrible experiences of the millions of Jews and other "inferior" peoples that it exterminated. Wagner's music has been informally banned in Israel so far as public performance is concerned, although his music is sometimes played on the radio and recordings of his music are on sale in Israeli shops. Somehow, to many Israeli Jews, Wagner's music—rich, extraordinarily complex, extraordinarily influential in the musical world—has come to symbolize the horrors of German anti-semitism.

I should also add that, even to many non-Jewish Europeans, Wagner is barely acceptable for some of the same reasons, particularly in countries that underwent a Nazi occupation during World War Two. Because some of his music sounds grandiose and "Germanic" (however one takes that misused adjective) and because he was a composer exclusively of operas, his work is so overbearing and so deeply concerned with the Germanic past, myths, traditions and achievements, and because he was such a tireless, verbose, pompous prose expounder of his mostly dubious ideas about

Al-Ahram, August 16–22, 2001; in *Al-Hayat,* August 15, 2001; in *Le Monde Diplomatique,* October 2001.

inferior races and sublime (Germanic) heroes, Wagner is a difficult person to accept, much less to like or admire. Nevertheless, he was an unquestionably great genius when it came to the theater and to music. He revolutionized our whole conception of opera; he totally transformed the tonal musical system; and he contributed ten great masterpieces, ten operas that remain among the very great summits of Western music. The challenge he presents, not just to Israeli Jews but to everyone, is how to admire and perform his music on the one hand, and, on the other hand, to separate from that his odious writings and the use made of them by the Nazis. As Barenboim has frequently pointed out, none of Wagner's operas have any immediately anti-semitic material in them; more bluntly, the Jews he hated and wrote about in his pamphlets are simply not at all to be found *as Jews* or Jewish characters in his musical works. Many critics have imputed an anti-semitic presence in some characters that Wagner treats with contempt and derision in his operas: but such accusations can only be imputations of anti-semitism, not instances of it, although the resemblance between caricatures of Jews that were common at the time and Beckmesser, a derisory character in Wagner's only comic opera *Die Meistersinger von Nürnberg* are actually quite close. Still, Beckmesser himself is a German Christian character in the opera, most certainly not Jewish. Clearly Wagner made the distinction in his own mind between Jews in reality and Jews in his music, since he was voluble about the former in his writing, and silent on them in the latter.

In any event, Wagner's works in Israel have by common consent been left unperformed, until July 7, 2001. Barenboim is head of the Chicago Symphony Orchestra, as well as the Berlin State Opera, whose orchestra he was leading on tour in Israel for the three consecutive concerts presented in Jerusalem. He had originally scheduled a performance of Act One of Wagner's opera *Die Walküre* for the July 7 concert, but had been asked to change it by the director of the Israel Festival, which had invited the German orchestra and Barenboim in the first place. Barenboim substituted a program of Schumann and Stravinsky, and then, after playing those, turned to the audience and proposed a short extract from Wagner's *Tristan und Isolde* as an encore. He opened the floor to a discussion, which ensued with people for and against. In the end, Barenboim said he would play the piece but suggested that those who were offended could leave, which some in fact did. By and large though, the Wagner was well received by a rapturous audience of about 2800 Israelis and, I am sure, extremely well performed.

Still, the attacks on Barenboim have not stopped. It was reported in the press on July 25 that the Knesset committee on culture and education "urged Israel's cultural bodies to boycott the conductor . . . for performing music by Hitler's favorite composer at Israel's premier cultural event until he apologises." The attacks on Barenboim by the minister of culture and other luminaries have been venomous, even though despite his birth and early childhood in Argentina, he himself has always thought of himself as an Israeli. He grew up there, he went to Hebrew schools, he carries an Israeli passport along with his Argentinian one. Besides, he has always been thought of as a major cultural asset to Israel, having been a central figure in the country's musical life for years and years, despite the fact that, since he was in his teens, he has lived in Europe and the United States most of the time, not in Israel. This has been a result of his work, which has afforded him many more important opportunities outside rather than inside Israel. After all, to have conducted and played the piano in Berlin, Paris, London, Vienna, Salzburg, Bayreuth, New York, Chicago, Buenos Aires, and places like them elsewhere has always overshadowed the mere fact of residence in one place. To some extent, as we shall see, this cosmopolitan and even iconoclastic life has been a source of the anger directed against him since the Wagner incident.

But he is a complex figure nonetheless, which also explains the furor over what he did. All societies are made up of a majority of average citizens—people who follow along all the major patterns—and a tiny number who by virtue of their talent and their independent inclinations are not at all average, and in many ways, are a challenge and even an affront to the usually docile majority. The problems occur when the perspective of the docile majority tries to reduce, simplify, and codify the complex and unroutine people who are a tiny minority. This clash inevitably occurs—large numbers of human beings cannot easily tolerate someone who is noticeably different, more talented, more original, than they are—and inevitably causes rage and irrationality in the majority. Look what Athens did to Socrates, because he was a genius who taught young people how to think independently and skeptically: he was sentenced to death. The Amsterdam Jews excommunicated Spinoza because his ideas were too much for them. Galileo was punished by the church. Al-Hallaj was crucified for his insights. And so it has gone for centuries. Barenboim is a gifted, extremely unusual figure who crossed too many lines and violated too many of the many taboos that bind Israeli society. Exactly how is worth detailing here.

It hardly needs repeating that musically speaking Barenboim is almost overwhelmingly unusual. He has every conceivable gift available to the individual who wants to be a great soloist and conductor—a perfect memory, competence and even brilliance in technical matters, a winning manner before the public, and above all, an enormous love of what he does. Nothing musical is beyond him or too difficult for him to master. He does it all with a seemingly effortless mastery, a talent that every musician alive today acknowledges about him. But it isn't that simple. His formative years were spent first in Spanish-speaking Argentina then in Hebrew-speaking Israel, so already he is neither one nor the other nationality purely and simply. Since his late teens he hasn't really lived in Israel, preferring instead the cosmopolitan and culturally more interesting atmosphere of Europe and the United States, where as I said earlier, he occupies two of the most prestigious positions in all music, one as conductor of arguably the best American orchestra (Chicago), the other as director of one of the greatest and oldest opera companies in the world (Berlin State Opera). Meanwhile he continues his career as a solo pianist. Quite obviously living that kind of itinerant life and achieving the kind of recognition he has had has come not with a studious compliance with standards set by ordinary people but by exactly the opposite, that is, a regular flouting of conventions and barriers. This is true of any unusual person who must live well beyond the conventions of ordinary bourgeois society. Few important achievements in matters of art or science are accomplished by living within the boundaries designed to regulate social and political life.

But it gets more complicated. Because he has lived and traveled so much, and because he has a gift for languages (he can speak seven fluently), Barenboim is in a sense at home everywhere and nowhere. One result is that his visits to Israel are limited to a few days a year, though he keeps in touch by phone and by reading the press. Another is that he has lived abroad, not just in the U.S. and Britain, but in Germany, which is where he spends most of his time now. One can imagine that for many Jews for whom Germany still represents what is most evil and anti-semitic, Barenboim's residence there is a difficult pill to swallow, more particularly in that his chosen area of music to perform (in this, he follows Wilhelm Furtwängler, the greatest German conductor of the 20th Century, very much also a complex political figure) is the classical Austro-Germanic repertory, in which Wagner's operas are at the very center. Aesthetically of course, this is a sound, not to say absolutely predictable area for a classical musician to concentrate on: it includes the great works of Mozart, Haydn, Beethoven, Brahms, Schumann, Bruckner, Mahler, Wagner, Richard Strauss, plus, of course, many other composers in the French, Russian and Spanish repertory at which Barenboim has excelled. But the core is Austrian and German music, music that for some Jewish philosophers and artists has sometimes presented a great problem, especially after World War Two. The great pianist Artur Rubinstein, a friend and mentor of Barenboim's, more or less refused ever to go to Germany and play there because, he would say, as a Jew, it was hard for him to be in a country that had slaughtered so many of his people. So already, there developed a sense of estrangement in many of his Israeli admirers about Barenboim's residence in Berlin, in the heart of the former capital of The Third Reich, which many living Jews still consider to bear within it today the marks of its former evil.

Now it is all very well for others to say, be broad-minded and remember that art is one thing, politics quite another. In actuality this is a nonsensical position, derided precisely by most artists and the very musicians whom we most revere. All of the great composers in one way or another were political, and held quite strong political ideas, some of them, in the case of the early Beethoven who adulated Napoleon as a great conqueror or Debussy who was a right-wing French nationalist, quite reprehensible from today's perspective. Haydn, as another example suggests, was a servile employee of his aristocratic patron Prince Esterhazy and even the greatest of all geniuses, Johann Sebastian Bach, was always fawning at the table or at the court of an archbishop or a duke.

We don't much care about these things today because they belong to a relatively remote and distant period. None of them offends us quite so sharply as one of Thomas Carlyle's racist pamphlets in the 1860's, but there are two other factors that need consideration as well. One is that music as an art form is not like language: notes don't mean something stable, the way a word like "cat" or "horse" does. Second, music for the most part is trans-national; it goes beyond the boundaries of a nation or a nationality and language. You don't have to know German to appreciate Mozart, and you don't have to be French to read a score by Berlioz. You have to know music, which is a very specialized technique acquired with painstaking care quite apart from subjects like history or literature, although I would argue that the context and traditions of individual works of music have to be understood for purposes of true comprehension and interpretation. In some ways, music is like algebra, but not quite, as the case of Wagner testifies.

Were he a minor composer or someone who composed his work hermetically or at least quietly, Wagner's contradictions would have been slightly easier to accept and tolerate. But he was incredibly voluble, filling Europe with his pronouncements, projects, and music, all of which went together and all of which were larger than life, more impressive, more deigned to overwhelm and compel the listener than those of every other composer. At the center of all his work was his own fantastically self-concerned, even narcissistic self, which he considered in no uncertain way to embody the essence of the German soul, its destiny, and its privileges. I obviously cannot enter a discussion here about Wagner's work, but it is important to insist on the fact that he sought controversy, he demanded attention, he did everything for the cause of Germany and himself which he conceived of in the most extreme revolutionary terms. His was to be a new music, a new art, a new aesthetic, and it was to embody the tradition of Beethoven and Goethe, and, typically, it was to transcend them in a new, universal synthesis. No one in the history of art has attracted more attention, no one more writing, no one more commentary. Wagner was ready made for the Nazis, but he was also—and this mustn't be forgotten—welcomed as a hero and a great genius by other musicians who understood that his contributions utterly changed the course of Western music. During his lifetime he had a special opera house, almost a shrine, built for him and the performance of his operas in the small town of Bayreuth, which is still the site of an annual festival where only Wagner's music is played. Bayreuth and the Wagner family were dear to Hitler's heart, and to add a further complexity to the matter, Richard Wagner's grandson Wolfgang still controls the summer festival at which Barenboim has conducted regularly for almost two decades.

Nor is this all. Barenboim is clearly an artist who overturns obstacles, crosses forbidden lines, and enters in taboo or forbidden territory. This doesn't automatically make him a fully-fledged political figure at all but he has made no secret of his unhappiness with Israel's occupation and went so far in early 1999 as to be the first Israeli to offer his services gratis to play a concert at Birzeit University on the West Bank. For the past three years, the first two at Weimar and this year in Chicago, he has brought together young Israeli and Arab musicians to play music together, in a daring enterprise that tries to rise above politics and conflict into the totally non-political art of interpreting music together. He is clearly fascinated by the Other, and categorically rejects the irrationality of a position that says that it is better not to know than to know. I agree with him that ignorance is not an adequate political strategy for a people, and therefore, each in his own way must understand and know the forbidden Other. Not many individuals think this way, but for me, as well as a growing number of others, this is the only intellectually coherent position to take. This doesn't diminish one's defense of justice or solidarity with the oppressed; it doesn't mean abandoning your identity; it doesn't involve looking the other way so far as real politics are concerned. It does mean that reason, understanding, and intellectual analysis, and not the organization and encouragement of collective passions such as those that seem to impel fundamentalists, are the way to be a citizen. I have long subscribed to these beliefs myself and perhaps this is one reason why Barenboim and I have our differences and yet have remained friends.

The total rejection, the utter irrational condemnation, the blanket denunciation of complex phenomena such as Wagner is an irrational and finally unacceptable thing, just as in our situation as Arabs, it has been a stupid and wasteful policy for so many years to use phrases like "the Zionist entity" and completely refuse to understand and analyze Israel and Israelis on the grounds that their existence must be denied because they caused the Palestinian *nakba*. History is a dynamic thing, and if we expect Israeli Jews not to use the Holocaust to justify appalling human rights abuses of the Palestinian people, we too have to go beyond such idiocies as saying that the Holocaust never took place, and that Israelis are all, man, woman, and child, doomed to our eternal enmity and hostility. Nothing historical is frozen in time; nothing in history is immune to change; nothing in history is beyond reason, beyond understanding, beyond analysis and influence. Politicians can say all the nonsense they wish and do what they want, and so can professional demagogues. But for intellectuals, artists, and free citizens, there must always be room for dissent, for alternative views, for ways and possibilities to challenge the tyranny of the majority and, at the same time and most important, to advance human enlightenment and liberty.

This idea is not easily dismissed as a "Western" import and therefore inapplicable to Arab and Muslim, or for that matter, Jewish societies and traditions. It is a universal value to be found in every tradition that I know of. Every society has conflicts in it between justice and injustice, ignorance and knowledge, freedom and oppression. The point is not simply to belong to one side or the other because one is told to be, but to choose carefully and to make judgments that render what is just and due to every aspect of the situation. The purpose of education is not to accumulate facts or memorize the "correct" answer, but rather to learn how to think critically *for oneself* and to understand the meaning of things *for oneself.*

In the Israeli case about Wagner and Barenboim, it would be easy to dismiss the conductor simply either as an opportunist or as an insensitive adventurer. Similarly, it is reductive to say that Wagner was a terrible man with reactionary ideas in general, and therefore his music, no matter how wonderful, is intolerable because it is infected with the same poison as his prose. How would that be demonstrated? How many writers, musicians, poets, painters would be left if their art was judged by their moral behavior? And who is to decide what level of ugliness and turpitude can be tolerated in the artistic production of any given artist? Once one starts to censor, there is no theoretical limit. Rather, I would think that it is incumbent on the mind to be able to analyze a complex phenomenon such as the question of Wagner in Israel (or, to give another example analyzed in a famous essay written by the brilliant Nigerian novelist Chinua Achebe, the question of how to read Conrad's *Heart of Darkness* for an African today) and to show where the evil is and where the art is. For a mature mind it should be possible to hold together in one's mind two contradictory facts, that Wagner was a great artist, and second, that Wagner was a disgusting human being. Unfortunately, one cannot have one fact without the other. Does that mean, therefore, that Wagner should not be listened to? Most assuredly not, although it is obvious that if an individual is still troubled by the association of Wagner with the Holocaust then there is no need at all to inflict Wagner on oneself. All I would say, however, is that an open attitude towards art is necessary. This is not to say that artists shouldn't be morally judged for their immorality or evil practices; it is to say that an artist's work cannot be judged solely on those grounds and banned accordingly.

One last point, as well as one further analogy with the Arab situation, is worth making. During the heated Knesset debate a year ago as to whether Israeli high school students should or should not have the option to read Mahmoud Darwish, many of us took the vehemence with which the idea was attacked as a sign of how closed-minded orthodox Zionism was. In deploring the opponents of the idea that young Israelis would benefit from reading a major Palestinian author, many people argued that history and reality couldn't be hidden forever, and that censorship of that kind had no place in the educational curriculum. Wagner's music presents a similar problem, although there can be no denying the fact that the terrible associations with his music and ideas are a genuine trauma for those who feel that the composer was, in a sense, ready-made for appropriation by the Nazis. Yet at some point with a major composer like Wagner, blocking out his existence will not work. If it hadn't been Barenboim who performed his music in Israel on July 7, it would have been someone else a little later. A complex reality always bursts in on attempts to seal it out. The question then becomes how to understand the Wagner phenomenon, rather than whether or not to recognize its existence, which is an inadequate and obviously insufficient response.

In the Arab context, the campaign against "normalization" with Israel, while more urgent and actual a challenge—after all, Israel is practicing modes of daily collective punishment and murder against an entire people, whose land it has illegally occupied for 34 years—has some similar features with the Israeli taboos against Palestinian poetry and Wagner. Our problem is that Arab governments have economic and political relationships with Israel while groups of individuals have tried to impose a blanket ban on all contacts with Israelis. The ban on normalization lacks coherence since its *raison d'être*, Israel's oppression of the Palestinian people, hasn't been alleviated by the campaign: how many Palestinian homes have been protected from demolition by anti-normalization measures, and how many Palestinian universities have been able to give their students instruction because anti-normalization has been in place? None at all, alas, which is why I have said that it is better for a distinguished Egyptian intellectual to come to Palestine in solidarity with his/her Palestinian comrades, perhaps to teach or give a lecture or help at a clinic, than it is to sit at home preventing others from doing so. Complete anti-normalization is not an effective weapon for the powerless: its symbolic value is low, and its actual effect is merely passive and negative. Successful weapons of the weak—as in India, the American South, Vietnam, Malaysia and elsewhere—have always been active, and even aggressive. The point is to make the powerful oppressor uncomfortable and vulnerable both morally as well as politically. Suicide bombing doesn't achieve this effect, and neither does anti-normalization, which in the case of the South African liberation struggle was used as a boycott against visiting academics in conjunction with a whole variety of other means.

That is why I believe we must try to penetrate the Israeli consciousness with everything at our disposal. Speaking or writing to Israeli audiences breaks *their* taboo against *us*. This fear of being addressed by what their collective memory has suppressed was what stirred up the whole debate about reading Palestinian literature. Zionism has tried to exclude non-Jews and we, by our unselective boycott of even the name "Israel," have actually *helped* rather than hindered this plan. And in a different context, it is why Barenboim's performance of Wagner, although genuinely painful for many who still suffer the real traumas of anti-semitic genocide, has the salutary effect of allowing mourning to move on to another stage, i.e. toward the living of life itself, which must go on and cannot be frozen in the past. Perhaps I haven't caught all the many nuances of this complex set of issues, but the main point has to be that real life cannot be ruled by taboos and prohibitions against critical understanding and emancipatory experience. Those must always be given the highest priority. Ignorance and avoidance cannot be adequate guides for the present.

CHAPTER 44

Untimely Meditations

MAYNARD SOLOMON'S *LATE BEETHOVEN*

B EETHOVEN HAS been particularly fortunate in his recent critics and biographers. As a start, Elliot Forbes's revised edition of
Alexander Thayer's standard early-twentieth-century five-volume
Life appeared to great acclaim in 1964 and was further revised by Forbes
in 1967. This was followed by a spate of biographical and critical studies
of a very high order, including works by Joseph Kerman, Scott Burnham,
Charles Rosen, William Kinderman, Martin Cooper and Lewis Lockwood,
the senior figure in Beethoven studies, whose magisterial *Beethoven: The
Music and the Life*, the culmination of years of monographic studies, has
also just appeared. But for sheer interpretive genius and an uncommon
gift for rendering in prose the complex, humanly compelling subtleties of
Beethoven's music and life, few approach Maynard Solomon. Aside from
an excellent critical biography of Mozart and some important work on
Schubert, Solomon has over the years focused his scholarly energies almost
entirely on Beethoven, producing over the past quarter-century three massive (but eminently readable) volumes on the great composer: a biography
(1977, revised in 1998), a collection, *Beethoven Essays* (1988), and now perhaps the most remarkable, *Late Beethoven*, which is also a collection uni-
fied around the composer's musical and spiritual concerns during the last
decade of his life (1816–27).

Before describing Solomon's book let me say something about late style,
which has been a great interest of mine for some years. There is first of all
the artist's connection to his or her own time, or historical period, society
and antecedents, how the aesthetic work, for all its irreducible individuality,
is nevertheless a part—or, paradoxically, not a part—of the era in which
it was produced. This is not simply a matter of sociological or political

The Nation, September 1–8, 2003.

synchrony but more interestingly has to do with rhetorical or formal style. Thus Mozart expresses in his music a style much more intimately related to the worlds of court and church than Beethoven or Wagner, both of whom emerge from a secular environment in which, by virtue of unreliable patronage and the romantic cult of individual creativity, the composer is no longer seen as a servant (like Bach or Mozart) but as a demanding genius who stands proudly, and perhaps even narcissistically, apart from his time. So not only can one often see an easily perceptible connection between, say, a realistic artist like Balzac and his social milieu; there is also an antithetical relationship in the case of artists whose work challenges the aesthetic and social norms of their eras and is, so to speak, too late for the times, in the sense of superseding or transcending them. This relationship is especially difficult to discern in the case of a musician like Beethoven or Brahms, whose art is neither mimetic nor theatrical.

Beethoven's late works, according to Solomon, exude a new sense of private striving and instability that is quite different from earlier works such as the "Eroica" Symphony and the five piano concertos that address the world with self-confident gregariousness. The masterpieces of Beethoven's final decade are late to the extent that they are beyond their own time, ahead of it in terms of daring and startling newness, later than it in that they describe a return or homecoming to realms forgotten or left behind by the relentless forward march of history.

Literary modernism itself can be seen as a late-style phenomenon insofar as artists such as Joyce and Eliot appear to be out of their time altogether, returning to ancient myth or antique forms such as the epic or ancient religious ritual for their inspiration. Among other figures, writers like Lampedusa, the Sicilian aristocrat who wrote only one, backward-looking novel, *The Leopard,* which interested no publishers at all while he was alive, or Constantine Cavafy, the Alexandrian Greek poet who also published next to nothing during his lifetime, suggest the rarefied, almost precious, but formidably difficult aesthetic of minds that refuse direct engagement with their own time while spinning out a semi-resistant, backward-looking artwork of considerable power nonetheless. In philosophy, Nietzsche is the great prototype of a similarly "untimely" stance. The words "late" or "belated" seem acutely appropriate for such figures.

The second, more problematic aspect of late style on which Solomon draws has a special pertinence to Beethoven, whose late works (notably the Ninth Symphony, the last five piano sonatas, the final handful of quartets, *Missa Solemnis*) form an identifiable group and show marked evidence of a considerable transformation in his actual compositional style from the romantic heroism of his middle-period works to a difficult, highly personal and (to the listener and even his contemporaries) a somewhat unattractive, not to say repellent, idiom. It is as if the earlier extrovert has turned inward, and now produces gnarled and eccentric pieces of music that make unprecedented demands on performer and listener alike, and at the same time convey a sense not of resignation but of an unusual rebelliousness, breaking barriers, transgressively exploring the basic elements of the art as if anew.

In an introduction he wrote for Rachel Bespaloff's *On the Iliad*, Hermann Broch, the distinguished Austrian man of letters and author of *The Sleepwalkers* and *The Death of Virgil*, speaks of what he calls the style of old age as follows:

> [It] is not always a product of the years; it is a gift implanted along with his other gifts in the artist, ripening, it may be, with time, often blossoming before its season under the foreshadow of death, or unfolding of itself even before the approach of age or death: it is the reaching of a new level of expression, such as the old Titian's discovery of the all-penetrating light which dissolves the human flesh and the human soul to a higher unity; or such as the finding by Rembrandt and Goya, both at the height of their manhood, of the metaphysical surface which underlies the visible in man and thing, and which nevertheless can be painted; or such as the *The Art of the Fugue* which Bach in his old age dictated without having a concrete instrument in mind, because what he had to express was either beneath or beyond the audible surface of music.

Theodor Adorno's severely rigorous short essay "Beethoven's Late Style" catches the gist of this style aphoristically in one of the chapters of his posthumously published and unfinished book on the composer, *Beethoven: The Philosophy of Music*. What characterizes the late style, Adorno writes in this early part of the book, is not Beethoven's biographical apprehension of death (which, if it appears at all, does so only in the figure of allegory) but rather a new aesthetic that is fragmentary, incomplete, elusive and surprisingly full of outworn conventions (trills, *fiorituras*, "ingenuously simple . . . accompaniments") that are "made visible in unconcealed, untransformed barrenness." Far from the ripeness of a mature fruit, this peculiar style and the late works it gives rise to "are not well rounded, but wrinkled, even fissured. They are apt to lack sweetness, fending off with prickly tartness those interested merely in sampling them." Adorno concludes with this bravura set of formulations:

> The caesurae, however, the abrupt stops which characterize the latest Beethoven more than any other feature, are those moments of breaking free;

the work falls silent as it is deserted, turning its hollowness outward. Only then is the next fragment added, ordered to its place by escaping subjectivity and colluding for better or worse with what has gone before, and can be exorcized only by the figure they form together. This illuminates the contradiction whereby the very late Beethoven is called both subjective and objective, while the light in which alone it glows is subjective. He does not bring about their harmonious synthesis. As a dissociative force he tears them apart in time, perhaps in order to preserve them for the eternal. In the history of art, late works are the catastrophes.

This may seem impossibly gnomic, and it is certainly complicated to decipher, but its main arguments are clear enough. First of all, late-style Beethoven is not, as one might expect, all about reconciliation and a kind of restful summing up of a long, productive career. That is what one finds, for example, in Shakespeare's late romances like *The Tempest, The Winter's Tale* and *Cymbeline,* or in Sophocles' *Oedipus at Colonus,* where, to borrow from another context, ripeness is all. In Adorno's account of late style, there is violence, experimental energy and, most important, a refusal to accept any idea of a healing, inclusive restfulness that comes at the end of a fruitful career. Second, and this is crucial for Solomon's book (which, oddly, mentions Adorno only in passing), the late-style phenomenon overturns our ideas and experiences about the coherence, organic completeness, the wholeness of the work, which is tied together (if that's the right way of putting it) in unexpected ways. Solomon shows, for example, that for a long time after Beethoven composed the choral finale to the Ninth Symphony, he was endlessly toying with the idea of replacing it with instrumental music and doing away entirely with the choral setting of Schiller's "Ode to Joy." And what we have now, Solomon continues, is hardly the unitary hymn to joy but rather a composition whose "fusion of styles and procedures is matched by the multivalence of its forms, which constitute a palimpsest of superimposed hybrid structures—a set of variations; one or another sonata form; a four-movement cycle superimposed on a sonata-allegro concerto form with double exposition . . . ; a cantata; a through-composed text-derived form; a suite; a divertimento; an operatic finale; and even a free fantasy." Everything about the work echoes "resistance to the given. That is why it begins with open fifths, tonal indeterminacy, a sense of the void."

Solomon's description of the late work's openness explains somewhat the Ninth's various cultural appropriations since its first Vienna performance in 1824. This amazingly persistent phenomenon has been studied with sociological rigor by Esteban Buch in *Beethoven's Ninth: A Political History,* which demonstrates how Beethoven's music played a major part in the formation of national identity (along with national anthems like "God Save the King" and "La Marseillaise"). The Ninth ended up tragically in the employ of twentieth-century German nationalism at its worst, but it also lent itself to the struggles against apartheid and totalitarianism. No other musical work has had as far-reaching political effect all over the world as the Ninth, especially its celebration of human fraternity and an empowering freedom.

Solomon's focus, however, is exclusively on the composer's own internal world, which, beginning in the years around 1810 and "gaining momentum as the decade proceeded . . . eventually amounted to a sweeping realignment of his understanding of nature, divinity, and human purpose, constituting a sea change in Beethoven's system of beliefs." Using the composer's prose jottings in his *Tagebuch,* an intimate diary kept between 1812 and 1818, Solomon tries to do nothing less than connect these quite explicitly verbal and often philosophical thoughts to the entirely musical, nondiscursive, nondenotative world of tones and abstract form.

In a series of twelve chapters and a prologue, Solomon sketches out the revolution in thought, feeling and musical form that Beethoven accomplished during his last years as an active composer. These were years of increasing deafness and solitude of political disillusionment (especially after the Congress of Vienna) and a heightened sense of his own mortality. During this period he withdrew into himself, seeking through intense concentration to come to terms with his art not in an adversarial but in a creatively cooperative way, at the same time that he felt he had to renounce urban life for "the quasi-monastic solitude of rural life, removed from the hurly-burly of the city." What might have become instead an unforgiving sacrificial imperative was tempered by Beethoven's unstilled need for human kinship: Solomon opines that that need accounts for the lonely bachelor's efforts to become his nephew's guardian and mentor. But this too became for Beethoven "another form of self-denial," while musically he worked out "possible reconfigurations of musical form . . . [in order] to sound unplumbed depths of expressivity."

Read this way, Beethoven's last compositions, his late style, undertake all sorts of unconventional excursions in content and form, from a leisurely pastoral setting in his last violin sonata, Opus 96, which moves toward "a restoration of the full range of classical pastoral experience that Virgil, Bion, and Theocritus had known, including its Elegiac and Bacchic strains, thereby rescuing musical pastoral from its ongoing slide into a picturesque, revitalized celebration of the bucolic," to a devotional journey in his [monumental piano work, the] 'Diabelli' Variations," and then finally to "a colossal symphony that resumed to dissolve boundaries between language and music, thus perhaps to restore the union of the arts rumored to have existed in ancient ritual drama." Many of these ideas are scattered in Beethoven's notebooks, letters and diaries of the period, but it is Solomon's ingenuity to have seen in that often inchoate and fragmentary material the adumbration of huge formal outlines that, in their philosophical challenge to students of Beethoven, go well beyond the fussy schematic formalism imposed traditionally on orthodox musicology.

To Solomon, it is clear that besides being a great artist, Beethoven is also a thinker, and what he does in music is to think, feel and survey new territory in order to produce sound that almost has the feel of a landscape, or that of a Dantesque voyage, all of it realized in an exactingly personal, even rebarbative musical language. Thus, the older Beethoven abandons an anthropocentric classical worldview inherited from the Enlightenment and, like the literary and philosophic Romantics who were his contemporaries, he returns again and again to a transfigured or renovated classical world, even to the point of adapting classical Greek meters to organize his great Seventh Symphony in an attempt to "evoke the ancient pagan world via a fantasy reconstruction of its music." This, says Solomon, is a Classic-Romantic revalidation of "the cultural, ethical, and aesthetic premises of Antiquity." It is also, we need to add, yet another instance of what E. M. Butler has called the tyranny of Greece over Germany.

If one major intellectual source for Beethoven's late style was the body of ideas and readings he shared with Schlegel, Goethe and Herder—much of it derived from romantic Orientalism, especially that branch of it concerned with ancient mystery cults and religions from the East and the Mediterranean, translations of the ancient Indian classics by William Jones, and of course a renewed interest in Homer and other antique authors—the other was the Masonic tradition, which was extraordinarily influential in early modern Europe. Mozart was a prominent Mason, and so too in much of his thought about ritual purification, initiatory trials of endurance and moral fortitude, a deep veneration of the highest humanistic Illuminist ideals (all of this memorably embodied in Mozart's *Sarastro*), was Beethoven. A fine chapter by Solomon on Beethoven's "Masonic Imagination" goes over this material with great sensitivity, since as with all other fields of endeavor, Beethoven was a vital, if also eccentric, solitary whose prodigious hallmark was to cannibalize everything he borrowed or read and make it his own. Solomon's method is to show the trends and the inflections that enter the music as music, rather than as programmatic ideas.

The range of material in this book is striking indeed. Solomon moves gracefully between literature, philosophy, literary theory, social history, musical analysis and informed intellectual speculation. What is so impressive about the writing is the extraordinary tact and precision of Solomon's prose, as he describes music—the most silent and enigmatic of the arts—in terms that relate both to the whole range of one of the most striking of human minds in its historical context while also allowing us to enter the music on its own formal and compositional terms. In analyzing, for example, Beethoven's "Diabelli" Variations, a complex late-style piano composition consisting of thirty-three variations on what has been usually considered to be a trivial waltz theme by Anton Diabelli, Solomon revises and overturns that conventional assumption by relating the tune instead to Wordsworth's concern with the "humble and rustic," and the romantic "valorization of folk art"; which in turn leads us to "the familiar [which] opens on the quotidian, the sphere of the quotidian itself opens, not only on the humble, the popular, the rustic, and every manifestation of the ordinary; but on larger issues of identity as well." From there, Solomon proceeds to an elegant account of the huge work as a journey, the many skillfully executed metamorphoses in it implying a narrator who "looks back to the theme, which is a link to the home that he left in favor of an arduous pursuit of every conceivable metaphor for a desired goal—toward God, Paradise, reason, wisdom, order, peace, achievement, perfection, healing, and love." And then, in a masterful turn of phrase, Solomon notes how Beethoven foils our expectations of arrival and chooses instead "to close with a wordless song, a spectral dance in tempo di minuetto, moderato, marked *grazioso e dolce*."

I wish there were more opportunity here to show how every chapter in Solomon's book is full of subtle, deeply satisfying accounts of what actually went into Beethoven's late-style works, but of course there isn't. Still, I can conclude here by suggesting the compelling nature of Solomon's achievement, which seems to me to provide a kind of humanistic inquiry on the highest level without ever scanting the technical demands of Beethoven's formidably complex music. How many musicologists today can, for instance, excavate the Romantic movement as thoroughly as Solomon does and then take from it its principal motifs and images as they are transformed by Beethoven according to the rigors of, say, a symphony, sonata, fugue or bagatelle?

What distinguishes so much of Solomon's work is his fearless way of connecting human concerns of the utmost importance with the exigencies of music: Thus a moving chapter on the use of music for healing purposes derives its power from reported actual performances by Beethoven and Schubert (his exact contemporary) of specific piano works, in whose sonic universe the composer placed a kind of therapeutic spell. Or, even more brilliant than that, there is a superb excursion on Beethoven's endings during his last period (for example, for transcendental works such as the Hammerklavier Sonata and the Ninth Symphony), which are shown to be far from the conclusive and triumphant cadences that we have all taken them for, but rather seen by Beethoven as alternatives among others for closing statements to these monuments in sound. Far from being airy speculations, Solomon's analyses rely on the archeological discipline of archival research, which he turns into evidence for what he unwaveringly regards as Beethoven's endless, unrelenting artistic vitality and creativity. "Ultimately, the coercive and subversive implications of [such works as] the Ninth Symphony may be inseparable, perhaps because Beethoven's futuristic impulse—to create things that had never before existed—warred with his yearning to belong to tradition."

My one nagging reservation about what Solomon does so well as an inventive critic and generously sympathetic cultural interpreter is that it isn't clear how his findings might be related to actual performances of Beethoven's music today. You can take Solomon's marvelously enlightening insights out of Beethoven's writing and his scores, but he does not quite provide us with a way of putting them back into musical realizations of the works themselves. Perhaps there is no direct indication of how that might be done, although, if the reader is a musician, he or she is filled with a sense of possible interpretive routes to take. Performance necessarily involves choices made and action taken. Solomon's reticence on this point somewhat undermines the attractive power of his overall insights, with their richness of allusion and the sense they convey of untapped possibility and as-yet-unthought alternatives buried inside the music, there to be discovered and deciphered with great intellectual pleasure. Perhaps that's enough of an achievement for one critic writing at the top of his form, but I must say that I feel tantalizingly close to an understanding of what I might do as a musician with Solomon there to guide me, along with the legions of performing artists who have so much to learn from his analyses. If only now he would.

APPENDIX

Bach/Beethoven

T HE MOST silent of the arts, music is also the most directly affecting and expressive as well as the most esoteric and difficult to discuss. Consequently Western classical music generally stands apart from cultural consideration of the sort that makes film, painting, photography and of course literature the common currency of intelligent discussion. Musicology is a highly specialized discipline; the "music world" with a few exceptions like Pierre Boulez is restricted to business, the cult of celebrity, very flashy performances, and an increasingly smaller repertory of an antiquarian or curatorial kind. Newness and originality are shunned for their rebarbative styles by the organizers of musical life: a new *Traviata* is infinitely preferable to a complete performance of Olivier Messiaen's *St. Francis.*

But this cannot be all there is and Bach/Beethoven is an attempt to remedy this impoverishing situation. We are in the 250th anniversary of Bach's death, and Beethoven very much remains the symbol of romantic, heroic music. Between them they define certain abiding musical as well as cultural concerns stretching from their own times into the present. How and in what ways? The point is to portray them doing something in music impossible in other forms yet essential to our contemporary sense of where we are today—globalized and multicultural, in addition to being obsessed with questions of identity, tradition and tumultuous change.

In the history of Western music Bach occupies a place of absolute priority and greatness for literally everyone who came after him, a strange but extraordinary position for someone who in effect was the culmination of the "old" polyphonic style in the amazing inclusiveness and variety of his music. For Bach's counterpoint is an art of combination and re-combination,

April 14, 2000.

horizontal lines flowing together in an endlessly varied pattern of consonance and dissonance, melody and harmony, rhythmically four square and syncopated, straight and inverted, forward and backward. He is in short a composer who is nothing less than a whole method for exploring and at the same time beautifully systematizing the world as a teacher, performer, worshipper, magician and supreme technician whose capacity to produce beautiful and even elegant sound was never compromised by the sheer erudite complexity of his music, which in its perfect order seems to stand just beyond the knowable. One returns to Bach as the symbol of invention and fully worked out elaboration.

Beethoven on the other hand is the greatest instance of development, breaking out of music towards the world in a sustained gesture whose force and astonishing propulsive, patterned energy endures till now. It is, I think, right to describe his work as making the first and most decisive step out of music (but always in it of course, even when he adds words to the music) based on the ego's personal force. Unlike Bach's, Beethoven's music is not about reconciliation and incorporation but about a constantly building sense of intensity through dramatic form (sonata form principally but also variation and song cycle). Thus his music is about bursting through, growing beyond bounds, crossing discrete borders and territories, traversing time as if it were opening territory that is being explored (violated) and charted and settled at the same time. Provocative, audacious, egoistic, and yet (in the final or third phase of his work) perhaps unreconciled and alienated.

These two composers are the two pillars, or panels, not just of Western music, but of major developments in modern culture, which it would be salutary—indeed possible *only* to see—in these musical terms, available for a rather special apprehension of the contemporary cultural world of the new century. Yes, Bach was a thoroughly Christian composer, and Beethoven the first really important Western bourgeois-artist of the modern era, and yes there they have been seen to represent everything that is Eurocentric, self-regarding and removed from the "uncontrollable mystery on the bestial floor" as Yeats called human experience.

But it isn't that simple or as cut and dry as this essay in interpretation and understanding argues. First of all the two great figures are prime examples of such polarities as tradition and innovation, system and originality, centrality and eccentricity, the impersonal and the personal. More, because music is so rare and silent, its movement and existence are the purest examples we have of what in Bach is complex inclusiveness and system (never dull or academic: Bach was everything but that) and in Beethoven is developmental energy arising out of self and threatening incoherence as well as expansion and affirmation. Today such matters face us in what is supposed to be postmodernist questioning as to the meaning of the past (through memory and the writing of acceptable narratives) which undergoes the unsettling challenge of the future. What do we keep, what jettison, what do we reconstruct? Moreoever, new configurations in the city and country have produced a sort of transnational landscape that both knits together the world, and—at "the ends of the earth"—divides it more profoundly. What are the limits of self and subjectivity in a time when privacy is dissipated through homogeneity and instant electronic communication? What is left behind and where does it go?

Finally the question of politics and culture is entailed by these two massive figures. The past millennium has allowed us (East and West, North and South) to conceive of history as accumulation and development, consolidation and growth, Bach and Beethoven. What if the ceaseless migration and endless transformations of our time no longer permit the old balance (and exchange) between the two modes represented by Bach and Beethoven, and what if a new hybrid identity is being slowly made apparent, one for whom neither territory nor traditional identity will serve as they once did?

These are some of the matters I take up in this short (175 page) book. My previous cultural, political, critical, literary, and musical writings provide me with an excellent background for such an undertaking, as, more specifically, does my complete knowledge of music. To the best of my awareness, this book brings an entirely fresh and original perspective to the extraordinary cultural challenges of the new millennium (hitherto unaddressed in the altogether more overtly economic and political studies of disparate gurus like Paul Kennedy, Fukuyama, Conor Cruise O'Brien, Thomas Friedman, Benjamin Barber).

Index